She stood still a moment, as if listening for some sound that
might direct her.

THE LAST DAYS OF POMPEII

BY

SIR EDWARD BULWER LYTTON

(Lord Lytton)

"Such is Vesuvius! and these things take place in it every year. But all eruptions which have happened since would be trifling, even if all summed into one, compared to what occurred at the period we refer to. . . . . .
. . . .
"Day was turned into night, and light into darkness;—an inexpressible quantity of dust and ashes was poured out, deluging land, sea, and air, and burying two entire cities, Herculaneum and Pompeii, while the people were sitting in the theatre."

—*Dion Cassius,* lib. lxvi.

THE SPENCER PRESS

MANUFACTURED IN THE UNITED STATES OF AMERICA
BY THE CUNEO PRESS, INC.

THE SPENCER PRESS

The avowed purpose of the Spencer Press is to publish classics which have survived the test of time. In the quest for enduring titles more than fifty famous lists of the finest books ever written were consulted. The findings were then tabulated and the list was found to include more than one thousand titles, some of which have been mentioned in the recommendations of as many as thirty-five different authorities. The first hundred titles which were most often mentioned by the critics, were selected on the assumption that any book which had been chosen so often and by so many eminent authorities must be exceptionally fine. Upon considering these titles, thirty books were discarded because they were either too heavy in style or subject matter to find popular favor.

The next problem was to select those twenty books which would form the cornerstone of a fine home library for people of discriminating taste; books with a cultural and educational background that would tend to broaden the vision and develop the inner resources of the reader . . . books that were sufficiently thrilling and popular in their appeal to capture the imagination and interest of every member of the family.

It seems significant to mention here that when the final list of twenty volumes was compiled it contained books which had been mentioned on almost every list of worthwhile reading. The titles of this set are submitted with the confidence that each and every volume merits the label "World's Greatest Literature."

The next problem of importance was the designing of a format worthy of the name "Spencer." The services of Mr. Leonard Mounteney, a master craftsman who had served for twenty years as a binder in the studios of Robert Riviere & Sons of London, England, were engaged for this artistic undertaking. Mounteney has in the last

V

ten years won for himself considerable acclaim as one of the world's most eminent binders. He approached the task of designing these books with all the fervor and interest of a skilled artisan who loves his work, applying the same thought to these volumes as is usually accorded the bindings of museum masterpieces, incunabula and priceless first editions. Mounteney was well aware that the name "Spencer" had become identified with handsome illustration, fine printing and exquisite binding and he was most anxious to create books of surpassing beauty.

"The Spencer Press" is named in honor of and as a tribute to the memory of William Augustus Spencer, the son of Lorillard Spencer and Sarah Johnson Griswold. Spencer was born in New York, was educated in Europe and made his home in Paris, frequently visiting the United States. Spencer became an inveterate book collector, specializing in fine French bindings. He soon became a patron of the fine binders of his day and his collection, now on permanent exhibition at the New York Public Library, is rated as one of the finest of modern collections. Unfortunately, Spencer perished in the sinking of the Titanic in 1912 cutting short a career of great promise.

The books collected by Spencer were mostly nineteenth century works. These volumes represent a definite advancement in many spheres of book production. The authors, publishers, printers, engravers and bookbinders are all representative of what is modern in their several arts, for Spencer was a true collector who insisted upon a high state of perfection in every creative phase of the bookmaking art.

This type of publishing depends more than anything else upon patronage for its existence. The history of fine bookmaking is linked with the social history of the countries where it is practised. The wealthy nobility were usually the patrons of this fine art. The Kings of France were notable collectors forming libraries of considerable merit. Jean Grolier, Viscount d'Aguisy (1479-1565), Treasurer-General of the Duchy of Milan, friend of Francis I, and ambassador to Pope Clement VII, friend of

Aldus, the great printer, was perhaps the most lavish patron of the art of binding and collecting books. To Grolier is accorded the first place among all the great names in book collecting history, and to him is owed the dignified standing in which book collecting is esteemed among the gentler arts. To Grolier also goes the honor for creating a most important and fundamental style in the decoration of book covers.

From Grolier to Spencer we find the names of many illustrious notables who have fostered and patronized the advancement of this art. Jean Baptiste Colbert, statesman and minister of finance under Louis XIV, was the founder of the Academy of Inscriptions which concerned itself greatly with book decoration. Then there was Mazarin, Italian and French cardinal and statesman, who founded one of the great libraries of the world which bears his name. During the intervening years there have been thousands of collectors who have patronized the art. In America one thinks of such great names as Weidner, Morgan, Huntington and Hay in this connection.

Such affluent patronage has given aid to many different interpretations of beauty. Books have been handsomely bound in paper, in wood, in parchment, in cloth and fine leathers. They have been inlaid with materials of contrasting colors, hand painted, encrusted with rare and valuable jewels. They have contained gorgeous end papers and fancy doublures. Men have spent years in the binding, tooling and decoration of a single volume.

These bibliophiles collected not only fine titles, bindings and illustrations but fine printing as well. Gutenberg, the father of fine printing, set an early standard which has been difficult if not impossible to excel. The books created by Gutenberg still rank as among the finest examples of book ornamentation ever produced. Then came the handsome volumes of the East with their arabesques, graceful lines and fleurons which found many an eager collector among the gentlemen of Venice. Aldus, the printer, patronized by Grolier, created many examples of fine printing influenced by these same Eastern designs. The history of fine binding and bookmaking is a long

VII

and interesting one filled with many glorious stories of exquisite books. In the creation of this set of the "World's Greatest Literature," Mounteney has copied the designs of Roger Payne, the one truly great English binder of the nineteenth century. Payne's work was known to have a French influence, a delicate decorative scheme of dots, lines and simple designs. Mounteney has added certain elegant refinements of his own and has endeavored to create a set of books that would be a credit to the memory and name of one of the greatest of all modern collectors . . . a set of books within the reach of the true book-lover so that the appreciation of fine and beautiful books need no longer be a kingly prerogative alone.

The publishers do not claim or even dare to hope that these books are to be compared for richness of binding or makeup with the volumes in the Spencer Library, for some of those books cost thousands of dollars and occupied many years in the lives of master craftsmen. It is true, however, that Mounteney in his careful designing has created books possessing rare beauty of design and exquisite good taste which vie in appearance and handsomeness with the Spencer masterpieces. It should be remembered that the original Spencer volumes were designed by hand, tooled by hand, and often printed by hand, whereas these books were created by one of the world's greatest printers employing every advancement of modern science and efficiency to bring to you books you will treasure over the years . . . books that will add to the richness and fullness of your life.

Reading, Pa. 1936.   LEONARD S. DAVIDOW.

CONTENTS

BOOK THE FOURTH

BOOK THE FIFTH

BOOK THE FIRST.

CHAPTER I.

The two gentlemen of Pompeii.

"Ho, Diomed, well met! Do you sup with Glaucus to-night?" said a young man of small stature, who wore his tunic in those loose and effeminate folds which proved him to be a gentleman and a coxcomb.

"Alas, no! dear Clodius; he has not invited me," replied Diomed, a man of portly frame and of middle age. "By Pollux, a scurvy trick! for they say his suppers are the best in Pompeii."

"Pretty well—though there is never enough of wine for me. It is not the old Greek blood that flows in his veins, for he pretends that wine makes him dull the next morning."

"There may be another reason for that thrift," said Diomed, raising his brows. "With all his conceit and extravagance he is not so rich, I fancy, as he affects to be, and perhaps loves to save his amphoræ better than his wit."

"An additional reason for supping with him while the sesterces last. Next year, Diomed, we must find another Glaucus."

"He is fond of the dice, too, I hear."

"He is fond of every pleasure; and while he likes the pleasure of giving suppers, we are all fond of *him*."

"Ha, ha, Clodius, that is well said! Have you ever seen my wine-cellars, by the bye?" "I think not, my good Diomed."

"Well, you must sup with me some evening; I have tolerable mu\ræn\æ* in my reservoir, and I will ask Pansa the ædile to meet you."

"Oh, no state with me!—*Persicos odi apparatus*, I am easily contented. Well, the day wanes; I am for the baths—and you——"

---

* *Muræne*—lampreys.

1

"To the questor—business of state—afterwards to the temple of Isis. *Vale!*"

"An ostentatious, bustling, ill-bred fellow," muttered Clodius to himself, as he sauntered slowly away. "He thinks with his feasts and his wine-cellars to make us forget that he is the son of a freedman:—and so we will, when we do him the honor of winning his money; these rich plebeians are a harvest for us spendthrift nobles."

Thus soliloquizing, Clodius arrived in the Via Domitiana, which was crowded with passengers and chariots, and exhibited all that gay and animated exuberance of life and motion which we find at this day in the streets of Naples.

The bells of the cars as they rapidly glided by each other, jingled merrily on the ear, and Clodius with smiles or nods claimed familiar acquaintance with whatever equipage was most elegant or fantastic: in fact, no idler was better known in Pompeii.

"What, Clodius! and how have you slept on your good fortune?" cried, in a pleasant and musical voice, a young man, in a chariot of the most fastidious and graceful fashion. Upon its surface of bronze were eleborately wrought, in the still exquisite workmanship of Greece, reliefs of the Olympian games: the two horses that drew the car were of the rarest breed of Parthia; their slender limbs seemed to disdain the ground and court the air, and yet at the slightest touch of the charioteer, who stood behind the young owner of the equipage, they paused motionless, as if suddenly transformed into stone —lifeless, but life-like, as one of the breathing wonders of Praxiteles. The owner himself was of that slender and beautiful symmetry from which the sculptors of Athens drew their models; his Grecian origin betrayed itself in his light but clustering locks, and the perfect harmony of his features. He wore no toga, which in the time of the emperors had indeed ceased to be the general distinction of the Romans, and was especially ridiculed by the pretenders to fashion; but his tunic glowed in the richest hues of the Tyrian dye, and the fibulæ, or buckles, by which it was fastened, sparkled with emeralds: around his neck was a chain of gold, which in the middle of his breast twisted itself into the form of a serpent's head, from the mouth of which hung pendent a large signet ring of elaborate and most exquisite workmanship; the sleeves of the tunic were loose, and fringed at the hand with gold: and across the waist a girdle wrought in arabesque designs, and of the same material as the fringe, served in lieu of pockets for the receptacle of the handkerchief and the purse, the stilus and the tablets.

"My dear Glaucus!" said Clodius, "I rejoice to see that your losses have so little affected your mien. Why, you seem as if you had been inspired by Apollo, and your face shines with happiness like a glory; any one might take you for the winner, and me for the loser."

"And what is there in the loss or gain of those dull pieces of metal that should change our spirit, my Clodius? By Venus, while yet young, we can cover our full locks with chaplets— while yet the cithara sounds on unsated ears—while yet the smile of Lydia or of Chloe flashes over our veins in which the blood runs so swiftly, so long shall we find delight in the sunny air, and make bald time itself but the treasurer of our joys. You sup with me to-night, you know."

"Who ever forgets the invitation of Glaucus!"

"But which way go you now?"

"Why, I thought of visiting the baths; but it wants yet an hour to the usual time."

"Well, I will dismiss my chariot, and go with you. So, so, my Phylias," stroking the horse nearest to him, which by a low neigh and with backward ears playfully acknowledged the courtesy: "a holiday for you to-day. Is he not handsome, Clodius?"

"Worthy of Phœbus," returned the noble parasite,—"or of Glaucus."

CHAPTER II.

The blind flower-girl, and the beauty of fashion.—The Athenian's confession. —The reader's introduction to Arbaces of Egypt.

TALKING lightly on a thousand matters, the two young men sauntered through the streets: they were now in that quarter which was filled with the gayest shops, their open interiors all and each radiant with the gaudy yet harmonious colors of frescoes, inconceivably varied in fancy and design.

The sparkling fountains, that at every vista threw upwards their grateful spray in the summer air; the crowd of passengers, or rather loiterers, mostly clad in robes of the Tyrian dye; the gay groups collected round each more attractive shop; the slaves passing to and fro with buckets of bronze, cast in the most graceful shapes, and borne upon their heads; the country girls stationed at frequent intervals with baskets of blushing fruit and flowers more alluring to the ancient Italians than to their descendants (with whom, indeed, *"latet anguis in herba,"* a disease seems lurking in every violet and rose), the numerous haunts which fulfilled with that idle people the office of cafés and clubs at this day; the shops, where on shelves of marble were ranged the vases of wine and oil, and before whose thresholds, seats, protected from the sun by a purple awning, invited the weary to rest and the indolent to lounge—made a scene of such glowing and vivacious excitement, as might well give the Athenian spirit of Glaucus an excuse for its susceptibility to joy.

"Talk to me no more of Rome," said he to Clodius. "Pleasure is too stately and ponderous in those mighty walls: even in the precincts of the court—even in the Golden House of Nero, and the incipient glories of the palace of Titus, there is a certain dulness of magnificence—the eye aches—the spirit is wearied; besides, my Clodius, we are discontented when we compare the enormous luxury and wealth of others with the mediocrity of our own state. But here we surrender ourselves easily to pleasure, and we have the brilliancy of luxury without the lassitude of its pomp."

"It was from that feeling that you chose your summer retreat at Pompeii?"

"It was. I prefer it to Baiæ: I grant the charms of the latter, but I love not the pedants who resort there, and who seem to weigh out their pleasures by the drachm."

"Yet you are fond of the learned, too; and as for poetry, why your house is literally eloquent with Æschylus and Homer, the epic and the drama."

"Yes, but those Romans who mimic my Athenian ancestors do everything so heavily. Even in the chase they make their slaves carry Plato with them; and whenever the boar is lost, out they take their books and their papyrus, in order not to lose their time too. When the dancing-girls swim before them in all the blandishment of Persian manners, some drone of a freedman, with a face of stone, reads them a section of Cicero "De Officiis." Unskilful pharmacists! pleasure and study are not elements to be thus mixed together—they must be enjoyed separately: the Romans lose both by this pragmatical affectation of refinement, and prove that they have no souls for either. Oh, my Clodius, how little your countrymen know of the true versatility of a Pericles, of the true witcheries of an Aspasia! It was but the other day that I paid a visit to Pliny: he was sitting in his summer-house writing, while an unfortunate slave played on the tibia. His nephew (oh! whip me such philosophical coxcombs!) was reading Thucydides' description of the plague, and nodding his conceited little head in time to the music, while his lips were repeating all the loathsome details of that terrible delineation. The puppy saw nothing incongruous in learning at the same time a ditty of love and a description of the plague."

"Why they *are* much the same thing," said Clodius.

"So I told him, in excuse for his coxcombry;—but my youth stared me rebukingly in the face, without taking the jest, and answered, that it was only the insensate ear that the music pleased, whereas the book (the description of the plague, mind you!) elevated the heart. 'Ah!' quoth the fat uncle, wheezing, 'my boy is quite an Athenian, always mixing the *utile* with the *dulce.*' O Minerva, how I laughed in my sleeve! While I was there, they came to tell the boy-sophist that his favorite freedman was just dead of a fever. 'Inexorable death!' cried he;—'get me my Horace. How beautifully the sweet poet consoles us for these misfortunes!' Oh, can these men love, my Clodius? Scarcely even with the senses. How rarely a Roman has a heart! He is but the mechanism of genius—he wants its bones and flesh."

Though Clodius was secretly a little sore at these remarks on his countrymen, he affected to sympathize with his friend, partly because he was by nature a parasite, and partly because it was the fashion among the dissolute young Romans to affect a little contempt for the very birth which, in reality, made them so arrogant: it was the mode to imitate the Greeks, and yet to laugh at their own clumsy imitation.

Thus conversing, their steps were arrested by a crowd gathered round an open space where three streets met; and, just where the porticos of a light and graceful temple threw their shade, there stood a young girl, with a flower-basket on her right arm, and a small three-stringed instrument of music in the left hand, to whose low and soft tones she was modulating a wild and half-barbaric air. At every pause in the music she gracefully waved her flower-basket round, inviting the loiterers to buy; and many a sesterce was showered into the basket, either in compliment to the music or in compassion to the songstress—for she was blind.

"It is my poor Thessalian," said Glaucus, stopping; "I have not seen her since my return to Pompeii. Hush! her voice is sweet; let us listen."

THE BLIND FLOWER-GIRL'S SONG.

I.

"Buy my flowers—O buy—I pray!
  The blind girl comes from afar;
If the earth be as fair as I hear them say,
  These flowers her children are!
Do they her beauty keep?
  They are fresh from her lap, I know;
For I caught them fast asleep
  In her arms an hour ago.
  With the air which is her breath—
  Her soft and delicate breath—
    Over them murmuring low!

On their lips her sweet kiss lingers yet,
And their cheeks with her tender tears are wet.
For she weeps—that gentle mother weeps—
(As morn and night her watch she keeps,
With a yearning heart and a passionate care)
To see the young things grow so fair;
  She weeps—for love she weeps;
  And the dews are the tears she weeps,
  From the well of a mother's love!

II.

Ye have a world of light,
  Where love in the loved rejoices;
But the blind girl's home is the House of Night,
  And its beings are empty voices.

As one in the realm below,
I stand by the streams of woe!
I hear the vain shadows glide,

I feel their soft breath at my side.
    And I thirst the loved forms to see,
And I stretch my fond arms around,
And I catch but a shapeless sound,
For the living are ghosts to me.

    Come buy—come buy!—
Hark! how the sweet things sigh
(For they have a voice like ours),
'The breath of the blind girl closes
The leaves of the saddening roses—
We are tender, we sons of light,
We shrink from this child of night;
From the grasp of the blind girl free us:
We yearn for the eyes that see us—
We are for night too gay,
In your eyes we behold the day—
O buy—O buy the flowers!' "

"I must have yon bunch of violets, sweet Nydia," said Glaucus, pressing through the crowd, and dropping a handful of small coins into the basket; "your voice is more charming than ever."

The blind girl started forward as she heard the Athenian's voice; then as suddenly paused, while the blood rushed violently over neck, cheek, and temples.

"So you are returned!" said she, in a low voice; and then repeated half to herself, "Glaucus is returned!"

"Yes, child, I have not been at Pompeii above a few days. My garden wants your care, as before; you will visit it, I trust, to-morrow. And mind, no garlands at my house shall be woven by any hands but those of the pretty Nydia."

Nydia smiled joyously, but did not answer, and Glaucus, placing in his breast the violets he had selected, turned gaily and carelessly from the crowd.

"So, she is a sort of client of yours, this child?" said Clodius.

"Ay—does she not sing prettily? She interests me, the poor slave! Besides, she is from the land of the Gods' hill— Olympus frowned upon her cradle—she is of Thessaly."

"The witches' country."

"True: but for my part I find every woman a witch; and at Pompeii, by Venus! the very air seems to have taken a love-philtre, so handsome does every face without a beard seem in my eyes."

"And lo! one of the handsomest in Pompeii, old Diomed's daughter, the rich Julia!" said Clodius, as a young lady her face covered by her veil, and attended by two female slaves, approached them, on her way to the bath.

"Fair Julia, we salute thee!" said Clodius.

Julia partly raised her veil, so as with some coquetry to display a bold Roman profile, a full dark bright eye and a cheek over whose natural olive art shed a fairer and softer rose.

"And Glaucus, too, is returned!" said she, glancing meaningly at the Athenian. "Has he forgotten," she added in a half-whisper, "his friends of the last year?"

"Beautiful Julia! even Lethe itself, if it disappear in one part of the earth, rises again in another. Jupiter does not allow us ever to forget for more than a moment; but Venus, more harsh still, vouchsafes not even a moment's oblivion."

"Glaucus is never at a loss for fair words."

"Who is, when the object of them is so fair?"

"We shall see you both at my father's villa soon," said Julia, turning to Clodius.

"We will mark the day in which we visit you with a white stone," answered the gamester.

Julia dropped her veil, but slowly, so that her last glance rested on the Athenian with affected timidity and real boldness; the glance bespoke tenderness and reproach.

The friends passed on.

"Julia is certainly handsome," said Glaucus.

"And last year you would have made that confession in a warmer tone."

"True: I was dazzled at the first sight, and mistook for a gem that which was but an artful imitation."

"Nay," returned Clodius, "all women are the same at heart. Happy he who weds a handsome face and a large dower. What more can he desire?"

Glaucus sighed.

They were now in a street less crowded than the rest, at the end of which they beheld that broad and most lovely sea, which upon those delicious coasts seems to have renounced its prerogative of terror,—so soft are the crisping winds that hover around its bosom, so glowing and so various are the hues which it takes from the rosy clouds, so fragrant are the perfumes which the breezes from the land scatter over its depths. From such a sea might you well believe that Aphrodité rose to take the empire of the earth.

"It is still early for the bath," said the Greek, who was the creature of every poetical impulse; "let us wander from the crowded city, and look upon the sea while the noon yet laughs along its billows."

"With all my heart," said Clodius; "and the bay, too, is always the most animated part of the city.

Pompeii was the miniature of the civilization of that age. Within the narrow compass of its walls was contained, as it were, a specimen of every gift which luxury offered to power. In its minute but glittering shops, its tiny palaces, its baths, its forum, its theatre, its circus—in the energy yet corruption, in the refinement yet the vice, of its people, you beheld a model of the whole empire. It was a toy, a plaything, a showbox, in which the gods seemed pleased to keep the representation of the great monarchy of earth, and which they afterwards hid from time, to give the wonder of posterity;—the moral of the maxim, that under the sun there is nothing new.

Crowded in the glassy bay were the vessels of commerce and the gilded galleys for the pleasures of the rich citizens. The boats of the fishermen glided rapidly to and fro; and afar off you saw the tall masts of the fleet under the command of Pliny. Upon the shore sat a Sicilian, who, with vehement gestures and flexile features, was narrating to a group of fishermen and peasants a strange tale of shipwrecked mariners and friendly dolphins:—just as at this day, in the modern neighborhood, you may hear upon the Mole of Naples.

Drawing his comrade from the crowd, the Greek bent his steps toward a solitary part of the beach, and the two friends, seated on a small crag which rose amidst the smooth pebbles, inhaled the voluptuous and cooling breeze, which, dancing over the waters, kept music with its invisible feet. There was, perhaps, something in the scene that invited them to silence and reverie. Clodius shading his eyes from the burning sky, was calculating the gains of the last week; and the Greek, leaning upon his hand, and shrinking not from that sun,— his nation's tutelary deity,—with whose fluent light of poesy, and joy, and love, his own veins were filled, gazed upon the broad expanse, and envied, perhaps, every wind that bent its pinions towards the shores of Greece.

"Tell me, Clodius," said the Greek at last, "hast thou ever been in love?" "Yes, very often."

"He who has loved often," answered Glaucus, "has loved never. There is but one Eros, though there are many counterfeits of him." "The counterfeits are not bad little gods, upon the whole," answered Clodius.

"I agree with you," returned the Greek. "I adore even the shadow of Love; but I adore himself yet more."

"Art thou, then, soberly and earnestly in love? Hast thou that feeling which the poets describe—a feeling that makes us neglect our suppers, forswear the theatre, and write elegies? I should never have thought it. You dissemble well."

"I am not far gone enough for that," returned Glaucus, smiling; "or rather I say with Tibullus,—

'He whom love rules, where'er his path may be,
Walks safe and sacred.'

In fact, I am not in love; but I could be if there were but occasion to see the object. Eros would light his torch, but the priests have given him no oil."

"Shall I guess the object?—Is it not Diomed's daughter? She adores you, and does not affect to conceal it; and, by Hercules, I say again and again, she is both handsome and rich. She will bind the door-posts of her husband with golden fillets."

"No, I do not desire to sell myself. Diomed's daughter is handsome, I grant; and at one time, had she not been the grandchild of a freedman, I might have—— Yet no—she carries all her beauty in her face; her manners are not maidenlike, and her mind knows no culture save that of pleasure."

"You are ungrateful. Tell me, then, who is the fortunate virgin?"

"You shall hear, my Clodius. Several months ago I was sojourning at Neapolis, a city utterly to my own heart, for it still retains the manners and stamp of its Grecian origin,— and it yet merits the name of Parthenope, from its delicious air and its beautiful shores. One day I entered the temple of Minerva, to offer up my prayers, not for myself more than for the city on which Pallas smiles no longer. The temple was

empty and deserted. The recollections of Athens crowded fast
and meltingly upon me: imagining myself still alone in the
temple, and absorbed in the earnestness of my devotion, my
prayer gushed from my heart to my lips, and I wept as I
prayed. I was startled in the midst of my devotions, however,
by a deep sigh; I turned suddenly round, and just behind me
was a female. She had raised her veil also in prayer: and when
our eyes met, methought a celestial ray shot from those dark
and smiling orbs at once into my soul. Never, my Clodius,
have I seen mortal face more exquisitely moulded: a certain
melancholy softened and yet elevated its expression; that unutterable something which springs from the soul, and which
our sculptors have imparted to the aspect of Psyche, gave her
beauty I know not what of divine and noble: tears were rolling
down her eyes. I guessed at once that she was also of Athenian lineage; and that in my prayer for Athens her heart had
responded to mine. I spoke to her, though with a faltering
voice—'Art thou not, too, Athenian?' said I, 'O beautiful
virgin!' At the sound of my voice she blushed, and half drew
her veil across her face,—'My forefathers' ashes,' said she,
'repose by the waters of Ilyssus: my birth is of Neapolis; but
my heart, as my lineage, is Athenian.'—'Let us, then,' said I,
'make our offerings together:' and, as the priest now appeared,
we stood side by side, while we followed the priest in his ceremonial prayer; together we touched the knees of the goddess
—together we laid our olive garlands on the altar. I felt a
strange emotion of almost sacred tenderness at this companionship. We, strangers from a far and fallen land, stood together and alone in that temple of our country's deity: was it
not natural that my heart should yearn to my countrywoman,
for so I might surely call her? I felt as if I had known her for
years; and that simple rite seemed, as by a miracle, to operate
on the sympathies and ties of time. Silently we left the temple,
and I was about to ask her where she dwelt, and if I might be
permitted to visit her, when a youth, in whose features there
was some kindred resemblance to her own, and who stood
upon the steps of the fane, took her by the hand. She turned
round and bade me farewell. The crowd separated us: I saw
her no more. On reaching my home I found letters, which
obliged me to set out for Athens, for my relations threatened
me with litigation concerning my inheritance. When that suit

was happily over, I repaired once more to Neapolis; I instituted inquiries throughout the whole city, I could discover no clue of my lost countrywoman, and, hoping to lose in gaiety all remembrance of that beautiful apparition, I hastened to plunge myself amidst the luxuries of Pompeii. This is all my history. I do not love; but I remember and regret."

As Clodius was about to reply, a slow and stately step approached them, and at the sound it made amongst the pebbles, each turned, and each recognized the new-comer.

It was a man who had scarcely reached his fortieth year, of tall stature, and of a thin but nervous and sinewy frame. His skin, dark and bronzed, betrayed his Eastern origin; and his features had something Greek in their outline, (especially in the chin, the lip, and the brow,) save that the nose was somewhat raised and aquiline; and the bones, hard and visible, forbade that fleshy and waving contour which on the Grecian physiognomy preserved even in manhood the round and beautiful curves of youth. His eyes, large and black as the deepest night, shone with no varying and uncertain lustre. A deep, thoughtful, and half-melancholy calm, seemed unalterably fixed in their majestic and commanding gaze. His step and mien were peculiarly sedate and lofty, and something foreign in the fashion and the sober hues of his sweeping garments added to the impressive effect of his quiet countenance and stately form. Each of the young men, in saluting the new-comer, made mechanically, and with care to conceal it from him, a slight gesture or sign with their fingers; for Arbaces, the Egyptian, was supposed to possess the fatal gift of the evil eye.

"The scene must, indeed, be beautiful," said Arbaces, with a cold though courteous smile, "which draws the gay Clodius, and Glaucus the all-admired, from the crowded thoroughfares of the city."

"Is Nature ordinarily so unattractive?" asked the Greek.

"To the dissipated—yes."

"An austere reply, but scarcely a wise one. Pleasure delights in contrasts; it is from dissipation that we learn to enjoy solitude, and from solitude dissipation."

"So think the young philosophers of the Garden," replied the Egyptian; "they mistake lassitude for meditation, and imagine that, because they are sated with others, they know the delight of loneliness. But not in such jaded bosoms can Nature awaken that enthusiasm which alone draws from her chaste reserve all her unspeakable beauty: she demands from you, not the exhaustion of passion, but all that fervor, from which you only seek, in adoring her, a release. When, young Athenian, the moon revealed herself in visions of light to Endymion, it was after a day passed, not amongst the feverish haunts of men, but on the still mountains and in the solitary valleys of the hunter."

"Beautiful simile!" cried Glaucus; "most unjust application! Exhaustion! that word is for age, not youth. By me, at least, one moment of satiety has never been known!"

Again the Egyptian smiled, but his smile was cold and blighting, and even the unimaginative Clodius froze beneath its light. He did not reply to the passionate exclamation of Glaucus; but, after a pause, he said, in a soft and melancholy voice,—

"After all, you do right to enjoy the hour while it smiles for you; the rose soon withers, the perfume soon exhales. And we, O Glaucus! strangers in the land, and far from our fathers' ashes, what is there left for us but pleasure or regret?—for you the first, perhaps for me the last."

The bright eyes of the Greek were suddenly suffused with tears. "Ah, speak not, Arbaces," he cried—"speak not of our ancestors. Let us forget that there were ever other liberties than those of Rome! And Glory!—oh, vainly would we call her ghost from the fields of Marathon and Thermopylæ!"

"Thy heart rebukes thee while thou speakest," said the Egyptian; "and in thy gaieties this night, thou wilt be more mindful of Leæna than of Lais. *Vale!*"

Thus saying, he gathered his robe around him, and slowly swept away.

"I breathe more freely," said Clodius. "Imitating the Egyptians, we sometimes introduce a skeleton at our feasts. In truth, the presence of such an Egyptian as yon gliding shadow were spectre enough to sour the richest grape of the Falernian."

"Strange man!" said Glaucus, musingly; "yet dead though he seem to pleasure, and cold to the objects of the world, scandal belies him, or his house and his heart could tell a different tale."

"Ah! there are whispers of other orgies than those of Osiris in his gloomy mansion. He is rich, too, they say. Can we not get him amongst us, and teach him the charms of dice? Pleasure of pleasures! hot fever of hope and fear! inexpressible unjaded passion! how fiercely beautiful thou art, O Gaming!"

"Inspired—inspired!" cried Glaucus, laughing; "the oracle speaks poetry in Clodius. What miracle next!"

CHAPTER III.

Parentage of Glaucus.—Description of the houses of Pompeii.—A classic revel.

HEAVEN had given to Glaucus every blessing but one: it had given him beauty, health, fortune, genius, illustrious descent, a heart of fire, a mind of poetry; but it had denied him the heritage of freedom. He was born in Athens, the subject of Rome. Succeeding early to an ample inheritance, he had indulged that inclination for travel so natural to the young, and had drunk deep of the intoxicating draught of pleasure amidst the gorgeous luxuries of the imperial court.

He was an Alcibiades without ambition. He was what a man if imagination, youth, fortune, and talents, readily becomes when you deprive him of the inspiration of glory. His house at Rome was the theme of the debauchees, but also of the lovers of art; and the sculptors of Greece delighted to task their skill in adorning the porticos and *exedra* of an Athenian. His retreat in Pompeii—alas! the colors are faded now, the walls stripped of their paintings!—its main beauty, its elaborate finish of grace and ornament, is gone; yet when first given once more to the day, what eulogies, what wonder, did its minute and glowing decorations create—its paintings —its mosaics! Passionately enamoured of poetry and the drama, which recalled to Glaucus the wit and the heroism of his race, that fairy mansion was adorned with representations of Æschylus and Homer. And antiquaries, who resolve taste to a trade, have turned the patron to the professor, and still (though the error is now acknowledged) they style in custom, as they first named in mistake, the disburied house of the Athenian Glaucus "THE HOUSE OF THE DRAMATIC POET."

Previous to our description of this house, it may be as well to convey to the reader a general notion of the houses of Pompeii, which we will find to resemble strongly the plans of Vitruvius; but with all those differences in detail, of caprice and taste, which being natural to mankind, have always puzzled antiquaries. We shall endeavor to make this description as clear and unpedantic as possible.

You enter then, usually, by a small entrance-passage (called *cestibulum*), into a hall, sometimes with (but more frequently without) the ornament of columns; around three sides of this hall are doors communicating with several bed-chambers (among which is the porter's), the best of these being usually appropriated to country visitors. At the extremity of the hall, on either side to the right and left, if the house is large, there are two small recesses, rather than chambers, generally devoted to the ladies of the mansion; and in the centre of the tessellated pavement of the hall is invariably a square, shallow reservoir for rain-water (classically termed *impluvium*), which was admitted by an aperture in the roof above; the said aperture being covered at will by an awning. Near this impluvium, which had a peculiar sanctity in the eyes of the ancients, were sometimes (but at Pompeii more rarely than at Rome) placed images of the household gods;—the hospitable hearth, often mentioned by the Roman poets, and consecrated to the Lares, was at Pompeii almost invariably formed by a movable *brazier;* while in some corner, often the most ostentatious place, was deposited a huge wooden chest, ornamented and strengthened by bands of bronze or iron, and secured by strong hooks upon a stone pedestal so firmly as to defy the attempts of any robber to detach it from its position. It is supposed that this chest was the money-box, or coffer, of the master of the house; though as no money has been found in any of the chests discovered at Pompeii, it is probable that it was sometimes rather designed for ornament than use.

In this hall (or *atrium,* to speak classically) the clients and visitors of inferior ranks were usually received. In the houses of the more "respectable," an *atriensis,* or slave peculiarly devoted to the service of the hall, was invariably retained, and his rank among his fellow-slaves was high and important. The reservoir in the centre must have been rather

a dangerous ornament, but the centre of the hall was like the
grass-plot of a college, and interdicted to the passers to and
fro, who found ample space in the margin. Right opposite the
entrance, at the other end of the hall, was an apartment
(tablinum), in which the pavement was usually adorned with
rich mosaics, and the walls covered with elaborate paintings.
Here were usually kept the records of the family, or those of
any public office that had been filled by the owner: on one side
of this saloon, if we may so call it, was often a dining-room,
or *triclinium;* on the other side, perhaps, what we should now
term a cabinet of gems, containing whatever curiosities were
deemed most rare and costly; and invariably a small passage
for the slaves to cross to the further parts of the house, without passing the apartments thus mentioned. These rooms all
opened on a square or oblong colonnade, technically termed
peristyle. If the house was small, its boundary ceased with
this colonnade; and in that case its centre, however diminutive, was ordinarily appropriated to the purpose of a garden,
and adorned with vases of flowers, placed upon pedestals:
while, under the colonnade, to the right and left, were doors,
admitting to bed-rooms, to a second *triclinium,* or eating-
room (for the ancients generally appropriated two rooms at
least to that purpose, one for summer, and one for winter
—or, perhaps, one for ordinary, the other for festive, occasions) ; and if the owner affected letters, a cabinet, dignified
by the name of library,—for a very small room was sufficient
to contain the few rolls of papyrus which the ancients deemed
a notable collection of books.

At the end of the peristyle was generally the kitchen.
Supposing the house was large, it did not end with the peristyle, and the centre thereof was not in that case a garden, but
might be, perhaps, adorned with a fountain, or basin for fish;
and at its end, exactly opposite to the tablinum, was generally
another eating-room, on either side of which were bed-rooms,
and, perhaps, a picture-saloon, or *pinacotheca.* These apartments communicated again with a square or oblong space,
usually adorned on three sides with a colonnade like the
peristyle, and very much resembling the peristyle, only usually
longer. This was the proper *viridarium,* or garden, being
commonly adorned with a fountain, or statues, and a profusion of gay flowers: at its extreme end was the gardener's

house; on either side, beneath the colonnade, were sometimes, if the size of the family required it, additional rooms.

At Pompeii, a second or third story was rarely of importance, being built only above a small part of the house, and containing rooms for the slaves; differing in this respect from the more magnificent edifices of Rome, which generally contained the principal eating-room (or *cœnaculum*) on the second floor. The apartments themselves were ordinarily of small size; for in those delightful climes they received any extraordinary number of visitors in the peristyle (or portico), the hall, or the garden;—and even their banquet-rooms, however elaborately adorned and carefully selected in point of aspect, were of diminutive proportions; for the intellectual ancients, being fond of society, not of crowds, rarely feasted more than nine at a time, so that large dinner-rooms were not so necessary with them as with us. But the suite of rooms seen at once from the entrance, must have had a very imposing effect: you beheld at once the hall richly paved and painted—the tablinum—the graceful peristyle, and (if the house extended farther) the opposite banquet-room and the garden, which closed the view with some gushing fount or marble statue.

The reader will now have a tolerable notion of the Pompeian houses, which resembled in some respects the Grecian, but mostly the Roman fashion of domestic architecture. In almost every house there is some difference in detail from the rest, but the principal outline is the same in all. In all you find the hall, the tablinum, and the peristyle, communicating with each other; in all you find the walls richly painted; and in all the evidence of a people fond of the refining elegancies of life. The purity of the taste of the Pompeians in decoration is, however, questionable: they were fond of the gaudiest colors, of fantastic designs; they often painted the lower half of their columns a bright red, leaving the rest uncolored; and where the garden was small, its wall was frequently tinted to deceive the eye as to its extent, imitating trees, birds, temples, &c., in perspective—a meretricious delusion which the graceful pedantry of Pliny himself adopted, with a complacent pride in its ingenuity.

But the house of Glaucus was at once one of the smallest, and yet one of the most adorned and finished of all the private mansions of Pompeii: it would be a model at this day for the house of "a single man in Mayfair"—the envy and despair of the cœlibian purchasers of buhl and marquetry.

You enter by a long and narrow vestibule, on the floor of which is the image of a dog in mosaic, with the well-known "Cave canem,"—or "Beware the dog." On either side is a chamber of some size; for the interior part of the house not being large enough to contain the two great divisions of private and public apartments, these two rooms were set apart for the reception of visitors who neither by rank nor familiarity were entitled to admission in the penetralia of the mansion.

Advancing up the vestibule you enter an atrium, that when first discovered was rich in paintings, which, *in point of expression,* would scarcely disgrace a Rafaele. You may see them now transplanted to the Neapolitan Museum; they are still the admiration of connoisseurs—they depict the parting of Achilles and Briseis. Who does not acknowledge the force, the vigor, the beauty, employed in delineating the forms and faces of Achilles and the immortal slave!

On one side the atrium, a small staircase admitted to the apartments for the slaves on the second floor; there also were two or three small bed-rooms, the walls of which portrayed the rape of Europa, the battle of the Amazons, &c.

You now enter the tablinum, across which, at either end, hung rich draperies of Tyrian purple, half withdrawn. On the walls was depicted a poet reading his verses to his friends; and in the pavement was inserted a small and most exquisite mosaic, typical of the instructions given by the director of the stage to his comedians.

You passed through this saloon and entered the peristyle; and here (as I have said before, was usually the case with the smaller houses of Pompeii) the mansion ended. From each of the seven columns that adorned this court hung festoons of garlands; the centre, supplying the place of a garden, bloomed with the rarest flowers placed in vases of white marble, that were supported on pedestals. At the left hand of this small garden was a diminutive fane, resembling one of those small chapels placed at the side of roads in Catholic countries, and dedicated to the Penates; before it stood a bronze tripod: to the left of the colonnade were two small cubicula, or bed-rooms; to the right was the triclinium, in which the guests were now assembled.

This room is usually termed by the antiquaries of Naples, "The Chamber of Leda;" and in the beautiful work of Sir William Gell, the reader will find an engraving from that most delicate and graceful painting of Leda presenting her new-born to her husband, from which the room derives its name. This charming apartment opened upon the fragrant garden. Round the table of citrean wood, highly polished and delicately wrought with silver arabesques, were placed the three couches, which were yet more common at Pompeii than the semicircular seat that had grown lately into fashion at Rome: and on these couches of bronze, studded with richer metals, were laid thick quiltings covered with elaborate broidery, and yielding luxuriously to the pressure.

"Well, I must own," said the ædile Pansa, "that your house, though scarcely larger than a case for one's fibulæ, is a gem of its kind. How beautifully painted is that parting of Achilles and Briseis!—what a style!—what heads!—what a —hem!"

"Praise from Pansa is indeed valuable on such subjects," said Clodius, gravely. "Why, the paintings on *his* walls!— Ah! there is, indeed, the hand of a Zeuxis!"

"You flatter me, my Clodius; indeed you do;" quoth the ædile, who was celebrated through Pompeii for having the worst paintings in the world; for he was patriotic, and patronized none but Pompeians. "You flatter me; but there is something pretty—Ædepol, yes—in the colors, to say nothing of the design;—and then for the kitchen, my friends—ah! that was all my fancy."

"What is the design?" said Glaucus. "I have not yet seen your kitchen, though I have often witnessed the excellence of its cheer."

"A cook, my Athenian—a cook sacrificing the trophies of his skill on the altar of Vesta, with a beautiful muræna (taken from the life) on a spit at a distance;—there is some invention there!"

At that instant the slaves appeared, bearing a tray covered with the first preparative initia of the feast. Amidst delicious figs, fresh herbs strewed with snow, anchovies, and eggs, were ranged small cups of diluted wine sparingly mixed with

honey. As these were placed on the table, young slaves bore
round to each of the five guests (for there were no more) the
silver basin of perfumed water, and napkins edged with a
purple fringe. But the ædile ostentatiously drew forth his own
napkin, which was not, indeed, of so fine a linen, but in which
the fringe was twice as broad, and wiped his hands with the
parade of a man who felt he was calling for admiration.

"A splendid *nappa* that of yours," said Clodius; "why, the
fringe is as broad as a girdle!"

"A trifle, my Clodius: a trifle! They tell me this stripe is
the latest fashion at Rome; but Glaucus attends to these
things more than I."

"Be propitious, O Bacchus!" said Glaucus, inclining
reverentially to a beautiful image of the god placed in the
centre of the table, at the corners of which stood the Lares
and the salt-holders. The guests followed the prayer, and
then, sprinkling the wine on the table, they performed the
wonted libation.

This over, the convivialists reclined themselves on the
couches, and the business of the hour commenced.

"May this cup be my last!" said the young Sallust, as the
table, cleared of its first stimulants, was now loaded with the
substantial part of the entertainment, and the ministering
slave poured forth to him a brimming cyathus—"May this
cup be my last, but it is the best wine I have drunk at Pompeii!"

"Bring hither the amphora," said Glaucus, "and read its
date and its character."

The slave hastened to inform the party that the scroll
fastened to the cork betokened its birth from Chios, and its
age a ripe fifty years.

"How deliciously the snow has cooled it!" said Pansa. "It
is just enough."

"It is like the experience of a man who has cooled his
pleasures sufficiently to give them a double zest," exclaimed
Sallust.

"It is like a woman's 'No,'" added Glaucus: "it cools, but
to inflame the more."

"When is our next wild-beast fight?" said Clodius to
Pansa.

"It stands fixed for the ninth ide of August," answered

Pansa: "on the day after the Vulcanalia;—we have a most lovely young lion for the occasion."

"Whom shall we get for him to eat?" asked Clodius. "Alas! there is a great scarcity of criminals. You must positively find some innocent or other to condemn to the lion, Pansa!"

"Indeed I have thought very seriously about it of late," replied the ædile, gravely. "It was a most infamous law that which forbade us to send our own slaves to the wild beasts. Not to let us do what we like with our own, that's what I call an infringement on property itself."

"Not so in the good old days of the Republic," sighed Sallust.

"And then this pretended mercy to the slaves is such a disappointment to the poor people. How they do love to see a good tough battle between a man and a lion; and all this innocent pleasure they may lose (if the gods don't send us a good criminal soon) from this cursed law!"

"What can be worse policy," said Clodius, sententiously, "than to interfere with the manly amusements of the people?"

"Well, thank Jupiter and the Fates! we have no Nero at present," said Sallust.

"He was, indeed, a tyrant; he shut up our amphitheatre for ten years."

"I wonder it did not create a rebellion," said Sallust.

"It very nearly did," returned Pansa, with his mouth full of wild boar.

Here the conversation was interrupted for a moment by a flourish of flutes, and two slaves entered with a single dish.

"Ah! what delicacy hast thou in store for us now, my Glaucus?" cried the young Sallust, with sparkling eyes.

Sallust was only twenty-four, but he had no pleasure in life like eating—perhaps he had exhausted all the others: yet had he some talent, and an excellent heart—as far as it went.

"I know its face, by Pollux!" cried Pansa. "It is an Ambracian Kid. Ho! [snapping his fingers, a usual signal to the slaves) we must prepare a libation in honor to the newcomer."

"I had hoped," said Glaucus, in a melancholy tone, "to have procured you some oysters from Britain; but the winds that were so cruel to Cæsar have forbid us the oysters."

"Are they in truth so delicious?" asked Lepidus, loosening to a yet more luxurious ease his ungirdled tunic.

"Why, in truth, I suspect it is the distance that gives the flavor; they want the richness of the Brundusium oyster. But at Rome, no supper is complete without them."

"The poor Britons! There is some good in them after all," said Sallust. "They produce an oyster!"

"I wish they would produce us a gladiator," said the ædile, whose provident mind was musing over the wants of the amphitheatre.

"By Pallus!" cried Glaucus, as his favorite slave crowned his streaming locks with a new chaplet, "I love these wild spectacles well enough when beast fights beast; but when a man, one with bones and blood like ours, is coldly put on the arena, and torn limb from limb, the interest is too horrid: I sicken—I gasp for breath—I long to rush and defend him. The yells of the populace seem to me more dire than the voices of the Furies chasing Orestes. I rejoice that there is so little chance of that bloody exhibition for our next show!"

The ædile shrugged his shoulders. The young Sallust, who was thought the best-natured man in Pompeii, stared in surprise. The graceful Lepidus, who rarely spoke for fear of disturbing his features, ejaculated "Hercle!" The parasite Clodius muttered "Ædepol!" and the sixth banqueter, who was the umbra of Clodius, and whose duty it was to echo his richer friend, when he could not praise him,—the parasite of a parasite,—muttered also "Ædepol!"

"Well, you Italians are used to these spectacles; we Greeks are more merciful. Ah, shade of Pindar!—the rapture of a true Grecian game—the emulation of man against man—the generous strife—the half-mournful triumph—so proud to contend with a noble foe, so sad to see him overcome! But ye understand me not."

"The kid is excellent," said Sallust. The slave, whose duty it was to carve, and who valued himself on his science, had just performed that office on the kid to the sound of music, his knife keeping time, beginning with a low tenor and accomplishing the arduous feat amidst a magnificent diapason.

"Your cook is, of course, from Sicily?" said Pansa.

"Yes, of Syracuse."

"I will play you for him," said Clodius. "We will have a game between the courses."

"Better that sort of game, certainly, than a beast fight; but I cannot stake my Sicilian—you have nothing so precious to stake me in return."

"My Phillida—my beautiful dancing-girl!"

"I never buy women," said the Greek, carelessly rearranging his chaplet.

The musicians, who were stationed in the portico without, had commenced their office with the kid; they now directed the melody into a more soft, a more gay, yet it may be a more intellectual strain; and they chanted that song of Horace beginning, "Persicos odi," &c., so impossible to translate, and which they imagined applicable to a feast that, effeminate as it seems to us, was simple enough for the gorgeous revelry of the time. We are witnessing the domestic, and not the princely feast—the entertainment of a gentleman, not an emperor or a senator.

"Ah, good old Horace!" said Sallust, compassionately; "he sang well of feasts and girls, but not like our modern poets."

"The immortal Fulvius, for instance," said Clodius.

"Ah, Fulvius, the immortal!" said the umbra.

"And Spuræna; and Caius Mutius, who wrote three epics in a year—could Horace do that, or Virgil either?" said Lepidus. "Those old poets all fell into the mistake of copying sculpture instead of painting. Simplicity and repose—that was their notion; but we moderns have fire, and passion, and energy—we never sleep, we imitate the colors of painting, its life, and its action. Immortal Fulvius!"

"By the way," said Sallust, "have you seen the new ode by Spuræna, in honor of our Egyptian Isis? It is magnificent—the true religious fervor."

"Isis seems a favorite divinity at Pompeii," said Glaucus.

"Yes!" said Pansa, "she is exceedingly in repute just at this moment; her statue has been uttering the most remarkable oracles. I am not superstitious, but I must confess that she has more than once assisted me materially in my magistracy with her advice. Her priests are so pious, too! none of your gay, none of your proud, ministers of Jupiter and Fortune: they walk barefoot, eat no meat, and pass the greater part of the night in solitary devotion!"

"An example to our other priesthoods, indeed!—Jupiter's temple wants reforming sadly," said Lepidus, who was a great reformer for all but himself.

"They say that Arbaces the Egyptian has imparted some most solemn mysteries to the priests of Isis," observed Sallust. "He boasts his descent from the race of Rameses, and declares that in his family the secrets of remotest antiquity are treasured."

"He certainly possesses the gift of the evil eye," said Clodius. "If I ever come upon that Medusa front without the previous charm, I am sure to lose a favorite horse, or throw the *canes* nine times running."

"The last would be indeed a miracle!" said Sallust, gravely.

"How mean you, Sallust?" returned the gamester, with flushed brow.

"I mean, what you would *leave* me if I played often with you; and that is—nothing."

Clodius answered only by a smile of disdain.

"If Arbaces were not so rich," said Pansa, with a stately air, "I should stretch my authority a little, and inquire into the truth of the report which calls him an astrologer and a sorcerer. Agrippa, when ædile of Rome, banished all such terrible citizens. But a rich man—it is the duty of an ædile to protect the rich!"

"What think you of this new sect, which I am told has even a few proselytes in Pompeii, these followers of the Hebrew God—Christus?"

"Oh, mere speculative visionaries," said Clodius; "they have not a single gentleman amongst them; their proselytes are poor, insignificant, ignorant people!"

"Who ought, however, to be crucified for their blasphemy," said Pansa, with vehemence; "they deny Venus and Jove! Nazarene is but another name for atheist. Let me catch them, that's all."

The second course was gone—the feasters fell back on their couches—there was a pause while they listened to the soft voices of the South, and the music of the Arcadian reed. Glaucus was the most rapt and the least inclined to break the silence, but Clodius began already to think that they had wasted time.

"*Bene vobis!* (your health) my Glaucus," said he, quaffing a cup to each letter of the Greek's name, with the ease of the practised drinker. "Will you not be avenged on your ill-fortune of yesterday? See the dice court us."

"As you will," said Glaucus.

"The dice in summer, and I an ædile!" said Pansa, magisterially; "it is against all law."

"Not in your presence, grave Pansa," returned Clodius, rattling the dice in a long box; "your presence restrains all license: it is not the thing, but the excess of the thing, that hurts." "What wisdom!" muttered the umbra.

"Well, I will look another way," said the ædile.

"Not yet, good Pansa: let us wait till we have supped," said Glaucus.

Clodius reluctantly yielded, concealing his vexation with a yawn. "He gapes to devour the gold," whispered Lepidus to Sallust, in a quotation from the *Aulularia* of Plautus. "Ah! how well I know these polypi, who hold all they touch," answered Sallust, in the same tone, and out of the same play.

The third course, consisting of a variety of fruits, pistachio nuts, sweetmeats, tarts, and confectionery tortured into a thousand fantastic and airy shapes, was now placed upon the table: and the ministri, or attendants, also set there the wine (which had hitherto been handed round to the guests) in large jugs of glass, each bearing upon it the schedule of its age and quality. "Taste this Lesbian, my Pansa," said Sallust; "it is excellent."

"It is not very old," said Glaucus, "but it has been made precocious, like ourselves, by being put to the fire:—the wine to the flames of Vulcan—we to those of his wife—to whose honor I pour this cup."

"It is delicate," said Pansa, "but there is perhaps the least particle too much of rosin in its flavor."

"What a beautiful cup!" cried Clodius, taking up one of transparent crystal, the handles of which were wrought with gems, and twisted in the shape of serpents, the favorite fashion at Pompeii.

"This ring," said Glaucus, taking a costly jewel from the first joint of his finger, and hanging it on the handle, "gives it a richer show, and renders it less unworthy of thy acceptance, my Clodius, on whom may the gods bestow health and fortune, long and oft to crown it to the brim!"

"You are too generous, Glaucus," said the gamester, handing the cup to his slave; "but your love gives it a double value."

"This cup to the Graces!" said Pansa, and he thrice emptied his calix. The guests followed his example.

"We have appointed no director to the feast," cried Sallust.

"Let us throw for him, then," said Clodius, rattling the dice-box.

"Nay," cried Glaucus, "no cold and trite director for us: no dictator of the banquet; no *rex convivii*. Have not the Romans sworn never to obey a king? Shall we be less free than your ancestors? Ho! musicians, let us have the song I composed the other night: it has a verse on this subject, 'The Bacchic hymn of the Hours.'"

The musicians struck their instruments to a wild Ionic air, while the youngest voices in the band chanted forth, in Greek words, as numbers, the following strain:—

THE EVENING HYMN OF THE HOURS.

I.

"Through the summer day, through the weary day,
    We have glided long;
Ere we speed to the Night through her portals grey,
    Hail us with song!—
    With song, with song,
    With a bright and joyous song;
Such as the Cretan maid,
    While the twilight made her bolder,
Woke, high through the ivy shade,
    When the wine-god first consoled her.
From the hush'd, low-breathing skies,
Half-shut look'd their starry eyes,
    And all around,
    With a loving sound,
    The Ægean waves were creeping:
On her lap lay the lynx's head;
Wild thyme was her bridal bed;
And aye through each tiny space,
In the green vine's green embrace,
The Fauns were slily peeping:—
    The Fauns, the prying Fauns—
    The arch, the laughing Fauns—
The Fauns were slily peeping!

II.

Flagging and faint are we
    With our ceaseless flight,
And dull shall our journey be
    Through the realm of night.
Bathe us, O bathe our weary wings,
In the purple wave, as it freshly springs
    To your cups from the fount of light—
From the fount of light—from the fount of light,
For there, when the sun has gone down in night,
        There in the bowl we find him.
The grape is the well of that summer sun,
Or rather the stream that he gazed upon,
Till he left in truth, like the Thespian youth,
        His soul, as he gazed, behind him.

III.

A cup to Jove, and a cup to Love,
    And a cup to the son of Maia;
And honor with three, the band zone-free,
    The band of the bright Aglaia.
But since every bud in the wreath of pleasure
    Ye owe to the sister Hours,
No stinted cups, in a formal measure,
    The Bromian law makes our.
He honors us most who gives us most,
And boasts, with a Bacchanal's honest boast,
    He never will *count* the treasure.
Fastly we fleet, then seize our wings,
And plunge us deep in the sparkling springs;
And aye, as we rise with a dripping plume,
We'll scatter the spray round the garland's bloom.
        We glow—we glow.
Behold, as the girls of the Eastern wave
Bore once with a shout to their crystal cave
    The prize of the Mysian Hylas,
        Even so—even so,
We have caught the young god in our warm embrace,
We hurry him on in our laughing race;
We hurry him on, with a whoop and song,
The cloudy rivers of night along—
    Ho, ho!—we have caught thee, Psilas!"

The guests applauded loudly. When the poet is your host,
his verses are sure to charm.

"Thoroughly Greek," said Lepidus: "the wildness, force,
and energy of that tongue, it is impossible to imitate in the
Roman poetry."

"It is, indeed, a great contrast," said Clodius, ironically at heart, though not in appearance, "to the old-fashioned and tame simplicity of that ode of Horace which we heard before. The air is beautifully Ionic: the word puts me in mind of a toast—Companions, I give you the beautiful Ione."

"Ione!—the name is Greek," said Glaucus, in a soft voice. "I drink the health with delight. But who is Ione?"

"Ah! you have but just come to Pompeii, or you would deserve ostracism for your ignorance," said Lepidus, conceitedly: "not to know Ione, is not to know the chief charm of our city."

"She is of the most rare beauty," said Pansa; "and what a voice!" "She can feed only on nightingales' tongues," said Clodius. "Nightingales' tongues!—beautiful thought!" sighed the umbra.

"Enlighten me, I beseech you," said Glaucus.

"Know then——" began Lepidus.

"Let me speak," cried Clodius; "you drawl out your words as if you spoke tortoises."

"And you speak stones," muttered the coxcomb to himself, as he fell back disdainfully on his couch.

"Know then, my Glaucus," said Clodius, "that Ione is a stranger who has but lately come to Pompeii. She sings like Sappho, and her songs are her own composing; and as for the tibia, and the cithara, and the lyre, I know not in which she most outdoes the Muses. Her beauty is most dazzling. Her house is perfect; such taste—such gems—such bronzes! She is rich, and generous as she is rich."

"Her lovers, of course," said Glaucus, "take care that she does not starve; and money lightly won is always lavishly spent." "Her lovers—ah, there is the enigma! Ione has but one vice—she is chaste. She has all Pompeii at her feet, and she has no lovers: she will not even marry."

"No lovers!" echoed Glaucus.

"No; she has the soul of Vesta, with the girdle of Venus."

"What refined expressions!" said the umbra.

"A miracle!" cried Glaucus. "Can we not see her?"

"I will take you there this evening," said Clodius; "meanwhile—," added he, once more rattling the dice.

"I am yours!" said the complaisant Glaucus. "Pansa, turn your face!"

Lepidus and Sallust played at odd and even, and the umbra looked on, while Glaucus and Clodius became gradually absorbed in the chances of the dice.

"By Pollux!" cried Glaucus, "this is the second time I have thrown the caniculæ" (the lowest throw).

"Now Venus befriend me!" said Clodius, rattling the box for several moments. "O Alma Venus—it is Venus herself!" as he threw the highest cast, named from that goddess,—whom he who wins money, indeed, usually propitiates!

"Venus is ungrateful to me," said Glaucus, gaily; "I have always sacrificed on her altar."

"He who plays with Clodius," whispered Lepidus, "will soon, like Plautus's Curculio, put his pallium for the stakes."

"Poor Glaucus!—he is as blind as Fortune herself," replied Sallust, in the same tone.

"I will play no more," said Glaucus; "I have lost thirty sestertia." "I am sorry——," began Clodius.

"Amiable man!" groaned the umbra.

"Not at all!" exclaimed Glaucus; "the pleasure I take in your gain compensates the pain of my loss."

The conversation now grew general and animated; the wine circulated more freely; and Ione once more became the subject of eulogy to the guests of Glaucus.

"Instead of outwatching the stars, let us visit one at whose beauty the stars grow pale," said Lepidus.

Clodius, who saw no chance of renewing the dice, seconded the proposal; and Glaucus, though he civilly pressed his guests to continue the banquet, could not but let them see that his curiosity had been excited by the praises of Ione: they therefore resolved to adjourn (all, at least, but Pansa and the umbra) to the house of the fair Greek. They drank, therefore, to the health of Glaucus and of Titus—they performed their last libation—they resumed their slippers—they descended the stairs—passed the illumined atrium—and walking unbitten over the fierce dog painted on the threshold, found themselves beneath the light of the moon just risen, in the lively and still crowded streets of Pompeii.

They passed the jewellers' quarter, sparkling with lights, caught and reflected by the gems displayed in the shops, and arrived at last at the door of Ione. The vestibule blazed with rows of lamps; curtains of embroidered purple hung on either aperture of the tablinum whose walls and mosaic pavement glowed with the richest colors of the artist; and under the portico which surrounded the odorous viridarium they found Ione, already surrounded by adoring and applauding guests!

"Did you say she was Athenian?" whispered Glaucus, ere he passed into the peristyle.

"No, she is from Neapolis."

"Neapolis!" echoed Glaucus; and at that moment the group, dividing on either side of Ione, gave to his view that bright, that nymph-like beauty, which for months had shone down upon the waters of his memory.

CHAPTER IV.

The Temple of Isis.—Its Priest.—The character of Arbaces develops itself.

THE story returns to the Egyptian. We left Arbaces upon the shores of the noon-day sea, after he had parted from Glaucus and his companion. As he approached to the more crowded part of the bay, he paused and gazed upon that animated scene with folded arms, and a bitter smile upon his dark features.

"Gulls, dupes, fools, that ye are!" muttered he to himself; "whether business or pleasure, trade or religion, be your pursuit, you are equally cheated by the passions that ye should rule! How I could loathe you, if I did not hate—yes, hate! Greek or Roman, it is from us, from the dark lore of Egypt, that ye have stolen the fire that gives you souls. Your knowledge—your poesy—your laws—your arts—your barbarous mastery of war (all how tame and mutilated, when compared with the vast original!)—ye have filched, as a slave filches the fragments of the feast, from us! And now, ye mimics of a mimic!—Romans, forsooth! the mushroom herd of robbers! ye are our masters! the pyramids look down no more on the race of Rameses—the eagle cowers over the serpent of the Nile. *Our* masters—no, not *mine.* My soul, by the power of its wisdom, controls and chains you, though the fetters are unseen. So long as craft can master force, so long as religion has a cave from which oracles can dupe mankind, the wise hold an empire over earth. Even from your vices Arbaces

distills his pleasures;—pleasures unprofaned by vulgar eyes—
pleasures vast, wealthy, inexhaustible, of which your enervate
minds, in their unimaginative sensuality, cannot conceive or
dream! Plod on, plod on, fools of ambition and of avarice!
your petty thirst for fasces and quæstorships, and all the mum-
mery of servile power, provokes my laughter and my scorn.
My power can extend wherever man believes. I ride over the
souls that the purple veils. Thebes may fall, Egypt be a name;
the world itself furnishes the subjects of Arbaces."

Thus saying, the Egyptian moved slowly on; and, entering
the town, his tall figure towered above the crowded throng of
the forum, and swept towards the small but graceful temple
consecrated to Isis.

That edifice was then but of recent erection; the ancient
temple had been thrown down in the earthquake sixteen years
before, and the new building had become as much in vogue
with the versatile Pompeians as a new church or a new
preacher may be with us. The oracles of the goddess at Pompeii were indeed remarkable, not more for the mysterious
language in which they were clothed, than for the credit which
was attached to their mandates and predictions. If they were
not dictated by a divinity, they were framed at least by a profound knowledge of mankind; they applied themselves exactly
to the circumstances of individuals, and made a notable contrast to the vague and loose generalities of their rival temples.
As Arbaces now arrived at the rails which separated the profane from the sacred place, a crowd, composed of all classes,
but especially of the commercial, collected, breathless and
reverential, before the many altars which rose in the open
court. In the walls of the cella, elevated on seven steps of
Parian marble, various statues stood in niches, and those walls
were ornamented with the pomegranate consecrated to Isis.
An oblong pedestal occupied the interior building, on which
stood two statues, one of Isis, and its companion represented
the silent and mystic Orus. But the building contained many
other deities to grace the court of the Egyptian deity: her
kindred and many-titled Bacchus, and the Cyprian Venus, a
Grecian disguise for herself, rising from her bath, and the
dog-headed Anubis, and the ox Apis, and various Egyptian
idols of uncouth form and unknown appellations.

But we must not suppose that, among the cities of Magna

Græcia, Isis was worshipped with those forms and ceremonies which were of right her own. The mongrel and modern
nations of the South, with a mingled arrogance and ignorance,
confounded the worships of all climes and ages. And the
profound mysteries of the Nile were degraded by a hundred
meretricious and frivolous admixtures from the creeds of
Cephisus and of Tibur. The temple of Isis in Pompeii was
served by Roman and Greek priests, ignorant alike of the
language and the customs of her ancient votaries; and the
descendant of the dread Egyptian kings, beneath the appearance of reverential awe, secretly laughed to scorn the puny
mummeries which imitated the solemn and typical worship
of his burning clime.

Ranged now on either side the steps was the sacrificial
crowd, arrayed in white garments, while at the summit stood
two of the inferior priests, the one holding a palm-branch, the
other a slender sheaf of corn. In the narrow passage in front
thronged the by-standers.

"And what," whispered Arbaces to one of the by-standers,
who was a merchant engaged in the Alexandrian trade, which
trade had probably first introduced in Pompeii the worship of
the Egyptian goddess—"What occasion now assembles you
before the altars of the venerable Isis? It seems, by the white
robes of the group before me, that a sacrifice is to be rendered;
and by the assembly of the priests, that ye are prepared for
some oracle. To what question is it to vouchsafe a reply?"

"We are merchants," replied the by-stander (who was no
other than Diomed) in the same voice, "who seek to know the
fate of our vessels, which sail for Alexandria to-morrow. We
are about to offer up a sacrifice and implore an answer from
the goddess. I am not one of those who have petitioned the
priest to sacrifice, as you may see by my dress, but I have some
interest in the success of the fleet;—by Jupiter! yes. I have a
pretty trade, else how could I live in these hard times?"

The Egyptian replied gravely—"That though Isis was
properly the goddess of agriculture, she was no less the patron
of commerce." Then turning his head towards the east, Arbaces seemed absorbed in silent prayer.

And now in the centre of the steps appeared a priest robed
in white from head to foot, the veil parting over the crown;
two new priests relieved those hitherto stationed at either

corner, being naked half-way down to the breast, and covered, for the rest, in white and loose robes. At the same time, seated at the bottom of the steps, a priest commenced a solemn air upon a long wind-instrument of music. Half-way down the steps stood another flamen, holding in one hand the votive wreath, and in the other a white wand; adding to the picturesque scene of that eastern ceremony, the stately ibis (bird sacred to Egyptian worship) looked mutely down the wall upon the rite, or stalked beside the altar at the base of the steps.

At that altar now stood the sacrificial flamen.

The countenance of Arbaces seemed to lose all its rigid calm while the aruspices inspected the entrails, and to be intent in pious anxiety—to rejoice and brighten as the signs were declared favorable, and the fire began bright and clearly to consume the sacred portion of the victim amidst odors of myrrh and frankincense. It was then that a dead silence fell over the whispering crowd, and the priests gathering round the cella, another priest, naked save by a cincture round the middle, rushed forward, and dancing with wild gestures, implored an answer from the goddess. He ceased at last in exhaustion, and a low murmuring noise was heard within the body of the statue; thrice the head moved, and the lips parted, and then a hollow voice uttered these mystic words:—

"There are waves like chargers that meet and glow,
There are graves ready wrought in the rocks below:
On the brow of the future the dangers lour,
But blest are your barks in the fearful hour."

The voice ceased—the crowd breathed more freely—the merchants looked at each other. "Nothing can be more plain," murmured Diomed; "there is to be a storm at sea, as there very often is at the beginning of autumn, but our vessels are to be saved. O beneficent Isis!"

"Lauded eternally be the goddess!" said the merchants: "what can be less equivocal than her prediction?"

Raising one hand in sign of silence to the people, for the rights of Isis enjoined what to the lively Pompeians was an impossible suspense from the use of the vocal organs, the chief priest poured his libation on the altar, and after a short concluding prayer the ceremony was over, and the congregation dismissed. Still, however, as the crowd dispersed themselves here and there, the Egyptian lingered by the railing, and when the space became tolerably cleared, one of the priests, approaching it, saluted him with great appearance of friendly familiarity.

The countenance of the priest was remarkably unprepossessing—his shaven skull was so low and narrow in the front as nearly to approach to the conformation of that of an African savage, save only towards the temples, where, in that organ styled acquisitiveness by the pupils of a science modern in name, but best practically known (as their sculpture teaches us) amongst the ancients, two huge and almost preternatural protuberances yet more distorted the unshapely head;—around the brows the skin was puckered into a web of deep and intricate wrinkles—the eyes, dark and small, rolled in a muddy and yellow orbit—the nose, short yet coarse, was distended at the nostrils like a satyr's—and the thick but pallid lips, the high cheek-bones, the livid and motley hues that struggled through the parchment skin, completed a countenance which none could behold without repugnance, and few without terror and distrust: whatever the wishes of the mind, the animal frame was well fitted to execute them; the wiry muscles of the throat, the broad chest, the nervous hands and lean gaunt arms, which were bared above the elbow, betokened a form capable alike of great active exertion and passive endurance.

"Calenus," said the Egyptian to this fascinating flamen, "you have improved the voice of the statue much by attending to my suggestion; and your verses are excellent. Always prophesy good fortune, unless there is an absolute impossibility of its fulfilment."

"Besides," added Calenus, "if the storm does come, and if it does overwhelm the accursed ships, have we not prophesied it? and are the barks not blest to be at rest?—for rest prays the mariner in the Ægean sea, or at least so says Horace;—can the mariner be more at rest in the sea than when he is at the bottom of it?"

"Right, my Calenus; I wish Apæcides would take a lesson from your wisdom. But I desire to confer with you relative to him and to other matters: you can admit me into one of your less sacred apartments?"

"Assuredly," replied the priest, leading the way to one of the small chambers which surrounded the open gate. Here they seated themselves before a small table spread with dishes containing fruit and eggs, and various cold meats, with vases of excellent wine, of which while the companions partook, a curtain, drawn across the entrance opening to the court, concealed them from view, but admonished them by the thinness of the partition to speak low, or to speak no secrets: they chose the former alternative.

"Thou knowest," said Arbaces, in a voice that scarcely stirred the air, so soft and inward was its sound, "that it has ever been my maxim to attach myself to the young. From their flexile and unformed minds I can carve out my fittest tools. I weave—I warp—I mould them at my will. Of the men I make merely followers or servants; of the women—"

"Mistresses," said Calenus, as a livid grin distorted his ungainly features.

"Yes, I do not disguise it; woman is the main object, the great appetite, of my soul. As *you* feed the victim for the slaughter, *I* love to rear the votaries of my pleasure. I love to train, to ripen their minds—to unfold the sweet blossom of their hidden passions, in order to prepare the fruit to my taste. I loathe your ready-made and ripened courtesans; it is in the soft and unconscious progress of innocence to desire that I find the true charm of love: it is thus that I defy satiety; and by contemplating the freshness of others, I sustain the freshness of my own sensations. From the young hearts of my victims I draw the ingredients of the caldron in which I reyouth myself. But enough of this: to the subject before us. You know, then, that in Neapolis some time since I encountered Ione and Apæcides, brother and sister, the children of Athenians who had settled at Neapolis. The death of their parents, who knew and esteemed me, constituted me their guardian. I was not unmindful of the trust. The youth, docile and mild, yielded readily to the impression I sought to stamp upon him. Next to woman, I love the old recollections of my ancestral land; I love to keep alive—to propagate on distant shores (which her colonies perchance yet people) her dark and mystic creeds. It may be, that it pleases me to delude mankind, while I thus serve the deities. To Apæcides I taught the solemn faith of Isis. I unfolded to him something of those sublime allegories which are couched beneath her worship. I excited in a soul peculiarly alive to religious fervor that enthusiasm which imagination begets on faith. I have placed him amongst you: he is one of you."

"He is so," said Calenus: "but in thus stimulating his faith, you have robbed him of wisdom. He is horror-struck that he is no longer duped: our sage delusions, our speaking statues and secret staircases dismay and revolt him; he pines; he wastes away; he mutters to himself; he refuses to share our ceremonies. He has been known to frequent the company of men suspected of adherence to that new and atheistical creed which denies all our gods, and terms our oracles the inspirations of that malevolent spirit of which eastern tradition speaks. Our oracles—alas! we know well whose inspirations *they* are!"

"This is what I feared," said Arbaces, musingly, "from various reproaches he made me when I last saw him. Of late he hath shunned my steps: I must find him: I must continue my lessons; I must lead him into the adytum of Wisdom. I must teach him that there are two stages of sanctity—the first, FAITH—the next, DELUSION; the one for the vulgar, the second for the sage." "I never passed through the first," said Calenus; "nor you either, I think, my Arbaces."

"You err," replied the Egyptian, gravely. "I believe at this day (not indeed that which I teach, but that which I teach not). Nature has a sanctity against which I cannot (nor would I) steel conviction. I believe in mine own knowledge, and that has revealed to me,—but no matter. Now to earthlier and more inviting themes. If I thus fulfilled my object with Apæcides, what was my design for Ione? Thou knowest already I intend her for my queen—my bride—my heart's Isis. Never till I saw her knew I all the love of which my nature is capable."

"I hear from a thousand lips that she is a second Helen," said Calenus; and he smacked his own lips, but whether at the wine or at the notion it is not easy to decide.

"Yes, she has a beauty that Greece itself never excelled," resumed Arbaces. "But that is not all: she has a soul worthy to match with mine. She has a genius beyond that of woman —keen—dazzling—bold. Poetry flows spontaneous to her lips: utter but a truth, and, however intricate and profound, her mind seizes and commands it. Her imagination and her reason are not at war with each other; they harmonize and direct her course as the winds and the waves direct some lofty bark.

With this she unites a daring independence of thought; she can stand alone in the world; she can be brave as she is gentle; this is the nature I have sought all my life in woman, and never found till now. Ione must be mine! In her I have a double passion; I wish to enjoy a beauty of spirit as of form."

"She is not yours yet, then?" said the priest.

"No; she loves me—but as a friend:—she loves me with her mind only. She fancies in me the paltry virtues which I have only the profounder virtue to disdain. But you must pursue with me her history. The brother and sister were young and rich: Ione is proud and ambitious—proud of her genius —the magic of her poetry—the charm of her conversation. When her brother left me, and entered your temple, in order to be near him she removed also to Pompeii. She has suffered her talents to be known. She summons crowds to her feasts; her voice enchants them; her poetry subdues. She delights in being thought the successor of Erinna." "Or of Sappho?"

"But Sappho without love! I encouraged her in this boldness of career—in this indulgence of vanity and of pleasure. I love to steep her amidst the dissipations and luxury of this abandoned city. Mark me, Calenus! I desired to enervate her mind!—it has been too pure to receive yet the breath which I wish not to pass, but burningly to eat into, the mirror. I wished her be surrounded by lovers, hollow, vain, and frivolous (lovers that her nature must despise), in order to feel the want of love. Then, in those soft intervals of lassitude that succeed to excitement, I can weave my spells—excite her interest— attract her passions—possess myself of her heart. For it is not the young, nor the beautiful, nor the gay, that should fascinate Ione; her imagination must be won, and the life of Arbaces has been one scene of triumph over the imaginations of his kind." "And hast thou no fear, then, of thy rivals? The gallants of Italy are skilled in the art to please."

"None! Her Greek soul despises the barbarian Romans, and would scorn itself if it admitted a thought of love for one of that upstart race."

"But thou art an Egyptian, not a Greek!"

"Egypt," replied Arbaces, "is the mother of Athens. Her tutelary Minerva is our deity; and her founder, Cecrops, was the fugitive of Egyptian Sais. This have I already taught to her; and in my blood she venerates the eldest dynasties of earth. But yet I will own that of late some uneasy suspicions have crossed my mind. She is more silent than she used to be; she loves melancholy and subduing music; she sighs without an outward cause. This may be the beginning of love—it may be the want of love. In either case it is time for me to begin my operations on her fancies and her heart: in the one case, to divert the source of love to me; in the other, in me to awaken it. It is for this that I have sought you."

"And how can I assist you?"

"I am about to invite her to a feast in my house: I wish to dazzle—to bewilder—to inflame her senses. Our arts—the arts by which Egypt trained her young novitiates—must be employed; and, under veil of the mysteries of religion, I will open to her the secrets of love."

"Ah! now I understand:—one of those voluptuous banquets that, despite our dull vows of mortified coldness, we, thy priests of Isis, have shared at thy house."

"No, no! Thinkest thou her chaste eyes are ripe for such scenes? No; but first we must ensnare the brother—an easier task. Listen to me, while I give you my instructions."

CHAPTER V.

More of the flower-girl.—The progress of love.

THE sun shone gaily into that beautiful chamber in the house of Glaucus, which I have before said is now called "the Room of Leda." The morning rays entered through rows of small casements at the higher part of the room, and through the door which opened on the garden, that answered to the inhabitants of the southern cities the same purpose that a greenhouse or conservatory does to us. The size of the garden did not adapt it for exercise, but the various and fragrant plants with which it was filled gave a luxury to that indolence so dear to the dwellers in a sunny clime. And now the odors, fanned by a gentle wind creeping from the adjacent sea, scattered themselves over that chamber, whose walls vied with the richest colors of the most glowing flowers. Besides the gem of the room—the painting of Leda and Tyndarus—in the centre of each compartment of the walls were set other pictures of exquisite beauty. In one you saw Cupid leaning on the knees of Venus; in another Ariadne sleeping on the beach, unconscious of the perfidy of Theseus. Merrily the sunbeams played to and fro on the tessellated floor and the brilliant walls—far more happily came the rays of joy to the heart of the young Glaucus.

"I have seen her, then," said he, as he paced that narrow chamber—"I have heard her—nay, I have spoken to her again—I have listened to the music of her song, and she sang of glory and of Greece. I have discovered the long-sought idol of my dreams; and like the Cyprian sculptor, I have breathed life into my own imaginings."

Longer, perhaps, had been the enamoured soliloquy of Glaucus, but at that moment a shadow darkened the threshold of the chamber, and a young female, still half a child in years, broke upon his solitude. She was dressed simply in a white tunic, which reached from the neck to the ankles; under her arm she bore a basket of flowers, and in the other hand she held a bronze water-vase; her features were more formed than exactly became her years, yet they were soft and feminine in their outline, and, without being beautiful in themselves, they were almost made so by their beauty of expression; there was something ineffably gentle, and you would say patient, in her aspect. A look of resigned sorrow, of tranquil endurance, had banished the smile, but not the sweetness, from her lips; something timid and cautious in her step —something wandering in her eyes, led you to suspect the affliction which she had suffered from her birth:—she was blind; but in the orbs themselves there was no visible defect— their melancholy and subdued light was clear, cloudless, and serene. "They tell me that Glaucus is here," said she; "may I come in?"

"Ah, my Nydia," said the Greek, "is that you? I knew you would not neglect my invitation."

"Glaucus did but justice to himself," answered Nydia, with a blush; "for he has always been kind to the poor blind girl." "Who could be otherwise?" said Glaucus, tenderly, and in the voice of a compassionate brother.

Nydia sighed and paused before she resumed, without replying to his remark. "You have but lately returned?"

"This is the sixth sun that hath shone upon me at Pompeii."

"And you are well? Ah, I need not ask—for who that sees the earth, which they tell me is so beautiful, can be ill?"

"I am well. And you, Nydia—how you have grown! Next year you will be thinking what answer to make your lovers."

A second blush passed over the cheek of Nydia, but this time she frowned as she blushed. "I have brought you some flowers," said she, without replying to a remark that she seemed to resent; and feeling about the room till she found the table that stood by Glaucus, she laid the basket upon it: "they are poor, but they are fresh-gathered."

"They might come from Flora herself," said he, kindly; "and I renew again my vow to the Graces, that I will wear no other garlands while thy hands can weave me such as these."

"And how find you the flowers in your viridarium?—are they thriving?"

"Wonderfully so—the Lares themselves must have tended them."

"Ah, now you give me pleasure; for I came, as often as I could steal the leisure, to water and tend them in your absence."

"How shall I thank thee, fair Nydia?" said the Greek. "Glaucus little dreamed that he left one memory so watchful over his favorites at Pompeii."

The hand of the child trembled, and her breast heaved beneath her tunic. She turned round in embarrassment. "The sun is hot for the poor flowers," said she, "to-day, and they will miss me; for I have been ill lately, and it is nine days since I visited them."

"Ill, Nydia!—yet your cheek has more color than it had last year."

"I am often ailing," said the blind girl, touchingly, "and as I grow up I grieve more that I am blind. But now to the flowers!" So saying, she made a slight reverence with her head, and passing into the viridarium, busied herself with watering the flowers.

"Poor Nydia," thought Glaucus, gazing on her; "thine is a hard doom! Thou seest not the earth—nor the sun—nor the ocean—nor the stars;—above all, thou canst not behold Ione."

At that last thought his mind flew back to the past evening, and was a second time disturbed in its reveries by the entrance of Clodius. It was a proof how much a single evening had sufficed to increase and to refine the love of the Athenian for Ione, that whereas he had confided to Clodius the secret of his first interview with her, and the effect it had produced on him, he now felt an invincible aversion even to mention to him her name. He had seen Ione, bright, pure, unsullied, in the midst of the gayest and most profligate gallants of Pompeii, charming rather than awing the boldest into respect, and changing the very nature of the most sensual and the least ideal:—as by her intellectual and refining spells she reversed the fable of Circe, and converted the animals into men. They who could not understand her soul were made spiritual, as it were, by the magic of her beauty;—they who had no heart for poetry had ears, at least, for the melody of her voice. Seeing her thus surrounded, purifying and brightening all things with her presence, Glaucus almost for the first time felt the nobleness of his own nature,—he felt how unworthy of the goddess of his dreams had been his companions and his pursuits. A veil seemed lifted from his eyes; he saw that immeasurable distance between himself and his associates which the deceiving mists of pleasure had hitherto concealed; he was refined by a sense of his courage in aspiring to Ione. He felt that henceforth it was his destiny to look upward and to soar. He could no longer breathe that name, which sounded to the sense of his ardent fancy as something sacred and divine, to lewd and vulgar ears. She was no longer the beautiful girl once seen and passionately remembered,— she was already the mistress, the divinity of his soul. This feeling who has not experienced?—If thou hast not, then thou hast never loved.

When Clodius therefore spoke to him in affected transports of the beauty of Ione, Glaucus felt only resentment and disgust that such lips should dare to praise her; he answered coldly, and the Roman imagined that his passion was cured instead of heightened. Clodius scarcely regretted it, for he was anxious that Glaucus should marry an heiress yet more richly endowed—Julia, the daughter of the wealthy Diomed, whose gold the gamester imagined he could readily divert into his own coffers. Their conversation did not flow with its usual ease; and no sooner had Clodius left him than Glaucus bent his way to the house of Ione. In passing by the threshold he again encountered Nydia, who had finished her graceful task. She knew his step on the instant.

"You are early abroad?" said she.

"Yes; for the skies of Campania rebuke the sluggard who neglects them."

"Ah, would I could see them!" murmured the blind girl, but so low that Glaucus did not overhear the complaint.

The Thessalian lingered on the threshold a few moments, and then guiding her steps by a long staff, which she used with great dexterity, she took her way homeward. She soon turned from the more gaudy streets, and entered a quarter of the town but little loved by the decorous and the sober. But from the low and rude evidences of vice around her she was saved by her misfortune. And at that hour the streets were quiet and silent, nor was her youthful ear shocked by the sounds which too often broke along the obscene and obscure haunts she patiently and sadly traversed.

She knocked at the back-door of a sort of tavern; it opened, and a rude voice bade her give an account of the sesterces. Ere she could reply, another voice, less vulgarly accented, said—

"Never mind those petty profits, my Burbo. The girl's voice will be wanted again soon at our rich friend's revels; and he pays, as thou knowest, pretty high for his nightingales' tongues."

"Oh, I hope not—I trust not," cried Nydia, trembling; "I will beg from sunrise to sunset, but send me not there."

"And why?" asked the same voice.

"Because—because I am young, and delicately born, and the female companions I meet there are not fit associates for one who—who——" "Is a slave in the house of Burbo," returned the voice ironically, and with a coarse laugh.

The Thessalian put down the flowers, and, leaning her face on her hands, wept silently.

Meanwhile, Glaucus sought the house of the beautiful Neapolitan. He found Ione sitting amidst her attendants, who were at work around her. Her harp stood at her side, for Ione herself was unusually idle, perhaps unusually thoughtful, that day. He thought her even more beautiful by the morning light, and in her simple robe, than amidst the blazing

lamps, and decorated with the costly jewels of the previous
night: not the less so from a certain paleness that overspread
her transparent hues—not the less so from the blush that
mounted over them when he approached. Accustomed to
flatter, flattery died upon his lips when he addressed Ione. He
felt it beneath her to *utter* the homage which every *look* con-
veyed. They spoke of Greece; this was a theme on which Ione
loved rather to listen than to converse: it was a theme on
which the Greek could have been eloquent for ever. He
described to her the silver olive groves that yet clad the banks
of Ilyssus, and the temples, already despoiled of half their
glories—but how beautiful in decay! He looked back on the
melancholy city of Harmodius the free, and Pericles the
magnificent, from the height of that distant memory, which
mellowed into one hazy light all the ruder and darker shades.
He had seen the land of poetry chiefly in the poetical age of
early youth; and the associations of patriotism were blended
with those of the flush and spring of life. And Ione listened
to him, absorbed and mute; dearer were those accents, and
those descriptions, than all the prodigal adulation of her
numberless adorers. Was it a sin to love her countryman?
she loved Athens in him—the gods of her race, the land of her
dreams, spoke to her in his voice! From that time they daily
saw each other. At the cool of the evening they made excursions on the placid sea. By night they met again in Ione's
porticos and halls. Their love was sudden, but it was strong;
it filled all the sources of their life. Heart—brain—sense—
imagination, all were its ministers and priests. As you take
some obstacle from two objects that have a mutual attraction,
they met, and united at once; their wonder was, that they had
lived separate so long. And it was natural that they should so
love. Young, beautiful, and gifted—of the same birth, and
the same souls;—there was poetry in their very union. They
imagined the heavens smiled upon their affection. As the
persecuted seek refuge at the shrine, so they recognized in the
altar of their love an asylum from the sorrows of earth; they
covered it with flowers—they knew not of the serpents that
lay coiled behind.

One evening, the fifth after their first meeting at Pompeii,
Glaucus and Ione, with a small party of chosen friends, were
returning from an excursion round the bay; their vessel

skimmed lightly over the twilight waters, whose lucid mirror was only broken by the dripping oars. As the rest of the party conversed gaily with each other, Glaucus lay at the feet of Ione, and he would have looked up in her face, but he did not dare. Ione broke the pause between them.

"My poor brother," said she, sighing, "how once he would have enjoyed this hour!"

"Your brother!" said Glaucus; "I have not seen him. Occupied with you, I have thought of nothing else, or I should have asked if that was not your brother for whose companionship you left me at the Temple of Minerva, in Neapolis?"

"It was."—"And is he here?"—"He is."—"At Pompeii! and not constantly with you? Impossible!"—"He has other duties," answered Ione, sadly; "he is a priest of Isis."

"So young, too; and that priesthood, in its laws at least, so severe!" said the warm and bright-hearted Greek, in surprise and pity. "What could have been his inducement?"

"He was always enthusiastic and fervent in religious devotion; and the eloquence of an Egyptian—our friend and guardian—kindled in him the pious desire to consecrate his life to the most mystic of our deities. Perhaps, in the intenseness of his zeal, he found in the severity of that peculiar priesthood its peculiar attraction."

"And he does not repent his choice?—I trust he is happy." Ione sighed deeply, and lowered her veil over her eyes.

"I wish," said she, after a pause, "that he had not been so hasty. Perhaps, like all who expect too much, he is revolted too easily!"

"Then he is not happy in his new condition. And this Egyptian, was he a priest himself? was he interested in recruits to the sacred band?"

"No. His main interest was in our happiness. He thought he promoted that of my brother. We were left orphans."

"Like myself," said Glaucus, with a deep meaning in his voice. Ione cast down her eyes as she resumed,—

"And Arbaces sought to supply the place of our parent. You must know him. He loves genius."

"Arbaces! I know him already; at least, we speak when we meet. But for your praise I would not seek to know more of him. My heart inclines readily to most of my kind. But that dark Egyptian, with his gloomy brow and icy smiles, seems to me to sadden the very sun. One would think that, like Epimenides the Cretan, he had spent forty years in a cave, and had found something unnatural in the daylight ever afterwards."

"Yet, like Epimenides, he is kind, and wise, and gentle," answered Ione.

"Oh, happy that he has thy praise! He needs no other virtues to make him dear to me."

"His calm, his coldness," said Ione, evasively pursuing the subject, "are perhaps but the exhaustion of past sufferings; as yonder mountain (and she pointed to Vesuvius), which we see dark and tranquil in the distance, once nursed the fires for ever quenched."

They both gazed on the mountain as Ione said these words; the rest of the sky was bathed in rosy and tender hues, but over that grey summit, rising amidst the woods and vineyards that then clomb half-way up the ascent there hung a black and ominous cloud, the single frown of the landscape. A sudden and unaccountable gloom came over each as they thus gazed; and in that sympathy which love had already taught them, and which bade them, in the slightest shadows of emotion, the faintest presentiment of evil, turn for refuge to each other, their gaze at the same moment left the mountain, and, full of unimaginable tenderness, met. What need had they of words to say they loved?

CHAPTER VI.

The fowler snares again the bird that had just escaped, and sets his nets for a new victim.

In the history I relate, the events are crowded and rapid as those of the drama. I write of an epoch in which days sufficed to ripen the ordinary fruits of years.

Meanwhile, Arbaces had not of late much frequented the house of Ione; and when he had visited her he had not encountered Glaucus, nor knew he, as yet, of that love which had so suddenly sprung up between himself and his designs. In his interest for the brother of Ione, he had been forced, too, a little while, to suspend his interest in Ione herself. His pride and his selfishness were aroused and alarmed at the

sudden change which had come over the spirit of the youth.
He trembled lest he himself should lose a docile pupil, and
Isis an enthusiastic servant. Apæcides had ceased to seek or
to consult him. He was rarely to be found; he turned sullenly
from the Egyptian,—nay, he fled when he perceived him in
the distance. Arbaces was one of those haughty and powerful
spirits accustomed to master others; he chafed at the notion
that one once his own should ever elude his grasp. He swore
inly that Apæcides should not escape him.

It was with this resolution that he passed through a thick
grove in the city, which lay between his house and that of
Ione, on his way to the latter; and there, leaning against a
tree, and gazing on the ground, he came unawares on the
young priest of Isis.

"Apæcides!" said he,—and he laid his hand affectionately
on the young man's shoulder.

The priest started; and his first instinct seemed to be that
of flight. "My son," said the Egyptian, "what has chanced
that you desire to shun me?"

Apæcides remained silent and sullen, looking down on the
earth, as his lips quivered, and his breast heaved with emotion.

"Speak to me, my friend," continued the Egyptian.
"Speak. Something burdens thy spirit. What hast thou to
reveal?" "To thee—nothing."

"And why is it to me thou art thus unconfidential?"

"Because thou hast been my enemy."

"Let us confer," said Arbaces, in a low voice; and drawing the reluctant arm of the priest in his own, he led him to
one of the seats which were scattered within the grove. They
sat down,—and in those gloomy forms there was something
congenial to the shade and solitude of the place.

Apæcides was in the spring of his years, yet he seemed to
have exhausted even more of life than the Egyptian; his delicate and regular features were wan and colorless; his eyes
were hollow, and shone with a brilliant and feverish glare;
his frame bowed prematurely, and in his hands, which were
small to effeminacy, the blue and swollen veins indicated the
lassitude and weakness of the relaxed fibres. You saw in his
face a strong resemblance to Ione, but the expression was
altogether different from that majestic and spiritual calm
which breathed so divine and classical a repose over his sis-

ter's beauty. In her, enthusiasm was visible, but it seemed always suppressed and restrained; this made the charm and sentiment of her countenance; you longed to awaken a spirit which reposed, but evidently did not sleep. In Apæcides the whole aspect betokened the fervor and passion of his temperament, and the intellectual portion of his nature seemed, by the wild fire of the eyes, the great breadth of the temples when compared with the height of the brow, the trembling restlessness of the lips, to be swayed and tyrannized over by the imaginative and ideal. Fancy, with the sister, had stopped short at the golden goal of poetry; with the brother, less happy and less restrained, it had wandered into visions more intangible and unembodied; and the faculties which gave genius to the one threatened madness to the other.

"You say I have been your enemy," said Arbaces.

"I know the cause of that unjust accusation: I have placed you amidst the priests of Isis—you are revolted at their trickeries and imposture—you think that I too have deceived you —the purity of your mind is offended—you imagine that I am one of the deceitful——"

"You knew the jugglings of that impious craft," answered Apæcides; "why did you disguise them from me?—When you excited my desire to devote myself to the office whose garb I bear, you spoke to me of the holy life of men resigning themselves to knowledge—you have given me for companions an ignorant and sensual herd, who have no knowledge but that of the grossest frauds;—you spoke to me of men sacrificing the earthlier pleasures to the sublime cultivation of virtue— you place me amongst men reeking with all the filthiness of vice;—you spoke to me of the friends, the enlighteners of our common kind—I see but their cheats and deluders! Oh! it was basely done!—you have robbed me of the glory of youth, of the convictions of virtue, of the sanctifying thirst after wisdom. Young as I was, rich, fervent, the sunny pleasures of earth before me, I resigned all without a sigh, nay, with happiness and exultation, in the thought that I resigned them for the abstruse mysteries of diviner wisdom, for the companionship of gods—for the revelations of Heaven—and now —now——"

Convulsive sobs checked the priest's voice; he covered his

face with his hands, and large tears forced themselves through the wasted fingers, and ran profusely down his vest.

"What I promised to thee, that will I give, my friend, my pupil: these have been but trials to thy virtue—it comes forth the brighter for thy novitiate,—think no more of those dull cheats—assort no more with those menials of the goddess, the atrienses of her hall—you are worthy to enter into the penetralia. I henceforth will be your priest, your guide, and you who now curse my friendship shall live to bless it."

The young man lifted up his head and gazed with a vacant and wondering stare upon the Egyptian.

"Listen to me," continued Arbaces, in an earnest and solemn voice, casting first his searching eyes around to see that they were still alone. "From Egypt came all the knowledge of the world; from Egypt came the lore of Athens, and the profound policy of Crete; from Egypt came those early and mysterious tribes which (long before the hordes of Romulus swept over the plains of Italy, and in the eternal cycle of events drove back civilization into barbarism and darkness) possessed all the arts of wisdom and the graces of intellectual life. From Egypt came the rites and the grandeur of that solemn Cære, whose inhabitants taught their iron vanquishers of Rome all that they yet know of elevated in religion and sublime in worship. And how deemest thou, young man, that that dread Egypt, the mother of countless nations, achieved her greatness, and soared to her cloud-capt eminence of wisdom?—it was the result of a profound and holy policy. Your modern nations owe their greatness to Egypt—Egypt her greatness to her priests. Rapt in themselves, coveting a sway over the nobler part of man, his soul and his belief, those ancient ministers of God were inspired with the grandest thought that ever exalted mortals. From the revolutions of the stars, from the seasons of the earth, from the round and unvarying circle of human destinies, they devised an august allegory; they made it gross and palpable to the vulgar by the signs of gods and goddesses, and that which in reality was Government they named Religion. Isis is a fable—start not!—that for which Isis is a type is a reality, an immortal being; Isis is nothing. Nature, which she represents, is the mother of all things—dark, ancient, inscrutable, save to the gifted few. 'None among mortals hath ever lifted up my veil,' so saith the Isis that you adore; but to the wise that veil *hath* been removed, and we have stood face to face with the solemn loveliness of Nature. The priests then were the benefactors, the civilizers of mankind; true, they were also cheats, impostors if you will. But think you, young man, that if they had not deceived their kind they could have served them? The ignorant and servile vulgar must be blinded to attain to their proper good; they would not believe a maxim—they revere an oracle. The Emperor of Rome sways the vast and various tribes of earth, and harmonizes the conflicting and disunited elements; thence come peace, order, law, the blessings of life. Think you it is the man, the emperor, that thus sways?—no, it is the pomp, the awe, the majesty that surround him—*these* are his impostures, his delusions; our oracles and our divinations, our rites and our ceremonies, are the means of *our* sovereignty and the engines of *our* power. They are the same means to the same end, the welfare and harmony of mankind. You listen to me rapt and intent—the light begins to dawn upon you."

Apæcides remained silent, but the changes rapidly passing over his speaking countenance betrayed the effect produced upon him by the words of the Egyptian—words made tenfold more eloquent by the voice, the aspect, and the manner of the man.

"While, then," resumed Arbaces, "our fathers of the Nile thus achieved the first elements by whose life chaos is destroyed, namely, the obedience and reverence of the multitude for the few, they drew from their majestic and starred meditations that wisdom which was *no* delusion: they invented the codes and regularities of law—the arts and glories of existence. They asked belief; they returned the gift by civilization. Were not their very cheats a virtue! Trust me, whosoever in yon far heavens of a diviner and more beneficent nature look down upon our world, smile approvingly on the wisdom which has worked such ends. But you wish me to apply these generalities to yourself; I hasten to obey the wish. The altars of the goddess of our ancient faith must be served, and served too by others than the stolid and soulless things that are but as pegs and hooks whereon to hang the fillet and the robe. Remember two sayings of Sextus the Pythagorean, sayings borrowed from the lore of Egypt. The first is, 'Speak not of God to the multitude;' the second is, 'The man worthy of God is a god among men.' As Genius gave to the ministers of Egypt worship, that empire in late ages so fearfully decayed, thus by Genius only can the dominion be restored. I saw in you, Apæcides, a pupil worthy of my lessons—a minister worthy of the great ends which may yet be wrought: your energy, your talents, your purity of faith, your earnestness of enthusiasm, all fitted you for that calling which demands so imperiously high and ardent qualities: I fanned, therefore, your sacred desires; I stimulated you to the step you have taken. But you blame me that I did not reveal to you the little souls and the juggling tricks of your companions. Had I done so, Apæcides, I had defeated my own object; your noble nature would have at once revolted, and Isis would have lost her priest."

Apæcides groaned aloud. The Egyptian continued, without heeding the interruption.

"I placed you, therefore, without preparation, in the temple; I left you suddenly to discover and to be sickened by all those mummeries which dazzle the herd. I desired that you should perceive how those engines are moved by which the fountain that refreshes the world casts its waters in the air. It was the trial ordained of old to all our priests. They who accustom themselves to the impostures of the vulgar, are left to practise them;—for those, like you, whose higher natures demand higher pursuit, religion opens more godlike secrets. I am pleased to find in you the character I had expected. You have taken the vows; you cannot recede. Advance—I will be your guide."

"And what wilt thou teach me, O singular and fearful man? New cheats—new——"

"No—I have thrown thee into the abyss of disbelief; I will lead thee now to the eminence of faith. Thou hast seen the false types: thou shalt learn now the realities they represent. There is no shadow, Apæcides, without its substance. Come to me this night. Your hand."

Impressed, excited, bewildered by the language of the Egyptian, Apæcides gave him his hand, and master and pupil parted.

It was true that for Apæcides there was no retreat. He had taken the vows of celibacy: he had devoted himself to a life that at present seemed to possess all the austerities of fanaticism, without any of the consolations of belief. It was natural that he should yet cling to a yearning desire to reconcile himself to an irrevocable career. The powerful and profound mind of the Egyptian yet claimed an empire over his young imagination; excited him with vague conjecture, and kept him alternately vibrating between hope and fear.

Meanwhile Arbaces pursued his slow and stately way to the house of Ione. As he entered the tablinum, he heard a voice from the porticos of the peristyle beyond, which, musical as it was, sounded displeasingly on his ear—it was the voice of the young and beautiful Glaucus, and for the first time an involuntary thrill of jealousy shot through the breast of the Egyptian. On entering the peristyle, he found Glaucus seated by the side of Ione. The fountain in the odorous garden cast up its silver spray in the air, and kept a delicious coolness in the midst of the sultry noon. The handmaids, almost invariably attendant on Ione, who with her freedom of life preserved the most delicate modesty, sat at a little distance; by the feet of Glaucus lay the lyre on which he had been playing to Ione one of the Lesbian airs. The scene—the group before Arbaces, was stamped by that peculiar and refined ideality of poesy which we yet, not erroneously, imagine to be the distinction of the ancients,—the marble columns, the vases of flowers, the statue, white and tranquil, closing every vista; and above all, the two living forms, from which a sculptor might have caught either inspiration or despair!

Arbaces, pausing for a moment, gazed on the pair with a brow from which all the usual stern serenity had fled; he recovered himself by an effort, and slowly approached them, but with a step so soft and echoless, that even the attendants heard him not; much less Ione and her lover.

"And yet," said Glaucus, "it is only before we love that we imagine that our poets have truly described the passion; the instant the sun rises, all the stars that had shone in his absence vanish into air. The poets exist only in the night of the heart; they are nothing to us when we feel the full glory of the god."

"A gentle and most glowing image, noble Glaucus."

Both started, and recognized behind the seat of Ione the cold and sarcastic face of the Egyptian.

"You are a sudden guest," said Glaucus, rising, and with a forced smile. "So ought all to be who know they are welcome," returned Arbaces, seating himself, and motioning to Glaucus to do the same. "I am glad," said Ione, "to see you at length together; for you are suited to each other, and you are formed to be friends."

"Give me back some fifteen years of life," replied the Egyptian, "before you can place me on an equality with Glaucus. Happy should I be to receive his friendship; but what can I give him in return? Can I make to him the same confidences that he would repose in me—of banquets and garlands—of Parthian steeds, and the chances of the dice? these pleasures suit his age, his nature, his career; they are not for mine."

So saying, the artful Egyptian looked down and sighed; but from the corner of his eye he stole a glance towards Ione, to see how she received these insinuations of the pursuits of her visitor. Her countenance did not satisfy him. Glaucus slightly coloring, hastened gaily to reply. Nor was he, perhaps, without the wish in his turn to disconcert and abash the Egyptian.

"You are right, wise Arbaces," said he; "we can esteem each other, but we cannot be friends. My banquets lack the secret salt, which, according to rumor, gives such zest to your own. And, by Hercules! when I have reached your age, if I, like you, may think it wise to pursue the pleasures of manhood, like you, I shall be doubtless sarcastic on the gallantries of youth."

The Egyptian raised his eyes to Glaucus with a sudden and piercing glance.

"I do not understand you," said he, coldly; "but it is the custom to consider that wit lies in obscurity." He turned from Glaucus as he spoke, with a scarcely perceptible sneer of contempt, and after a moment's pause addressed himself to Ione. "I have not, beautiful Ione," said he, "been fortunate enough to find you within doors the last two or three times that I have visited your vestibule."

"The smoothness of the sea has tempted me much from home," replied Ione, with a little embarrassment.

The embarrassment did not escape Arbaces; but without seeming to heed it, he replied with a smile: "You know the old poets says, that 'Women should keep within doors, and there converse.'"

"The poet was a cynic," said Glaucus, "and hated women."

"He spoke according to the customs of his country, and that country is your boasted Greece."

"To different periods different customs. Had our forefathers known Ione, they had made a different law."

"Did you learn these pretty gallantries at Rome?" said Arbaces, with ill-suppressed emotion.

"One certainly would not go for gallantries to Egypt," retorted Glaucus, playing carelessly with his chain.

"Come, come," said Ione, hastening to interrupt a conversation which she saw, to her great distress, was so little likely to cement the intimacy she had desired to effect between Glaucus and her friend, "Arbaces must not be so hard upon his poor pupil. An orphan, and without a mother's care, I may be to blame for the independent and almost masculine liberty of life that I have chosen: yet it is not greater than the Roman women are accustomed to—it is not greater than the Grecian ought to be. Alas! is it only to be among *men* that freedom and virtue are to be deemed united? Why should the slavery that destroys you be considered the only method to preserve us? Ah! believe me, it has been the great error of men—and one that has worked bitterly on their destinies— to imagine that the nature of women is (I will not say inferior, that may be so, but) so different from their own, in making laws unfavorable to the intellectual advancement of women. Have they not, in so doing, made laws against their children, whom women are to rear?—against the husbands, of whom women are to be the friends, nay, sometimes the advisers?" Ione stopped short suddenly, and her face was suffused with the most enchanting blushes. She feared lest her enthusiasm had led her too far: yet she feared the austere Arbaces less than the courteous Glaucus, for she loved the last, and it was not the custom of the Greeks to allow their women (at least such of their women as they most honored) the same liberty and the same station as those of Italy enjoyed. She felt, therefore, a thrill of delight as Glaucus earnestly replied,—

"Ever mayst thou think thus, Ione—ever be your pure heart your unerring guide! Happy it had been for Greece if she had given to the chaste the same intellectual charms that are so celebrated amongst the less worthy of her women. No state falls from freedom—from knowledge, while your sex smile only on the free, and by appreciating, encourage the wise."

Arbaces was silent, for it was neither his part to sanction the sentiment of Glaucus, nor to condemn that of Ione; and, after a short and embarrassed conversation, Glaucus took his leave of Ione.

When he was gone, Arbaces, drawing his seat nearer to the fair Neapolitan's, said in those bland and subdued tones, in which he knew so well how to veil the mingled art and fierceness of his character,—

"Think not, my sweet pupil, if so I may call you, that I wish to shackle that liberty you adorn while you assume: but which, if not greater, as you rightly observe, than that possessed by the Roman women, must at least be accompanied by great circumspection, when arrogated by one unmarried. Continue to draw crowds of the gay, the brilliant, the wise themselves, to your feet—continue to charm them with the conversation of an Aspasia, the music of an Erinna—but reflect, at least, on those censorious tongues which can so easily blight the tender reputation of a maiden; and while you provoke admiration, give, I beseech you, no victory to envy."

"What mean you, Arbaces?" said Ione, in an alarmed and trembling voice: "I know you are my friend, that you desire only my honor and my welfare. What is it you would say?"

"Your friend—ah, how sincerely! May I speak then as a friend, without reserve and without offence?"

"I beseech you do so."

"This young profligate, this Glaucus, how didst thou know him? Hast thou seen him often?" And as Arbaces spoke, he fixed his gaze steadfastly upon Ione, as if he sought to penetrate into her soul.

Recoiling before that gaze, with a strange fear which she could not explain, the Neapolitan answered with confusion and hesitation—"He was brought to my house as a countryman of my father's, and I may say of mine. I have known him only within this last week or so: but why these questions?"

"Forgive me," said Arbaces; "I thought you might have known him longer. Base insinuator that he is!"

"How! what mean you? Why that term?"

"It matters not: let me not rouse your indignation against one who does not deserve so grave an honor."

"I implore you speak. What has Glaucus insinuated? or rather, in what do you *suppose* he has offended?"

Smothering his resentment at the last part of Ione's question, Arbaces continued—"You know his pursuits, his companions, his habits; the comissatio and the alea (the revel and the dice) make his occupation;—and amongst the associates of vice, how can he dream of virtue?"

"Still you speak riddles. By the gods! I entreat you, say the worst at once."

"Well, then, it must be so. Know, my Ione, that it was but yesterday that Glaucus boasted openly—yes, in the public baths, of your love to him. He said it amused him to take advantage of it. Nay, I will do him justice, he praised your beauty. Who could deny it? But he laughed scornfully when his Clodius, or his Lepidus, asked him if he loved you enough for marriage, and when he purposed to adorn his door-posts with flowers?"

"Impossible! How heard you this base slander?"

"Nay, would you have me relate to you all the comments of the insolent coxcombs with which the story has circled through the town? Be assured that I myself disbelieved at first, and that I have now painfully been convinced by several ear-witnesses of the truth of what I have reluctantly told thee."

Ione sank back, and her face was whiter than the pillar against which she leaned for support.

"I own it vexed—it irritated me, to hear your name thus lightly pitched from lip to lip, like some mere dancing-girl's fame. I hastened this morning to seek and to warn you. I found Glaucus here. I was stung from my self-possession. I could not conceal my feelings; nay, I was uncourteous in thy presence. Canst thou forgive thy friend, Ione?"

Ione placed her hand in his, but replied not.

"Think no more of this," said he; "but let it be a warning voice, to tell thee how much prudence thy lot requires. It cannot hurt thee, Ione, for a moment; for a gay thing like this could never have been honored by even a serious thought from Ione. These insults only wound when they come from one we love; far different is he indeed whom the lofty Ione shall stoop to love." "Love!" muttered Ione, with an hysterical laugh. "Ay, indeed."

It is not without interest to observe in those remote times, and under a social system so widely different from the modern, the same small causes that ruffle and interrupt the "course of love," which operate so commonly at this day;—the same inventive jealousy, the same cunning slander, the same crafty and fabricated retailings of petty gossip, which so often now suffice to break the ties of the truest love, and counteract the tenor of circumstances most apparently propitious. When the bark sails on over the smoothest wave, the fable tells us of the diminutive fish that can cling to the keel and arrest its progress: so is it ever with the great passions of mankind; and we should paint life but ill if, even in times the most prodigal of romance, and of the romance of which we most largely avail ourselves, we did not also describe the mechanism of those trivial and household springs of mischief which we see every day at work in our chambers and at our hearths. It is in these, the lesser intrigues of life, that we mostly find ourselves at home with the past.

Most cunningly had the Egyptian appealed to Ione's ruling foible—most dexterously had he applied the poisoned dart to her pride. He fancied he had arrested what he hoped, from the shortness of the time she had known Glaucus, was, at most, but an incipient fancy; and hastening to change the subject, he now led her to talk of her brother. Their conversation did not last long. He left her, resolved not again to trust so much to absence, but to visit—to watch her—every day.

No sooner had his shadow glided from her presence, than woman's pride—her sex's dissimulation—deserted his intended victim, and the haughty Ione burst into passionate tears.

CHAPTER VII.

The gay life of the Pompeian lounger.—A miniature likeness of the Roman baths.

WHEN Glaucus left Ione, he felt as if he trod upon air. In the interview with which he had just been blessed, he had for the first time gathered from her distinctly that his love was not unwelcome to, and would not be unrewarded by, her. This hope filled him with a rapture for which earth and heaven seemed too narrow to afford a vent. Unconscious of the sudden enemy he had left behind, and forgetting not only his taunts but his very existence, Glaucus passed through the gay streets, repeating to himself, in the wantonness of joy, the music of the soft air to which Ione had listened with such intentness; and now he entered the Street of Fortune, with its raised foot-path—its houses painted without, and the open doors admitting the view of the glowing frescoes within. Each end of the street was adorned with a triumphal arch: and as Glaucus now came before the Temple of Fortune, the jutting portico of that beautiful fane (which is supposed to have been built by one of the family of Cicero, perhaps by the orator himself) imparted a dignified and venerable feature to a scene otherwise more brilliant than lofty in its character. That temple was one of the most graceful specimens of Roman architecture. It was raised on a somewhat lofty podium; and between two flights of steps ascending to a platform stood the altar of the goddess. From this platform another flight of broad stairs led to the portico, from the height of whose fluted columns hung festoons of the richest flowers. On either side the extremities of the temple were placed statues of Grecian workmanship; and at a little distance from the temple rose the triumphal arch crowned with an equestrian statue of Caligula, which was flanked by trophies of bronze. In the space before the temple a lively throng were assembled—some seated on benches and discussing the politics of the empire, some conversing on the approaching spectacle of the amphitheatre. One knot of young men were lauding a new beauty, another discussing the merits of the last play; a third group, more stricken in age, were speculating on the chance of the trade with Alexandria, and amidst these were many merchants in the Eastern costume, whose loose and peculiar robes, painted and gemmed slippers, and composed and serious countenances, formed a striking contrast to the tunicked forms and animated gestures of the Italians. For that impatient and lively people had, as now, a language distinct from speech—a language of signs and motions inexpressibly significant and vivacious: their descendants retain it, and the learned Jorio hath written a most entertaining work upon that species of hieroglyphical gesticulation.

Sauntering through the crowd, Glaucus soon found himself amidst a group of his merry and dissipated friends.

"Ah!" said Sallust, "it is a lustrum since I saw you."

"And how have you spent the lustrum? What new dishes have you discovered?"

"I have been scientific," returned Sallust, "and have made some experiments in the feeding of lampreys; I confess I despair of bringing them to the perfection which our Roman ancestors attained." "Miserable man! and why?"

"Because," returned Sallust, with a sigh, "it is no longer lawful to give them a slave to eat. I am very often tempted to make away with a very fat carptor (butler) whom I possess, and pop him slily into the reservoir. He would give the fish a most oleaginous flavor! But slaves are not slaves now-a-days, and have no sympathy with their masters' interest—or Davus would destroy himself to oblige me!"

"What news from Rome?" said Lepidus, as he languidly joined the group.

"The emperor has been giving a splendid supper to the senators," answered Sallust.

"He is a good creature," quoth Lepidus; "they say he never sends a man away without granting his request."

"Perhaps he would let me kill a slave for my reservoir?" returned Sallust, eagerly.

"Not unlikely," said Glaucus; "for he who grants a favor to one Roman, must always do it at the expense of another. Be sure, that for every smile Titus has caused, a hundred eyes have wept."

"Long live Titus!" cried Pansa, overhearing the emperor's name, as he swept patronizingly through the crowd; "he has promised my brother a quæstorship, because he had run through his fortune."

"And wishes now to enrich himself among the people, my Pansa," said Glaucus. "Exactly so," said Pansa.

"That is putting the people to some use," said Glaucus.

"To be sure," returned Pansa. "Well, I must go and look after the ærarium—it is a little out of repair;" and followed by a long train of clients, distinguished from the rest of the throng by the togas they wore (for togas, once the sign of freedom in a citizen, were now the badge of servility to a patron), the ædile fidgeted fussily away.

"Poor Pansa!" said Lepidus: "he never has time for pleasure. Thank Heaven I am not an ædile!"

"Ah, Glaucus! how are you? gay as ever!" said Clodius, joining the group.

"Are you come to sacrifice to Fortune?" said Sallust.

"I sacrifice to her every night," returned the gamester.

"I do not doubt it. No man has made more victims!"

"By Hercules, a biting speech!" cried Glaucus, laughing.

"The dog's letter is never out of your mouth, Sallust," said Clodius, angrily: "you are always snarling."

"I may well have the dog's letter in my mouth, since, whenever I play with you, I have the dog's throw in my hand," returned Sallust.

"Hist!" said Glaucus, taking a rose from a flower-girl, who stood beside.

"The rose is the token of silence," replied Sallust; "but I love only to see it at the supper-table."

"Talking of that, Diomed gives a grand feast next week," said Sallust: "are you invited, Glaucus?"

"Yes, I received an invitation this morning."

"And I, too," said Sallust, drawing a square piece of papyrus from his girdle: "I see that he asks us an hour earlier than usual: an earnest of something sumptuous."

"Oh! he is rich as Crœsus," said Clodius; "and his bill of fare is as long as an epic."

"Well, let us to the baths," said Glaucus: "this is the time when all the world is there; and Fulvius, whom you admire so much, is going to read us his last ode."

The young men assented readily to the proposal, and they strolled to the baths.

Although the public thermæ, or baths, were instituted rather for the poorer citizens than the wealthy (for the last had baths in their own houses), yet, to the crowds of all ranks who resorted to them, it was a favorite place for conversation, and for that indolent lounging so dear to a gay and thoughtless people. The baths at Pompeii differed, of course, in plan and construction from the vast and complicated thermæ of Rome; and, indeed, it seems that in each city of the empire there was always some slight modification of arrangement in the general architecture of the public baths. This mightily puzzles the learned,—as if architects and fashion were not capricious before the nineteenth century! Our party entered by the principal porch in the Street of Fortune. At the wing of the portico sat the keeper of the baths, with his two boxes before him, one for the money he received, one for the tickets he dispensed. Round the walls of the portico were seats crowded with persons of all ranks; while others, as the regimen of the physicians prescribed, were walking briskly to and fro the portico, stopping every now and then to gaze on the innumerable notices of shows, games, sales, exhibitions, which were painted or inscribed upon the walls. The general subject of conversation was, however, the spectacle announced in the amphitheatre; and each new-comer was fastened upon by a group eager to know if Pompeii had been so fortunate as to produce some monstrous criminal, some happy case of sacrilege or of murder, which would allow the ædiles to provide a man for the jaws of the lion: all other more common exhibitions seemed dull and tame, when compared with the possibility of this fortunate occurrence.

"For my part," said one jolly-looking man, who was a goldsmith, "I think the emperor, if he is as good as they say, might have sent us a Jew."

"Why not take one of the new sect of Nazarenes?" said a philosopher. "I am not cruel: but an atheist, one who denies Jupiter himself, deserves no mercy."

"I care not how many gods a man likes to believe in," said the goldsmith; "but to deny all gods is something monstrous."

"Yet I fancy," said Glaucus, "that these people are not absolutely atheists. I am told that they believe in a God—nay, in a future state."

"Quite a mistake, my dear Glaucus," said the philosopher. "I have conferred with them—they laughed in my face when I talked of Pluto and Hades."

"O ye gods!" exclaimed the goldsmith, in horror; "are there any of these wretches in Pompeii?"

"I know there are a few: but they meet so privately that it is impossible to discover who they are."

As Glaucus turned away, a sculptor, who was a great enthusiast in his art, looked after him admiringly.

"Ah!" said he, "if we could get *him* on the arena—there would be a model for you! What limbs! what a head! he ought to have been a gladiator! A subject—a subject—worthy of our art! Why don't they give him to the lion?"

Meanwhile Fulvius, the Roman poet, whom his contemporaries declared immortal, and who, but for this history, would never have been heard of in our neglectful age, came eagerly up to Glaucus: "Oh, my Athenian, my Glaucus, you have come to hear my ode! That is indeed an honor; you, a Greek—to whom the very language of common life is poetry. How I thank you! It is but a trifle; but if I secure your approbation, perhaps I may get an introduction to Titus. Oh, Glaucus! a poet without a patron is an amphora without a label; the wine may be good, but nobody will laud it! And what says Pythagoras?—'Frankincense to the gods, but praise to man.' A patron then, is the poet's priest: he procures him the incense, and obtains him his believers."

"But all Pompeii is your patron, and every portico an altar in your praise."

"Ah! the poor Pompeians are very civil—they love to honor merit. But they are only the inhabitants of a petty town —*spero meliora!* Shall we within?"

"Certainly; we lose time till we hear your poem."

At this instant there was a rush of some twenty persons from the baths into the portico; and a slave stationed at the door of a small corridor now admitted the poet, Glaucus, Clodius, and a troop of the bard's other friends, into the passage.

"A poor place this, compared with the Roman thermæ!" said Lepidus, disdainfully.

"Yet is there some taste in the ceiling," said Glaucus, who was in a mood to be pleased with everything; pointing to the stars which studded the roof.

Lepidus shrugged his shoulders, but was too languid to reply.

They now entered a somewhat spacious chamber, which served for the purposes of the apoditerium (that is, a place where the bathers prepared themselves for their luxurious ablutions). The vaulted ceiling was raised from a cornice, glowingly colored with motley and grotesque paintings; the ceiling itself was panelled in white compartments bordered with rich crimson; the unsullied and shining floor was paved with white mosaics, and along the walls were ranged benches for the accommodation of the loiterers. This chamber did not possess the numerous and spacious windows which Vitruvius attributes to his more magnificent *frigidarium.* The Pompeians, as all the southern Italians, were fond of banishing the

light of their sultry skies, and combined in their voluptuous
associations the idea of luxury with darkness. Two windows
of glass alone admitted the soft and shaded ray; and the compartment in which one of these casements was placed was
adorned with a large relief of the destruction of the Titans.

In this apartment Fulvius seated himself with a magisterial
air, and his audience gathering round him, encouraged him to
commence his recital.

The poet did not require much pressing. He drew forth
from his vest a roll of papyrus, and after hemming three times,
as much to command silence as to clear his voice, he began
that wonderful ode, of which, to the great mortification of the
author of this history, no single verse can be discovered.

By the plaudits he received, it was doubtless worthy of his
fame; and Glaucus was the only listener who did not find it
excel the best odes of Horace.

The poem concluded, those who took only the cold bath
began to undress; they suspended their garments on hooks
fastened in the wall, and receiving, according to their condition, either from their own slaves or those of the thermæ,
loose robes in exchange, withdrew into that graceful and circular building which yet exists, to shame the unlaving posterity
of the south.

The more luxurious departed by another door to the tepidarium, a place which was heated to a voluptuous warmth,
partly by a movable fire-place, principally by a suspended
pavement, beneath which was conducted the caloric of the
laconicum.

Here this portion of the intended bathers, after unrobing
themselves, remained for some time enjoying the artificial
warmth of the luxurious air. And this room, as befitted its
important rank in the long process of ablution, was more
richly and elaborately decorated than the rest; the arched roof
was beautifully carved and painted; the windows above, of
ground glass, admitted but wandering and uncertain rays; below the massive cornices were rows of figures in massive and
bold relief; the walls glowed with crimson, the pavement was
skilfully tessellated in white mosaics. Here the habituated
bathers, men who bathed seven times a day, would remain in
a state of enervate and speechless lassitude, either before or
(mostly) after the water-bath; and many of these victims of

the pursuit of health turned their listless eyes on the new-comers, recognizing their friends with a nod, but dreading the fatigue of conversation.

From this place the party again diverged, according to their several fancies, some to the sudatorium, which answered the purpose of our vapor-baths, and thence to the warm-bath itself; those more accustomed to exercise, and capable of dispensing with so cheap a purchase of fatigue, resorted at once to the calidarium, or water-bath.

In order to complete this sketch, and give to the reader an adequate notion of this, the main luxury of the ancients, we will accompany Lepidus, who regularly underwent the whole process, save only the cold-bath, which had gone lately out of fashion. Being then gradually warmed in the tepidarium, which has just been described, the delicate steps of the Pompeian *élégant* were conducted to the sudatorium. Here let the reader depict to himself the gradual process of the vapor-bath, accompanied by an exhalation of spicy perfumes. After our bather had undergone this operation, he was seized by his slaves, who always awaited him at the baths, and the dews of heat were removed by a kind of scraper, which (by the way) a modern traveller has gravely declared to be used only to remove the dirt, not one particle of which could ever settle on the polished skin of the practised bather. Thence, somewhat cooled, he passed into the water-bath, over which fresh perfumes were profusely scattered, and on emerging from the opposite part of the room, a cooling shower played over his head and form. Then wrapping himself in a light robe, he returned once more to the tepidarium, where he found Glaucus, who had not encountered the sudatorium; and now, the main delight and extravagance of the bath commenced. Their slaves anointed the bathers from the vials of gold, of alabaster, or of crystal, studded with profusest gems, and containing the rarest unguents gathered from all quarters of the world. The number of these smegmata used by the wealthy would fill a modern volume—especially if the volume were printed by a fashionable publisher; *Amoracinum, Megalium, Nardum— omne quod exit in um:*—while soft music played in an adjacent chamber, and such as used the bath in moderation, refreshed and restored by the grateful ceremony, conversed with all the zest and freshness of rejuvenated life.

"Blessed be he who invented baths!" said Glaucus, stretching himself along one of those bronze seats (then covered with soft cushions) which the visitor to Pompeii sees at this day in that same tepidarium. "Whether he were Hercules or Bacchus, he deserved deification."

"But tell me," said a corpulent citizen, who was groaning and wheezing under the operation of being rubbed down, "tell me, O Glaucus!—evil chance to thy hands, O slave! why so rough?—tell me—ugh—ugh!—are the baths at Rome really so magnificent?" Glaucus turned, and recognized Diomed, though not without some difficulty, so red and so inflamed were the good man's cheeks by the sudatory and the scraping he had so lately undergone. "I fancy they must be a great deal finer than these. Eh?" Suppressing a smile, Glaucus replied—

"Imagine all Pompeii converted into baths, and you will then form a notion of the size of the imperial thermæ of Rome. But a notion of the *size* only. Imagine every entertainment for mind and body—enumerate all the gymnastic games our fathers invented—repeat all the books Italy and Greece have produced—suppose places for all these games, admirers for all these works—add to this, baths of the vastest size, the most complicated construction—intersperse the whole with gardens, with theatres, with porticos, with schools—suppose, in one word, a city of the gods, composed but of palaces and public edifices, and you may form some faint idea of the glories of the great baths of Rome."

"By Hercules!" said Diomed, opening his eyes, "why it would take a man's whole life to bathe!"

"At Rome, it often does so," replied Glaucus, gravely. "There are many who live only at the baths. They repair there the first hour in which the doors are opened, and remain till that in which the doors are closed. They seem as if they knew nothing of the rest of Rome, as if they despised all other existence." "By Pollux! you amaze me."

"Even those who bathe only thrice a day contrive to consume their lives in this occupation. They take their exercise in the tennis-court or the porticos, to prepare them for the first bath; they lounge into the theatre, to refresh themselves after it. They take their prandium under the trees, and think over their second bath. By the time it is prepared, the prandium is digested. From the second bath they stroll into one of the peristyles, to hear some new poet recite; or into the library, to sleep over an old one. Then comes the supper, which they still consider but a part of the bath; and then a third time they bathe again, as the best place to converse with their friends."

"Per Hercle! but we have their imitators at Pompeii."

"Yes, and without their excuse. The magnificent voluptuaries of the Roman baths are happy; they see nothing but gorgeousness and splendor; they visit not the squalid parts of the city; they know not that there is poverty in the world. All Nature smiles for them, and her only frown is the last one which sends them to bathe in Cocytus. Believe me, they are your only true philsophers."

While Glaucus was thus conversing, Lepidus, with closed eyes and scarce perceptible breath, was undergoing all the mystic operations, not one of which he ever suffered his attendants to omit. After the perfumes and the unguents, they scattered over him the luxurious powder which prevented any farther accession of heat; and this being rubbed away by the smooth surface of the pumice, he began to indue, not the garments he had put off, but those more festive ones termed "the synthesis," with which the Romans marked their respect for the coming ceremony of supper, if rather, from its hour (three o'clock in our measurement of time), it might not be more fitly denominated dinner. This done, he at length opened his eyes and gave signs of returning life.

At the same time, too, Sallust betokened by a long yawn the evidence of existence.

"It is supper-time," said the epicure; "you, Glaucus and Lepidus, come and sup with me."

"Recollect you are all three engaged to my house next week," cried Diomed, who was mightily proud of the acquaintance of men of fashion.

"Ah, ah! we recollect," said Sallust: "the seat of memory, my Diomed, is certainly in the stomach."

Passing now once again into the cooler air, and so into the street, our gallants of that day concluded the ceremony of a Pompeian bath.

CHAPTER VIII.

Arbaces cogs his dice with pleasure, and wins the game.

THE evening darkened over the restless city, as Apæcides took his way to the house of the Egyptian. He avoided the more lighted and populous streets; and as he strode onward with his head buried in his bosom, and his arms folded within his robe, there was something startling in the contrast, which his solemn mien and wasted form presented to the thoughtless brows and animated air of those who occasionally crossed his path.

At length, however, a man of a more sober and staid demeanor, and who had twice passed him with a curious but doubting look, touched him on the shoulder.

"Apæcides!" said he, and he made a rapid sign with his hands: it was the sign of the cross.

"Well, Nazarene," replied the priest, and his face grew paler: "what wouldst thou?"

"Nay," returned the stranger, "I would not interrupt thy meditations; but the last time we met, I seemed not to be so unwelcome."

"You are not unwelcome, Olinthus; but I am sad and weary: nor am I able this evening to discuss with you those themes which are most acceptable to you."

"O backward of heart!" said Olinthus, with bitter fervor; "and art thou sad and weary, and wilt thou turn from the very springs that refresh and heal?"

"O earth!" cried the young priest, striking his breast passionately, "from what regions shall my eyes open to the true Olympus, where thy gods really dwell? Am I to believe with this man, that none whom for so many centuries my fathers worshipped have a being or a name? Am I to break down, as something blasphemous and profane, the very altars which I have deemed most sacred? or am I to think with Arbaces—what?"

He paused, and strode rapidly away in the impatience of a man who strives to get rid of himself. But the Nazarene was

66

one of those hardy, vigorous, and enthusiastic men, by whom God in all times has worked the revolutions of earth, and those, above all, in the establishment and in the reformation of His own religion;—men who were formed to convert, because formed to endure. It is men of this mould whom nothing discourages, nothing dismays; in the fervor of belief they are inspired and they inspire. Their reason first kindles their passion, but the passion is the instrument they use; they force themselves into men's hearts, while they appear only to appeal to their judgment. Nothing is so contagious as enthusiasm; it it the real allegory of the tale of Orpheus—it moves stones, it charms brutes. Enthusiasm is the genius of sincerity, and truth accomplishes no victories without it.

Olinthus did not then suffer Apæcides thus easily to escape him. He overtook, and addressed him thus:—

"I do not wonder, Apæcides, that I distress you; that I shake all the elements of your mind: that you are lost in doubt; that you drift here and there in the vast ocean of uncertain and benighted thought. I wonder not at this, but bear with me a little; watch and pray,—the darkness shall vanish, the storm sleep, and God himself, as He came of yore on the seas of Samaria, shall walk over the lulled billows, to the delivery of your soul. Ours is a religion jealous in its demands, but how infinitely prodigal in its gifts! It troubles you for an hour, it repays you by immortality."

"Such promises," said Apæcides, sullenly, "are the tricks by which man is ever gulled. Oh, glorious were the promises which led me to the shrine of Isis!"

"But," answered the Nazarene, "ask thy reason, can that religion be sound which outrages all morality? You are told to worship your gods. What are those gods, even according to yourselves? What their actions, what their attributes? Are they not all represented to you as the blackest of criminals? yet you are asked to serve them as the holiest of divinities. Jupiter himself is a parricide and an adulterer. What are the meaner deities but imitators of his vices? You are told not to murder, but you worship murderers; you are told not to commit adultery, and you make your prayers to an adulterer. Oh! what is this but a mockery of the holiest part of man's nature, which is faith? Turn now to the God, the one, the true God, to whose shrine I would lead you. If He seem to you too sublime, too shadowy, for those human associations, those touching connections between Creator and creature, to which the weak heart clings—contemplate Him in his Son, who put on mortality like ourselves. His mortality is not indeed declared, like that of your fabled gods, by the vices of our nature, but by the practice of all its virtues. In Him are united the austerest morals with the tenderest affections. If He were but a mere man, He had been worthy to become a god. You honor Socrates—he has his sect, his disciples, his schools. But what are the doubtful virtues of the Athenian, to the bright, the undisputed, the active, the unceasing, the devoted holiness of Christ? I speak to you now only of His human character. He came in that as the pattern of future ages, to show us the form of virtue which Plato thirsted to see embodied. This was the true sacrifice that He made for man; but the halo that encircled His dying hour not only brightened earth, but opened to us the sight of heaven! You are touched—you are moved. God works in your heart. His Spirit is with you. Come, resist not the holy impulse: come at once—unhesitatingly. A few of us are now assembled to expound the word of God. Come, let me guide you to them. You are sad, you are weary. Listen, then, to the words of God;—'Come to me,' saith He, 'all ye that are heavy laden, and I will give you rest!'"

"I cannot now," said Apæcides; "another time."

"Now—now!" exclaimed Olinthus, earnestly, and clasping him by the arm.

But Apæcides, yet unprepared for the renunciation of that faith—that life, for which he had sacrificed so much, and still haunted by the promises of the Egyptian, extricated himself forcibly from the grasp; and feeling an effort necessary to conquer the irresolution which the eloquence of the Christian had begun to effect in his heated and feverish mind, he gathered up his robes, and fled with a speed that defied pursuit.

Breathless and exhausted, he arrived at last in a remote and sequestered part of the city, and the lone house of the Egyptian stood before him. As he paused to recover himself, the moon emerged from a silver cloud, and shone full upon the walls of that mysterious habitation.

No other house was near—the darksome vines clustered far and wide in front of the building, and behind it rose a copse of lofty forest trees, sleeping in the melancholy moonlight;

beyond stretched the dim outline of the distant hills, and amongst them the quiet crest of Vesuvius, not then so lofty as the traveller beholds it now.

Apæcides passed through the arching vines, and arrived at the broad and spacious portico. Before it, on either side of the steps, reposed the image of the Egyptian sphinx, and the moonlight gave an additional and yet more solemn calm to those large, and harmonious, and passionless features, in which the sculptors of that type of wisdom united so much of loveliness with awe; half way up the extremities of the steps darkened the green and massive foliage of the aloe, and the shadow of the eastern palm cast its long and unwaving boughs partially over the marble surface of the stairs.

Something there was in the stillness of the place, and the strange aspect of the sculptured sphinxes, which thrilled the blood of the priest with a nameless and ghostly fear, and he longed even for an echo to his noiseless steps as he ascended to the threshold.

He knocked at the door, over which was wrought an inscription in characters unfamiliar to his eyes; it opened without a sound, and a tall Ethiopian slave without question or salutation, motioned to him to proceed.

The wide hall was lighted by lofty candelabra of elaborate bronze, and round the walls were wrought vast hieroglyphics, in dark and solemn colors, which contrasted strangely with the bright hues and graceful shapes with which the inhabitants of Italy decorated their abodes. At the extremity of the hall, a slave, whose countenance, though not African, was darker by many shades than the usual color of the south, advanced to meet him.

"I seek Arbaces," said the priest, but his voice trembled even in his own ear. The slave bowed his head in silence, and leading Apæcides to a wing without the hall, conducted him up a narrow staircase, and then traversing several rooms, in which the stern and thoughtful beauty of the sphinx still made the chief and most impressive object of the priest's notice, Apæcides found himself in a dim and half-lighted chamber, in the presence of the Egyptian.

Arbaces was seated before a small table, on which lay unfolded several scrolls of papyrus, impressed with the same character as that on the threshold of the mansion. A small tripod stood at a little distance, from the incense in which the smoke slowly rose. Near this was a vast globe, depicting the signs of heaven; and upon another table lay several instruments, of curious and quaint shape, whose uses were unknown to Apæcides. The farther extremity of the room was concealed by a curtain, and the oblong window in the roof admitted the rays of the moon, mingling sadly with the single lamp which burned in the apartment.

"Seat yourself, Apæcides," said the Egyptian, without rising. The young man obeyed.

"You ask me," resumed Arbaces, after a short pause, in which he seemed absorbed in thought,—"You ask me, or would do so, the mightiest secrets which the soul of man is fitted to receive; it is the enigma of life itself that you desire me to solve. Placed like children in the dark, and but for a little while, in this dim and confined existence, we shape our spectres in the obscurity; our thoughts now sink back into ourselves in terror, now wildly plunge themselves into the guideless gloom, guessing what it may contain;—stretching our helpless hands here and there, lest, blindly, we stumble upon some hidden danger; not knowing the limits of our boundary, now feeling them suffocate us with compression, now seeing them extend far away till they vanish into eternity. In this state, all wisdom consists necessarily in the solution of two questions—'What are we to believe? and What are we to reject?' These questions you desire me to decide?" Apæcides bowed his head in assent.

"Man *must* have some belief," continued the Egyptian, in a tone of sadness. "He must fasten his hope to something: it is our common nature that you inherit when, aghast and terrified to see that in which you have been taught to place your faith swept away, you float over a dreary and shoreless sea of incertitude, you cry for help, you ask for some plank to cling to, some land, however dim and distant, to attain. Well, then, listen. You have not forgotten our conversation of to-day?"

"Forgotten!"

"I confessed to you that those deities for whom smoke so many altars were but inventions. I confessed to you that our rites and ceremonies were but mummeries, to delude and lure the herd to their proper good. I explained to you that from those delusions came the bonds of society, the harmony of the world, the power of the wise; that power is in the obedience of the vulgar. Continue we then these salutary delusions—if man must have some belief, continue to him that which his fathers have made dear to him, and which custom sanctifies and strengthens. In seeking a subtler faith for us, whose senses are too spiritual for the gross one, let us leave others that support which crumbles from ourselves. This is wise—it is benevolent." "Proceed."

"This being settled," resumed the Egyptian, "the old landmarks being left uninjured for those whom we are about to desert, we gird up our loins and depart to new climes of faith. Dismiss at once from your recollection, from your thought, all that you have believed before. Suppose the mind a blank, an unwritten scroll, fit to receive impressions for the first time. Look round the world—observe its order—its regularity—its design. Something must have created it—the design speaks a designer: in that certainty we first touch land. But what is that something?—A god, you cry. Stay—no confused and confusing names. Of that which created the world, we know, we can know, nothing, save these attributes —power and unvarying regularity;—stern, crushing, relentless regularity—heeding no individual cases—rolling—sweeping—burning on;—no matter what scattered hearts, severed from the general mass, fall ground and scorched beneath its wheels. The mixture of evil with good—the existence of suffering and of crime—in all times have perplexed the wise. They created a god—they supposed him benevolent. How then came this evil? why did he permit—nay, why invent, why perpetuate it? To account for this, the Persian creates a second spirit, whose nature is evil, and supposes a continual war between that and the god of good. In our own shadowy and tremendous Typhon, the Egyptians image a similar demon. Perplexing blunder that yet more bewilders us!—folly that arose from the vain delusion that makes a palpable, a corporeal, a human being, of this unknown power—that clothes the Invisible with attributes and a nature similar to the Seen. No: to this designer let us give a name that does not command our bewildering associations, and the mystery becomes more clear—that name is NECESSITY. Necessity, say the Greeks, compels the gods. Then why the gods?—their agency becomes unnecessary—dismiss them at once. Necessity is the ruler of all we see;—power, regularity—these two qualities make its nature.

Would you ask more?—you can learn nothing: whether it be
eternal—whether it compel us, its creatures, to new careers
after that darkness which we call death—we cannot tell. There
leave we this ancient, unseen, unfathomable power, and come
to that which, to our eyes, is the great minister of its func-
tions. This we can task more, from this we can learn more: its
evidence is around us—its name is NATURE. The error of the
sages has been to direct their researches to the attributes of
necessity, where all is gloom and blindness. Had they confined their researches to Nature—what of knowledge might we
not already have achieved? Here patience, examination, are
never directed in vain. We see what we explore; our minds
ascend a palpable ladder of causes and effects. Nature is the
great agent of the external universe, and Necessity imposes
upon it the laws by which it acts, and imparts to us the powers
by which we examine; those powers are curiosity and memory—their union is reason, their perfection is wisdom. Well,
then, I examine by the help of these powers this inexhaustible
Nature. I examine the earth, the air, the ocean, the heaven: I
find that all have a mystic sympathy with each other—that the
moon sways the tides—that the air maintains the earth, and
is the medium of the life and sense of things—that by the
knowledge of the stars we measure the limits of the earth—
that we portion out the epochs of time—that by their pale
light we are guided into the abyss of the past—that in their
solemn lore we discern the destinies of the future. And thus,
while we know not that which Necessity is, we learn, at least,
her decrees. And now, what morality do we glean from this
religion?—for religion it is. I believe in two deities, Nature and
Necessity; I worship the last by reverence, the first by investi-
gation. What is the morality my religion teaches? This—all
things are subject but to general rules; the sun shines for the
joy of the many—it may bring sorrow to the few; the night
sheds sleep on the multitude—but it harbors murder as well
as rest; the forests adorn the earth—but shelter the serpent
and the lion; the ocean supports a thousand barks—but it en-
gulfs the one. It is only thus for the general, and not for the
universal benefit, that Nature acts, and Necessity speeds on
her awful course. This is the morality of the dread agents of
the world—it is mine, who am their creature. I would preserve the delusions of priestcraft, for they are serviceable to

the multitude; I would impart to man the arts I discover, the sciences I perfect: I would speed the vast career of civilizing lore:—in this I serve the mass, I fulfil the general law, I execute the great moral that Nature preaches. For myself I claim the individual exception; I claim it for the wise—satisfied that my individual actions are nothing in the great balance of good and evil; satisfied that the product of my knowledge can give greater blessings to the mass than my desires can operate evil on the few (for the first can extend to remotest regions and humanize nations yet unborn), I give to the world wisdom, to myself freedom. I enlighten the lives of others, and I enjoy my own. Yes; our wisdom is eternal, but our life is short: make the most of it while it lasts. Surrender thy youth to pleasure, and thy senses to delight. Soon comes the hour when the wine-cup is shattered, and the garlands shall cease to bloom. Enjoy while you may. Be still, O Apæcides, my pupil and my follower! I will teach thee the mechanism of Nature, her darkest and her wildest secrets—the lore which fools call magic—and the mighty mysteries of the stars. By this shalt thou discharge thy duty to the mass; by this shalt thou enlighten thy race. But I will lead thee also to pleasures of which the vulgar do not dream; and the day which thou givest to men shall be followed by the sweet night which thou surrenderest to thyself."

As the Egyptian ceased there rose about, around, beneath, the softest music that Lydia ever taught, or Ionia ever perfected. It came like a stream of sound, bathing the senses unawares; enervating, subduing with delight. It seemed the melodies of invisible spirits, such as the shepherd might have heard in the golden age, floating through the vales of Thessaly, or in the noontide glades of Paphos. The words which had rushed to the lip of Apæcides, in answer to the sophistries of the Egyptian, died trembling away. He felt it as a profanation to break upon that enchanted strain—the susceptibility of his excited nature, the Greek softness and ardor of his secret soul, were swayed and captured by surprise. He sank on the seat with parted lips and thirsting ear; while in a chorus of voices, bland and melting as those which waked Psyche in the halls of love, rose the following song:—

THE HYMN OF EROS.

"By the cool banks where soft Cephisus flows,
　　A voice sail'd trembling down the waves of air;
The leaves blushed brighter in the Teian's rose,
　　The doves couch'd breathless in their summer lair.;

While from their hands the purple flowerets fell,
　　The laughing Hours stood listening in the sky;—
From Pan's green cave to Ægle's haunted cell,
　　Heaved the charm'd earth in one delicious sigh.

'Love, sons of earth! I am the Power of Love!
　　Eldest of all the gods, with Chaos born;
My smile sheds light along the courts above,
　　My kisses wake the eyelids of the Morn.

'Mine are the stars—there, ever as ye gaze,
　　Ye meet the deep spell of my haunting eyes;
Mine is the moon—and, mournful if her rays,
　　'Tis that she lingers where her Carian lies.

'The flowers are mine—the blushes of the rose,
　　The violet-charming Zephyr to the shade;
Mine the quick light that in the Maybeam glows,
　　And mine the day-dream in the lonely glade.

'Love, sons of earth—for love is earth's soft lore,
　　Look where ye will—earth overflows with ME;
Learn from the waves that ever kiss the shore,
　　And the winds nestling on the heaving sea.

'All teaches love!'—The sweet voice, like a dream,
　　Melted in light; yet still the airs above,
The waving sedges, and the whispering stream,
　　And the green forest rustling, murmur'd 'LOVE!'"

As the voices died away, the Egyptian seized the hand of
Apæcides, and led him, wondering, intoxicated, yet half-reluc-
tant, across the chamber towards the curtain at the far end;
and now, from behind that curtain, there seemed to burst a
thousand sparkling stars; the veil itself, hitherto dark, was
now lighted by these fires behind into the tenderest blue of
heaven. It represented heaven itself—such a heaven, as in the
nights of June might have shone down over the streams of
Castaly. Here and there were painted rosy and aërial clouds,
from which smiled, by the limner's art, faces of divinest
beauty, and on which reposed the shapes of which Phidias and

Apelles dreamed. And the stars which studded the transparent azure rolled rapidly as they shone, while the music, that again woke with a livelier and lighter sound, seemed to imitate the melody of the joyous spheres.

"Oh! what miracle is this, Arbaces?" said Apæcides in faltering accents. "After having denied the gods, art thou about to reveal to me——"

"Their pleasures!" interrupted Arbaces, in a tone so different from its usual cold and tranquil harmony that Apæcides started, and thought the Egyptian himself transformed; and now, as they neared the curtain, a wild—a loud—an exulting melody burst from behind its concealment. With that sound the veil was rent in twain—it parted—it seemed to vanish into air: and a scene, which no Sybarite ever more than rivalled, broke upon the dazzled gaze of the youthful priest. A vast banquet-room stretched beyond, blazing with countless lights, which filled the warm air with the scents of frankincense, of jasmine, of violets, of myrrh; all that the most odorous flowers, all that the most costly spices could distil, seemed gathered into one ineffable and ambrosial essence: from the light columns that sprang upwards to the airy roof, hung draperies of white, studded with golden stars. At the extremities of the room two fountains cast up a spray, which, catching the rays of the roseate light, glittered like countless diamonds. In the centre of the room as they entered there rose slowly from the floor, to the sound of unseen minstrelsy, a table spread with all the viands which sense ever devoted to fancy, and vases of that lost Myrrhine fabric,* so glowing in its colors, so transparent in its material, were crowned with the exotics of the East. The couches, to which this table was the centre, were covered with tapestries of azure and gold; and from invisible tubes in the vaulted roof descended showers of fragrant waters, that cooled the delicious air, and contended with the lamps, as if the spirits of wave and fire disputed which element could furnish forth the most delicious odors. And now, from behind the snowy draperies, trooped such forms as Adonis beheld when he lay on the lap of Venus. They came, some with garlands, others with lyres; they surrounded the youth, they led his steps to the banquet. They flung the chap-

---

* Which, however, was possibly the porcelain of China,—though this is a matter which admits of considerable dispute.

lets round him in rosy chains. The earth—the thought of earth, vanished from his soul. He imagined himself in a dream, and suppressed his breath lest he should wake too soon; the senses, to which he had never yielded as yet, beat in his burning pulse, and confused his dizzy and reeling sight. And while thus amazed and lost, once again, but in brisk and Bacchic measures, rose the magic strain:—

ANACREONTIC.

"In the veins of the calix foams and glows
  The blood of the mantling vine,
But oh! in the bowl of Youth there glows
  A Lesbium, more divine!
    Bright, bright.
    As the liquid light,
  Its waves through thine eyelids shine!

Fill up, fill up, to the sparkling brim,
  The juice of the young Lyæus;

The grape is the key that we owe to him
  From the gaol of the world to free us.
    Drink, drink!
    What need to shrink,
  When the lamps alone can see us?

Drink, drink, as I quaff from thine eyes,
  The wine of a softer tree;
Give the smiles to the god of the grape—thy sighs,
  Beloved one, give to me.
    Turn, turn,
    My glances burn,
  And thirst for a look from thee!"

As the song ended, a group of three maidens, entwined with a chain of starred flowers, and who, while they imitated, might have shamed the Graces, advanced towards him in the gliding measures of the Ionian dance: such as the Nereids wreathed in moonlight on the yellow sands of the Ægean wave—such as Cytherea taught her handmaids in the marriage-feast of Psyche and her son.

Now approaching, they wreathed their chaplet round his head; now kneeling, the youngest of the three proffered him the bowl, from which the wine of Lesbos foamed and sparkled. The youth resisted no more, he grasped the intoxicating cup, the blood mantled fiercely through his veins. He sank upon the breast of the nymph who sat beside him, and turning with swimming eyes to seek for Arbaces, whom he had lost in the whirl of his emotions, he beheld him seated beneath a canopy at the upper end of the table, and gazing upon him with a smile that encouraged him to pleasure. He beheld him, but not as he had hitherto seen, with dark and sable garments, with a brooding and solemn brow: a robe that dazzled the sight, so studded was its whitest surface with gold and gems, blazed upon his majestic form; white roses, alternated with the emerald and the ruby, and shaped tiara-like, crowned his raven locks. He appeared, like Ulysses, to have gained the glory of a second youth—his features seemed to have exchanged thought for beauty, and he towered amidst the loveliness that surrounded him, in all the beaming and relaxing benignity of the Olympian god.

"Drink, feast, love, my pupil!" said he; "blush not that thou art passionate and young. That which thou art, thou feelest in thy veins: that which thou shalt be, survey!"

With this he pointed to a recess, and the eyes of Apæcides, following the gesture, beheld on a pedestal, placed between the statues of Bacchus and Idalia, the form of a skeleton.

"Start not," resumed the Egyptian; "that friendly guest admonishes us but of the shortness of life. From its jaws I hear a voice that summons us to ENJOY."

As he spoke, a group of nymphs surrounded the statue; they laid chaplets on its pedestal, and, while the cups were emptied and refilled at that glowing board, they sang the following strain:—

BACCHIC HYMNS TO THE IMAGE OF DEATH.

I.

"Thou art in the land of the shadowy Host,
Thou that didst drink and love:
By the Solemn River, a gliding ghost.
But thy thought is ours above!
If memory yet can fly,
Back to the golden sky,
And mourn the pleasures lost!
By the ruin'd hall these flowers we lay,
Where thy soul once held its palace;
When the rose to thy scent and sight was gay,

> And the smile was in the chalice,
> 　　And the cithara's silver voice
> 　　Could bid thy heart rejoice
> When night eclipsed the day."

Here a new group advancing, turned the tide of the music
into a quicker and more joyous strain:—

ii.

> "Death, death, is the gloomy shore,
> 　　Where we all sail—
> Soft, soft, thou gliding oar;
> 　　Blow soft, sweet gale!
> Chain with bright wreaths the Hours
> 　　Victims if all,
> Ever, 'mid song and flowers,
> 　　Victims should fall!"

Pausing for a moment, yet quicker and quicker danced the
silver-footed music:—

> "Since Life's so short, we'll live to laugh,
> 　　Ah, wherefore waste a minute!
> If youth's the cup we yet can quaff,
> 　　Be love the pearl within it!"

A third band now approached with brimming cups, which
they poured in libation upon that strange altar; and once more,
slow and solemn, rose the changeful melody:—

iii.

> "Thou art welcome, Guest of gloom,
> 　　From the far and fearful sea!
> When the last rose sheds its bloom,
> 　　Our board shall be spread with thee!
> 　　　　All hail, dark Guest!
> 　　Who hath so fair a plea
> 　　Our welcome Guest to be,
> 　　As thou, whose solemn hall
> 　　At last shall feast us all
> 　　In the dim and dismal coast?
> 　　Long yet be *we* the Host!
> 　　And thou, Dead Shadow, thou,
> 　　All joyless though thy brow,
> 　　　　Thou—but our passing *Guest!*

At this moment, she who sat beside Apæcides suddenly took up the song:—

IV.

"Happy is yet our doom,
   The earth and the sun are ours!
And far from the dreary tomb
   Speed the wings of the rosy Hours—
Sweet is for thee the bowl,
   Sweet are thy looks, my love;
I fly to thy tender soul,
   As the bird to its mated dove!
   Take me, ah, take!
Clasp'd to thy guardian breast,
Soft let me sink to rest:
   But wake me—ah, wake!
And tell me with words and sighs,
But more with thy melting eyes,
   That my sun is not set—
That the Torch is not quench'd at the Urn,
That we love, and we breathe, and burn,
   Tell me—thou lov'st me yet!"

BOOK THE SECOND.
CHAPTER I.

A flash house in Pompeii, and the gentlemen of the classic ring.

To one of those parts of Pompeii, which were tenanted not by the lords of pleasure, but by its minions and its victims; the haunt of gladiators and prize-fighters; of the vicious and the penniless; of the savage and the obscene; the Alsatia of an ancient city—we are now transported.

It was a large room, that opened at once on the confined and crowded lane. Before the threshold was a group of men, whose iron and well-strung muscles, whose short and Herculean necks, whose hardy and reckless countenances, indicated the champions of the arena. On a shelf, without the shop, were ranged jars of wine and oil; and right over this was inserted in the wall a coarse painting, which exhibited gladiators drinking—so ancient and so venerable is the custom of signs! Within the room were placed several small tables, arranged somewhat in the modern fashion of "boxes," and round these were seated several knots of men, some drinking, some playing at dice, some at that more skilful game called *"duodecim scriptæ,"* which certain of the blundering learned have mistaken for chess, though it *rather,* perhaps, resembled back-gammon of the two, and was usually though not always, played by the assistance of dice. The hour was in the early forenoon, and nothing better, perhaps, than that unseasonable time itself denoted the habitual indolence of these tavern-loungers. Yet, despite the situation of the house and the character of its inmates, it indicated none of that sordid squalor which would have characterized a similar haunt in a modern city. The gay disposition of all the Pompeians, who sought, at least, to gratify the sense even where they neglected the mind, was typified by the gaudy colors which decorated the walls, and the shapes, fantastic but not inelegant, in which the lamps, the drinking-cups, the commonest household utensils, were wrought.

"By Pollux!" said one of the gladiators, as he leaned against the wall of the threshold, "the wine thou sellest us, old Silenus,"—and as he spoke he slapped a portly personage on the back,—"is enough to thin the best blood in one's veins."

The man thus caressingly saluted, and whose bared arms, white apron, and keys and napkin tucked carelessly within his girdle, indicated him to be the host of the tavern, was already passed into the autumn of his years; but his form was still so robust and athletic, that he might have shamed even the sinewy shapes beside him, save that the muscles had seeded, as it were, into flesh, that the cheeks were swelled and bloated, and the increasing stomach threw into shade the vast and massive chest which rose above it.

"None of thy scurrilous blusterings with me," growled the gigantic landlord, in the gentle semi-roar of an insulted tiger; "my wine is good enough for a carcass which shall so soon soak the dust of the spoliarium."

"Croakest thou thus, old raven!" returned the gladiator, laughing scornfully; "thou shalt live to hang thyself with despite when thou seest me win the palm crown; and when I get the purse at the amphitheatre, as I certainly shall, my first vow to Hercules shall be to forswear thee and thy vile potations evermore."

"Hear to him—hear to this modest Pyrgopolinices! He has certainly served under Bombochides Cluninstaridysarhides," cried the host. "Sporus, Niger, Tetraides, he declares he shall win the purse from you. Why, by the gods! each of your muscles is strong enough to stifle all his body, or I know nothing of the arena!"

"Ha!" said the gladiator, coloring with rising fury, "our lanista would tell a different story."

"What story could he tell against me, vain Lydon?" said Tetraides, frowning.

"Or me, who have conquered in fifteen fights?" said the gigantic Niger, stalking up to the gladiator.

"Or me?" grunted Sporus, with eyes of fire.

"Tush!" said Lydon, folding his arms, and regarding his rivals with a reckless air of defiance. "The time of trial will soon come; keep your valor till then."

"Ay, do," said the surly host; "and if I press down my thumb to save you, may the Fates cut my thread!"

"Your rope, you mean," said Lydon, sneeringly: "here is a sesterce to buy one."

The Titan wine-vender seized the hand extended to him, and griped it in so stern a vise that the blood spirted from the fingers' ends over the garments of the bystanders.

They set up a savage laugh.

"I will teach thee, young braggart, to play the Macedonian with me! I am no puny Persian, I warrant thee! What, man! have I not fought twenty years in the ring, and never lowered my arms once? And have I not received the rod from the editor's own hand as a sign of victory, and as a grace to retirement on my laurels! And am I now to be lectured by a boy?" So saying, he flung the hand from him in scorn.

Without changing a muscle, but with the same smiling face with which he had previously taunted mine host, did the gladiator brave the painful grasp he had undergone. But no sooner was his hand released, than, crouching for one moment as a wild cat crouches, you might see his hair bristle on his head and beard, and with a fierce and shrill yell he sprang on the throat of the giant, with an impetus that threw him, vast and sturdy as he was, from his balance;—and down, with the crash of a falling rock, he fell;—while over him fell also his ferocious foe.

Our host, perhaps, had had no need of the rope so kindly recommended to him by Lydon, had he remained three minutes longer in that position. But, summoned to his assistance by the noise of his fall, a woman, who had hitherto kept in an inner apartment, rushed to the scene of battle. This new ally was in herself a match for the gladiator; she was tall, lean, and with arms that could give other than soft embraces. In fact, the gentle helpmate of Burbo the wine-seller had, like himself, fought in the lists—nay, under the emperor's eye. And Burbo himself—Burbo, the unconquered in the field, according to report, now and then yielded the palm to his soft Stratonice. This sweet creature no sooner saw the imminent peril that awaited her worse half, than without other weapons than those with which Nature had provided her, she darted upon the incumbent gladiator, and, clasping him round the waist with her long and snake-like arms, lifted him by a sudden wrench from the body of her husband, leaving only his hands still clinging to the throat of his foe. So have we seen a dog snatched by the hind legs from the strife with a fallen rival in the arms of some envious groom; so have we seen one half of him high in air—passive and offenceless—while the other half, head, teeth, eyes, claws, seemed buried and engulfed in the mangled and prostrate enemy. Meanwhile the gladiators, lapped, and pampered, and glutted upon blood, crowded delightedly round the combatants—their nostrils distended—their lips grinning—their eyes gloatingly fixed on the bloody throat of the one, and the indented talons of the other.

"Habet!" (he has got it!) *habet!"* cried they, with a sort of yell, rubbing their nervous hands.

"Non habeo, ye liars; I have not *got* it!" shouted the host, as with a mighty effort he wrenched himself from those deadly hands, and rose to his feet, breathless, panting, lacerated, bloody; and fronting, with reeling eyes, the glaring look and grinning teeth of his baffled foe, now struggling (but struggling with disdain) in the gripe of the sturdy amazon.

"Fair play!" cried the gladiators: "one to one;" and, crowding round Lydon and the woman, they separated our pleasing host from his courteous guest.

But Lydon, feeling ashamed at his present position, and endeavoring in vain to shake off the grasp of the virago, slipped his hand into his girdle, and drew forth a short knife. So menacing was his look, so brightly gleamed the blade, that Stratonice, who was used only to that fashion of battle which we moderns call the pugilistic, started back in alarm.

"O gods!" cried she, "the ruffian!—he has concealed weapons! Is that fair? Is that like a gentleman and a gladiator? No, indeed, I scorn such fellows!" With that she contemptuously turned her back on the gladiator, and hastened to examine the condition of her husband.

But he, as much inured to the constitutional exercise as an English bull-dog is to a contest with a more gentle antagonist, had already recovered himself. The purple hues receded from the crimson surface of his cheek, the veins of the forehead retired into their wonted size. He shook himself with a complacent grunt, satisfied that he was still alive, and then looking at his foe from head to foot with an air of more approbation than he had ever bestowed upon him before——

"By Castor!" said he, "thou art a stronger fellow than I took thee for! I see thou art a man of merit and virtue; give me thy hand, my hero!"

"Jolly old Burbo!" cried the gladiators, applauding; "stanch to the back-bone. Give him thy hand, Lydon."

"Oh, to be sure," said the gladiator; "but now I have tasted his blood, I long to lap the whole."

"By Hercules!" returned the host, quite unmoved, "that is the true gladiator feeling. Pollux! to think what good training may make a man; why a beast could not be fiercer!"

"A beast! O dullard! we beat the beasts hollow," cried Tetraides.

"Well, well," said Stratonice, who was now employed in smoothing her hair and adjusting her dress, "if ye are all good friends again, I recommend you to be quiet and orderly; for some young noblemen, your patrons and backers, have sent to say they will come here to pay you a visit; they wish to see you more at their ease than at the schools, before they make up their bets on the great fight at the amphitheatre. So they always come to my house for that purpose: they know we only receive the best gladiators in Pompeii—our society is very select, praised be the gods!"

"Yes," continued Burbo, drinking off a bowl, or rather a pail of wine, "a man who has won my laurels can only encourage the brave. Lydon, drink, my boy; may you have an honorable old age like mine!"

"Come here," said Stratonice, drawing her husband to her affectionately by the ears, in that caress which Tibullus has so prettily described—"Come here!"

"Not so hard, she-wolf! thou art worse than the gladiator," murmured the huge jaws of Burbo.

"Hist!" said she, whispering him; "Calenus has just stole in, disguised, by the back way. I hope he has brought the sesterces."

"Ho! ho! I will join him," said Burbo; "meanwhile, I say, keep a sharp eye on the cups—attend to the score. Let them not cheat thee, wife; they are heroes, to be sure, but then they are arrant rogues: Cacus was nothing to them."

"Never fear me, fool!" was the conjugal reply; and Burbo, satisfied with the dear assurance, strode through the apartment, and sought the penetralia of his house.

"So those soft patrons are coming to look at our muscles," said Niger. "Who sent to previse thee of it, my mistress?"

"Lepidus. He brings with him Clodius, the surest better in Pompeii, and the young Greek, Glaucus."

"A wager on a wager," cried Tetraides; "Clodius bets on me, for twenty sesterces! What say you, Lydon?"

"He bets on *me!*" said Lydon.

"No, on *me!*" grunted Sporus.

"Dolts! do you think he would prefer any of you to Niger?" said the athlete, thus modestly naming himself.

"Well, well," said Stratonice, as she pierced a huge amphora for her guests, who had now seated themselves before one of the tables, "great men and brave, as ye all think yourselves, which of you will fight the Numidian lion in case no malefactor should be found to deprive you of the option?"

"I who have escaped your arms, stout Stratonice," said Lydon, "might safely, I think, encounter the lion."

"But tell me," said Tetraides, "where is that pretty young slave of yours—the blind girl, with bright eyes? I have not seen her a long time."

"Oh! she is too delicate for you, my son of Neptune," said the hostess, "and too nice even for us, I think. We send her into the town to sell flowers and sing to the ladies; she makes us more money so than she would by waiting on you. Besides, she has often other employments which lie under the rose." "Other employments!" said Niger; "why, she is too young for them."

"Silence, beast!" said Stratonice; "you think there is no play but the Corinthian. If Nydia were twice the age she is at present, she would be equally fit for Vesta—poor girl!"

"But, hark ye, Stratonice," said Lydon; "how didst thou come by so gentle and delicate a slave? She were more meet for the handmaid of some rich matron of Rome than for thee."

"That is true," returned Stratonice; "and some day or other I shall make my fortune by selling her. How came I by Nydia, thou askest?" "Ay!"

"Why, thou seest, my slave Staphyla—thou rememberest Staphyla, Niger?"

"Ay, a large-handed wench, with a face like a comic mask.

How should I forget her, by Pluto, whose handmaid she doubtless is at this moment!"

"Tush, brute!—Well, Staphyla died one day, and a great loss she was to me, and I went into the market to buy me another slave. But, by the gods! they were all grown so dear since I had bought poor Staphyla, and money was so scarce, that I was about to leave the place in despair, when a merchant plucked me by the robe. 'Mistress,' said he, 'dost thou want a slave cheap? I have a child to sell—a bargain. She is but little, and almost an infant, it is true; but she is quick and quiet, docile and clever, sings well, and is of good blood, I assure you.' 'Of what country?' said I. 'Thessalian.' Now I knew the Thessalians were acute and gentle; so I said I would see the girl. I found her just as you see her now, scarcely smaller and scarcely younger in appearance. She looked patient and resigned enough, with her hands crossed on her bosom, and her eyes downcast. I asked the merchant his price: it was moderate, and I bought her at once. The merchant brought her to my house, and disappeared in an instant. Well, my friends, guess my astonishment when I found she was blind! Ha! ha! a clever fellow that merchant! I ran at once to the magistrates, but the rogue was already gone from Pompeii. So I was forced to go home in a very ill humor, I assure you; and the poor girl felt the effects of it too. But it was not her fault that she was blind, for she had been so from her birth. By degrees, we got reconciled to our purchase. True, she had not the strength of Staphyla, and was of very little use in the house, but she could soon find her way about the town, as well as if she had the eyes of Argus; and when one morning she brought us home a handful of sesterces, which she said she had got from selling some flowers she had gathered in our poor little garden, we thought the gods had sent her to us. So from that time we let her go out as she likes, filling her basket with flowers, which she wreathes into garlands after the Thessalian fashion, which pleases the gallants; and the great people seem to take a fancy to her, for they always pay her more than they do any other flower-girl, and she brings all of it home to us, which is more than any other slave would do. So I work for myself, but I shall soon afford from her earnings to buy me a second Staphyla; doubtless, the Thessalian kidnapper had stolen the blind girl from gentle parents. Besides her skill in the garlands, she sings and plays on the cithara, which also brings money; and lately ——but *that* is a secret." "*That* is a secret! What!" cried Lydon; "art thou turned sphinx?" "Sphinx, no—why sphinx?"

"Cease thy gabble, good mistress, and bring us our meat —I am hungry," said Sporus, impatiently.

"And I, too," echoed the grim Niger, whetting his knife on the palm of his hand.

The amazon stalked away to the kitchen, and soon returned with a tray laden with large pieces of meat half-raw: for so, as now, did the heroes of the prize-fight imagine they best sustained their hardihood and ferocity; they drew round the table with the eye of famished wolves—the meat vanished, the wine flowed. So leave we those important personages of classic life to follow the steps of Burbo.

CHAPTER II.

Two worthies.

IN the earlier times of Rome the priesthood was a profession, not of lucre but of honor. It was embraced by the noblest citizens—it was forbidden to the plebeians. Afterwards, and long previous to the present date, it was equally open to all ranks; at least, that part of the profession which embraced the flamens, or priests,—not of religion generally, but of peculiar gods. Even the priest of Jupiter (the Flamen Dialis), preceded by a lictor, and entitled by his office to the entrance of the senate, at first the especial dignitary of the patricians, was subsequently the choice of the people. The less national and less honored deities were usually served by plebeian ministers; and many embraced the profession, as now the Roman Catholic Christians enter the monastic fraternity, less from the impulse of devotion than the suggestions of a calculating poverty. Thus Calenus, the priest of Isis, was of the lowest origin. His relations, though not his parents, were freedmen. He had received from them a liberal education, and from his father a small patrimony, which he had soon exhausted. He embraced the priesthood as a last resource from distress. Whatever the state emoluments of the sacred profession, which at that time were probably small, the officers of a popular temple could never complain of the profits of their calling. There is no profession so lucrative as that which practises on the superstition of the multitude.

Calenus had but one surviving relative at Pompeii, and that was Burbo. Various dark and disreputable ties, stronger than those of blood, united together their hearts and interests; and often the minister of Isis stole disguised and furtively from the supposed austerity of his devotions;—and gliding through the back door of the retired gladiator, a man infamous alike by vices and by profession, rejoiced to throw off the last rag of an hyprocrisy which, but for the dictates of avarice, his ruling passion, would at all times have sat clumsily upon a nature too brutal for even the mimicry of virtue.

Wrapped in one of those large mantles which came in use among the Romans in proportion as they dismissed the toga, whose ample folds well concealed the form, and in which a sort of hood (attached to it) afforded no less a security to the features, Calenus now sat in the small and private chamber of the wine-cellar, whence a small passage ran at once to that back entrance, with which nearly all the houses of Pompeii were furnished.

Opposite to him sat the sturdy Burbo, carefully counting on a table between them a little pile of coins which the priest had just poured from his purse—for purses were as common then as now, with this difference—they were usually better furnished!

"You see," said Calenus, "that we pay you handsomely, and you ought to thank me for recommending you to so advantageous a market."

"I do, my cousin, I do," replied Burbo, affectionately, as he swept the coins into a leathern receptacle, which he then deposited in his girdle, drawing the buckle round his capacious waist more closely than he was wont to do in the lax hours of his domestic avocations. "And by Isis, Pisis, and Nisis, or whatever other gods there may be in Egypt, my little Nydia is a very Hesperides—a garden of gold to me."

"She sings well, and plays like a muse," returned Calenus; "those are virtues that he who employs me always pays liberally."

"He is a god," cried Burbo, enthusiastically; "every rich

man who is generous deserves to be worshipped. But come, a cup of wine, old friend: tell me more about it. What does she do? she is frightened, talks of her oath, and reveals nothing."

"Nor will I, by my right hand! I, too, have taken that terrible oath of secrecy." "Oath! what are oaths to men like us?"

"True, oaths of a common fashion; but this!"—and the stalwart priest shuddered as he spoke. "Yet," he continued, in emptying a huge cup of unmixed wine, "I will own to thee, that it is not so much the oath that I dread as the vengeance of him who proposed it. By the gods! he is a mighty sorcerer, and could draw my confession from the moon, did I dare to make it to her. Talk no more of this. By Pollux! wild as those banquets are which I enjoy with him, I am never quite at my ease there. I love, my boy, one jolly hour with thee, and one of the plain, unsophisticated, laughing girls that I meet in this chamber, all smoke-dried though it be, better than whole nights of those magnificent debauches."

"Ho! sayest thou so! To-morrow night, please the gods, we will have then a snug carousal."

"With all my heart," said the priest, rubbing his hands, and drawing himself nearer to the table.

At this moment they heard a slight noise at the door, as of one feeling the handle. The priest lowered the hood over his head. "Tush!" whispered the host, "it is but the blind girl," as Nydia opened the door, and entered the apartment.

"Ho! girl, and how durst thou? thou lookest pale—thou hast kept late revels? No matter, the young must be always the young," said Burbo, encouragingly.

The girl made no answer, but she dropped on one of the seats with an air of lassitude. Her color went and came rapidly: she beat the floor impatiently with her small feet, then she suddenly raised her face, and said, with a determined voice—"Master, you may starve me if you will—you may beat me—you may threaten me with death—but I will go no more to that unholy place!"

"How, fool!" said Burbo, in a savage voice, and his heavy brows met darkly over his fierce and bloodshot eyes; "how, rebellious! Take care." "I have said it," said the poor girl, crossing her hands on her breast.

"What! my modest one, sweet vestal, thou wilt go no more! Very well, thou shalt be carried."

"I will raise the city with my cries," said she, passionately; and the color mounted to her brow.

"We will take care of that, too; thou shalt go gagged."

"Then may the gods help me!" said Nydia, rising; "I will appeal to the magistrates."

"*Thine oath remember!*" said a hollow voice, as for the first time Calenus joined in the dialogue.

At these words a trembling shook the frame of the unfortunate girl; she clasped her hands imploringly. "Wretch that I am!" she cried, and burst violently into sobs.

Whether or not it was the sound of that vehement sorrow which brought the gentle Stratonice to the spot, her grisly form at this moment appeared in the chamber.

"How now? what hast thou been doing with my slave, brute?" said she, angrily, to Burbo.

"Be quiet, wife," said he, in a tone half-sullen, half-timid; "you want new girdles and fine clothes, do you? Well then, take care of your slave, or you may want them long. *Væ capiti tuo*—vengeance on thy head, wretched one!" "What is this?" said the hag, looking from one to the other.

Nydia started as by a sudden impulse from the wall against which she had leaned; she threw herself at the feet of Stratonice; she embraced her knees, and looking up at her with those sightless but touching eyes—

"O my mistress!" sobbed she, "you are a woman—you have had sisters,—you have been young like me,—feel for me, —save me! I will go to those horrible feasts no more!"

"Stuff!" said the hag, dragging her up rudely by one of those delicate hands, fit for no harsher labor than that of weaving the flowers which made her pleasure or her trade;—"stuff! these fine scruples are not for slaves."

"Hark ye," said Burbo, drawing forth his purse, and chinking its contents: "you hear this music, wife; by Pollux! if you do not break in yon colt with a tight rein, you will hear it no more."

"The girl is tired," said Stratonice, nodding to Calenus; "she will be more docile when you next want her."

"*You! you!* who is here?" cried Nydia, casting her eyes round the apartment with so fearful and straining a survey, that Calenus rose in alarm from his seat,—

"She *must* see with those eyes!" muttered he.

"Who is here? Speak, in heaven's name! Ah, if you were blind like me, you would be less cruel," said she; and she again burst into tears. "Take her away," said Burbo, impatiently; "I hate these whimperings." "Come!" said Stratonice, pushing the poor child by the shoulders. Nydia drew herself aside, with an air to which resolution gave dignity.

"Hear me," she said; "I have served you faithfully,—I, who was brought up—Ah! my mother, my poor mother! didst thou dream I should come to this?" She dashed the tear from her eyes, and proceeded:—"Command me in aught else, and I will obey; but I tell you now, hard, stern, inexorable as you are,—I tell you that I will go there no more; or, if I am forced there, that I will implore the mercy of the prætor himself—I have said it. Hear me, ye gods, I swear!"

The hag's eyes glowed with fire; she seized the child by the hair with one hand, and raised on high the other—that formidable right hand, the least blow of which seemed capable to crush the frail and delicate form that trembled in her grasp. That thought itself appeared to strike her, for she suspended the blow, changed her purpose, and dragging Nydia to the wall, seized from a hook a rope, often, alas! applied to a similar purpose, and the next moment the shrill, the agonized shrieks of the blind girl rang piercingly through the house.

CHAPTER III.

Glaucus makes a purchase that afterwards costs him dear.

"HOLLA, my brave fellows!" said Lepidus, stooping his head, as he entered the low doorway of the house of Burbo. "We have come to see which of you most honors your lanista." The gladiators rose from the table in respect to three gallants known to be among the gayest and richest youths of Pompeii, and whose voices were therefore the dispensers of amphitheatrical reputation.

"What fine animals!" said Clodius to Glaucus: "worthy to be gladiators!"

"It is a pity they are not warriors," returned Glaucus.

A singular thing it was to see the dainty and fastidious Lepidus, whom in a banquet a ray of daylight seemed to blind,

—whom in the bath a breeze of air seemed to blast,—in whom Nature seemed twisted and perverted from every natural impulse, and curdled into one dubious thing of effeminacy and art;—a singular thing was it to see this Lepidus, now all eagerness, and energy, and life, patting the vast shoulders of the gladiators with a blanched and girlish hand, feeling with a mincing gripe their great brawn and iron muscles, all lost in calculating admiration at that manhood which he had spent his life in carefully banishing from himself.

So have we seen at this day the beardless flutterers of the saloons of London thronging round the heroes of the Fivescourt;—so have we seen them admire, and gaze, and calculate a bet;—so have we seen them meet together, in ludicrous yet in melancholy assemblage, the two extremes of civilized society, —the patrons of pleasure and its slaves—vilest of all slaves— at once ferocious and mercenary; male prostitutes, who sell their strength as women their beauty; beasts in act, but baser than beasts in motive, for the last, at least, do not mangle themselves for money!

"Ha! Niger, how will you fight?" said Lepidus; "and with whom?" "Sporus challenges me," said the grim giant; "we shall fight to the death, I hope." "Ah! to be sure," grunted Sporus, with a twinkle of his small eye.

"He takes the sword, I the net and the trident: it will be rare sport. I hope the survivor will have enough to keep up the dignity of the crown."

"Never fear, we'll fill the purse, my Hector," said Clodius: "let me see,—you fight against Niger? Glaucus, a bet—I back Niger."

"I told you so," cried Niger exultingly. "The noble Clodius knows me; count yourself dead already, my Sporus." Clodius took out his tablet.—"A bet,—ten sestertia. What say you?"

"So be it," said Glaucus. "But whom have we here? I never saw this hero before;" and he glanced at Lydon, whose limbs were slighter than those of his companions and who had something of grace, and something even of nobleness, in his face, which his profession had not yet wholly destroyed.

"It is Lydon, a youngster, practised only with the wooden sword as yet," answered Niger, condescendingly. "But he has the true blood in him, and has challenged Tetraides."

"*He* challenged *me*," said Lydon: "I accept the offer."

"And how do you fight?" asked Lepidus. "Chut, my boy, wait a while before you contend with Tetraides." Lydon smiled disdainfully. "Is he a citizen or a slave?" said Clodius.

"A citizen;—we are all citizens here," quoth Niger.

"Stretch out your arm, my Lydon," said Lepidus, with the air of a connoisseur.

The gladiator, with a significant glance at his companions, extended an arm, which, if not so huge in its girth as those of his comrades, was so firm in its muscles, so beautifully symmetrical in its proportions, that the three visitors uttered simultaneously an admiring exclamation. "Well, man, what is your weapon?" said Clodius, tablet in hand.

"We are to fight first with the cestus; afterwards, if both survive, with swords," returned Tetraides, sharply, and with an envious scowl.

"With the cestus!" cried Glaucus; "there you are wrong, Lydon; the cestus is the Greek fashion: I know it well. You should have encouraged flesh for that contest; you are far too thin for it—avoid the cestus." "I cannot," said Lydon. "And why?" "I have said—because he has challenged me."

"But he will not hold you to the precise weapon."

"My honor holds me!" returned Lydon, proudly.

"I bet on Tetraides, two to one, at the cestus," said Clodius; "shall it be, Lepidus?—even betting, with swords."

"If you give me three to one, I will not take the odds," said Lepidus: "Lydon will never come to the swords. You are mighty courteous." "What say you, Glaucus?" said Clodius. "I will take the odds three to one." "Ten sestertia to thirty." "Yes." Clodius wrote the bet in his book.

"Pardon me, noble sponsor mine," said Lydon, in a low voice to Glaucus: "but how much think you the victor will gain?" "How much? why, perhaps seven sestertia."

"You are sure it will be as much?"

"At least. But out on you!—a Greek would have thought of the honor, and not the money. O Italians! everywhere ye are Italians!"

A blush mantled over the bronzed cheek of the gladiator.

"Do not wrong me, noble Glaucus; I think of both, but I should never have been a gladiator but for the money."

"Base! mayest thou fall! A miser never was a hero."

"I am not a miser," said Lydon, haughtily, and he withdrew to the other end of the room.

"But I don't see Burbo; where is Burbo? I must talk with Burbo," cried Clodius. "He is within," said Niger, pointing to the door at the extremity of the room. "And Stratonice, the brave old lass, where is she?" quoth Lepidus.

"Why, she was here just before you entered; but she heard something that displeased her yonder, and vanished. Pollux! old Burbo had perhaps caught hold of some girl in the back room. I heard a female's voice crying out; the old dame is as jealous as Juno."

"Ho! excellent!" cried Lepidus, laughing. "Come, Clodius let us go shares with Jupiter; perhaps he has caught a Leda."

At this moment a loud cry of pain and terror startled the group. "Oh, spare me! spare me! I am but a child, I am blind—is not *that* punishment enough?"

"O Pallas! I know that voice, it is my poor flower-girl!" exclaimed Glaucus, and he darted at once into the quarter whence the cry rose.

He burst the door; he beheld Nydia writhing in the grasp of the infuriate hag; the cord, already dabbled with blood, was raised in the air—it was suddenly arrested.

"Fury!" said Glaucus, and with his left hand he caught Nydia from her grasp; "how dare you use thus a girl—one of your own sex, a child! My Nydia, my poor infant!"

'Oh! is that you—is that Glaucus?" exclaimed the flower-girl, in a tone almost of transport; the tears stood arrested on her cheek; she smiled, she clung to his breast, she kissed his robe as she clung.

"And how dare you, pert stranger! interfere between a free woman and her slave. By the gods! despite your fine tunic and your filthy perfumes, I doubt whether you are even a Roman citizen, my mannikin."

"Fair words, mistress—fair words!" said Clodius, now entering with Lepidus. "This is my friend and sworn brother: he must be put under shelter of your tongue, sweet one; it rains stones!" "Give me my slave!" shrieked the virago, placing her mighty grasp on the breast of the Greek. "Not if all your sister Furies could help you," answered Glaucus. "Fear not, sweet Nydia; an Athenian never forsook distress!"

"Holla!" said Burbo, rising reluctantly, "what turmoil is

all this about a slave? Let go the young gentleman, wife—let him go: for his sake the pert thing shall be spared this once." So saying, he drew, or rather dragged off, his ferocious helpmate. "Methought when we entered," said Clodius, "there was another man present?" "He is gone." For the priest of Isis had indeed thought it high time to vanish.

"Oh, a friend of mine! a brother cupman, a quiet dog, who does not love these snarlings," said Burbo, carelessly. "But go, child, you will tear the gentleman's tunic if you cling to him so tight; go, you are pardoned." "Oh, do not—do not forsake me!" cried Nydia, clinging yet closer to the Athenian.

Moved by her forlorn situation, her appeal to him, her own innumerable and touching graces, the Greek seated himself on one of the rude chairs. He held her on his knees—he wiped the blood from her shoulders with his long hair—he kissed the tears from her cheeks—he whispered to her a thousand of those soothing words with which we calm the grief of a child;—and so beautiful did he seem in his gentle and consoling task, that even the fierce heart of Stratonice was touched. His presence seemed to shed light over that base and obscene haunt—young, beautiful, glorious, he was the emblem of all that earth made most happy, comforting one that earth had abandoned. "Well, who could have thought our blind Nydia had been so honored?" said the virago, wiping her heated brow.

Glaucus looked up at Burbo.

"My good man," said he, "this is your slave; she sings well, she is accustomed to the care of flowers—I wish to make a present of such a slave to a lady. Will you sell her to me?" As he spoke, he felt the whole frame of the poor girl tremble with delight; she started up, she put her dishevelled hair from her eyes, she looked around, as if, alas! she had the power to *see!* "Sell our Nydia! no, indeed," said Stratonice, gruffly.

Nydia sank back with a long sigh, and again clasped the robe of her protector.

"Nonsense!" said Clodius, imperiously; "you must oblige me. What, man! what, old dame! offend me, and your trade is ruined. Is not Burbo my kinsman Pansa's client? Am I not the oracle of the amphitheatre and its heroes? If I say the word, Break up your wine-jars—you sell no more. Glaucus, the slave is yours."

Burbo scratched his huge head in evident embarrassment.

"The girl is worth her weight in gold to me."

"Name your price, I am rich," said Glaucus.

The ancient Italians were like the modern, there was nothing they would not sell, much less a poor blind girl.

"I paid six sestertia for her, she is worth twelve now," muttered Stratonice.

"You shall have twenty; come to the magistrates at once, and then to my house for your money."

"I would not have sold the dear girl for a hundred but to oblige noble Clodius," said Burbo, whiningly. "And you will speak to Pansa about the place of *designator* at the amphitheatre, noble Clodius? it would just suit me."

"Thou shalt have it," said Clodius; adding in a whisper to Burbo, "Yon Greek can make your fortune; money runs through him like a sieve: mark to-day with white chalk, my Priam."

"*An dabis?*" said Glaucus, in the formal question of sale and barter. "*Dabitur,*" answered Burbo.

"Then, then, I am to go with you—with you? O happiness!" murmured Nydia.

"Pretty one, yes; and thy hardest task henceforth shall be to sing thy Grecian hymns to the loveliest lady in Pompeii."

The girl sprang from his clasp; a change came over her whole face, so bright the instant before; she sighed heavily, and then once more taking his hand, she said—

"I thought I was to go to *your* house?"

"And so thou shalt for the present; come, we lose time."

CHAPTER IV.

The rival of Glaucus presses onward in the race.

IONE was one of those brilliant characters which, but once or twice, flash across our career. She united in the highest perfection the rarest of earthly gifts,—Genius and Beauty. No one ever possessed superior intellectual qualities without knowing them,—the alliteration of modesty and merit is pretty enough, but where merit is great, the veil of that modesty you admire never disguises its extent from its possessor. It is the proud consciousness of certain qualities that it cannot reveal to

the every-day world, that gives to genius that shy, and reserved, and troubled air, which puzzles and flatters you when
you encounter it.

Ione, then, knew her genius; but, with that charming
versatility that belongs of right to women, she had the faculty,
so few of a kindred genius in the less malleable sex can claim—
the faculty to bend and model her graceful intellect to all
whom it encountered. The sparkling fountain threw its waters
alike upon the strand, the cavern, and the flowers; it refreshed,
it smiled, it dazzled everywhere. That pride, which is the necessary result of superiority, she wore easily—in her breast
it concentred itself in independence. She pursued thus her own
bright and solitary path. She asked no aged matron to direct
and guide her,—she walked alone by the torch of her own
unflickering purity. She obeyed no tyrannical and absolute
custom. She moulded custom to her own will, but this so delicately and with so feminine a grace, so perfect an exemption
from error, that you could not say she *outraged* custom, but
commanded it. The wealth of her graces was inexhaustible—
she beautified the commonest action; a word, a look from her,
seemed magic. Love her, and you entered into a new world,
you passed from this trite and common-place earth. You were
in a land in which your eyes saw everything through an enchanted medium. In her presence you felt as if listening to
exquisite music; you were steeped in that sentiment which has
so little of earth in it, and which music so well inspires,—that
intoxication which refines and exalts, which seizes, it is true,
the senses, but gives them the character of the soul.

She was peculiarly formed, then, to command and fascinate the less ordinary and the bolder natures of men; to love
her was to unite two passions, that of love and of ambition,—
you aspired when you adored her. It was no wonder that she
had completely chained and subdued the mysterious but burning soul of the Egyptian, a man in whom dwelt the fiercest
passions. Her beauty and her soul alike enthralled him.

Set apart himself from the common world, he loved that
daringness of character which also made itself, among common things, aloof and alone. He did not, or he would not see,
that that very isolation put her yet more from him than from
the vulgar. Far as the poles—far as the night from day, his
solitude was divided from hers. He was solitary from his dark

and solemn vices—she from her beautiful fancies and her
purity of virtue.

If it was not strange that Ione thus enthralled the Egyptian, far less strange was it that she had captured, as suddenly
as irrevocably, the bright and sunny heart of the Athenian.
The gladness of a temperament which seemed woven from the
beams of light had led Glaucus into pleasure. He obeyed no
more vicious dictates when he wandered into the dissipations
of his time, than the exhilarating voices of youth and health.
He threw the brightness of his nature over every abyss and
cavern through which he strayed. His imagination dazzled
him, but his heart never was corrupted. Of far more penetration than his companions deemed, he saw that they sought to
prey upon his riches and his youth: but he despised wealth
save as the means of enjoyment, and youth was the great sympathy that united him to them. He felt, it is true, the impulse
of nobler thoughts and higher aims than in pleasure could be
indulged: but the world was one vast prison, to which the
Sovereign of Rome was the Imperial gaoler; and the very
virtues, which in the free days of Athens would have made
him ambitious, in the slavery of earth made him inactive and
supine. For in that unnatural and bloated civilization, all that
was noble in emulation was forbidden. Ambition in the regions
of a despotic and luxurious court was but the contest of flattery and craft. Avarice had become the sole ambition,—men
desired prætorships and provinces only as the license to pillage,
and government was but the excuse of rapine. It is in small
states that glory is most active and pure,—the more confined
the limits of the circle, the more ardent the patriotism. In
small states, opinion is concentrated and strong,—every eye
reads your actions—your public motives are blended with your
private ties,—every spot in your narrow sphere is crowded
with forms familiar since your childhood,—the applause of
your citizens is like the caresses of your friends. But in large
states, the city is but the court: the provinces—unknown to
you, unfamiliar in customs, perhaps in language,—have no
claim on your patriotism, the ancestry of their inhabitants is
not yours. In the court you desire favor instead of glory; at a
distance from the court, public opinion has vanished from you,
and self-interest has no counterpoise.

Italy, Italy, while I write, your skies are over me—your

seas flow beneath my feet, listen not to the blind policy which would unite all your crested cities, mourning for their republics, into one empire; false, pernicious delusion! your only hope of regeneration is in division. Florence, Milan, Venice, Genoa, may be free once more, if each is free. But dream not of freedom for the whole while you enslave the parts; the heart must be the centre of the system, the blood must circulate freely everywhere; and in vast communities you behold but a bloated and feeble giant, whose brain is imbecile, whose limbs are dead, and who pays in disease and weakness the penalty of transcending the natural proportions of health and vigor.

Thus thrown back upon themselves, the more ardent qualities of Glaucus found no vent, save in that overflowing imagination which gave grace to pleasure, and poetry to thought. Ease was less despicable than contention with parasites and slaves, and luxury could yet be refined though ambition could not be ennobled. But all that was best and brightest in his soul woke at once when he knew Ione. Here was an empire, worthy of demigods to attain—here was a glory, which the reeking smoke of a foul society could not soil or dim. Love, in every time, in every state, can thus find space for its golden altars. And tell me if there ever, even in the ages most favorable to glory, could be a triumph more exalted and elating than the conquest of one noble heart?

And whether it was that this sentiment inspired him, his ideas glowed more brightly, his soul seemed more awake and more visible, in Ione's presence. If natural to love her, it was natural that she should return the passion. Young, brilliant, eloquent, enamoured, and Athenian, he was to her as the incarnation of the poetry of her father's land. They were not like creatures of a world in which strife and sorrow are the elements; they were like things to be seen only in the holiday of nature, so glorious and so fresh were their youth, their beauty, and their love. They seemed out of place in the harsh and every-day earth; they belonged of right to the Saturnian age, and the dreams of demigod and nymph. It was as if the poetry of life gathered and fed itself in them, and in their hearts were concentrated the last rays of the sun of Delos and of Greece.

But if Ione was independent in her choice of life, so was her modest pride proportionably vigilant and easily alarmed. The falsehood of the Egyptian was invented by a deep knowledge of her nature. The story of coarseness, of indelicacy, in Glaucus, stung her to the quick. She felt it a reproach upon her character and her career, a punishment above all to her love; she felt, for the first time, how suddenly she had yielded to that love; she blushed with shame at a weakness, the extent of which she was startled to perceive: she imagined it was that weakness which had incurred the contempt of Glaucus; she endured the bitterest curse of noble natures—*humiliation!* Yet her love, perhaps, was no less alarmed than her pride. If one moment she murmured reproaches upon Glaucus—if one moment she renounced, she almost hated him—at the next she burst into passionate tears, her heart yielded to its softness, and she said in the bitterness of anguish, "He despises me—he does not love me."

From the hour the Egyptian had left her, she had retired to her most secluded chamber, she had shut out her handmaids, she had denied herself to the crowds that besieged her door. Glaucus was excluded with the rest; he wondered, but he guessed not why! He never attributed to his Ione—his queen —his goddess—that woman-like caprice of which the love-poets of Italy so unceasingly complain. He imagined her, in the majesty of her candor, above all the arts that torture. He was troubled, but his hopes were not dimmed, for he knew already that he loved and was beloved; what more could he desire as an amulet against fear?

At deepest night, then, when the streets were hushed, and the high moon only beheld his devotions, he stole to that temple of his heart—her home;* and wooed her after the beautiful fashion of his country. He covered her threshold with the richest garlands, in which every flower was a volume of sweet passion; and he charmed the long summer-night with the sound of the Lycian lute; and verses, which the inspiration of the moment sufficed to weave.

But the window above opened not; no smile made yet more holy the shining air of night. All was still and dark. He knew not if his verse was welcome and his suit was heard.

Yet Ione slept not, nor disdained to hear. Those soft strains ascended to her chamber; they soothed, they subdued her. While she listened, she believed nothing against her lover; but when they were stilled at last, and his step departed, the spell

---

* Athenæus—"The true temple of Cupid is the house of the beloved one."

ceased; and, in the bitterness of her soul, she almost conceived in that delicate flattery a new affront.

I said she was denied to all; but there was one exception, there was one person who would not be denied, assuming over her actions and her house something like the authority of a parent; Arbaces, for himself, claimed an exemption from all the ceremonies observed by others. He entered the threshold with the license of one who feels that he is privileged and at home. He made his way to her solitude, and with that sort of quiet and unapologetic air which seemed to consider the right as a thing of course. With all the independence of Ione's character, his art had enabled him to obtain a secret and powerful control over her mind. She could not shake it off; sometimes she desired to do so; but she never actively struggled against it. She was fascinated by his serpent eye. He arrested, he commanded her, by the magic of a mind long accustomed to awe and to subdue. Utterly unaware of his real character or his hidden love, she felt for him the reverence which genius feels for wisdom, and virtue for sanctity. She regarded him as one of those mighty sages of old, who attained to the mysteries of knowledge by an exemption from the passions of their kind. She scarcely considered him as a being, like herself, of the earth, but as an oracle at once dark and sacred. She did not love him, but she feared. His presence was unwelcome to her; it dimmed her spirit even in its brightest mood; he seemed, with his chilling and lofty aspect, like some eminence which casts a shadow over the sun. But she never thought of forbidding his visits. She was passive under the influence which created in her breast, not the repugnance, but something of the stillness of terror.

Arbaces himself now resolved to exert all his arts to possess himself of that treasure he so burningly coveted. He was cheered and elated by his conquests over her brother. From the hour in which Apæcides fell beneath the voluptuous sorcery of that fête which we have described, he felt his empire over the young priest triumphant and insured. He knew that there is no victim so thoroughly subdued as a young and fervent man for the first time delivered to the thraldom of the senses.

When Apæcides recovered, with the morning light, from the profound sleep which succeeded to the delirium of wonder and of pleasure, he was, it is true, ashamed—terrified—appalled. His vows of austerity and celibacy echoed in his ear; his thirst after holiness—had it been quenched at so unhallowed a stream? But Arbaces knew well the means by which to confirm his conquest. From the arts of pleasure he led the young priest at once to those of his mysterious wisdom. He bared to his amazed eyes the initiatory secrets of the sombre philosophy of the Nile—those secrets plucked from the stars, and the wild chemistry, which, in those days, when Reason herself was but the creature of Imagination, might well pass for the lore of a diviner magic. He seemed to the young eyes of the priest as a being above mortality, and endowed with supernatural gifts. That yearning and intense desire for the knowledge which is not of earth—which had burned from his boyhood in the heart of the priest—was dazzled, until it confused and mastered his clearer sense. He gave himself to the art which thus addressed at once the two strongest of human passions, that of pleasure and that of knowledge. He was loth to believe that one so wise could err, that one so lofty could stoop to deceive. Entangled in the dark web of metaphysical moralities, he caught at the excuse by which the Egyptian converted vice into a virtue. His pride was insensibly flattered that Arbaces had deigned to rank him with himself, to set him apart from the laws which bound the vulgar, to make him an august participator, both in the mystic studies and the magic fascinations of the Egyptian's solitude. The pure and stern lessons of that creed to which Olinthus had sought to make him convert, were swept away from his memory by the deluge of new passions. And the Egyptian, who was versed in the articles of that true faith, and who soon learned from his pupil the effect which had been produced upon him by its believers, sought, not unskillfully, to undo that effect, by a tone of reasoning, half-sarcastic and half-earnest.

"This faith," said he, "is but a borrowed plagiarism from one of the many allegories invented by our priests of old. Observe," he added, pointing to a hieroglyphical scroll,—"observe in these ancient figures the origin of the Christian's Trinity. Here are also three gods—the Deity, the Spirit, and the Son. Observe that the epithet of the Son is 'Saviour,'—observe, that the sign by which his human qualities are denoted is the cross. Note here, too, the mystic history of Osiris, how he put on death; how he lay in the grave; and how, thus fulfilling a solemn atonement, he rose again from the dead! In these stories we but design to paint an allegory from the operations of nature and the evolutions of the eternal heavens. But, the allegory unknown, the types themselves have furnished to credulous nations the materials of many creeds. They have travelled to the vast plains of India; they have mixed themselves up in the visionary speculations of the Greek: becoming more and more gross and embodied, as they emerge farther from the shadows of their antique origin, they have assumed a human and palpable form in this novel faith; and the believers of Galilee are but the unconscious repeaters of one of the superstitions of the Nile!"

This was the last argument which completely subdued the priest. It was necessary to him, as to all, to believe in something; and undivided and, at last, unreluctant, he surrendered himself to that belief which Arbaces inculcated, and which all that was human in passion—all that was flattering in vanity —all that was alluring in pleasure, served to invite to, and contributed to confirm.

This conquest, thus easily made, the Egyptian could now give himself wholly up to the pursuit of a far dearer and mightier object; and he hailed, in his success with the brother, an omen of his triumph over the sister.

He had seen Ione on the day following the revel we have witnessed; and which was also the day after he had poisoned her mind against his rival. The next day, and the next, he saw her also: and each time he laid himself out with consummate art, partly to conform her impression against Glaucus, and principally to prepare her for the impressions he desired her to receive. The proud Ione took care to conceal the anguish she endured; and the pride of woman has an hypocrisy which can deceive the most penetrating, and shame the most astute. But Arbaces was no less cautious not to recur to a subject which he felt it was most politic to treat as of the lightest importance. He knew that by dwelling much upon the fault of a rival, you only give him dignity in the eyes of your mistress: the wisest plan is, neither loudly to hate, nor bitterly to contemn; the wisest plan is to lower him by an indifference of tone, as if you could not dream that *he* could be loved. Your safety is in concealing the wound to your own pride, and imperceptibly alarming that of the umpire, whose voice is fate! Such, in all times, will be the policy of one who knows the science of the sex—it was now the Egyptian's.

He recurred no more, then, to the presumption of Glaucus; he mentioned his name, but not more often than that of Clodius or of Lepidus. He affected to class them together, as things of a low and ephemeral species; as things wanting nothing of the butterfly, save its innocence and its grace. Sometimes he slightly alluded to some invented debauch, in which he declared them companions; sometimes he adverted to them as the antipodes of those lofty and spiritual natures, to whose order that of Ione belonged. Blinded alike by the pride of Ione, and, perhaps, by his own, he dreamed not that she already loved; but he dreaded lest she might have formed for Glaucus the first fluttering prepossessions that *lead* to love. And, secretly, he ground his teeth in rage and jealousy, when he reflected on the youth, the fascinations, and the brilliancy of that formidable rival whom he pretended to undervalue.

It was on the fourth day from the date of the close of the previous book, that Arbaces and Ione sat together.

"You wear your veil at home," said the Egyptian; "that is not fair to those whom you honor with your friendship."

"But to Arbaces," answered Ione, who, indeed, had cast the veil over her features to conceal eyes red with weeping,— "to Arbaces, who looks only to the mind, what matters it that the face is concealed?"

"I do look only to the mind," replied the Egyptian: "show me then your face—for there I shall see it!"

"You grow gallant in the air of Pompeii," said Ione, with a forced tone of gaiety.

"Do you think, fair Ione, that it is only at Pompeii that I have learned to value you?" The Egyptian's voice trembled— he paused for a moment, and then resumed.

"There is a love, beautiful Greek, which is not the love only of the thoughtless and the young—there is a love which sees not with the eyes, which hears not with the ears; but in which soul is enamoured of soul. The countryman of thy ancestors, the cave-nursed Plato, dreamed of such a love—his followers have sought to imitate it; but it is a love that is not for the herd to echo—it is a love that only high and noble natures can conceive—it hath nothing in common with the sympathies and ties of coarse affection;—wrinkles do not revolt it—homeliness of feature does not deter; it asks youth, it is true, but it asks it only in the freshness of the emotions; it asks beauty, it is true, but it is the beauty of the thought and of the spirit. Such is the love, O Ione, which is a worthy offering to thee from the cold and the austere. Austere and cold thou deemest me—such is the love that I venture to lay upon thy shrine—thou canst receive it without a blush."

"And its name is Friendship!" replied Ione: her answer was innocent, yet it sounded like the reproof of one conscious of the design of the speaker.

"Friendship!" said Arbaces, vehemently. "No; that is a word too often profaned to apply to a sentiment so sacred. Friendship! it is a tie that binds fools and profligates! Friendship! it is the bond that unites the frivolous hearts of a Glaucus and a Clodius! Friendship! no, *that* is an affection of earth, of vulgar habits and sordid sympathies; the feeling of which I speak is borrowed from the stars—it partakes of that mystic and ineffable yearning, which we feel when we gaze on them—it burns, yet it purifies,—it is the lamp of naphtha in the alabaster vase, glowing with fragrant odors, but shining only through the purest vessels. No; it is not love, and it is not friendship, that Arbaces feels for Ione. Give it no name— earth has no name for it—it is not of earth—why debase it with earthly epithets and earthly associations?"

Never before had Arbaces ventured so far, yet he felt his ground step by step; he knew that he uttered a language which, if at this day of affected platonisms it would speak unequivocally to the ears of beauty, was at that time strange and unfamiliar, to which no precise idea could be attached, from which he could imperceptibly advance or recede, as occasion suited, as hope encouraged or fear deterred. Ione trembled, though she knew not why; her veil hid her features, and masked an expression, which, if seen by the Egyptian, would have at once damped and enraged him; in fact, he never was more displeasing to her—the harmonious modulation of the most suasive voice that ever disguised unhallowed thought fell discordantly on her ear. Her whole soul was still filled with the image of Glaucus; and the accent of tenderness from another only revolted and dismayed; yet she did not conceive that any passion more ardent than that platonism which Arbaces expressed lurked beneath his words. She thought that he, in truth, spoke only of the affection and sympathy of the soul; but was it not precisely that affection and that sympathy which had made a part of those emotions she felt for Glaucus; and could any other footstep than his approach the haunted adytus of her heart?

Anxious at once to change the conversation, she replied, therefore, with a cold and indifferent voice, "Whomsoever Arbaces honors with the sentiment of esteem, it is natural that his elevated wisdom should color that sentiment with its own hues; it is natural that his friendship should be purer than that of others, whose pursuits and errors he does not deign to share. But tell me, Arbaces, hast thou seen my brother of late? He has not visited me for several days; and when I last saw him, his manner disturbed and alarmed me much. I fear lest he was too precipitate in the severe choice that he has adopted, and that he repents an irrevocable step."

"Be cheered, Ione," replied the Egyptian. "It is true, that some little time since he was troubled and sad of spirit; those doubts beset him which were likely to haunt one of that fervent temperament, which ever ebbs and flows, and vibrates between excitement and exhaustion. But *he,* Ione, *he* came to me in his anxieties and his distress; he sought one who pitied and loved him; I have calmed his mind—I have removed his doubts—I have taken him from the threshold of Wisdom into its temple; and before the majesty of the goddess his soul is hushed and soothed. Fear not, he will repent no more; they who trust themselves to Arbaces never repent but for a moment."

"You rejoice me," answered Ione. "My dear brother! in his contentment I am happy."

The conversation then turned upon lighter subjects; the Egyptian exerted himself to please, he condescended even to entertain; the vast variety of his knowledge enabled him to adorn and light up every subject on which he touched; and Ione, forgetting the displeasing effect of his former words, was carried away, despite her sadness, by the magic of his intellect. Her manner became unrestrained and her language fluent; and Arbaces, who had waited his opportunity, now hastened to seize it.

"You have never seen," said he, "the interior of my home; it may amuse you to do so: it contains some rooms that may explain to you what you have often asked me to describe—the fashion of an Egyptian house; not, indeed, that you will perceive in the poor and minute proportions of Roman architecture the massive strength, the vast space, the gigantic magnificence, or even the domestic construction of the palaces of Thebes and Memphis; but something there is, here and there, that may serve to express to you some notion of that antique civilization which has humanized the world. Devote, then, to the austere friend of your youth, one of these bright summer evenings, and let me boast that my gloomy mansion has been honored with the presence of the admired Ione."

Unconscious of the pollutions of the mansion, of the danger that awaited her, Ione readily assented to the proposal. The next evening was fixed for the visit; and the Egyptian, with a serene countenance, and a heart beating with fierce and unholy joy, departed. Scarce had he gone, when another visitor claimed admission.—But now we return to Glaucus.

CHAPTER V.

The poor tortoise.—New changes for Nydia.

THE morning sun shone over the small and odorous den enclosed within the peristyle of the house of the Athenian. He lay reclined, sad and listlessly, on the smooth grass which intersected the viridarium; and a slight canopy stretched above, broke the fierce rays of the summer sun.

When that fairy mansion was first disinterred from the earth, they found in the garden the shell of a tortoise that had been its inmate. That animal, so strange a link in the creation, to which Nature seems to have denied all the pleasures of life, save life's passive and dream-like perception, had been the guest of the place for years before Glaucus purchased it; for years, indeed, which went beyond the memory of man, and to which tradition assigned an almost incredible date. The house had been built and rebuilt—its possessors had changed and fluctuated—generations had flourished and decayed—and still the tortoise dragged on its slow and unsympathizing existence. In the earthquake, which sixteen years before had overthrown many of the public buildings of the city, and scared away the amazed inhabitants, the house now inhabited by Glaucus had been terribly shattered. The possessors deserted it for many days; on their return they cleared away the ruins which encumbered the viridarium, and found still the tortoise, unharmed and unconscious of the surrounding destruction. It seemed to bear a charmed life in its languid blood and imperceptible motions; yet was it not so inactive as it seemed: it held a regular and monotonous course; inch by inch it traversed the little orbit of its domain, taking months to accomplish the whole gyration. It was a restless voyager, that tortoise!—patiently, and with pain, did it perform its self-appointed journeys, evincing no interest in the things around it—a philosopher concentrated in itself. There was something grand in its solitary selfishness!—the sun in which it basked—the waters poured daily over it—the air, which it insensibly inhaled, were its sole and unfailing luxuries. The mild changes of the season, in that lovely clime, affected it not. It covered itself with its shell—as the saint in his piety—as the sage in his wisdom —as the lover in his hope.

It was impervious to the shocks and mutations of time— it was an emblem of time itself: slow, regular, perpetual: unwitting of the passions that fret themselves around—of the wear and tear of mortality. The poor tortoise! nothing less than the bursting of volcanoes, the convulsions of the riven world, could have quenched its sluggish spark! The inexorable Death, that spared not pomp or beauty, passed unheedingly by a thing to which death could bring so insignificant a change.

For this animal, the mercurial and vivid Greek felt all the wonder and affection of contrast. He could spend hours in surveying its creeping progress, in moralizing over its mechanism. He despised it in joy—he envied it in sorrow.

Regarding it now as he lay along the sward, its dull mass moving while it seemed motionless, the Athenian murmured to himself:—

"The eagle dropped a stone from his talons, thinking to break thy shell: the stone crushed the head of a poet. This is the allegory of Fate! Dull thing! Thou hadst a father and a mother; perhaps, ages ago, thou thyself hadst a mate. Did thy parents love, or didst thou? Did thy slow blood circulate more gladly when thou didst creep to the side of thy wedded one? Wert thou capable of affection? Could it distress thee if she were away from thy side? Couldst thou feel when she

was present? What would I not give to know tne history of
thy mailed breast—to gaze upon the mechanism of thy faint
desires—to mark what hair-breadth difference separates thy
sorrow from thy joy! Yet, methinks, thou wouldst know if
Ione were present! Thou wouldst feel her coming like a happier air—like a gladder sun. I envy thee now, for thou
knowest not that she is absent; and I—would I could be like
thee—between the intervals of seeing her! What doubt, what
presentiment, haunts me! why will she not admit me? Days
have passed since I heard her voice. For the first time, life
grows flat to me. I am as one who is left alone at a banquet,
the lights dead, and the flowers faded. Ah! Ione, couldst thou
dream how I adore thee!"

From these enamoured reveries, Glaucus was interrupted
by the entrance of Nydia. She came with her light, though
cautious step, along the marble tablinum. She passed the portico, and paused at the flowers which bordered the garden.
She had her water-vase in her hand, and she sprinkled the
thirsting plants, which seemed to brighten at her approach.
She bent to inhale their odor. She touched them timidly and
caressingly. She felt, along their stems, if any withered leaf
or creeping insect marred their beauty. And as she hovered
from flower to flower, with her earnest and youthful countenance and graceful motions, you could not have imagined a
fitter handmaid for the goddess of the garden.

"Nydia, my child!" said Glaucus.

At the sound of his voice she paused at once—listening,
blushing, breathless; with her lips parted, her face upturned
to catch the direction of the sound, she laid down the vase—
she hastened to him; and wonderful it was to see how unerringly she threaded her dark way through the flowers, and
came by the shortest path to the side of her new lord.

"Nydia," said Glaucus, tenderly stroking back her long
and beautiful hair, "it is now three days since thou hast been
under the protection of my household gods. Have they smiled
on thee? Art thou happy?"

"Ah! so happy!" sighed the slave.

"And now," continued Glaucus, "that thou hast recovered
somewhat from the hateful recollections of thy former state,
—and now that they have fitted thee [touching her broidered
tunic] with garments more meet for thy delicate shape,—

and now, sweet child, that thou hast accustomed thyself to a happiness, which may the gods grant thee ever! I am about to pray at thy hands a boon."

"Oh! what can I do for thee?" said Nydia, clasping her hands.

"Listen," said Glaucus, "and young as thou art, thou shalt be my confidant. Hast thou ever heard the name of Ione?"

The blind girl gasped for breath, and turning pale as one of the statues which shone upon them from the peristyle, she answered with an effort, and after a moment's pause,——

"Yes! I have heard that she is of Neapolis, and beautiful."

"Beautiful! her beauty is a thing to dazzle the day! Neapolis! nay, she is Greek by origin; Greece only could furnish forth such shapes. Nydia, I love her!"

"I thought so," replied Nydia, calmly.

"I love, and thou shalt tell her so. I am about to send thee to her. Happy Nydia, thou wilt be in her chamber—thou wilt drink the music of her voice—thou wilt bask in the sunny air of her presence!"

"What! what! wilt thou send me from thee?"

"Thou wilt go to Ione," answered Glaucus, in a tone that said, "What more canst thou desire?"

Nydia burst into tears. Glaucus, raising himself, drew her towards him with the soothing caresses of a brother.

"My child, my Nydia, thou weepest in ignorance of the happiness I bestow on thee. She is gentle, and kind, and soft as the breeze of spring. She will be a sister to thy youth— she will appreciate thy winning talents—she will love thy simple graces as none other could, for they are like her own. Weepest thou still, fond fool? I will not force thee, sweet. Wilt thou not do for me this kindness?" "Well, if I can serve thee, command. See, I weep no longer—I am calm."

"That is my own Nydia," continued Glaucus, kissing her hand. "Go, then, to her: if thou art disappointed in her kindness—if I have deceived thee, return when thou wilt. I do not *give* thee to another; I but lend. My home ever be thy refuge, sweet one. Ah! would it could shelter all the friendless and distressed! But if my heart whispers truly, I shall claim thee again soon, my child. My home and Ione's will become the same, and thou shalt dwell with both."

A shiver passed through the slight frame of the blind girl, but she wept no more—she was resigned.

"Go, then, my Nydia, to Ione's house—they shall show thee the way. Take her the fairest flowers thou canst pluck; the vase which contains them I will give thee: thou must excuse its unworthiness. Thou shalt take, too, with thee the lute that I gave thee yesterday, and from which thou knowest so well to awaken the charming spirit. Thou shalt give her also this letter, in which, after a hundred efforts, I have embodied something of my thoughts. Let thy ear catch every accent—every modulation of her voice, and tell me, when we meet again, if its music should flatter me or discourage. It is now, Nydia, some days since I have been admitted to Ione; there is something mysterious in this exclusion. I am distracted with doubts and fears; learn—for thou art quick, and thy care for me will sharpen tenfold thy acuteness—learn the cause of this unkindness; speak of me as often as thou canst; let my name come ever to thy lips; *insinuate* how I love, rather than *proclaim* it; watch if she sighs whilst thou speakest, if she answer thee; or, if she reproves, in what accents she reproves. Be my friend, plead for me; and oh! how vastly wilt thou overpay the little I have done for thee! Thou comprehendest, Nydia; thou art yet a child—have I said more than thou canst understand?" "No."

"And thou wilt serve me?" "Yes."

"Come to me when thou hast gathered the flowers, and I will give thee the vase I speak of; seek me in the chamber of Leda. Pretty one, thou dost not grieve now?" "Glaucus, I am a slave; what business have I with grief or joy?"

"Sayest thou so? No, Nydia, be free. I give thee freedom; enjoy it as thou wilt, and pardon me that I reckoned on thy desire to serve me."

"You are offended. Oh! I would not, for that which no freedom can give, offend you, Glaucus. My guardian, my saviour, my protector, forgive the poor blind girl! She does not grieve even in leaving thee, if she can contribute to thy happiness."

"May the gods bless this grateful heart!" said Glaucus, greatly moved; and, unconscious of the fires he excited, he repeatedly kissed her forehead.

"Thou forgivest me," said she, "and thou wilt talk no more of freedom; my happiness is to be thy slave: thou hast promised thou wilt not give me to another——"

"I have promised."

"And now, then, I will gather the flowers."

Silently, Nydia took from the hand of Glaucus, the costly and jewelled vase, in which the flowers vied with each other in hue and fragrance; tearlessly she received his parting admonition. She paused for a moment when his voice ceased—she did not trust herself to reply—she sought his hand—she raised it to her lips, dropped her veil over her face, and passed at once from his presence. She paused again as she reached the threshold; she stretched her hands towards it, and murmured,—

"Three happy days—days of unspeakable delight, have I known since I passed thee—blessed threshold! may peace dwell ever with thee when I am gone! And now, my heart tears itself from thee, and the only sound it utters bids me—die!"

CHAPTER VI.

The happy beauty and the blind slave

A slave entered the chamber of Ione. A messenger from Glaucus desired to be admitted.

Ione hesitated an instant.

"She is blind, that messenger," said the slave; "she will do her commission to none but thee."

Base is that heart which does not respect affliction! The moment she heard the messenger was blind, Ione felt the impossibility of returning a chilling reply. Glaucus had chosen a herald that was indeed sacred—a herald that could not be denied.

"What can he want with me? what message can he send?" and the heart of Ione beat quick. The curtain across the door was withdrawn; a soft and echoless step fell upon the marble; and Nydia, led by one of the attendants, entered with her precious gift.

She stood still a moment, as if listening for some sound that might direct her.

"Will the noble Ione," said she, in a soft and low voice, "deign to speak, that I may know whither to steer these benighted steps, and that I may lay my offerings at her feet?"

"Fair child," said Ione, touched and soothingly, "give not thyself the pain to cross these slippery floors, my attendant will bring to me what thou hast to present;" and she motioned to the handmaid to take the vase.

"I may give these flowers to none but thee," answered Nydia; and, guided by her ear, she walked slowly to the place where Ione sat, and kneeling when she came before her, proffered the vase.

Ione took it from her hand, and placed it on the table at her side. She then raised her gently, and would have seated her on the couch, but the girl modestly resisted.

"I have not yet discharged my office," said she; and she drew the letter of Glaucus from her vest. "This will, perhaps, explain why he who sent me chose so unworthy a messenger to Ione."

The Neapolitan took the letter with a hand, the trembling of which Nydia at once felt and sighed to feel. With folded arms, and downcast looks, she stood before the proud and stately form of Ione;—no less proud, perhaps, in her attitude of submission. Ione waved her hand, and the attendants withdrew; she gazed again upon the form of the young slave in surprise and beautiful compassion; then, retiring a little from her, she opened and read the following letter:—

"Glaucus to Ione sends more than he dares to utter. Is Ione ill? thy slaves tell me 'No,' and that assurance comforts me. Has Glaucus offended Ione?—ah! that question I may not ask from *them*. For five days I have been banished from thy presence. Has the sun shone?—I know it not. Has the sky smiled?—it has had no smile for me. My sun and my sky are Ione. Do I offend thee? Am I too bold? Do I say that on the tablet which my tongue has hesitated to breathe? Alas! it is in thine absence that I feel most the spells by which thou hast subdued me. And absence, that deprives me of joy, brings me courage. Thou wilt not see me; thou hast banished also the common flatterers that flock around thee. Canst thou

confound me with them? It is not possible! Thou knowest
too well that I am not of them—that their clay is not mine.
For even were I of the humblest mould, the fragrance of the
rose has penetrated me, and the spirit of thy nature hath
passed within me, to embalm, to sanctify, to inspire. Have
they slandered me to thee, Ione? Thou wilt not believe them.
Did the Delphic oracle itself tell me thou wert unworthy, I
would not believe it; and am I less incredulous than thou? I
think of the last time we met—of the song which I sang to
thee—of the look that thou gavest me in return. Disguise it
as thou wilt, Ione, there is something kindred between us, and
our eyes acknowledged it, though our lips were silent. Deign
to see me, to listen to me, and after that exclude me if thou
wilt. I meant not so soon to say I loved. But those words rush
to my heart—they will have way. Accept, then, my homage
and my vows. We met first at the shrine of Pallas; shall we
not meet before a softer and a more ancient altar?

"Beautiful! adored Ione! If my hot youth and my Athenian blood have misguided and allured me, they have but
taught my wanderings to appreciate the rest—the haven they
have attained. I hang up my dripping robes on the Sea-god's
shrine. I have escaped shipwreck. I have found THEE. Ione,
deign to see me; thou art gentle to strangers, wilt thou be less
merciful to those of thine own land? I await thy reply. Accept the flowers which I send—their sweet breath has a language more eloquent than words. They take from the sun
the odors they return—they are the emblem of the love that
receives and repays tenfold—the emblem of the heart that
drank thy rays, and owes to thee the germ of the treasures
that it proffers to thy smile. I send these by one whom thou
wilt receive for her own sake, if not for mine. She, like us,
is a stranger; her fathers' ashes lie under brighter skies: but,
less happy than we, she is blind and a slave. Poor Nydia!
I seek as much as possible to repair to her the cruelties of
Nature and of Fate, in asking permission to place her with
thee. She is gentle, quick, and docile. She is skilled in music
and the song; and she is a very Chloris to the flowers. She
thinks, Ione, that thou wilt love her: if thou dost not, send
her back to me.

"One word more—let me be bold, Ione. Why thinkest

thou so highly of yon dark Egyptian! he hath not about him the air of honest men. We Greeks learn mankind from our cradle; we are not the less profound, in that we affect no sombre mien: our lips smile, but our eyes are grave—they observe —they note—they study. Arbaces is not one to be credulously trusted: can it be that he hath wronged me to thee? I think it, for I left him with thee; thou sawest how my presence stung him; since then thou hast not admitted me. Believe nothing that he can say to my disfavor; if thou dost, tell me so at once; for this Ione owes to Glaucus. Farewell! this letter touches thy hand; these characters meet thine eyes—shall they be more blessed than he who is their author. Once more, farewell!"

It seemed to Ione, as she read this letter, as if a mist had fallen from her eyes. What had been the supposed offence of Glaucus—that he had not really loved! And now, plainly, and in no dubious terms, he confessed that love. From that moment, his power was fully restored. At every tender word in that letter, so full of romantic and trustful passion, her heart smote her. And had she doubted his faith, and had she believed another? and had she not, at least, allowed to him the culprit's right to know his crime, to plead in his defence?— the tears rolled down her cheeks—she kissed the letter—she placed it in her bosom; and, turning to Nydia, who stood in the same place and in the same posture: —

"Wilt thou sit, my child," said she, "while I write an answer to this letter?"

"You will answer it, then!" said Nydia, coldly. "Well, the slave that accompanied me will take back your answer."

"For you," said Ione, "stay with me—trust me, your service shall be light." Nydia bowed her head.

"What is your name, fair girl?" "They call me Nydia."

"Your country?" "The land of Olympus—Thessaly."

"Thou shalt be to me a friend," said Ione, caressingly, "as thou art already half a countrywoman. Meanwhile, I beseech thee, stand not on these cold and glassy marbles.— There! now that thou art seated, I can leave thee for an instant."

"Ione to Glaucus greeting.—Come to me, Glaucus," wrote

Ione—"come to me to-morrow. I may have been unjust to thee; but I will tell thee, at least, the fault that has been imputed to thy charge. Fear not, henceforth, the Egyptian—fear none. Thou sayest thou hast expressed too much—alas! in these hasty words I have already done so. Farewell!"

As Ione reappeared with the letter, which she did not dare to read after she had written (Ah! common rashness, common timidity of love!)—Nydia started from her seat.

"You have written to Glaucus?" "I have."

"And will he thank the messenger who gives to him thy letter?"

Ione forgot that her companion was blind; she blushed from the brow to the neck, and remained silent.

"I mean this," added Nydia, in a calmer tone; "the lightest word of coldness from thee will sadden him—the lightest kindness will rejoice. If it be the first, let the slave take back thine answer; if it be the last, let me—I will return this evening."

"And why, Nydia," asked Ione, evasively, "wouldst thou be the bearer of my letter?"

"It is so, then!" said Nydia. "Ah! how could it be otherwise; who could be unkind to Glaucus?"

"My child," said Ione, a little more reservedly than before, "thou speakest warmly—Glaucus, then, is amiable in thine eyes?" "Noble Ione! Glaucus has been that to me which neither fortune nor the gods have been—a friend!"

The sadness mingled with dignity with which Nydia uttered these simple words, affected the beautiful Ione; she bent down and kissed her. "Thou art grateful, and deservedly so; why should I blush to say that Glaucus is worthy of thy gratitude? Go, my Nydia—take to him thyself this letter—but return again. If I am from home when thou returnest—as this evening, perhaps, I shall be—thy chamber shall be prepared next my own. Nydia, I have no sister—wilt thou be one to me?"

The Thessalian kissed the hand of Ione, and then said, with some embarrassment—

"One favor, fair Ione—may I dare to ask it?"

"Thou canst not ask what I will not grant," replied the Neapolitan.

"They tell me," said Nydia, "that thou art beautiful beyond the loveliness of earth. Alas! I cannot see that which gladdens the world! Wilt thou suffer me, then, to pass my hand over thy face?—that is my sole criterion of beauty, and I usually guess aright."

She did not wait for the answer of Ione, but, as she spoke, gently and slowly passed her hand over the bending and half-averted features of the Greek—features which but one image in the world can yet depicture and recall—that image is the mutilated, but all-wondrous, statue in her native city—her own Neapolis;—that Parian face, before which all the beauty of the Florentine Venus is poor and earthly—that aspect so full of harmony—of youth—of genius—of the soul—which modern critics have supposed the representation of Psyche.

Her touch lingered over the braided hair and polished brow—over the downy and damask cheek—over the dimpled lip—the swan-like and whitest neck. "I know, now, that thou art beautiful," she said; "and I can picture thee to my darkness henceforth, and for ever!"

When Nydia left her, Ione sank into a deep but delicious reverie. Glaucus then loved her; he owned it—yes, he loved her. She drew forth again that dear confession; she paused over every word, she kissed every line; she did not ask why he had been maligned, she only felt assured that he had been so. She wondered how she had ever believed a syllable against him; she wondered how the Egyptian had been enabled to exercise a power against Glaucus; she felt a chill creep over her as she again turned to his warning against Arbaces, and her secret fear of that gloomy being darkened into awe. She was awakened from these thoughts by her maidens, who came to announce to her that the hour appointed to visit Arbaces was arrived; she started, she had forgotten the promise. Her first impression was to renounce it; her second, was to laugh at her own fears of her eldest surviving friend. She hastened to add the usual ornaments to her dress, and doubtful whether she should yet question the Egyptian more closely with respect to his accusation of Glaucus, or whether she should wait till, without citing the authority, she should insinuate to Glaucus the accusation itself, she took her way to the gloomy mansion of Arbaces.

CHAPTER VII.

Ione entrapped.—The mouse tries to gnaw the net.

"O DEAREST Nydia!" exclaimed Glaucus, as he read the letter of Ione, "whitest-robed messenger that ever passed between earth and heaven—how, how shall I thank thee?"

"I am rewarded," said the poor Thessalian. "To-morrow —to-morrow! how shall I while the hours till then?"

The enamoured Greek would not let Nydia escape him, though she sought several times to leave the chamber; he made her recite to him over and over again every syllable of the brief conversation that had taken place between her and Ione; a thousand times, forgetting her misfortune, he questioned her of the looks, of the countenance of his beloved; and then quickly again excusing his fault, he bade her recommence the whole recital which he had thus interrupted. The hours thus painful to Nydia passed rapidly and delightfully to him, and the twilight had already darkened ere he once more dismissed her to Ione with a fresh letter and with new flowers. Scarcely had she gone, than Clodius and several of his gay companions broke in upon him; they rallied him on his seclusion during the whole day, and his absence from his customary haunts; they invited him to accompany them to the various resorts in that lively city, which night and day proffered diversity to pleasure. Then, as now, in the south (for no land, perhaps, losing more of greatness has retained more of custom), it was the delight of the Italians to assemble at the evening; and, under the porticos of temples or the shade of the groves that interspersed the streets, listening to music or the recitals of some inventive tale-teller, they hailed the rising moon with libations of wine and the melodies of song. Glaucus was too happy to be unsocial; he longed to cast off the exuberance of joy that oppressed him. He willingly accepted the proposal of his comrades, and laughingly they sallied out together down the populous and glittering streets.

In the meantime Nydia once more gained the house of

118

Ione, who had long left it; she inquired indifferently whither Ione had gone. The answer arrested and appalled her. "To the house of Arbaces—of the Egyptian? Impossible!"

"It is true, my little one," said the slave, who had replied to her question. "She has known the Egyptian long."

"Long! ye gods, yet Glaucus loves her!" murmured Nydia to herself. "And has," asked she aloud,—"has she often visited him before?"

"Never till now," answered the slave. "If all the rumored scandal of Pompeii be true, it would be better, perhaps, if she had not ventured there at present. But she, poor mistress mine, hears nothing of that which reaches us; the talk of the vestibulum reaches not to the peristyle."

"Never till now!" repeated Nydia. "Art thou sure?"

"Sure, pretty one: but what is that to thee or to us?"

Nydia hesitated a moment, and then, putting down the flowers with which she had been charged, she called to the slave who had accompanied her, and left the house without saying another word.

Not till she had got half-way back to the house of Glaucus did she break silence, and even then she only murmured inly:—

"She does not dream—she cannot—of the dangers into which she has plunged. Fool that I am,—shall I save her!—yes, for I love Glaucus better than myself."

When she arrived at the house of the Athenian, she learnt that he had gone out with a party of his friends, and none knew whither. He probably would not be home before midnight.

The Thessalian groaned; she sank upon a seat in the hall, and covered her face with her hands as if to collect her thoughts. "There is no time to be lost," thought she, starting up. She turned to the slave who had accompanied her.

"Knowest thou," said she, "if Ione has any relative, any intimate friend at Pompeii?"

"Why, by Jupiter!" answered the slave, "art thou silly enough to ask the question? Every one in Pompeii knows that Ione has a brother who, young and rich, has been—under the rose I speak—so foolish as to become a priest of Isis."

"A priest of Isis! O Gods! his name?" "Apæcides."

"I know it all," muttered Nydia: "brother and sister, then, are to be both victims! Apæcides! yes, that was the name I heard in—— Ha! he well, then, knows the peril that surrounds his sister; I will go to him."

She sprang up at that thought, and taking the staff which always guided her steps, she hastened to the neighboring shrine of Isis. Till she had been under the guardianship of the kindly Greek, that staff had sufficed to conduct the poor blind girl from corner to corner of Pompeii. Every street, every turning in the more frequented parts, was familiar to her; and as the inhabitants entertained a tender and half-superstitious veneration for those subject to her infirmity, the passengers had always given way to her timid steps. Poor girl, she little dreamed that she should, ere very many days were passed, find her blindness her protection, and a guide far safer than the keenest eyes!

But since she had been under the roof of Glaucus, he had ordered a slave to accompany her always; and the poor devil thus appointed, who was somewhat of the fattest, and who, after having twice performed the journey to Ione's house, now saw himself condemned to a third excursion (whither the gods only knew), hastened after her, deploring his fate, and solemnly assuring Castor and Pollux that he believed the blind girl had the talaria of Mercury as well as the infirmity of Cupid.

Nydia, however, required but little of his assistance to find her way to the popular temple of Isis: the space before it was now deserted, and she won without obstacle to the sacred rails.

"There is no one here," said the fat slave. "What dost thou want, or whom? Knowest thou not that the priests do not live in the temple?"

"Call out!" said she, impatiently; "night and day there is always one flamen, at least, watching in the shrines of Isis."

The slave called,—no one appeared. "Seest thou no one?"

"No one." "Thou mistakest; I hear a sigh: look again."

The slave, wondering and grumbling, cast round his heavy eyes, and before one of the altars, whose remains still crowd the narrow space, he beheld a form bending as in meditation.

"I see a figure," said he; "and by the white garments, it is a priest." "O flamen of Isis!" cried Nydia; "servant of the Most Ancient, hear me!" "Who calls?" said a low and melancholy voice.

"One who has no common tidings to impart to a member of your body; I come to declare and not to ask oracles."

"With whom wouldst thou confer? This is no hour for thy conference; depart, disturb me not: the night is sacred to the gods, the day to men."

"Methinks I know thy voice! thou art he whom I seek; yet I have heard thee speak but once before. Art thou not the priest Apæcides?"

"I am that man," replied the priest, emerging from the altar, and approaching the rail.

"Thou art! the gods be praised!" Waving her hand to the slave, she bade him withdraw to a distance; and he, who naturally imagined some superstition connected, perhaps, with the safety of Ione, could alone lead her to the temple, obeyed, and seated himself on the ground at a little distance. "Hush!" said she, speaking quick and low; "art thou indeed Apæcides?"

"If thou knowest me, canst thou not recall my features?"

"I am blind," answered Nydia; "my eyes are in my ear, and *that* recognizes thee: yet swear that thou art he."

"By the gods I swear it, by my right hand, and by the moon!"

"Hush! speak low—bend near—give me thy hand: knowest thou Arbaces? Hast thou laid flowers at the feet of the dead? Ah! thy hand is cold—hark yet!—hast thou taken the awful vow?"

"Who art thou, whence comest thou, pale maiden?" said Apæcides, fearfully: "I know thee not; thine is not the breast on which this head hath lain; I have never seen thee before."

"But thou hast heard my voice: no matter, those recollections it should shame us both to recall. Listen, thou hast a sister." "Speak! speak! what of her?"

"Thou knowest the banquets of the dead, stranger,—it pleases thee, perhaps, to share them—would it please thee to have thy sister a partaker? Would it please thee that Arbaces was her host?"

"O gods, he dare not! Girl, if thou mockest me, tremble! I will tear thee limb from limb!"

"I speak the truth; and while I speak, Ione is in the halls of Arbaces—for the first time his guest. Thou knowest if there be peril in that first time! Farewell! I have fulfilled my charge."

"Stay! stay!" cried the priest, passing his wan hand over his brow. "If this be true, what—what can be done to save her? They may not admit me. I know not all the mazes of that intricate mansion. O Nemesis! justly am I punished!"

"I will dismiss yon slave, be thou my guide and comrade; I will lead thee to the private door of the house: I will whisper to thee the word which admits. Take some weapon: it may be needful!"

"Wait an instant," said Apæcides, retiring into one of the cells that flank the temple, and reappearing in a few moments wrapped in a large cloak, which was then much worn by all classes, and which concealed his sacred dress. "Now," he said, grinding his teeth, "if Arbaces hath dared to—but he dare not! he dare not! Why should I suspect him? Is he so base a villain? I will not think it—yet, sophist! dark bewilderer that he is! O gods protect!—hush! *are* there gods? Yes, there is one goddess, at least, whose voice I can command; and that is—Vengeance."

Muttering these disconnected thoughts, Apæcides, followed by his silent and sightless companion, hastened through the most solitary paths to the house of the Egyptian.

The slave, abruptly dismissed by Nydia, shrugged his shoulders, muttered an adjuration, and, nothing loath, rolled off to his cubiculum.

CHAPTER VIII.

The solitude and soliloquy of the Egyptian.—His character analyzed.

WE must go back a few hours in the progress of our story. At the first grey dawn of the day, which Glaucus had already marked with white, the Egyptian was seated, sleepless and alone, on the summit of the lofty and pyramidal tower which flanked his house. A tall parapet around it served as a wall, and conspired, with the height of the edifice and the gloomy trees that girded the mansion, to defy the prying eyes of curiosity or observation. A table, on which lay a scroll, filled with mystic figures, was before him. On high, the stars waxed dim and faint, and the shades of night melted from the sterile mountain-tops; only above Vesuvius there rested a deep and massy cloud, which for several days past had gathered darker and more solid over its summit. The struggle of night and day was more visible over the broad ocean, which stretched calm, like a gigantic lake, bounded by the circling shores that, covered with vines and foliage, and gleaming here and there with the white walls of sleeping cities, sloped to the scarce rippling waves.

It was the hour above all others most sacred to the daring science of the Egyptian—the science which would read our changeful destinies in the stars.

He had filled his scroll, he had noted the moment and the sign; and, leaning upon his hand, he had surrendered himself to the thoughts which his calculation excited.

"*Again* do the stars forewarn me! Some danger, then, assuredly awaits me!" said he, slowly; "some danger, violent and sudden in its nature. The stars wear for me the same mocking menace which, if our chronicles do not err, they once wore for Pyrrhus—for him, doomed to strive for all things, to enjoy none—all attacking, nothing gaining—battles without fruit, laurels without triumph, fame without success; at last made craven by his own superstitions, and slain like a dog by a tile from the hand of an old woman! Verily, the stars flatter when they give me a type in this fool of war,—when they promise to the ardor of my wisdom the same results as to the madness of his ambition;—perpetual exercise—no certain goal;—the Sisyphus task, the mountain and the stone!—the stone, a gloomy image!—it reminds me that I am threatened with somewhat of the same death as the Epirote. Let me look again. 'Beware,' say the shining prophets, 'how thou passest under ancient roofs, or besieged walls, or overhanging cliffs— a stone, hurled from above, is charged by the curses of destiny against thee!' And, at no distant date from this, comes the peril: but I cannot, of a certainty, read the day and hour. Well! if my glass runs low, the sands shall sparkle to the last. Yet, if I escape this peril—ay, if I escape—bright and clear as the moonlight track along the waters glows the rest of my existence. I see honors, happiness, success, shining upon every billow of the dark gulf beneath which I must sink at last. What, then, with such destinies *beyond* the peril, shall I succumb *to* the peril? My soul whispers hope, it sweeps exultingly beyond the boding hour, it revels in the future,—its own courage is its fittest omen. If I were to perish so suddenly and so soon, the shadow of death would darken over me, and I should feel the icy presentiment of my doom. My soul would express, in sadness and in gloom, its forecast of the dreary Orcus. But it smiles—it assures me of deliverance."

As he thus concluded his soliloquy, the Egyptian involuntarily rose. He paced rapidly the narrow space of that star-roofed floor, and, pausing at the parapet, looked again upon the grey and melancholy heavens. The chills of the faint dawn came refreshingly upon his brow, and gradually his mind resumed its natural and collected calm. He withdrew his gaze from the stars, as, one after one, they receded into the depths of heaven; and his eyes fell over the broad expanse below. Dim in the silenced port of the city rose the masts of the galleys: along that mart of luxury and of labor was stilled the mighty hum. No lights, save here and there from before the columns of a temple, or in the porticos of the voiceless forum, broke the wan and fluctuating light of the struggling morn. From the heart of the torpid city, so soon to vibrate with a thousand passions, there came no sound: the streams of life circulated not; they lay locked under the ice of sleep. From the huge space of the amphitheatre, with its stony seats rising one above the other—coiled and round as some slumbering monster—rose a thin and ghastly mist, which gathered darker, and more dark, over the scattered foliage that gloomed in its vicinity. The city seemed as, after the awful change of seventeen ages, it seems now to the traveller,—a City of the Dead.

The ocean itself—that serene and tideless sea—lay scarce less hushed, save that from its deep bosom came, softened by the distance, a faint and regular murmur, like the breathing of its sleep; and curving far, as with outstretched arms, into the green and beautiful land, it seemed unconsciously to clasp to its breast the cities sloping to its margin—Stabiæ, and Herculaneum, and Pompeii—those children and darlings of the deep. "Ye slumber," said the Egyptian, as he scowled over the cities, the boast and flower of Campania; "ye slumber!— would it were the eternal repose of death! As ye now—jewels in the crown of empire—so once were the cities of the Nile! Their greatness hath perished from them, they sleep amidst ruins, their palaces and their shrines are tombs, the serpent coils in the grass of their streets, the lizard basks in their solitary halls. By that mysterious law of Nature, which humbles one to exalt the other, ye have thriven upon their ruins; thou, haughty Rome, hast usurped the glories of Sesostris and Semiramis—thou art a robber, clothing thyself with their spoils! And these—slaves in thy triumph—that I (the last son of forgotten monarchs) survey below, reservoirs of thine all-pervading power and luxury, I curse as I behold! The time shall come when Egypt shall be avenged! when the barbarian's steed shall make his manger in the Golden House of Nero! and thou that hast sown the wind with conquest shalt reap the harvest in the whirlwind of desolation!"

As the Egyptian uttered a prediction which fate so fearfully fulfilled, a more solemn and boding image of ill omen never occurred to the dreams of painter or of poet. The morning light, which can pale so wanly even the young cheek of beauty, gave his majestic and stately features almost the colors of the grave, with the dark hair falling massively around them, and the dark robes flowing long and loose, and the arm outstretched from that lofty eminence, and the glittering eyes, fierce with a savage gladness—half prophet and half fiend!

He turned his gaze from the city and the ocean; before him lay the vineyards and meadows of the rich Campania. The gate and walls—ancient, half Pelasgic—of the city, seemed not to bound its extent. Villas and villages stretched on every side up the ascent of Vesuvius, not nearly then so steep or so lofty as at present. For as Rome itself is built on an exhausted volcano, so in similar security the inhabitants of the South tenanted the green and vine-clad places around a volcano whose fires they believed at rest for ever. From the gate stretched the long street of tombs, various in size and architecture, by which, on that side, the city is yet approached. Above all, rose the cloud-capped summit of the Dread Mountain, with the shadows, now dark, now light, betraying the mossy caverns and ashy rocks, which testified the past conflagrations, and might have prophesied—but man is blind—that which was to come!

Difficult was it then and there to guess the causes why the tradition of the place wore so gloomy and stern a hue; why, in those smiling plains, for miles around—to Baiæ and Misenum—the poets had imagined the entrance and thresholds of their hell—their Acheron, and their fabled Styx: why, in those Phlegræ, now laughing with the vine, they placed the battles of the gods, and supposed the daring Titans to have sought the victory of heaven—save, indeed, that yet, in yon seared and blasted summit, fancy might think to read the characters of the Olympian thunderbolt.

But it was neither the rugged height of the still volcano, nor the fertility of the sloping fields, nor the melancholy avenue of tombs, nor the glittering villas of a polished and luxurious people, that now arrested the eye of the Egyptian. On one part of the landscape, the mountain of Vesuvius descended to the plain in a narrow and uncultivated ridge, broken here and there by jagged crags and copses of wild foliage. At the base of this lay a marshy and unwholesome pool; and the intent gaze of Arbaces caught the outline of some living form moving by the marshes, and stooping ever and anon as if to pluck its rank produce.

"Ho!" said he, aloud, "I have, then, another companion in these unworldly night-watches. The witch of Vesuvius is abroad. What! doth she, too, as the credulous imagine—doth she, too, learn the lore of the great stars? Hath she been uttering foul magic to the moon, or culling (as her pauses betoken) foul herbs from the venomous marsh? Well, I must see this fellow-laborer. Whoever strives to know learns that no human lore is despicable. Despicable only you—ye fat and bloated things—slaves of luxury—sluggards in thought—who, cultivating nothing but the barren sense, dream that its poor soil can produce alike the myrtle and the laurel. No, the wise only can enjoy—to us only *true* luxury is given, when mind, brain, invention, experience, thought, learning, imagination, all contribute like rivers to swell the seas of SENSE!—Ione!"

As Arbaces uttered that last and charmed word, his thoughts sunk at once into a more deep and profound channel. His steps paused; he took not his eyes from the ground; once or twice he smiled joyously, and then, as he turned from his place of vigil, and sought his couch, he muttered, "If death frowns so near, I will say at least that I have lived—Ione shall be mine!"

The character of Arbaces was one of those intricate and varied webs, in which even the mind that sat within it was sometimes confused and perplexed. In him, the son of a fallen dynasty, the outcast of a sunken people, was that spirit of discontented pride, which ever rankles in one of a sterner mould, who feels himself inexorably shut from the sphere in which his fathers shone, and to which Nature as well as birth no less entitles himself. This sentiment hath no benevolence; it wars with society, it sees enemies in mankind. But with this sentiment did not go its common companion, poverty. Arbaces possessed wealth which equalled that of most of the Roman nobles; and this enabled him to gratify to the utmost the passions which had no outlet in business or ambition. Travelling from clime to clime, and beholding still Rome everywhere, he increased both his hatred of society and his passion for pleasure. He was in a vast prison, which, however, he could fill with the ministers of luxury. He could not escape from the prison, and his only object, therefore, was to give it the character of the palace. The Egyptians, from the earliest time, were devoted to the joys of sense; Arbaces inherited both their appetite for sensuality and the glow of imagination which struck light from its rottenness. But still, unsocial in his pleasures as in his graver pursuits, and brooking neither superior nor equal, he admitted few to his companionship, save the willing slaves of his profligacy. He was the solitary lord of a crowded harem; but, with all, he felt condemned to that satiety which is the constant curse of men whose intellect is above their pursuits, and that which once had been the impulse of passion froze down to the ordinance of custom. From the disappointments of sense he sought to raise himself by the cultivation of knowledge; but as it was not his object to serve mankind, so he despised that knowledge which is practical and useful. His dark imagination loved to exercise itself in those more visionary and obscure researches which are ever the most delightful to a wayward and solitary mind, and to which he himself was invited by the daring pride of his disposition and the mysterious traditions of his clime. Dismissing faith in the confused creeds of the heathen world, he reposed the greatest faith in the power of human wisdom. He did not know (perhaps no one in that age distinctly did) the limits which Nature imposes upon our discoveries. Seeing that the higher we mount in knowledge the more wonders we behold, he imagined that Nature not only worked miracles in her ordinary course, but that she might, by the cabala of some master soul, be diverted from that course itself. Thus he pursued Science, across her appointed boundaries, into the land of perplexity and shadow. From the truths of astronomy he wandered into astrological fallacy; from the secrets of chemistry he passed into the spectral labyrinth of magic; and he who could be sceptical as to the power of the gods, was credulously superstitious as to the power of man.

The cultivation of magic, carried at that day to a singular height among the would-be wise, was especially Eastern in its origin: it was alien to the early philosophy of the Greeks, nor had it been received by them with favor until Ostanes, who accompanied the army of Xerxes, introduced, amongst the simple credulities of Hellas, the solemn superstitions of Zoroaster. Under the Roman emperors it had become, however, naturalized at Rome (a meet subject for Juvenal's fiery wit). Intimately connected with magic was the worship of Isis, and the Egyptian religion was the means by which was extended the devotion to Egyptian sorcery. The theurgic, or benevolent magic—the goetic, or dark and evil necromancy—were alike in pre-eminent repute during the first century of the Christian era; and the marvels of Faustus are not comparable to those of Apollonius. Kings courtiers, and sages, all trembled before the professors of the dread science. And not the least remarkable of his tribe was the formidable and profound Arbaces. His fame and his discoveries were known to all the cultivators of magic; they even survived himself. But it was not by his real name that he was honored by the sorcerer and the sage: his real name, indeed, was unknown in Italy, for "Arbaces" was not a genuinely Egyptian but a Median appellation, which, in the admixture and unsettlement of the ancient races, had become common in the country of the Nile; and there were various reasons, not only of pride, but of policy (for in youth he had conspired against the majesty of Rome), which induced him to conceal his true name and rank. But neither by the name he had borrowed from the Mede, nor by that which in the colleges of Egypt would have attested his origin from kings, did the cultivators of magic acknowledge the potent master. He received from their homage a more mystic appellation, and was long remembered in Magna Græcia and the Eastern plains by the name of "Hermes, the Lord of the Flaming Belt." His subtle speculations and boasted attributes of wisdom, recorded in various volumes, were among those tokens "of the curious arts" which the Christian converts most joyfully, yet most fearfully, burned at Ephesus, depriving posterity of the proofs of the cunning of the fiend.

The conscience of Arbaces was solely of the intellect— it was awed by no moral laws. If man imposed these checks upon the herd, so he believed that man, by superior wisdom, could raise himself above them. "If [he reasoned] I have the genius to impose laws, have I not the right to command my own creations? Still more, have I not the right to control— to evade—to scorn—the fabrications of yet meaner intellects than my own?" Thus, if he were a villain, he justified his villainy by what ought to have made him virtuous—namely, the elevation of his capacities.

Most men have more or less the passion for power; in Arbaces that passion corresponded exactly to his character. It was not the passion for an external and brute authority. He desired not the purple and the fasces, the insignia of vulgar command. His youthful ambition once foiled and defeated, scorn had supplied its place—his pride, his contempt for Rome—Rome, which had become the synonym of the world (Rome, whose haughty name he regarded with the same disdain as that which Rome herself lavished upon the barbarian), did not permit him to aspire to sway over others, for that would render him at once the tool or creature of the emperor. He, the Son of the Great Race of Rameses—*he* execute the orders of, and receive his power from, another!—the mere notion filled him with rage. But in rejecting an ambition that coveted nominal distinctions, he but indulged the more in the ambition to rule the heart. Honoring mental power as the greatest of earthly gifts, he loved to feel that power palpably in himself, by extending it over all whom he encountered. Thus had he ever sought the young—thus had he ever fascinated and controlled them. He loved to find subjects in men's

souls—to rule over an invisible and immaterial empire!—had
he been less sensual and less wealthy, he might have sought
to become the founder of a new religion. As it was, his ener-
gies were checked by his pleasures. Besides, however, the
vague love of this moral sway (vanity so dear to sages!) he
was influenced by a singular and dreamlike devotion to all that
belonged to the mystic Land his ancestors had swayed.
Although he disbelieved in her deities, he believed in the
allegories they represented (or rather he interpreted those
allegories anew). He loved to keep alive the *worship* of Egypt,
because he thus maintained the shadow and the recollection
of her *power*. He loaded, therefore, the altars of Osiris and
of Isis with regal donations, and was ever anxious to dignify
their priesthood by new and wealthy converts. The vow taken
—the priesthood embraced—he usually chose the comrades of
his pleasures from those whom he had made his victims,
partly because he thus secured to himself their secrecy—
partly because he thus yet more confirmed to himself his
peculiar power. Hence the motives of his conduct to Apæcides,
strengthened as these were, in that instance, by his passion
for Ione.

He had seldom lived long in one place; but as he grew
older, he grew more wearied of the excitement of new scenes,
and he had sojourned among the delightful cities of Campania
for a period which surprised even himself. In fact, his pride
somewhat crippled his choice of residence. His unsuccessful
conspiracy excluded him from those burning climes which he
deemed of right his own hereditary possessions, and which
now cowered, supine and sunken, under the wings of the
Roman eagle. Rome herself was hateful to his indignant soul;
nor did he love to find his riches rivalled by the minions of the
court, and cast into comparative poverty by the mighty magnificence of the court itself. The Campanian cities proffered
to him all that his nature craved—the luxuries of an un-
equalled climate—the imaginative refinements of a voluptuous
civilization. He was removed from the sight of a superior
wealth; he was without rivals to his riches; he was free from
the spies of a jealous court. As long as he was rich, none pried
into his conduct. He pursued the dark tenor of his way undisturbed and secure.

It is the curse of sensualists never to love till the pleasures of sense begin to pall; their ardent youth is frittered away in countless desires—their hearts are exhausted. So, ever chasing love, and taught by a restless imagination to exaggerate, perhaps, its charms, the Egyptian had spent all the glory of his years without attaining the object of his desires. The beauty of to-morrow succeeded the beauty of to-day, and the shadows bewildered him in his pursuit of the substance. When, two years before the present date, he beheld Ione, he saw, for the first time, one whom he imagined he could *love*. He stood, then, upon that bridge of life, from which man sees before him distinctly a wasted youth on the one side, and the darkness of approaching age upon the other: a time in which we are more than ever anxious, perhaps, to secure to ourselves, ere it be yet too late, whatever we have been taught to consider necessary to the enjoyment of a life of which the brighter half is gone.

With an earnestness and a patience which he had never before commanded for his pleasures, Arbaces had devoted himself to win the heart of Ione. It did not content him to love, he desired to be loved. In this hope he had watched the expanding youth of the beautiful Neapolitan; and, knowing the influence that the mind possesses over those who are taught to cultivate the mind, he had contributed willingly to form the genius and enlighten the intellect of Ione, in the hope that she would be thus able to appreciate what he felt would be his best claim to her affection; viz. a character which, however criminal and perverted, was rich in its original elements of strength and grandeur. When he felt that character to be acknowledged, he willingly allowed, nay, encouraged her, to mix among the idle votaries of pleasure, in the belief that her soul, fitted for higher commune, would miss the companionship of his own, and that, in comparison with others, she would learn to love herself. He had forgot, that as the sunflower to the sun, so youth turns to youth, until his jealousy of Glaucus suddenly apprised him of his error. From that moment, though, as we have seen, he knew not the extent of his danger, a fiercer and more tumultuous direction was given to a passion long controlled. Nothing kindles the fire of love like a sprinkling of the anxieties of jealousy; it takes then a wilder, a more resistless flame; it forgets its softness; it ceases to be tender; it assumes something of the intensity—of the ferocity—of hate.

Arbaces resolved to lose no farther time upon cautious and perilous preparations: he resolved to place an irrevocable barrier between himself and his rivals: he resolved to possess himself of the person of Ione: not that in his present love, so long nursed and fed by hopes purer than those of passion alone, he would have been contented with that mere possession. He desired the heart, the soul, no less than the beauty, of Ione; but he imagined that once separated by a daring crime from the rest of mankind—once bound to Ione by a tie that memory could not break, she would be driven to concentrate her thoughts in him—that his arts would complete his conquest, and that, according to the true moral of the Roman and the Sabine, the empire obtained by force would be cemented by gentler means. This resolution was yet more confirmed in him by his belief in the prophecies of the stars: they had long foretold to him this year, and even the present month, as the epoch of some dread disaster, menacing life itself. He was driven to a certain and limited date. He resolved to crowd, monarch-like, on his funeral pyre all that his soul held most dear. In his own words, if he were to die, he resolved to feel that he had lived, and that Ione should be his own.

CHAPTER IX.

What becomes of Ione in the house of Arbaces.—The first signal of the wrath of the dread foe.

When Ione entered the spacious hall of the Egyptian, the same awe which had crept over her brother impressed itself also upon her: there seemed to her as to him something ominous and warning in the still and mournful faces of those dread Theban monsters, whose majestic and passionless features the marble so well portrayed:

> "Their look, with the reach of past ages, was wise,
> And the soul of eternity thought in their eyes."

The tall Æthiopian slave grinned as he admitted her, and motioned to her to proceed. Half-way up the hall she was met by Arbaces himself, in festive robes, which glittered with jewels. Although it was broad day without, the mansion, according to the practice of the luxurious, was artificially darkened, and the lamps cast their still and odor-giving light over the rich floors and ivory roofs.

"Beautiful Ione," said Arbaces, as he bent to touch her hand, "it is you that have eclipsed the day—it is your eyes that light up the halls—it is your breath which fills them with perfumes."

"You must not talk to me thus," said Ione, smiling: "you forget that your lore has sufficiently instructed my mind to render these graceful flatteries to my person unwelcome. It was you who taught me to disdain adulation: will you unteach your pupil?"

There was something so frank and charming in the manner of Ione, as she thus spoke, that the Egyptian was more than ever enamoured, and more than ever disposed to renew the offence he had committed; he, however, answered quickly and gaily, and hastened to renew the conversation.

He led her through the various chambers of a house, which seemed to contain to her eyes, inexperienced to other splendor than the minute elegance of Campanian cities, the treasures of the world.

In the walls were set pictures of inestimable art, the lights shone over statues of the noblest age of Greece. Cabinets of gems, each cabinet itself a gem, filled up the interstices of the columns; the most precious woods lined the thresholds and composed the doors; gold and jewels seemed lavished all around. Sometimes they were alone in these rooms—sometimes they passed through silent rows of slaves, who, kneeling as she passed, proffered to her offerings of bracelets, of chains, of gems, which the Egyptian vainly entreated her to receive.

"I have often heard," said she, wonderingly, "that you were rich: but I never dreamed of the amount of your wealth."

"Would I could coin it all," replied the Egyptian, "into one crown, which I might place upon that snowy brow!"

"Alas! the weight would crush me; I should be a second Tarpeia," answered Ione, laughingly.

"But thou dost not disdain riches, O Ione! they know not what life is capable of who are not wealthy. Gold is the great magician of earth—it realizes our dreams—it gives them the power of a god—there is a grandeur, a sublimity, in its possession; it is the mightiest, yet the most obedient of our slaves."

The artful Arbaces sought to dazzle the young Neapolitan by his treasures and his eloquence; he sought to awaken in her the desire to be mistress of what she surveyed: he hoped that she would confound the owner with the possessions, and that the charms of his wealth would be reflected on himself. Meanwhile, Ione was secretly somewhat uneasy at the gallantries which escaped from those lips, which, till lately, had seemed to disdain the common homage we pay to beauty: and with that delicate subtlety, which woman alone possesses, she sought to ward off shafts deliberately aimed, and to laugh or to talk away the meaning from his warming language. Nothing in the world is more pretty than that same species of defence; it is the charm of the African necromancer who professed with a feather to turn aside the winds.

The Egyptian was intoxicated and subdued by her grace even more than by her beauty; it was with difficulty that he suppressed his emotions; alas! the feather was only powerful against the summer breezes—it would be the sport of the storm.

Suddenly, as they stood in one hall, which was surrounded by draperies of silver and white, the Egyptian clapped his hands, and as if by enchantment, a banquet rose from the floor—a couch or throne, with a crimson canopy, ascended simultaneously at the feet of Ione,—and at the same instant from behind the curtains swelled the invisible and softest music.

Arbaces placed himself at the feet of Ione, and children, young and beautiful as Loves, ministered to the feast.

The feast was over, the music sank into a low and subdued strain, and Arbaces thus addressed his beautiful guest:—

"Hast thou never in this dark and uncertain world—hast thou never aspired, my pupil, to look beyond—hast thou never wished to put aside the veil of futurity, and to behold on the shores of Fate the shadowy images of things to be? For it is not the past alone that has its ghosts: each event *to come* has also its spectrum—its shade; when the hour arrives, life enters it, the shadow becomes corporeal, and walks the world. Thus, in the land beyond the grave, are ever two impalpable and spiritual hosts—the things to be, the things that have been! If by our wisdom we can penetrate that land, we see the one as the other, and learn, as *I* have learned, not alone the mysteries of the dead, but also the destiny of the living."

"As thou hast learned!—Can wisdom attain so far?"

"Wilt thou prove my knowledge, Ione, and behold the representation of thine own fate? It is a drama more striking than those of Æschylus; it is one I have prepared for thee, if thou wilt see the shadows perform their part."

The Neapolitan trembled; she thought of Glaucus, and sighed as well as trembled; were their destinies to be united? Half incredulous, half believing, half awed, half alarmed by the words of her strange host, she remained for some moments silent, and then answered—

"It may revolt—it may terrify; the knowledge of the future will perhaps only embitter the present!"

"Not so, Ione. I have myself looked upon thy future lot, and the ghosts of thy Future bask in the gardens of Elysium: amidst the asphodel and the rose they prepare the garlands of thy sweet destiny, and the Fates, so harsh to others, weave only for thee the web of happiness and love. Wilt thou then come and behold thy doom, so that thou mayst enjoy it beforehand?"

Again the heart of Ione murmured *"Glaucus;"* she uttered a half audible assent; the Egyptian rose, and taking her by the hand, he led her across the banquet-room—the curtains withdrew, as by magic hands, and the music broke forth in a louder and gladder strain; they passed a row of columns, on either side of which fountains cast aloft their fragrant waters; they descended by broad and easy steps into a garden. The eve had commenced; the moon was already high in heaven, and those sweet flowers that sleep by day, and fill, with ineffable odors, the airs of night, were thickly scattered amidst alleys cut through the star-lit foliage;—or, gathered in baskets, lay like offerings at the feet of the frequent statues that gleamed along their path.

"Whither wouldst thou lead me, Arbaces?" said Ione, wonderingly.

"But yonder," said he, pointing to a small building which stood at the end of the vista. "It is a temple consecrated to the Fates—our rites require such holy ground."

They passed into a narrow hall, at the end of which hung a

sable curtain. Arbaces lifted it; Ione entered, and found herself in total darkness.

"Be not alarmed," said the Egyptian, "the light will rise instantly." While he so spoke, a soft, and warm, and gradual light diffused itself around; as it spread over each object, Ione perceived that she was in an apartment of moderate size, hung everywhere with black; a couch with draperies of the same hue was beside her. In the centre of the room was a small altar, on which stood a tripod of bronze. At one side, upon a lofty column of granite, was a colossal head of the blackest marble, which she perceived, by the crown of wheat-ears that encircled the brow, represented the great Egyptian goddess. Arbaces stood before the altar: he had laid his garland on the shrine, and seemed occupied with pouring into the tripod the contents of a brazen vase; suddenly from that tripod leaped into life a blue, quick, darting, irregular flame; the Egyptian drew back to the side of Ione, and muttered some words in a language unfamiliar to her ear; the curtain at the back of the altar waved tremulously to and fro—it parted slowly, and in the aperture which was thus made, Ione beheld an indistinct and pale landscape, which gradually grew brighter and clearer as she gazed; at length she discovered plainly trees, and rivers, and meadows, and all the beautiful diversity of the richest earth. At length, before the landscape, a dim shadow glided; it rested opposite to Ione; slowly the same charm seemed to operate upon it as over the rest of the scene; it took form and shape, and lo!—in its feature and in its form Ione beheld herself!

Then the scene behind the spectre faded away, and was succeeded by the representation of a gorgeous palace; a throne was raised in the centre of its hall—the dim forms of slaves and guards were ranged around it, and a pale hand held over the throne the likeness of a diadem.

A new actor now appeared; he was clothed from head to foot in a dark robe—his face was concealed—he knelt at the feet of the shadowy Ione—he clasped her hand—he pointed to the throne, as if to invite her to ascend it.

The Neapolitan's heart beat violently. "Shall the shadow disclose itself?" whispered a voice beside her—the voice of Arbaces. "Ah, yes!" answered Ione, softly.

Arbaces raised his hand—the spectre seemed to drop the

mantle that concealed its form—and Ione shrieked—it was Arbaces himself that thus knelt before her.

"This is, indeed, thy fate!" whispered again the Egyptian's voice in her ear. "And thou art destined to be the bride of Arbaces."

Ione started—the black curtain closed over the phantasmagoria: and Arbaces himself—the real, the living Arbaces—was at her feet.

"Oh, Ione!" said he, passionately gazing upon her; "listen to one who has long struggled vainly with his love. I adore thee! The Fates do not lie—thou art destined to be mine—I have sought the world around, and found none like thee. From my youth upward, I have sighed for such as thou art. I have dreamed till I saw thee—I wake, and I behold thee. Turn not away from me, Ione; think not of me as thou hast thought; I am not that being—cold, insensate, and morose, which I have seemed to thee. Never woman had lover so devoted—so passionate as I will be to Ione. Do not struggle in my clasp: see—I release thy hand. Take it from me if thou wilt—well, be it so! But do not reject me, Ione—do not rashly reject—judge of thy power over him whom thou canst thus transform. I who never knelt to mortal being, kneel to thee. I who have commanded fate, receive from thee my own. Ione, tremble not, thou art my queen—my goddess:—be my bride! All the wishes thou canst form shall be fulfilled. The ends of the earth shall minister to thee—pomp, power, luxury, shall be thy slaves. Arbaces shall have no ambition, save the pride of obeying thee. Ione, turn upon me those eyes—shed upon me thy smile. Dark is my soul when thy face is hid from it; —shine over me, my sun—my heaven—my daylight!—Ione, Ione—do not reject my love!"

Alone, and in the power of this singular and fearful man, Ione was not yet terrified; the respect of his language, the softness of his voice, reassured her; and, in her own purity, she felt protection. But she was confused, astonished: it was some moments before she could recover the power to reply.

"Rise, Arbaces!" said she at length; and she resigned to him once more her hand, which she as quickly withdrew again, when she felt upon it the burning pressure of his lips. "Rise! and if thou art serious, if thy language be in earnest—"

"*If!*" said he, tenderly.

"Well, then, listen to me: you have been my guardian, my friend, my monitor; for this new character I was not prepared;—think not," she added quickly, as she saw his dark eyes glitter with the fierceness of his passion—"think not, that I scorn—that I am untouched—that I am not honored by this homage; but, say—canst thou hear me calmly?"

"Ay, though thy words were lightning, and could blast me!"

"*I love another!*" said Ione, blushingly, but in a firm voice.

"By the gods—by hell!" shouted Arbaces, rising to his fullest height; "dare not tell me that—dare not mock me:—it is impossible!—Whom hast thou seen—whom known! Oh, Ione! it is thy woman's invention, thy woman's art that speaks—thou wouldst gain time: I have surprised—I have terrified thee. Do with me as thou wilt—say that thou lovest not me; but say not that thou lovest another!"

"Alas!" began Ione; and then, appalled before his sudden and unlooked-for violence, she burst into tears.

Arbaces came nearer to her—his breath glowed fiercely on her cheek; he wound his arms round her—she sprang from his embrace. In the struggle a tablet fell from her bosom on the ground: Arbaces perceived, and seized it—it was the letter that morning received from Glaucus. Ione sank upon the couch, half dead with terror.

Rapidly the eyes of Arbaces ran over the writing; the Neapolitan did not dare to gaze upon him: she did not see the deadly paleness that came over his countenance—she marked not his withering frown, nor the quivering of his lip, nor the convulsions that heaved his breast. He read it to the end, and then, as the letter fell from his hand, he said, in a voice of deceitful calmness,—

"Is the writer of this the man thou lovest?" Ione sobbed, but answered not. "Speak!" he rather shrieked than said. "It is—it is!" "And his name—it is written here—his name is Glaucus!" Ione, clasping her hands, looked around as if for succor or escape.

"Then hear me," said Arbaces, sinking his voice into a whisper; "thou shalt go to thy tomb rather than to his arms! What! thinkest thou Arbaces will brook a rival such as this puny Greek? What! thinkest thou that he has watched the fruit ripen, to yield it to another! Pretty fool—no! Thou art

mine—all—only mine: and thus—thus I seize and claim thee!"
As he spoke, he caught Ione in his arms; and, in that ferocious
grasp, was all the energy—less of love than of revenge.

But to Ione despair gave supernatural strength; she again
tore herself from him—she rushed to that part of the room
by which she had entered—she half withdrew the curtain—
he seized her—again she broke away from him—and fell,
exhausted, and with a loud shriek, at the base of the column
which supported the head of the Egyptian goddess. Arbaces
paused for a moment, as if to regain his breath; and then once
more darted upon his prey.

At that instant the curtain was rudely torn aside, the
Egyptian felt a fierce and strong grasp upon his shoulder. He
turned—he beheld before him the flashing eyes of Glaucus,
and the pale, worn, but menacing, countenance of Apæcides.
"Ah!" he muttered, as he glared from one to the other, "what
Fury hath sent ye hither?"

"Atè" answered Glaucus; and he closed at once with the
Egyptian. Meanwhile, Apæcides raised his sister, now lifeless,
from the ground; his strength, exhausted by a mind long
overwrought, did not suffice to bear her away, light and delicate though her shape: he placed her, therefore, on the couch,
and stood over her with a brandishing knife, watching the
contest between Glaucus and the Egyptian, and ready to
plunge his weapon in the bosom of Arbaces should he be victorious in the struggle. There is, perhaps, nothing on earth
so terrible as the naked and unarmed contest of animal
strength, no weapon but those which Nature supplies to rage.
Both the antagonists were now locked in each other's grasp
—the hand of each seeking the throat of the other—the face
drawn back—the fierce eyes flashing—the muscles strained—
the veins swelled—the lips apart—the teeth set;—both were
strong beyond the ordinary power of men, both animated by
relentless wrath; they coiled, they wound, around each other;
they rocked to and fro—they swayed from end to end of their
confined arena:—they uttered cries of ire and revenge;—they
were now before the altar—now at the base of the column
where the struggle had commenced: they drew back for breath
—Arbaces leaning against the column—Glaucus a few paces
apart.

"O ancient goddess!" exclaimed Arbaces, clasping the

column, and raising his eyes toward the sacred image it supported, "protect thy chosen,—proclaim thy vengeance against
this thing of an upstart creed, who with sacrilegious violence
profanes thy resting-place and assails thy servant."

As he spoke, the still and vast features of the goddess
seemed suddenly to glow with life; through the black marble,
as through a transparent veil, flushed luminously a crimson
and burning hue; around the head played and darted corusca-
tions of livid lightning; the eyes became like balls of lurid fire,
and seemed fixed in withering and intolerable wrath upon the
countenance of the Greek. Awed and appalled by this sudden
and mystic answer to the prayer of his foe, and not free from
the hereditary superstitions of his race, the cheeks of Glaucus
paled before that strange and ghastly animation of the marble,
—his knees knocked together,—he stood, seized with a divine
panic, dismayed, aghast, half unmanned before his foe!
Arbaces gave him not breathing time to recover his stupor:
"Die, wretch!" he shouted, in a voice of thunder, as he sprang
upon the Greek; "the Mighty Mother claims thee as a living
sacrifice!" Taken thus by surprise in the first consternation
of his superstitious fears, the Greek lost his footing—the
marble floor was as smooth as glass—he slid—he fell. Arbaces
planted his foot on the breast of his fallen foe. Apæcides,
taught by his sacred profession, as well as by his knowledge of
Arbaces, to distrust all miraculous interpositions, had not
shared the dismay of his companion; he rushed forward,—his
knife gleamed in the air,—the watchful Egyptian caught his
arm as it descended,—one wrench of his powerful hand tore
the weapon from the weak grasp of the priest,—one sweeping
blow stretched him to the earth—with a loud and exulting yell
Arbaces brandished the knife on high. Glaucus gazed upon
his impending fate with unwinking eyes, and in the stern and
scornful resignation of a fallen gladiator, when, at that awful
instant, the floor shook under them with a rapid and convulsive
throe,—a mightier spirit than that of the Egyptian was
abroad!—a giant and crushing power, before which sunk into
sudden impotence his passion and his arts. It woke—it
stirred—that Dread Demon of the Earthquake—laughing to
scorn alike the magic of human guile and the malice of human
wrath. As a Titan, on whom the mountains are piled, it roused
itself from the sleep of years,—it moved on its tortured couch,

—the caverns below groaned and trembled beneath the motion
of its limbs. In the moment of his vengeance and his power,
the self-prized demigod was humbled to his real clay. Far
and wide along the soil went a hoarse and rumbling sound,—
the curtains of the chamber shook as at the blast of a storm,
—the altar rocked—the tripod reeled,—and, high over the
place of contest, the column trembled and waved from side to
side,—the sable head of the goddess tottered and fell from its
pedestal;—and as the Egyptian stooped above his intended
victim, right upon his bended form, right between the
shoulder and the neck, struck the marble mass! the shock
stretched him like the blow of death, at once, suddenly, without sound or motion, or semblance of life, upon the floor,
apparently crushed by the very divinity he had impiously
animated and invoked!

"The Earth has preserved her children," said Glaucus,
staggering to his feet. "Blessed be the dread convulsion! Let
us worship the providence of the gods!" He assisted Apæcides
to rise, and then turned upward the face of Arbaces; it seemed
locked as in death; blood gushed from the Egyptian's lips over
his glittering robes; he fell heavily from the arms of Glaucus,
and the red stream trickled slowly along the marble. Again
the earth shook beneath their feet; they were forced to cling
to each other; the convulsion ceased as suddenly as it came:
they tarried no longer; Glaucus bore Ione lightly in his arms,
and they fled from the unhallowed spot. But scarce had they
entered the garden when they were met on all sides by flying
and disordered groups of women and slaves, whose festive and
glittering garments contrasted in mockery the solemn terror
of the hour; they did not appear to heed the strangers,—they
were occupied only with their own fears. After the tranquillity of sixteen years, that burning and treacherous soil again
menaced destruction; they uttered but one cry, "THE EARTH-
QUAKE! THE EARTHQUAKE!" and passing unmolested from
the midst of them, Apæcides and his companions, without entering the house, hastened down one of the alleys, passed a
small open gate, and there, sitting on a little mound over
which spread the gloom of the dark green aloes, the moonlight
fell on the bended figure of the blind girl,—she was weeping
bitterly.

BOOK THE THIRD.
CHAPTER I.

The Forum of the Pompeians;—The first rude machinery by which the new era of the world was wrought.

It was early noon, and the forum was crowded alike with the busy and the idle. As at Paris at this day, so at that time in the cities of Italy, men lived almost wholly out of doors: the public buildings, the forum, the porticos, the baths, the temples themselves, might be considered their real homes; it was no wonder that they decorated so gorgeously these favorite places of resort,—they felt for them a sort of domestic affection as well as a public pride. And animated was, indeed, the aspect of the forum of Pompeii at that time! Along its broad pavement, composed of large flags of marble, were assembled various groups, conversing in that energetic fashion which appropriates a gesture to every word, and which is still the characteristic of the people of the south. Here, in seven stalls on one side the colonnade, sat the money-changers, with their glittering heaps before them, and merchants and seamen in various costumes crowding round their stalls. On one side, several men in long togas were seen bustling rapidly up to a stately edifice, where the magistrates administered justice;—these were the lawyers, active, chattering, joking, and punning, as you may find them at this day in Westminster. In the center of the space, pedestals supported various statues, of which the most remarkable was the stately form of Cicero. Around the court ran a regular and symmetrical colonnade of Doric architecture; and there several, whose business drew them early to the place, were taking the slight morning repast which made an Italian breakfast, talking vehemently on the earthquake of the preceding night as they dipped pieces of bread in their cups of diluted wine. In the open space, too, you might perceive various petty traders exercising the arts of their calling. Here one man

142

was holding out ribands to a fair dame from the country; another man was vaunting to a stout farmer the excellence of his shoes; a third, a kind of stall-restaurateur, still so common in the Italian cities, was supplying many a hungry mouth with hot messes from his small and itinerant stove, while—contrast strongly typical of the mingled bustle and intellect of the time—close by, a schoolmaster was expounding to his puzzled pupils the elements of the Latin grammar. A gallery above the portico, which was ascended by small wooden staircases had also its throng; though, as here the immediate business of the place was mainly carried on, its groups wore a more quiet and serious air.

Every now and then the crowd below respectfully gave way as some senator swept along to the Temple of Jupiter (which filled up one side of the forum, and was the senators' hall of meeting), nodding with ostentatious condescension to such of his friends or clients as he distinguished amongst the throng. Mingling amidst the gay dresses of the better orders you saw the hardy forms of the neighboring farmers, as they made their way to the public granaries. Hard by the temple you caught a view of the triumphal arch, and the long street beyond swarming with inhabitants; in one of the niches of the arch a fountain played, cheerily sparkling in the sunbeams; and above its cornice rose the bronzed and equestrian statue of Caligula, strongly contrasting the gay summer skies. Behind the stalls of the money-changers was that building now called the Pantheon, and a crowd of the poorer Pompeians passed through the small vestibule which admitted to the interior, with panniers under their arms, pressing on towards a platform, placed between two columns, where such provisions as the priests had rescued from sacrifice were exposed for sale.

At one of the public edifices appropriated to the business of the city, workmen were employed upon the columns, and you heard the noise of their labor every now and then rising above the hum of the multitude:—*the columns are unfinished to this day!*

All, then, united, nothing could exceed in variety the costumes, the ranks, the manners, the occupations of the crowd;—nothing could exceed the bustle, the gaiety, the animation, the flow and flush of life all around. You saw there all the myriad signs of a heated and feverish civilization,—where pleasure and commerce, idleness and labor, avarice and ambition, mingled in one gulf their motley, rushing, yet harmonious, streams.

Facing the steps of the Temple of Jupiter, with folded arms, and a knit and contemptuous brow, stood a man of about fifty years of age. His dress was remarkably plain,—not so much from its material, as from the absence of all those ornaments which were worn by the Pompeians of every rank,—partly from the love of show, partly, also, because they were chiefly wrought into those shapes deemed most efficacious in resisting the assaults of magic and the influence of the evil eye. His forehead was high and bald; the few locks that remained at the back of the head were concealed by a sort of cowl, which made a part of his cloak, to be raised or lowered at pleasure, and was now drawn half-way over the head, as a protection from the rays of the sun. The color of his garments was brown, no popular hue with the Pompeians; all the usual admixtures of scarlet or purple seemed carefully excluded. His belt, or girdle, contained a small receptacle for ink, which hooked on to the girdle, a stilus (or implement of writing), and tablets of no ordinary size. What was rather remarkable, the cincture held no purse, which was the almost indispensable appurtenance of the girdle, even when that purse had the misfortune to be empty!

It was not often that the gay and egotistical Pompeians busied themselves with observing the countenances and actions of their neighbors; but there was that in the lip and eye of this by-stander so remarkably bitter and disdainful, as he surveyed the religious procession sweeping up the stairs of the temple, that it could not fail to arrest the notice of many.

"Who is yon cynic?" asked a merchant of his companion, a jeweller.

"It is Olinthus," replied the jeweller; "a reputed Nazarene."

The merchant shuddered. "A dread sect!" said he, in a whispered and fearful voice. "It is said, that when they meet at nights they always commence their ceremonies by the murder of a new-born babe: they profess a community of goods, too,—the wretches! A community of goods! What would become of merchants, or jewellers either, if such notions were in fashion?"

"That is very true," said the jeweller; "besides, they wear no jewels,—they mutter imprecations when they see a serpent; and at Pompeii all our ornaments are serpentine."

"Do but observe," said a third, who was a fabricant of bronze, "how yon Nazarene scowls at the piety of the sacrificial procession. He is murmuring curses on the temple, be sure. Do you know, Celcinus, that this fellow, passing by my shop the other day, and seeing me employed on a statue of Minerva, told me with a frown that, had it been marble, he would have broken it; but the bronze was too strong for him. 'Break a goddess!' said I. 'A goddess!' answered the atheist; 'it is a demon,—an evil spirit!' Then he passed on his way cursing. Are such things to be borne? What marvel that the earth heaved so fearfully last night, anxious to reject the atheist from her bosom?—An atheist, do I say? worse still, —a scorner of the Fine Arts! Woe to us fabricants of bronze, if such fellows as this give the law to society!"

"These are the incendiaries that burnt Rome under Nero," groaned the jeweller.

While such were the friendly remarks provoked by the air and faith of the Nazarene, Olinthus himself became sensible of the effect he was producing; he turned his eyes round, and observed the intent faces of the accumulating throng, whispering as they gazed; and surveying them for a moment with an expression, first of defiance, and afterwards of compassion, he gathered his cloak round him and passed on, muttering audibly, "Deluded idolaters!—did not last night's convulsion warn ye? Alas! how will ye meet the last day?"

The crowd that heard these boding words gave them different interpretations, according to their different shades of ignorance and of fear; all, however, concurred in imagining them to convey some awful imprecation. They regarded the Christian as the enemy of mankind; the epithets they lavished upon him, of which "Atheist" was the most favored and frequent, may serve, perhaps, to warn us, believers of that same creed now triumphant, how we indulge the persecution of opinion Olinthus then underwent, and how we apply to those whose notions differ from our own the terms at that day lavished on the fathers of our faith.

As Olinthus stalked through the crowd, and gained one of the more private places of egress from the forum, he perceived gazing upon him a pale and earnest countenance, which he was not slow to recognize.

Wrapped in a pallium that partially concealed his sacred robes, the young Apæcides surveyed the disciple of that new and mysterious creed, to which at one time he had been half a convert.

"Is *he,* too, an impostor? Does this man, so plain and simple in life, in garb, in mien—does he too, like Arbaces, make austerity the robe of the sensualist? Does the veil of Vesta hide the vices of the prostitute?"

Olinthus, accustomed to men of all classes, and combining with the enthusiasm of his faith a profound experience of his kind, guessed, perhaps, by the index of the countenance, something of what passed within the breast of the priest. He met the survey of Apæcides with a steady eye, and a brow of serene and open candor.

"Peace be with thee!" said he, saluting Apæcides.

"Peace!" echoed the priest, in so hollow a tone that it went at once to the heart of the Nazarene.

"In that wish," continued Olinthus, "all good things are combined—without virtue thou canst not have peace. Like the rainbow, Peace rests upon the earth, but its arch is lost in heaven! Heaven bathes it in hues of light—it springs up amidst tears and clouds,—it is a reflection of the Eternal Sun, —it is an assurance of calm—it is the sign of a great covenant between Man and God. Such peace, O young man! is the smile of the soul; it is an emanation from the distant orb of immortal light. Peace be with you!"

"Alas!" began Apæcides, when he caught the gaze of the curious loiterers, inquisitive to know what could possibly be the theme of conversation between a reputed Nazarene and a priest of Isis. He stopped short, and then added in a low tone —"We cannot converse here, I will follow thee to the banks of the river; there is a walk which at this time is usually deserted and solitary."

Olinthus bowed assent. He passed through the streets

with a hasty step, but a quick and observant eye. Every now and then he exchanged a significant glance, a slight sign, with some passenger, whose garb usually betokened the wearer to belong to the humbler classes; for Christianity was in this the type of all other and less mighty revolutions—the grain of mustard-seed was in the hearts of the lowly. Amidst the huts of poverty and labor, the vast stream which afterwards poured its broad waters beside the cities and palaces of earth, took its neglected source.

CHAPTER II.

The noonday excursion on the Campanian seas.

"BUT tell me, Glaucus," said Ione, as they glided down the rippling Sarnus in their boat of pleasure, "how camest thou with Apæcides to my rescue from that bad man?"

"Ask Nydia yonder," answered the Athenian, pointing to the blind girl, who sat at a little distance from them, leaning pensively over her lyre:—"she must have thy thanks, not we. It seems that she came to my house, and finding me from home, sought thy brother in his temple; he accompanied her to Arbaces; on their way they encountered me, with a company of friends, whom thy kind letter had given me a spirit cheerful enough to join. Nydia's quick ear detected my voice —a few words sufficed to make me the companion of Apæcides; I told not my associates why I left them—could I trust thy name to their light tongues and gossiping opinion?— Nydia led us to the garden-gate, by which we afterwards bore thee—we entered, and were about to plunge into the mysteries of that evil house, when we heard thy cry in another direction. Thou knowest the rest."

Ione blushed deeply. She then raised her eyes to those of Glaucus, and he felt all the thanks she could not utter. "Come hither, my Nydia," said she, tenderly to the Thessalian.

"Did I not tell thee that thou shouldst be my sister and friend? Hast thou not already been more?—my guardian, my preserver!"

"It is nothing," answered Nydia coldly, and without stirring.

"Ah! I forgot," continued Ione,—"I should come to thee;" and she moved along the benches till she reached the place where Nydia sat, and flinging her arms caressingly round her, covered her cheeks with kisses.

Nydia was that morning paler than her wont, and her countenance grew even more wan and colorless as she submitted to the embrace of the beautiful Neapolitan. "But how camest thou, Nydia," whispered Ione, "to surmise so faithfully the danger I was exposed to? Didst thou know aught of the Egyptian!" "Yes, I knew of his vices." "And how?"

"Noble Ione, I have been a slave to the vicious—those whom I served were his minions."

"And thou hast entered his house, since thou knewest so well that private entrance?"

"I have played on my lyre to Arbaces," answered the Thessalian, with embarrassment.

"And thou hast escaped the contagion from which thou hast saved Ione!" returned the Neapolitan, in a voice too low for the ear of Glaucus.

"Noble Ione, I have neither beauty nor station; I am a child, and a slave, and blind. The despicable are ever safe."

It was with a pained, and proud, and indignant tone that Nydia made this humble reply; and Ione felt that she only wounded Nydia by pursuing the subject. She remained silent, and the bark now floated into the sea.

"Confess that I was right, Ione," said Glaucus, "in prevailing on thee not to waste this beautiful noon in thy chamber—confess that I was right."

"Thou wert right, Glaucus," said Nydia, abruptly.

"The dear child speaks for thee," returned the Athenian.

"But permit me to move opposite to thee, or our light boat will be overbalanced."

So saying, he took his seat exactly opposite to Ione, and leaning forward, he fancied that it was her breath, and not the winds of summer, that flung fragrance over the sea.

"Thou wert to tell me," said Glaucus, "why for so many days thy door was closed to me?"

"Oh, think of it no more!" answered Ione, quickly; "I

gave my ear to what I now know was the malice of slander."

"And my slanderer was the Egyptian?"

Ione's silence assented to the question.

"His motives are sufficiently obvious."

"Talk not of him," said Ione, covering her face with her hands, as if to shut out his very thought.

"Perhaps, he may be already by the banks of the slow Styx," resumed Glaucus; "yet in that case we should probably have heard of his death. Thy brother, methinks, hath felt the dark influence of his gloomy soul. When we arrived last night at thy house, he left me abruptly. Will he ever vouchsafe to be my friend?"

"He is consumed with some secret care," answered Ione, tearfully. "Would that we could lure him from himself! Let us join in that tender office."

"He shall be my brother," returned the Greek.

"How calmly," said Ione, rousing herself from the gloom into which her thoughts of Apæcides had plunged her—"How calmly the clouds seem to repose in heaven; and yet you tell me, for I knew it not myself, that the earth shook beneath us last night."

"It did, and more violently, they say, than it has done since the great convulsion sixteen years ago: the land we live in yet nurses mysterious terror; and the reign of Pluto, which spreads beneath our burning fields, seems rent with unseen commotion. Didst thou not feel the earth quake, Nydia, where thou wert seated last night? and was it not the fear that it occasioned thee that made thee weep?"

"I felt the soil creep and heave beneath me, like some monstrous serpent," answered Nydia; "but as I saw nothing, I did not fear: I imagined the convulsion to be a spell of the Egyptian's. They say he has power over the elements."

"Thou art a Thessalian, my Nydia," replied Glaucus, "and hast a national right to believe in magic."

"Magic!—who doubts it?" answered Nydia simply: "dost thou?"

"Until last night (when a necromantic prodigy did indeed appal me), methinks I was not credulous in any other magic save that of love!" said Glaucus, in a tremulous voice, and fixing his eyes on Ione.

"Ah!" said Nydia, with a sort of shiver, and she awoke mechanically a few pleasing notes from her lyre; the sound suited well the tranquillity of the waters and the sunny stillness of the noon.

"Play to us, dear Nydia," said Glaucus,—"play, and give us one of thine old Thessalian songs; whether it be of magic or not, as thou wilt—let it, at least, be of love!"

"Of love!" repeated Nydia, raising her large, wandering eyes, that ever thrilled those who saw them with a mingled fear and pity; you could never familiarize yourself to their aspect: so strange did it seem that those dark wild orbs were ignorant of the day, and either so fixed with their deep mysterious gaze, or so restless and perturbed their glance, that you felt, when you encountered them, that same vague, and chilling, and half-preternatural impression, which comes over you in the presence of the insane,—of those who having a life outwardly like your own, have a life within life—dissimilar—unsearchable—unguessed!

"Will you that I should sing of love?" said she, fixing those eyes upon Glaucus.

"Yes," replied he, looking down.

She moved a little way from the arm of Ione, still cast round her, as if that soft embrace embarrassed: and placing her light and graceful instrument on her knee, after a short prelude, she sang the following strain:—

NYDIA'S LOVE SONG

I.

"The Wind and the Beam loved the Rose,
    And the Rose loved one;
For who recks the wind where it blows?
    Or loves not the sun?

II.

None knew whence the humble Wind stole,
    Poor sport of the skies—
None dreamt that the Wind had a soul,
    In its mournful sighs!

III.

Oh, happy Beam! how canst thou prove
    That bright love of thine?
In thy light is the proof of thy love,
    Thou hast but—to shine!

IV.

How its love can the Wind reveal?
    Unwelcome its sigh:
Mute—mute to its Rose let it steal—
    Its proof is—to die!"

"Thou singest but sadly, sweet girl," said Glaucus; "thy youth only feels as yet the dark shadow of Love; far other inspiration doth he wake, when he himself bursts and brightens upon us."

"I sing as I was taught," replied Nydia, sighing.

"Thy master was love-crossed then—try thy hand at a gayer air. Nay, girl, give the instrument to me." As Nydia obeyed, her hand touched his, and, with that slight touch, her breast heaved—her cheek flushed. Ione and Glaucus, occupied with each other, perceived not those signs of strange and premature emotions, which preyed upon a heart that, nourished by imagination, dispensed with hope.

And now, broad, blue, bright before them, spread that halcyon sea, fair as at this moment, seventeen centuries from that date, I behold it rippling on the same divinest shores. Clime that yet enervates with a soft and Circean spell—that moulds us insensibly, mysteriously, into harmony with thyself, banishing the thought of austerer labor, the voices of wild ambition, the contests and the roar of life; filling us with gentle and subduing dreams, making necessary to our nature that which is its least earthly portion, so that the very air inspires us with the yearning and thirst of love! Whoever visits thee seems to leave earth and its harsh cares behind— to enter by the Ivory Gate into the Land of Dreams. The young and laughing Hours of the PRESENT—the Hours, those children of Saturn, which he hungers ever to devour, seem snatched from his grasp. The past—the future—are forgotten; we enjoy but the breathing time. Flower of the world's garden—Fountain of Delight—Italy of Italy—beautiful, benign Campania!—vain were, indeed, the Titans, if on this spot they yet struggled for another heaven. Here, if God meant this working-day life for a perpetual holiday, who would not sigh to dwell for ever—asking nothing, hoping nothing, fearing nothing, while thy skies shine over him—while thy seas sparkle at his feet—while thine air brought him sweet messages from the violet and the orange—and while the heart, resigned to—beating with—but one emotion, could find the lips and the eyes, which flatter it (vanity of vanities!) that love can defy custom, and be eternal?

It was then in this clime—on those seas, that the Athenian gazed upon a face that might have suited the nymph, the spirit of the place: feeding his eyes on the changeful roses of that softest cheek, happy beyond the happiness of common life, loving, and knowing himself beloved.

In the tale of human passion, in past ages, there is something of interest even in the remoteness of the time. We love to feel within us the bond which unites the most distant eras —men, nations, customs, perish; THE AFFECTIONS ARE IM-MORTAL!—they are the sympathies which unite the ceaseless generations. The past lives again, when we look upon its emotions—it lives in our own! That which was, ever is! The magician's gift, that revives the dead—that animates the dust of forgotten graves, is not in the author's skill—it is in the heart of the reader!

Still vainly seeking the eyes of Ione, as, half downcast, half averted, they shunned his own, the Athenian, in a low and soft voice, thus expressed the feelings inspired by happier thoughts than those which had colored the song of Nydia.

THE SONG OF GLAUCUS

I.

"As the bark floateth on o'er the summer-lit sea,
Floats my heart o'er the deeps of its passion for thee;
All lost in the space, without terror it glides,
For bright with thy soul is the face of the tides.
Now heaving, now hush'd, is that passionate ocean,
　　As it catches thy smile or thy sighs;
And the twin-stars that shine on the wanderer's devotion,
　　Its guide and its god—are thine eyes!

II.

The bark may go down, should the cloud sweep above,
For its being is bound to the light of thy love.
As thy faith and thy smile are its life and its joy,

So thy frown or thy change are the storms that destroy:
Ah! sweeter to sink while the sky is serene,
  If time hath a change for thy heart!
  If to live be to weep over what thou hast been,
  Let me die while I know what thou art!"

As the last words of the song trembled over the sea, Ione raised her looks—they met those of her lover. Happy Nydia! —happy in thy affliction, that thou couldst not see that fascinated and charmed gaze, that said so much—that made the eye the voice of the soul—that promised the impossibility of change!

But, though the Thessalian could not detect that gaze, she divined its meaning by their silence—by their sighs. She pressed her hands tightly across her breast, as if to keep down its bitter and jealous thoughts; and then she hastened to speak —for that silence was intolerable to her.

"After all, O Glaucus!" said she, "there is nothing very mirthful in your strain!"

"Yet I meant it to be so, when I took up the lyre, pretty one. Perhaps happiness will not permit us to be mirthful."

"How strange is it," said Ione, changing a conversation which oppressed her while it charmed,—"that for the last several days yonder cloud has hung motionless over Vesuvius! Yet not indeed motionless, for sometimes it changes its form; and now methinks it looks like some vast giant, with an arm outstretched over the city. Dost thou see the likeness—or is it only to my fancy?"

"Fair Ione! I see it also. It is astonishingly distinct. The giant seems seated on the brow of the mountain, the different shades of the cloud appear to form a white robe that sweeps over its vast breast and limbs; it seems to gaze with a steady face upon the city below, to point with one hand, as thou sayest, over its glittering streets, and to raise the other (dost thou note it?) towards the higher heaven. It is like the ghost of some huge Titan brooding over the beautiful world he lost; sorrowful for the past—yet with something of menace for the future."

"Could that mountain have any connection with the last night's earthquake? They say that, ages ago, almost in the earliest era of tradition, it gave forth fires as Ætna still. Perhaps the flames yet lurk and dart beneath."

"It is possible," said Glaucus, musingly.

"Thou sayest thou art slow to believe in magic?" said Nydia suddenly. "I have heard that a potent witch dwells amongst the scorched caverns of the mountain, and yon cloud may be the dim shadow of the demon she confers with."

"Thou art full of the romance of thy native Thessaly," said Glaucus; "and a strange mixture of sense and all conflicting superstitions."

"We are ever superstitious in the dark," replied Nydia. "Tell me," she added, after a slight pause, "tell me, O Glaucus! do all that are beautiful resemble each other? They say you are beautiful, and Ione also. Are your faces then the same? I fancy not, yet it ought to be so!"

"Fancy no such grievous wrong to Ione," answered Glaucus, laughing. "But we do not, alas! resemble each other, as the homely and the beautiful sometimes do. Ione's hair is dark, mine light; Ione's eyes are—what color, Ione? I cannot see, turn them to me. Oh, are they black? no, they are too soft. Are they blue? no they are too deep: they change with every ray of the sun—I know not their color: but mine, sweet Nydia, are grey, and bright only when Ione shines on them! Ione's cheek is—"

"I do not understand one word of thy description," interrupted Nydia, peevishly. "I comprehend only that you do not resemble each other, and I am glad of it."

"Why, Nydia?" said Ione.

Nydia colored slightly. "Because," she replied coldly, "I have always imagined you under different forms, and one likes to know one is right."

"And what hast thou imagined Glaucus to resemble?" asked Ione, softly.

"Music!" replied Nydia, looking down.

"Thou art right," thought Ione.

"And what likeness hast thou ascribed to Ione?"

"I cannot tell yet," answered the blind girl; "I have not yet known her long enough to find a shape and sign for my guesses."

"I will tell thee, then," said Glaucus, passionately: "she is like the sun that warms—like the wave that refreshes."

"The sun sometimes scorches, and the wave sometimes drowns," answered Nydia.

"Take then these roses," said Glaucus; "let their fragrance suggest to thee Ione."

"Alas, the roses will fade!" said the Neapolitan, archly.

Thus conversing, they wore away the hours; the lovers, conscious only of the brightness and smiles of love; the blind girl feeling only its darkness—its tortures;—the fierceness of jealousy and its woe!

And now, as they drifted on, Glaucus once more resumed the lyre, and woke its strings with a careless hand to a strain, so wildly and gladly beautiful, that even Nydia was aroused from her reverie, and uttered a cry of admiration.

"Thou seest, my child," cried Glaucus, "that I can yet redeem the character of love's music, and that I was wrong in saying happiness could not be gay. Listen, Nydia! listen, dear Ione! and hear

THE BIRTH OF LOVE

I.

"Like a Star in the seas above,
  Like a Dream to the waves of sleep
Up—up—THE INCARNATE LOVE—
  She rose from the charmed deep!
And over the Cyprian Isle
The skies shed their silent smile;
And the Forest's green heart was rife
With the stir of the gushing life—
The life that had leap'd to birth,
In the veins of the happy earth!
      Hail! oh, hail!
The dimmest sea-cave below thee,
  The farthest sky-arch above,
In their innermost stillness know thee:
  And heave with the Birth of Love
      Gale! soft Gale!
Thou comest on thy silver winglets,
  From thy home in the tender west;
Now fanning her golden ringlets,
  Now hush'd on her heaving breast.
And afar on the murmuring sand,
The Seasons wait hand in hand
To welcome thee, Birth Divine,
To the earth which is henceforth thine.

II.

Behold! how she kneels in the shell,
Bright pearl in its floating cell!
Behold! how the shell's rose-hues
            The cheek and the breast of snow,
And the delicate limbs suffuse
            Like a blush, with a bashful glow,
Sailing on, slowly sailing
    O'er the wild water;
All hail! as the fond light is hailing
        Her daughter,
                    All hail!
We are thine, all thine evermore:
Not a leaf on the laughing shore,
Not a wave on the heaving sea,
            Nor a single sigh
            In the boundless sky,
But is vow'd evermore to thee!

III.

And thou, my beloved one—thou,
As I gaze on thy soft eyes now,
Methinks from their depths I view
The Holy Birth born anew;
Thy lids are the gentle cell
            Where the young Love blushing lies;
See! she breaks from the mystic shell,
            She comes from thy tender eyes!
            Hail! all hail!
She comes, as she came from the sea,
To my soul as it looks on thee;
            She comes, she comes!
She comes, as she came from the sea,
To my soul as it looks on thee!
            Hail! all hail!"

CHAPTER III.

The congregation.

FOLLOWED by Apæcides, the Nazarene gained the side of
the Sarnus;—that river, which now has shrunk into a petty
stream, then rushed gaily into the sea, covered with countless
vessels, and reflecting on its waves the gardens, the vines, the
palaces, and the temples of Pompeii. From its more noisy and

frequented banks, Olinthus directed his steps to a path which
ran amidst a shady vista of trees, at the distance of a few
paces from the river. This walk was in the evening a favorite
resort of the Pompeians, but during the heat and business of
the day was seldom visited, save by some groups of playful
children, some meditative poet, or some disputative philosophers. At the side farthest from the river, frequent copses of
box interspersed the more delicate and evanescent foliage,
and these were cut into a thousand quaint shapes, sometimes
into the forms of fauns and satyrs, sometimes into the mimicry of Egyptian pyramids, sometimes into the letters that
composed the name of a popular or eminent citizen. Thus the
false taste is equally ancient as the pure; and the retired
traders of Hackney and Paddington, a century ago, were little
aware, perhaps, that in their tortured yews and sculptured
box, they found their models in the most polished period of
Roman antiquity, in the gardens of Pompeii, and the villas of
the fastidious Pliny.

This walk now, as the noonday sun shone perpendicularly
through the chequered leaves, was entirely deserted; at least
no other forms than those of Olinthus and the priest infringed
upon the solitude. They sat themselves on one of the benches,
placed at intervals between the trees, and facing the faint
breeze that came languidly from the river, whose waves
danced and sparkled before them;—a singular and contrasted
pair; the believer in the latest—the priest of the most ancient
—worship of the world!

"Since thou leftst me so abruptly," said Olinthus, "hast
thou been happy? has thy heart found contentment under these
priestly robes? hast thou, still yearning for the voice of God,
heard it whisper comfort to thee from the oracles of Isis?
That sigh, that averted countenance, give me the answer my
soul predicted."

"Alas!" answered Apæcides, sadly, "thou seest before thee
a wretched and distracted man! From my childhood upward
I have idolized the dreams of virtue! I have envied the holiness of men who, in caves and lonely temples, have been admitted to the companionship of beings above the world; my
days have been consumed with feverish and vague desires;
my nights with mocking but solemn visions. Seduced by the
mystic prophecies of an impostor, I have indued these robes;

—my nature (I confess it to thee frankly)—my nature has revolted at what I have seen and been doomed to share in! Searching after truth, I have become but the minister of falsehoods. On the evening in which we last met, I was buoyed by hopes created by that same impostor, whom I ought already to have better known. I have—no matter—no matter! suffice it, I have added perjury and sin to rashness and to sorrow. The veil is now rent for ever from my eyes; I behold a villain where I obeyed a demigod; the earth darkens in my sight; I am in the deepest abyss of gloom; I know not if there be gods above; if we are the things of chance; if beyond the bounded and melancholy present there is annihilation or an hereafter —tell me, then, thy faith; solve me these doubts, if thou hast indeed the power!"

"I do not marvel," answered the Nazarene, "that thou hast thus erred, or that thou art thus sceptic. Eighty years ago there was no assurance to man of God, or of a certain and definite future beyond the grave. New laws are declared to him who has ears—a heaven, a true Olympus, is revealed to him who has eyes—heed then, and listen."

And with all the earnestness of a man believing ardently himself, and zealous to convert, the Nazarene poured forth to Apæcides the assurances of Scriptural promise. He spoke first of the sufferings and miracles of Christ—he wept as he spoke: he turned next to the glories of the Saviour's ascension—to the clear predictions of Revelation. He described that pure and unsensual heaven destined to the virtuous—those fires and torments that were the doom of guilt.

The doubts which spring up to the mind of later reasoners, in the immensity of the sacrifice of God to man, were not such as would occur to an early heathen. He had been accustomed to believe that the gods had lived upon earth, and taken upon themselves the forms of men; had shared in human passions, in human labors, and in human misfortunes. What was the travail of his own Alcmæna's son, whose altars now smoked with the incense of countless cities, but a toil for the human race. Had not the great Dorian Apollo expiated a mystic sin by descending to the grave? Those who were the deities of heaven had been the law-givers or benefactors on earth, and gratitude had led to worship. It seemed therefore, to the heathen, a doctrine neither new nor strange, that Christ had been sent from heaven, that an immortal had indued mortality, and tasted the bitterness of death. And the end for which He thus toiled and thus suffered—how far more glorious did it seem to Apæcides than that for which the deities of old had visited the nether world, and passed through the gates of death! Was it not worthy of a God to descend to these dim valleys, in order to clear up the clouds gathered over the dark mount beyond—to satisfy the doubts of sages—to convert speculation into certainty—by example to point out the rules of life—by revelation to solve the enigma of the grave—and to prove that the soul did not yearn in vain when it dreamed of an immortality? In this last was the great argument of those lowly men destined to convert the earth. As nothing is more flattering to the pride and the hopes of man than the belief in a future state, so nothing could be more vague and confused than the notions of the heathen sages upon that mystic subject. Apæcides had already learned that the faith of the philosophers was not that of the herd; that if they secretly professed a creed in some diviner power, it was not the creed which they thought it wise to impart to the community. He had already learned, that even the priest ridiculed what he preached to the people—that the notions of the few and the many were never united. But, in this new faith, it seemed to him that philosopher, priest, and people, the expounders of the religion and its followers, were alike accordant: they did not speculate and debate upon immortality, they spoke of it as a thing certain and assured; the magnificence of the promise dazzled him—its consolations soothed. For the Christian faith made its early converts among sinners! many of its fathers and its martyrs were those who had felt the bitterness of vice, and who were therefore no longer tempted by its false aspect from the paths of an austere and uncompromising virtue. All the assurances of this healing faith invited to repentance— they were peculiarly adapted to the bruised and sore of spirit; the very remorse which Apæcides felt for his late excesses, made him incline to one who found holiness in that remorse, and who whispered of the joy in heaven over one sinner that repenteth.

"Come," said the Nazarene, as he perceived the effect he had produced, "come to the humble hall in which we meet— a select and a chosen few; listen there to our prayers; note the

sincerity of our repentant tears; mingle in our simple sacrifice
—not of victims, nor of garlands, but offered by white-robed
thoughts upon the altar of the heart. The flowers that we lay
there are imperishable—they bloom over us when we are no
more; nay, they accompany us beyond the grave, they spring
up beneath our feet in heaven, they delight us with an eternal
odor, for they are of the soul, they partake of its nature; these
offerings are temptations overcome, and since repented.
Come, oh, come! lose not another moment; prepare already
for the great, the awful journey, from darkness to light, from
sorrow to bliss, from corruption to immortality! This is the
day of the Lord the Son, a day that we have set apart for our
devotions. Though we meet usually at night, yet some
amongst us are gathered together even now. What joy, what
triumph, will be with us all, if we can bring one stray lamb
into the sacred fold!"

There seemed to Apæcides, so naturally pure of heart,
something ineffably generous and benign in that spirit of conversion which animated Olinthus—a spirit that found its own
bliss in the happiness of others—that sought in its wide so-
ciality to make companions for eternity. He was touched,
softened, and subdued. He was not in that mood which can
bear to be left alone; curiosity, too, mingled with his purer
stimulants—he was anxious to see those rites of which so
many dark and contradictory rumors were afloat. He paused
a moment, looked over his garb, thought of Arbaces, shuddered with horror, lifted his eyes to the broad brow of the
Nazarene, intent, anxious, watchful—but for *his* benefit, for
his salvation! He drew his cloak round him, so as wholly to
conceal his robes, and said, "Lead on, I follow thee."

Olinthus pressed his hand joyfully, and then descending
to the river-side, hailed one of the boats that plyed there constantly; they entered it; an awning overhead, while it sheltered
them from the sun, screened also their persons from observation: they rapidly skimmed the wave. From one of the boats
that passed them floated a soft music, and its prow was decorated with flowers—it was gliding towards the sea.

"So," said Olinthus, sadly, "unconscious and mirthful in
their delusions, sail the votaries of luxury into the great
ocean of storm and shipwreck; we pass them, silent and un-
noticed to gain the land."

Apæcides, lifting his eyes, caught through the aperture in the awning a glimpse of the face of one of the inmates of that gay bark—it was the face of Ione. The lovers were embarked on the excursion at which we have been made present. The priest sighed, and once more sunk back upon his seat. They reached the shore where, in the suburbs, an alley of small and mean houses stretched towards the bank; they dismissed the boat, landed, and Olinthus, preceding the priest, threaded the labyrinth of lanes, and arrived at last at the closed door of a habitation somewhat larger than its neighbors. He knocked thrice—the door was opened and closed again, as Apæcides followed his guide across the threshold.

They passed a deserted atrium, and gained an inner chamber of moderate size, which, when the door was closed, received its only light from a small window cut over the door itself. But, halting at the threshold of this chamber, and knocking at the door, Olinthus said, "Peace be with you!" A voice from within returned, "Peace with whom?" "The Faithful!" answered Olinthus, and the door opened; twelve or fourteen persons were sitting in a semicircle, silent, and seemingly absorbed in thought, and opposite to a crucifix rudely carved in wood.

They lifted up their eyes when Olinthus entered, without speaking; the Nazarene himself, before he accosted them, knelt suddenly down, and by his moving lips, and his eyes fixed steadfastly on the crucifix, Apæcides saw that he prayed inly. This rite performed, Olinthus turned to the congregation—"Men and brethren," said he, "start not to behold amongst you a priest of Isis; he hath sojourned with the blind, but the Spirit hath fallen on him—he desires to see, to hear, and to understand."

"Let him," said one of the assembly; and Apæcides beheld in the speaker a man still younger than himself, of a countenance equally worn and pallid, of an eye which equally spoke of the restless and fiery operations of a working mind.

"Let him," repeated a second voice, and he who thus spoke was in the prime of manhood; his bronzed skin and Asiatic features bespoke him a son of Syria—he had been a robber in his youth.

"Let him," said a third voice; and the priest, again turning to regard the speaker, saw an old man with a long grey beard, whom he recognized as a slave to the wealthy Diomed.

"Let him," repeated simultaneously the rest—men who, with two exceptions, were evidently of the inferior ranks. In these exceptions, Apæcides noted an officer of the guard, and an Alexandrian merchant.

"We do not," recommenced Olinthus—"we do not bind you to secrecy; we impose on you no oaths (as some of our weaker brethren would do) not to betray us. It is true, indeed, that there is no absolute law against us; but the multitude, more savage than their rulers, thirst for our lives. So, my friends, when Pilate would have hesitated, it was *the people* who shouted 'Christ to the cross!' But we bind you not to our safety—no! Betray us to the crowd—impeach, calumniate, malign us if you will:—we are above death, we should walk cheerfully to the den of the lion, or the rack of the torturer—we can trample down the darkness of the grave, and what is death to a criminal is eternity to the Christian."

A low and applauding murmur ran through the assembly.

"Thou comest amongst us as an examiner, mayest thou remain a convert! Our religion? you behold it! Yon cross our sole image, yon scroll the mysteries of our Cære and Eleusis! Our morality? it is in our lives!—sinners we all have been; who now can accuse us of a crime? we have baptized ourselves from the past. Think not that this is of us, it is of God. Approach, Medon," beckoning to the old slave who had spoken third for the admission of Apæcides, "thou art the sole man amongst us who is not free. But in heaven, the last shall be first: so with us. Unfold your scroll, read and explain."

Useless would it be for us to accompany the lecture of Medon, or the comments of the congregation. Familiar now are those doctrines, then strange and new. Eighteen centuries have left us little to expound upon the lore of Scripture or the life of Christ. To us, too, there would seem little congenial in the doubts that occurred to a heathen priest, and little learned in the answers they received from men uneducated, rude, and simple, possessing only the knowledge that they were greater than they seemed.

There was one thing that greatly touched the Neapolitan; when the lecture was concluded, they heard a very gentle knock at the door; the password was given, and replied to; the door opened, and two young children, the eldest of whom might have told its seventh year, entered timidly; they were the children of the master of the house, that dark and hardy Syrian, whose youth had been spent in pillage and bloodshed. The eldest of the congregation (it was that old slave) opened to them his arms; they fled to the shelter—they crept to his breast —and his hard features smiled as he caressed them. And then these bold and fervent men, nursed in vicissitude, beaten by the rough winds of life—men of mailed and impervious fortitude, ready to affront a world, prepared for torment and armed for death—men, who presented all imaginable contrast to the weak nerves, the light hearts, the tender fragility of childhood, crowded round the infants, smoothing their rugged brows and composing their bearded lips to kindly and fostering smiles: and then the old man opened the scroll, and he taught the infants to repeat after him that beautiful prayer which we still dedicate to the Lord, and still teach to our children; and then he told them, in simple phrase, of God's love to the young, and how not a sparrow falls but His eye sees it. This lovely custom of infant initiation was long cherished by the early Church, in memory of the words which said, "Suffer little children to come unto me, and forbid them not;" and was perhaps the origin of the superstitious calumny which ascribed to the Nazarenes the crime which the Nazarene, when victorious, attributed to the Jew, viz. the decoying children to hideous rites, at which they were secretly immolated.

And the stern paternal penitent seemed to feel in the innocence of his children a return into early life—life ere yet it sinned: he followed the motion of their young lips with an earnest gaze; he smiled as they repeated, with hushed and reverent looks, the holy words; and when the lesson was done, and they ran, released, and gladly to his knee, he clasped them to his breast, kissed them again and again, and tears flowed fast down his cheek—tears, of which it would have been impossible to trace the source, so mingled they were with joy and sorrow, penitence and hope—remorse for himself and love for them!

Something, I say, there was in this scene which peculiarly affected Apæcides: and, in truth, it is difficult to conceive a ceremony more appropriate to the religion of benevolence, more appealing to the household and every-day affections, striking a more sensitive chord in the human breast.

It was at this time that an inner door opened gently, and a very old man entered the chamber, leaning on a staff. At his presence, the whole congregation rose; there was an expression of deep, affectionate respect upon every countenance; and Apæcides, gazing on his countenance, felt attracted towards him by an irresistible sympathy. No man ever looked upon that face without love; for there had dwelt the smile of the Deity, the incarnation of divinest love;—and the glory of the smile had never passed away.

"My children, God be with you!" said the old man, stretching his arms; and as he spoke, the infants ran to his knee. He sat down, and they nestled fondly to his bosom. It was beautiful to see that mingling of the extremes of life—the rivers gushing from their early source—the majestic stream gliding to the ocean of eternity! As the light of declining day seems to mingle earth and heaven, making the outline of each scarce visible, and blending the harsh mountain-tops with the sky, even so did the smile of that benign old age appear to hallow the aspect of those around, to blend together the strong distinctions of varying years, and to diffuse over infancy and manhood the light of that heaven into which it must so soon vanish and be lost.

"Father," said Olinthus, "thou on whose form the miracle of the Redeemer worked; thou who wert snatched from the grave to become the living witness of His mercy and His power; behold! a stranger in our meeting—a new lamb gathered to the fold!"

"Let me bless him," said the old man: the throng gave way. Apæcides approached him as by an instinct: he fell on his knees before him—the old man laid his hand on the priest's head, and blessed him, but not aloud. As his lips moved, his eyes were upturned, and tears—those tears that good men only shed in the hope of happiness to another—flowed fast down his cheeks.

The children were on either side of the convert; his heart was theirs—he had become as one of them—to enter into the kingdom of Heaven.

CHAPTER IV.

The stream of love runs on—whither?

Days are like years in the love of the young, when no bar, no obstacle, is between their hearts—when the sun shines, and the course runs smooth—when their love is prosperous and confessed. Ione no longer concealed from Glaucus the attachment she felt for him, and their talk now was only of their love. Over the rapture of the present, the hopes of the future glowed like the heaven above the gardens of spring. They went in their trustful thoughts far down the stream of time; they laid out the chart of their destiny to come; they suffered the light of to-day to suffuse the morrow. In the youth of their hearts it seemed as if care, and change, and death, were as things unknown. Perhaps they loved each other the more, because the condition of the world left to Glaucus no aim and no wish but love; because the distractions common in free states to men's affection existed not for the Athenian; because his country wooed him not to the bustle of civil life; because ambition furnished no counterpoise to love: and, therefore, over their schemes and their projects, love only reigned. In the iron age they imagined themselves of the golden, doomed only to live and to love.

To the superficial observer, who interests himself only in characters strongly marked and broadly colored, both the lovers may seem of too slight and commonplace a mould: in the delineation of characters purposely subdued the reader sometimes imagines that there is a want of character; perhaps, indeed, I wrong the real nature of these two lovers by not painting more impressively their stronger individualities. But in dwelling so much on their bright and bird-like existence, I am influenced almost insensibly by the forethought of the changes that await them, and for which they were so ill prepared. It was this very softness and gaiety of life that contrasted most strongly the vicissitudes of their coming fate. For the oak without fruit or blossom, whose hard and rugged heart is fitted for the storm, there is less fear than for the delicate branches of the myrtle, and the laughing clusters of the vine.

They had now advanced far into August—the next month their marriage was fixed, and the threshold of Glaucus was already wreathed with garlands; and nightly, by the door of Ione, he poured forth the rich libations. He existed no longer for his gay companions; he was ever with Ione. In the mornings they beguiled the sun with music; in the evenings they forsook the crowded haunts of the gay for excursions on the water, or along the fertile and vine-clad plains that lay beneath the fatal mount of Vesuvius. The earth shook no more; the lively Pompeians forgot even that there had gone forth so terrible a warning of their approaching doom. Glaucus imagined that convulsion, in the vanity of his heathen religion, an especial interposition of the gods, less in behalf of his own safety than that of Ione. He offered up the sacrifices of gratitude at the temples of his faith; and even the altar of Isis was covered with his votive garlands;—as to the prodigy of the animated marble, he blushed at the effect it had produced on him. He believed it, indeed, to have been wrought by the magic of man; but the result convinced him that it betokened not the anger of a goddess.

Of Arbaces, they heard only that he still lived; stretched on the bed of suffering, he recovered slowly from the effect of the shock he had sustained—he left the lovers unmolested —but it was only to brood over the hour and the method of revenge.

Alike in their mornings at the house of Ione, and in their evening excursions, Nydia was usually their constant, and often their sole companion. They did not guess the secret fires which consumed her:—the abrupt freedom with which she mingled in their conversation—her capricious and often her peevish moods found ready indulgence in the recollection of the service they owed her, and their compassion for her affliction. They felt an interest in her, perhaps the greater and more affectionate from the very strangeness and waywardness of her nature, her singular alternations of passion and soft- ness—the mixture of ignorance and genius—of delicacy and rudeness—of the quick humors of the child, and the proud calmness of the woman. Although she refused to accept of freedom, she was constantly suffered to be free; she went where she listed: so curb was put either on her words or actions; they felt for one so darkly fated, and so susceptible of every wound, the same pitying and compliant indulgence the mother feels for a spoiled and sickly child,—dreading to impose authority, even where they imagined it for her benefit. She availed herself of this license by refusing the companionship of the slave whom they wished to attend her. With the slender staff by which she guided her steps, she went now, as in her former unprotected state, along the populous streets: it was almost miraculous to perceive how quickly and how dexterously she threaded every crowd, avoiding every danger, and could find her benighted way through the most intricate windings of the city. But her chief delight was still in visiting the few feet of ground which made the garden of Glaucus;—in tending the flowers that at least repaid her love. Sometimes she entered the chamber where he sat, and sought a conversation, which she nearly always broke off abruptly—for conversation with Glaucus only tended to one subject—*Ione;* and that name from his lips inflicted agony upon her. Often she bitterly repented the service she had rendered to Ione; often she said inly, "If she had fallen, Glaucus could have loved her no longer;" and then dark and fearful thoughts crept into her breast.

She had not experienced fully the trials that were in store for her, when she had been thus generous. She had never before been present when Glaucus and Ione were together; she had never heard that voice so kind to her, so much softer to another. The shock that crushed her heart with the tidings that Glaucus loved, had at first only saddened and benumbed;—by degrees jealousy took a wilder and fiercer shape; it partook of hatred—it whispered revenge. As you see the wind only agitate the green leaf upon the bough, while the leaf which has lain withered and seared on the ground, bruised and trampled upon, till the sap and life are gone, is suddenly whirled aloft— now here—now there—without stay and without rest; so the love which visits the happy and the hopeful hath but freshness on its wings! its violence is but sportive. But the heart that hath fallen from the green things of life, that is without hope, that hath no summer in its fibres, is torn and whirled by the same wind that but caresses its brethren;—it hath no bough to cling to—it is dashed from path to path—till the winds fall, and it is crushed into the mire for ever.

The friendless childhood of Nydia had hardened prematurely her character; perhaps the heated scenes of profligacy through which she had passed, seemingly unscathed, had ripened her passions, though they had not sullied her purity. The orgies of Burbo might only have disgusted, the banquets of the Egyptian might only have terrified, at the moment; but the winds that pass unheeded over the soil leave seeds behind them. As darkness, too, favors the imagination, so, perhaps, her very blindness contributed to feed with wild and delirious visions the love of the unfortunate girl. The voice of Glaucus had been the first that had sounded musically to her ear; his kindness made a deep impression upon her mind; when he had left Pompeii in the former year, she had treasured up in her heart every word he had uttered; and when any one told her that this friend and patron of the poor flower-girl was the most brilliant and the most graceful of the young revellers of Pompeii, she had felt a pleasing pride in nursing his recollection. Even the task which she imposed upon herself, of tending his flowers, served to keep him in her mind; she associated him with all that was most charming to her impressions; and when she had refused to express what image she fancied Ione to resemble, it was partly, perhaps, that whatever was bright and soft in nature she had already combined with the thought of Glaucus. If any of my readers ever loved at an age which they would now smile to remember—an age in which fancy forestalled the reason; let them say whether that love, among all its strange and complicated delicacies, was not, above all other and later passions, susceptible of jealousy? I seek not here the cause: I know that it is commonly the fact.

When Glaucus returned to Pompeii, Nydia had told another year of life; that year, with its sorrows, its loneliness, its trials, had greatly developed her mind and heart; and when the Athenian drew her unconsciously to his breast, deeming her still in soul as in years a child—when he kissed her smooth cheek, and wound his arm round her trembling frame, Nydia felt suddenly, and as by revelation, that those feelings she had long and innocently cherished were of love. Doomed to be rescued from tyranny by Glaucus—doomed to take shelter under his roof—doomed to breathe, but for so brief a time, the same air—and doomed, in the first rush of a thousand happy, grateful, delicious sentiments of an overflowing heart, to hear that he loved another; to be commissioned to that other, the messenger, the minister; to feel all at once that utter nothingness which she' was—which she ever must be, but which, till then, her young mind had not taught her,—that utter nothingness to him who was all to her; what wonder that, in her wild and passionate soul, all the elements jarred discordant; that if love reigned over the whole, it was not the love which is born of the more sacred and soft emotions? Sometimes she dreaded only lest Glaucus should discover her secret; sometime's she felt indignant that it was *not* suspected; it was a sign of contempt—could he imagine that she presumed so far? Her feelings to Ione ebbed and flowed with every hour; now she loved her because *he* did; now she hated her for the same cause. There were moments when she could have murdered her unconscious mistress; moments when she could have laid down life for her. These fierce and tremulous alternations of passion were too severe to be borne long. Her health gave way, though she felt it not—her cheek paled—her step grew feebler —tears came to her eyes more often, and relieved her less.

One morning, when she repaired to her usual task in the garden of the Athenian, she found Glaucus under the columns of the peristyle, with a merchant of the town; he was selecting jewels for his destined bride. He had already fitted up her apartment; the jewels he bought that day were placed also within it—they were never fated to grace the fair form of Ione; they may be seen at this day among the disinterred treasures of Pompeii, in the chambers of the studio at Naples.

"Come hither, Nydia; put down thy vase, and come hither. Thou must take this chain from me—stay—there, I have put it on.—There, Servilius, does it not become her?"

"Wonderfully!" answered the jeweller: for jewellers were well-bred and flattering men, even at that day. "But when these ear-rings glitter in the ears of the noble Ione, *then,* by Bacchus! you will see whether my art adds anything to beauty."

"Ione?" repeated Nydia, who had hitherto acknowledged by smiles and blushes the gift of Glaucus.

"Yes," replied the Athenian, carelessly toying with the

gems; "I am choosing a present for Ione, but there are none worthy of her."

He was startled as he spoke by an abrupt gesture of Nydia; she tore the chain violently from her neck, and dashed it on the ground. "How is this? What, Nydia, dost thou not like the bauble? art thou offended?"

"You treat me ever as a slave and as a child," replied the Thessalian, with a breast heaving with ill-suppressed sobs, and she turned hastily away to the opposite corner of the garden.

Glaucus did not attempt to follow, or to soothe; he was offended; he continued to examine the jewels and to comment on their fashion—to object to this and to praise that, and finally to be talked by the merchant into buying all; the safest plan for a lover, and a plan that any one will do right to adopt,—provided always that he can obtain an Ione!

When he had completed his purchase and dismissed the jeweller, he retired into his chamber, dressed, mounted his chariot, and went to Ione. He thought no more of the blind girl, or her offence; he had forgotten both the one and the other.

He spent the forenoon with his beautiful Neapolitan, repaired thence to the baths, supped (if, as we have said before, we can justly so translate the three o'clock *cœna* of the Romans) alone, and abroad, for Pompeii had its restaurateurs: —and returning home to change his dress ere he again repaired to the house of Ione, he passed the peristyle, but with the absorbed reverie and absent eyes of a man in love, and did not note the form of the poor blind girl, bending exactly in the same place where he had left her. But though he saw her not, her ear recognized at once the sound of his step. She had been counting the moments to his return. He had scarcely entered his favorite chamber, which opened on the peristyle, and seated himself musingly on his couch, when he felt his robe timorously touched, and turning, he beheld Nydia kneeling before him, and holding up to him a handful of flowers— a gentle and appropriate peace-offering;—her eyes, darkly upheld to his own, streamed with tears.

"I have offended thee," said she, sobbing, "and for the first time. I would die rather than cause thee a moment's pain

—say that thou wilt forgive me. See! I have taken up the chain; I have put it on; I will never part from it—it is thy gift."

"My dear Nydia," returned Glaucus, and raising her, he kissed her forehead, "think of it no more! But why, my child, wert thou so suddenly angry? I could not divine the cause!"

"Do not ask!" said she, coloring violently. "I am a thing full of faults and humors; you know I am but a child—you say so often: is it from a child that you can expect a reason for every folly?"

"But, prettiest, you will soon be a child no more; and if you would have us treat you as a woman, you must learn to govern these singular impulses and gales of passion. Think not I chide: no, it is for your happiness only I speak."

"It is true," said Nydia, "I must learn to govern myself. I must hide, I must suppress, my heart. This is a woman's task and duty; methinks her virtue is hypocrisy."

"Self-control is not deceit, my Nydia," returned the Athenian; "and that is the virtue necessary alike to man and to woman: it is the true senatorial toga, the badge of the dignity it covers."

"Self-control! self-control! Well, well, what you say is right! When I listen to you, Glaucus, my wildest thoughts grow calm and sweet, and a delicious serenity falls over me. Advise, ah! guide me ever, my preserver!"

"Thy affectionate heart will be thy best guide, Nydia, when thou hast learned to regulate its feelings."

"Ah! that will be never," sighed Nydia, wiping away her tears. "Say not so: the first effort is the only difficult one."

"I have made many first efforts," answered Nydia, innocently. "But you, my Mentor, do you find it so easy to control yourself? Can you conceal, can you even regulate, your love for Ione?"

"Love! dear Nydia: ah! that is quite another matter," answered the young preceptor.

"I thought so!" returned Nydia, with a melancholy smile. "Glaucus, wilt thou take my poor flowers? Do with them as thou wilt—thou canst give them to Ione," added she, with a little hesitation.

"Nay, Nydia," answered Glaucus, kindly, divining something of jealousy in her language, though he imagined it only the jealousy of a vain and susceptible child; "I will not give thy pretty flowers to any one. Sit here and weave them into a garland; I will wear it this night: it is not the first those delicate fingers have woven for me."

The poor girl delightedly sat down beside Glaucus. She drew from her girdle a ball of the many-colored threads, or rather slender ribands, used in the weaving of garlands, and which (for it was her professional occupation) she carried constantly with her, and began quickly and gracefully to commence her task. Upon her young cheeks the tears were already dried, a faint but happy smile played round her lips;—childlike, indeed, she was sensible only of the joy of the present hour: she was reconciled to Glaucus: he had forgiven her—she was beside him—he played caressingly with her silken hair—his breath fanned her cheek,—Ione, the cruel Ione, was not by—none other demanded, divided, his care. Yes, she was happy and forgetful; it was one of the few moments in her brief and troubled life that it was sweet to treasure, to recall. As the butterfly, allured by the winter sun, basks for a little while in the sudden light, ere yet the wind awakes and the frost comes on, which shall blast it before the eve,—she rested beneath a beam, which, by contrast with the wonted skies, was not chilling; and the instinct which should have warned her of its briefness, bade her only gladden in its smile.

"Thou hast beautiful locks," said Glaucus. "They were once, I ween well, a mother's delight."

Nydia sighed; it would seem that she had not been born a slave; but she ever shunned the mention of her parentage, and, whether obscure or noble, certain it is that her birth was never known by her benefactors, nor by any one in those distant shores, even to the last. The child of sorrow and of mystery, she came and went as some bird that enters our chamber for a moment; we see it flutter for a while before us, we know not whence it flew or to what region it escapes.

Nydia sighed, and after a short pause, without answering the remark, said,—"But do I weave too many roses in my wreath, Glaucus? They tell me it is thy favorite flower."

"And ever favored, my Nydia, be it by those who have the soul of poetry: it is the flower of love, of festivals; it is also the flower we dedicate to silence and to death; it blooms on our brows in life, while life be worth the having; it is scattered above our sepulchre when we are no more."

"Ah! would," said Nydia, "instead of this perishable wreath, that I could take thy web from the hand of the Fates, and insert the roses *there!*"

"Pretty one! thy wish is worthy of a voice so attuned to song; it is uttered in the spirit of song; and, whatever my doom, I thank thee."

"Whatever thy doom! is it not already destined to all things bright and fair? My wish was vain. The Fates will be as tender to thee as I should."

"It might not be so, Nydia, were it not for love. While youth lasts, I may forget my country for a while. But what Athenian, in his graver manhood, can think of Athens as she was, and be contented that *he* is happy while *she* is fallen?— fallen, and for ever!" "And why for ever?"

"As ashes cannot be rekindled—as love once dead never can revive, so freedom departed from a people is never regained. But talk we not of these matters unsuited to thee."

"To me, oh! thou errest. I, too, have my sighs for Greece; my cradle was rocked at the feet of Olympus; the gods have left the mountain, but their traces may be seen—seen in the hearts of their worshippers, seen in the beauty of their clime: they tell me it *is* beautiful, and *I* have felt its airs, to which even these are harsh—its sun, to which these skies are chill. Oh! talk to me of Greece! Poor fool that I am, I can comprehend thee! and methinks, had I yet lingered on those shores, had I been a Grecian maid whose happy fate it was to love and to be loved, I myself could have armed my lover for another Marathon, a new Platæa. Yes, the hand that now weaves the roses should have woven thee the olive crown!"

"If such a day could come!" said Glaucus, catching the enthusiasm of the blind Thessalian, and half-rising.—"But no! the sun has set, and the night only bids us be forgetful,— and in forgetfulness be gay:—weave still the roses!"

But it was with a melancholy tone of forced gaiety that the Athenian uttered the last words: and sinking into a gloomy reverie, he was only wakened from it, a few minutes afterwards, by the voice of Nydia, as she sang in a low tone the following words, which he had once taught her.

THE APOLOGY FOR PLEASURE.

I.

"Who will assume the bays
    That the hero wore?
Wreaths on the Tomb of Days
    Gone evermore!
Who shall disturb the brave,
Or one leaf on their holy grave?
The laurel is vow'd to them,
Leave the bay on its sacred stem!
        But this, the rose, the fading rose,
        Alike for slave and freeman grows!

II.

If Memory sit beside the dead
    With tombs her only treasure;
If Hope is lost and Freedom fled,
    The more excuse for Pleasure.
Come, weave the wreath, the roses weave,
    The rose at least is ours;
To feeble hearts our fathers leave,
    In pitying scorn, the flowers!

III.

On the summit, worn and hoary,
Of Phyle's solemn hill,
The tramp of the brave is still!
And still in the saddening Mart,
The pulse of that mighty heart,
    Whose very blood was glory!
Glaucopis forsakes her own,
    The angry gods forget us;
But yet, the blue streams along,
Walk the feet of the silver Song;
And the night-bird wakes the moon;
And the bees in the blushing noon
    Haunt the heart of the old Hymettus!
We are fallen, but not forlorn,
    If something is left to cherish;
As Love was the earliest born;
    So Love is the last to perish.

IV.

Wreathe then the roses, wreathe
    The BEAUTIFUL still is ours,
While the stream shall flow, and the sky
    shall glow,

The BEAUTIFUL still is ours!
Whatever is fair, or soft, or bright,
In the lap of day or the arms of night,
Whispers our soul of Greece—of Greece,
And hushes our care with a voice of peace.
Wreathe then the roses, wreathe!
They tell me of earlier hours;
And I hear the heart of my Country breathe
From the lips of the Stranger's flowers."

CHAPTER V.

Nydia encounters Julia.—Interview of the heathen sister and converted brother.—
An Athenian's notion of Christianity.

"WHAT happiness to Ione! what bliss to be ever by the side of Glaucus, to hear his voice!—And *she* too can see him!"

Such was the soliloquy of the blind girl, as she walked alone and at twilight to the house of her new mistress, whither Glaucus had already preceded her. Suddenly she was interrupted in her fond thoughts by a female voice.

"Blind flower-girl, whither goest thou? There is no pannier under thine arm; hast thou sold all thy flowers?"

The person thus accosting Nydia was a lady of a handsome, but a bold and unmaidenly, countenance; it was Julia, the daughter of Diomed. Her veil was half raised as she spoke; she was accompanied by Diomed himself, and by a slave carrying a lantern before them—the merchant and his daughter were returning home from a supper at one of their neighbors'.

"Dost thou not remember my voice?" continued Julia. "I am the daughter of Diomed the wealthy."

"Ah! forgive me; yes, I recall the tones of your voice. No, noble Julia, I have no flowers to sell."

"I heard that thou wert purchased by the beautiful Greek, Glaucus; is that true, pretty slave?" asked Julia.

"I serve the Neapolitan, Ione," replied Nydia, evasively.

"Ah! and it is true, then——"

"Come, come!" interrupted Diomed, with his cloak up to his mouth, "the night grows cold; I cannot stay here while you prate to that blind girl: come, let her follow you home, if you wish to speak to her."

"Do, child," said Julia, with the air of one not accustomed to be refused; "I have much to ask of thee: come."

"I cannot this night, it grows late," answered Nydia. "I must be at home; I am not free, noble Julia."

"What! the meek Ione will chide thee?—Ay, I doubt not she is a second Thalestris. But come, then, to-morrow: do—remember I have been thy friend of old."

"I will obey thy wishes," answered Nydia; and Diomed again impatiently summoned his daughter: she was obliged to proceed, with the main question she had desired to put to Nydia, unasked.

Meanwhile we return to Ione. The interval of time that had elapsed that day between the first and second visit of Glaucus had not been too gayly spent: she had received a visit from her brother. Since the night he had assisted in saving her from the Egyptian, she had not before seen him.

Occupied with his own thoughts,—thoughts of so serious and intense a nature,—the young priest had thought little of his sister: in truth, men perhaps of that fervent order of mind which is ever aspiring *above* earth, are but little prone to the earthlier affections; and it had been long since Apæcides had sought those soft and friendly interchanges of thought, those sweet confidences, which in his earlier youth had bound him to Ione, and which are so natural to that endearing connection which existed between them.

Ione, however, had not ceased to regret his estrangement: she attributed it, at present, to the engrossing duties of his severe fraternity. And often, amidst all her bright hopes, and her new attachment to her betrothed—often, when she thought of her brother's brow prematurely furrowed, his unsmiling lip, and bended frame, she sighed to think that the service of the gods could throw so deep a shadow over that earth which the gods created.

But this day when he visited her there was a strange calmness on his features, a more quiet and self-possessed expression on his sunken eyes, than she had marked for years. This apparent improvement was but momentary—it was a false calm, which the least breeze could ruffle.

"May the gods bless thee, my brother!" said she, embracing him. "The gods! Speak not thus vaguely; perchance there is but *one* God!" "My brother!"

"What if the sublime faith of the Nazarene be true? What if God be a monarch—One—Invisible—Alone? What if these numerous, countless deities, whose altars fill the earth, be but evil demons, seeking to wean us from the true creed? This may be the case, Ione!"

"Alas! can we believe it? or if we believed, would it not be a melancholy faith?" answered the Neapolitan. "What! all this beautiful world made only human!—the mountain disenchanted of its Oread—the waters of their Nymph—that beautiful prodigality of faith, which makes everything divine, consecrating the meanest flowers, bearing celestial whispers in the faintest breeze—wouldst thou deny this, and make the earth mere dust and clay? No, Apæcides; all that is brightest in our hearts is that very credulity which peoples the universe with gods."

Ione answered as a believer in the poesy of the old mythology would answer. We may judge by that reply how obstinate and hard the contest which Christianity had to endure among the heathens. The Graceful Superstition was never silent; every, the most household, action of their lives was entwined with it,—it was a portion of life itself, as the flowers are a part of the thyrsus. At every incident they recurred to a god, every cup of wine was prefaced by a libation: the very garlands on their thresholds were dedicated to some divinity; their ancestors themselves, made holy, presided as Lares over their hearth and hall. So abundant was belief with them, that in their own climes, at this hour, idolatry has never thoroughly been outrooted: it changes but its objects of worship; it appeals to innumerable saints where once it resorted to divinities; and it pours its crowds, in listening reverence, to oracles at the shrines of St. Januarius or St. Stephen, instead of to those of Isis or Apollo.

But these superstitions were not to the early Christians the object of contempt so much as of horror. They did not believe, with the quiet scepticism of the heathen philosopher, that the gods were inventions of the priests; nor even, with the vulgar, that, according to the dim light of history, they had been mortals like themselves. They imagined the heathen divinities to be evil spirits—they transplanted to Italy and to Greece the gloomy demons of India and the East; and in Jupiter or in

Mars they shuddered at the representative of Moloch or of Satan.

Apæcides had not yet adopted formally the Christian faith, but he was already on the brink of it. He already participated the doctrines of Olinthus—he already imagined that the lively imaginations of the heathen were the suggestions of the arch-enemy of mankind. The innocent and natural answer of Ione made him shudder. He hastened to reply vehemently, and yet so confusedly, that Ione feared for his reason more than she dreaded his violence.

"Ah, my brother!" said she, "these hard duties of thine have shattered thy very sense. Come to me, Apæcides, my brother, my own brother; give me thy hand, let me wipe the dew from thy brow;—chide me not now, I understand thee not; think only that Ione could not offend thee!"

"Ione," said Apæcides, drawing her towards him, and regarding her tenderly, "can I think that this beautiful form, this kind heart, may be destined to an eternity of torment?"

"Dii meliora! the gods forbid!" said Ione, in the customary form of words by which her contemporaries thought an omen might be averted.

The words, and still more the superstition they implied, wounded the ear of Apæcides. He rose, muttering to himself, turned from the chamber, then, stopping half-way, gazed wistfully on Ione, and extended his arms.

Ione flew to them in joy; he kissed her earnestly, and then he said,—

"Farewell, my sister! when we next meet, thou mayst be to me as nothing; take thou, then, this embrace—full yet of all the tender reminiscences of childhood, when faith and hope, creeds, customs, interests, objects, were the same to us. Now, the tie is to be broken!"

With these strange words he left the house.

The great and severest trial of the primitive Christians was indeed this; their conversion separated them from their dearest bonds. They could not associate with beings whose commonest actions, whose commonest forms of speech, were impregnated with idolatry. They shuddered at the blessing of love; to their ears it was uttered in a demon's name. This, their misfortune, was their strength; if it divided them from the rest of the world, it was to unite them proportionally to each other. They were men of iron who wrought forth the Word of God, and verily the bonds that bound them were of iron also!

Glaucus found Ione in tears; he had already assumed the sweet privilege to console. He drew from her a recital of her interview with her brother; but in her confused account of language, itself so confused to one not prepared for it, he was equally at a loss with Ione to conceive the intentions or the meaning of Apæcides.

"Hast thou ever heard much," asked she, "of this new sect of the Nazarenes, of which my brother spoke?"

"I have often heard enough of the votaries," returned Glaucus, "but of their exact tenets know I nought, save that in their doctrine there seemeth something preternaturally chilling and morose. They live apart from their kind; they affect to be shocked even at our simple uses of garlands; they have no sympathies with the cheerful amusements of life; they utter awful threats of the coming destruction of the world: they appear, in one word, to have brought their unsmiling and gloomy creed out of the cave of Trophonius. Yet," continued Glaucus, after a slight pause, "they have not wanted men of great power and genius, nor converts, even among the Areopagites of Athens. Well do I remember to have heard my father speak of one strange guest at Athens, many years ago; methinks his name was PAUL. My father was amongst a mighty crowd that gathered on one of our immemorial hills to hear this sage of the East expound: through the wide throng there rang not a single murmur!—the jest and the roar, with which our native orators are received, were hushed for him;—and when on the loftiest summit of that hill, raised above the breathless crowd below, stood this mysterious visitor, his mien and his countenance awed every heart, even before a sound left his lips. He was a man, I have heard my father say, of no tall stature, but of noble and impressive mien; his robes were dark and ample; the declining sun, for it was evening, shone aslant upon his form as it rose aloft, motionless and commanding; his countenance was much worn and marked, as of one who had braved alike misfortune and the sternest vicissitudes of many climes; but his eyes were bright with an almost unearthly fire; and when he raised his arm to speak, it was with the majesty of a man into whom the Spirit of a God hath rushed!

" 'Men of Athens!' he is reported to have said, 'I find amongst ye an altar with this inscription—To the unknown God. Ye worship in ignorance the same Deity I serve. To you *unknown* till now, to you be it now revealed.'

"Then declared that solemn man how this great Maker of all things, who had appointed unto man his several tribes and his various homes—the Lord of earth and the universal heaven, dwelt not in temples made with hands; that His presence, His spirit, were in the air we breathed:—our life and our being were with Him. 'Think you,' he cried, 'that the Invisible is like your statues of gold and marble? Think you that He needeth sacrifice from you: He who made heaven and earth?' Then spoke he of fearful and coming times, of the end of the world, of a second rising of the dead, whereof an assurance had been given to man in the resurrection of the mighty Being whose religion he came to preach.

"When he thus spoke, the long-pent murmur went forth, and the philosophers that were mingled with the people, muttered their sage contempt; there might you have seen the chilling frown of the Stoic, and the Cynic's sneer;—and the Epicurean, who believeth not even in our own Elysium, muttered a pleasant jest, and swept laughing through the crowd: but the deep heart of the people was touched and thrilled; and they trembled, though they knew not why, for verily the stranger had the voice and majesty of a man to whom 'The Unknown God' had committed the preaching of His faith."

Ione listened with rapt attention, and the serious and earnest manner of the narrator betrayed the impression that he himself had received from one who had been amongst the audience that on the hill of the heathen Mars had heard the first tidings of the word of Christ!

CHAPTER VI.

The porter—the girl—and the gladiator.

The door of Diomed's house stood open, and Medon, the old slave, sat at the bottom of the steps by which you ascended to the mansion. That luxurious mansion of the rich merchant of Pompeii is still to be seen just without the gates of the city, at the commencement of the Street of Tombs; it was a gay neighborhood, despite the dead. On the opposite side, but at some yards nearer the gate, was a spacious hostelry, at which those brought by business or by pleasure to Pompeii often stopped to refresh themselves. In the space before the entrance of the inn now stood wagons, and carts, and chariots, some just arrived, some just quitting, in all the bustle of an animated and popular resort of public entertainment. Before the door, some farmers, seated on a bench by a small circular table, were talking over their morning cups, on the affairs of their calling. On the side of the door itself was painted gaily and freshly the eternal sign of the chequers. By the roof of the inn stretched a terrace, on which some females, wives of the farmers above mentioned, were, some seated, some leaning over the railing, and conversing with their friends below. In a deep recess, at a little distance, was a covered seat, in which some two or three poorer travellers were resting themselves, and shaking the dust from their garments. On the other side stretched a wide space, originally the burial-ground of a more ancient race than the present denizens of Pompeii, and now converted into the Ustrinum, or place for the burning of the dead. Above this rose the terraces of a gay villa, half hid by trees. The tombs themselves, with their graceful and varied shapes, the flowers and the foliage that surrounded them, made no melancholy feature in the prospect. Hard by the gate of the city, in a small niche, stood the still form of the well-disciplined Roman sentry, the sun shining brightly on his polished crest, and the lance on which he leaned. The gate itself was divided into three arches, the centre one for vehicles, the others for the foot-passengers; and on either side rose the massive walls which girt the city, composed, patched, repaired at a thousand different epochs, according as war, time, or the earthquake, had shattered that vain protection. At frequent intervals rose square towers, whose summits broke in picturesque rudeness the regular line of the wall, and contrasted well with the modern buildings gleaming whitely by.

The curving road, which in that direction leads from Pompeii to Herculaneum, wound out of sight amidst hanging vines, above which frowned the sullen majesty of Vesuvius.

"Hast thou heard the news, old Medon?" said a young woman, with a pitcher in her hand, as she paused by Diomed's door to gossip a moment with the slave, ere she repaired to the neighboring inn to fill the vessel, and coquet with the travellers. "The news! what news?" said the slave, raising his eyes moodily from the ground. "Why, there passed through the gate this morning, no doubt ere thou wert well awake, such a visitor to Pompeii!" "Ay," said the slave, indifferently. "Yes, a present from the noble Pomponianous."

"A present! I thought thou saidst a visitor!"

"It is both visitor and present. Know, O dull and stupid! that it is a most beautiful young tiger, for our approaching games in the amphitheatre. Hear you that, Medon? Oh, what pleasure! I declare I shall not sleep a wink till I see it; they say it has such a roar!"

"Poor fool!" said Medon, sadly and cynically.

"Fool me no fool, old churl! It is a pretty thing, a tiger, especially if we could but find somebody for him to eat. We have now a lion and a tiger: only consider that, Medon! and, for want of two good criminals, perhaps we shall be forced to see them eat each other. By the by, your son is a gladiator, a handsome man and a strong; can you not persuade him to fight the tiger? Do now, you would oblige me mightily; nay, you would be a benefactor to the whole town."

"Vah! vah!" said the slave, with great asperity; "think of thine own danger ere thou thus pratest of my poor boy's death."

"My own danger!" said the girl, frightened and looking hastily round—"Avert the omen! let thy words fall on thine own head!" And the girl as she spoke touched a talisman suspended round her neck. " 'Thine own danger!' what danger threatens me?"

"Had the earthquake but a few nights since no warning?" said Medon. "Has it not a voice? Did it not say to us all, 'Prepare for death; the end of all things is at hand?' "

"Bah, stuff!" said the young woman, settling the folds of her tunic. "Now thou talkest as they say the Nazarenes talk—methinks thou art one of them. Well, I can prate with thee, grey croaker, no more: thou growest worse and worse—*Vale!* O Hercules, send us a man for the lion—and another for the tiger!

"Ho! ho! for the merry, merry show,
With a forest of faces in every row!
Lo, the swordsmen, bold as the son of Alcmæna,
Sweep, side by side, o'er the hushed arena;
Talk while you may—you will hold your breath
When they meet in the grasp of the glowing death.
Tramp, tramp, how gaily they go!
Ho! ho! for the merry, merry show!"

Chanting in a silver and clear voice this feminine ditty, and holding up her tunic from the dusty road, the young woman stepped lightly across to the crowded hostelry.

"My poor son!" said the slave, half aloud, "is it for things like this thou art to be butchered? Oh! faith of Christ, I could worship thee in all sincerity, were it but for the horror which thou inspirest for these bloody lists."

The old man's head sank dejectedly on his breast. He remained silent and absorbed, but every now and then with the corner of his sleeve he wiped his eyes. His heart was with his son; he did not see the figure that now approached from the gate with a quick step, and a somewhat fierce and reckless gait and carriage. He did not lift his eyes till the figure paused opposite the place where he sat, and with a soft voice addressed the name of—"Father!"

"My boy! my Lydon! is it indeed thou?" said the old man, joyfully. "Ah, thou wert present to my thoughts."

"I am glad to hear it, my father," said the gladiator, respectfully touching the knees and beard of the slave; "and soon may I be always present with thee, not in thoughts only."

"Yes, my son—but not in this world," replied the slave, mournfully.

"Talk not thus, O my sire! look cheerfully, for I feel so— I am sure that I shall win the day; and then, the gold I gain buys thy freedom. Oh! my father, it was but a few days since that I was taunted, by one too whom I would gladly have undeceived, for he is more generous than the rest of his equals. He is not Roman—he is of Athens—by him I was taunted with the lust of gain—when I demanded what sum was the prize of victory. Alas, he little knew the soul of Lydon!"

"My boy! my boy!" said the old slave, as, slowly ascending the steps, he conducted his son to his own little chamber, com-

municating with the entrance hall (which in this villa was
the peristyle, not the atrium) :—you may see it now: it is the
third door to the right on entering. (The first door conducts
to the staircase; the second is but a false recess, in which there
stood a statue of bronze.) "Generous, affectionate, pious as
are thy motives," said Medon, when they were thus secured
from observation, "thy deed itself is guilt: thou art to risk thy
blood for thy father's freedom—that might be forgiven;
but the prize of victory is the blood of another. Oh, *that* is a
deadly sin; no object can purify it. Forbear! forbear! rather
would I be a slave for ever than purchase liberty on such
terms!"

"Hush, my father!" replied Lydon, somewhat impatiently;
"thou hast picked up in this new creed of thine, of which I
pray thee not to speak to me, for the gods that gave me
strength denied me wisdom, and I understand not one word of
what thou often preachest to me,—thou hast picked up, I say,
in this new creed, some singular fantasies of right and wrong.
Pardon me, if I offend thee: but reflect! Against whom shall I
contend? Oh! couldst thou know those wretches with whom,
for thy sake, I assort, thou wouldst think I purified earth by
removing one of them. Beasts, whose very lips drop blood;
things, all savage, unprincipled in their very courage; ferocious, heartless, senseless; no tie of life can bind them: they
know not fear, it is true—but neither know they gratitude, nor
charity, nor love; they are made but for their own career, to
slaughter without pity, to die without dread! Can thy gods,
whosoever they be, look with wrath on a conflict with such as
these, and in such a cause? Oh, my father, wherever the powers above gaze down on earth, they behold no duty so sacred,
so sanctifying, as the sacrifice offered to an aged parent by
the piety of a grateful son!"

The poor old slave, himself deprived of the lights of
knowledge, and only late a convert to the Christian faith, knew
not with what arguments to enlighten an ignorance at once so
dark, and yet so beautiful in its error. His first impulse was to
throw himself on his son's breast—his next to start away—to
wring his hands; and in the attempt to reprove, his broken
voice lost itself in weeping.

"And if," resumed Lydon,—"if thy Deity (methinks thou

wilt own but one?) be indeed that benevolent and pitying Power which thou assertest Him to be, He will know also that thy very faith in Him first confirmed me in that determination thou blamest." "How! what mean you?" said the slave.

"Why, thou knowest that I, sold in my childhood as a slave, was set free at Rome by the will of my master, whom I had been fortunate enough to please. I hastened to Pompeii to see thee—I found thee already aged and infirm, under the yoke of a capricious and pampered lord—thou hadst lately adopted this new faith, and its adoption made thy slavery doubly painful to thee: it took away all the softening charm of custom, which reconciles us so often to the worst. Didst thou not complain to me, that thou wert compelled to offices that were not odious to thee as a slave, but guilty as a Nazarene? Didst thou not tell me that thy soul shook with remorse when thou wert compelled to place even a crumb of cake before the Lares that watch over yon impluvium? that thy soul was torn by a perpetual struggle? Didst thou not tell me, that even by pouring wine before the threshold, and calling on the name of some Grecian deity, thou didst fear thou wert incurring penalties worse than those of Tantalus, an eternity of torture more terrible than those of the Tartarian fields? Didst thou not tell me this? I wondered, I could not comprehend: nor, by Hercules! can I now: but I was thy son, and my sole task was to compassionate and relieve. Could I hear thy groans, could I witness thy mysterious horrors, thy constant anguish, and remain inactive? No! by the immortal gods! the thought struck me like light from Olympus! I had no money, but I had strength and youth—these were thy gifts—I could sell these in my turn for thee! I learned the amount of thy ransom—I learned that the usual prize of a victorious gladiator would doubly pay it. I became a gladiator—I linked myself with those accursed men, scorning, loathing, while I joined—I acquired their skill—blessed be the lesson!—it shall teach me to free my father!"

"Oh, that thou couldst hear Olinthus!" sighed the old man, more and more affected by the virtue of his son, but not less strongly convinced of the criminality of his purpose.

"I will hear the whole world talk, if thou wilt," answered the gladiator, gaily; "but not till thou art a slave no more. Beneath thy own roof, my father, thou shalt puzzle this dull brain all day long, ay, and all night too, if it give thee pleasure. Oh, such a spot as I have chalked out for thee!—it is one of the nine hundred and ninety-nine shops of old Julia Felix, in the sunny part of the city, where thou mayst bask before the door in the day—and I will sell the oil and the wine for thee, my father—and then, please Venus (or if it does not please her, since thou lovest not her name, it is all one to Lydon;) —then I say, perhaps thou mayst have a daughter, too, to tend thy grey hairs, and hear shrill voices at thy knee, that shall call thee 'Lydon's father!' Ah! we shall be so happy—the prize can purchase all. Cheer thee! cheer up, my sire;—And now I must away—day wears—the lanista waits me. Come! thy blessing!"

As Lydon thus spoke, he had already quitted the dark chamber of his father; and speaking eagerly, though in a whispered tone, they now stood at the same place in which we introduced the porter at his post.

"O bless thee! bless thee, my brave boy!" said Medon, fervently; "and may the great Power that reads all hearts see the nobleness of thine, and forgive its error!"

The tall shape of the gladiator passed swiftly down the path; the eyes of the slave followed its light but stately steps, till the last glimpse was gone: and then sinking once more on his seat, his eyes again fastened themselves on the ground. His form, mute and unmoving, as a thing of stone. His heart!—who, in our happier age, can even imagine its struggles—its commotion?

"May I enter?" said a sweet voice. "Is thy mistress Julia within?"

The slave mechanically motioned to the visitor to enter, but she who addressed him could not see the gesture—she repeated her question timidly, but in a louder voice.

"Have I not told thee!" said the slave, peevishly: "enter."

"Thanks," said the speaker, plaintively; and the slave, roused by the tone, looked up, and recognized the blind flower-girl. Sorrow can sympathize with affliction—he raised himself, and guided her steps to the head of the adjacent staircase (by which you descended to Julia's apartment), where, summoning a female slave, he consigned to her the charge of the blind girl.

CHAPTER VII.

The dressing-room of a Pompeian beauty.—Important conversation between Julia and Nydia.

THE elegant Julia sat in her chamber, with her slaves around her;—like the cubiculum which adjoined it, the room was small, but much larger than the usual apartments appropriated to sleep, which were so diminutive, that few who have not seen the bed-chambers, even in the gayest mansions, can form any notion of the petty pigeon-holes in which the citizens of Pompeii evidently thought it desirable to pass the night. But, in fact, "bed" with the ancients was not that grave, serious, and important part of domestic mysteries which it is with us. The couch itself was more like a very narrow and small sofa, light enough to be transported easily, and by the occupant himself, from place to place; and it was, no doubt, constantly shifted from chamber to chamber, according to the caprices of the inmate, or the changes of the season; for that side of the house which was crowded in one month, might, perhaps, be carefully avoided in the next. There was also among the Italians of that period a singular and fastidious apprehension of too much daylight; their darkened chambers, which first appear to us the result of a negligent architecture, were the effect of the most elaborate study. In their porticos and gardens, they courted the sun whenever it so pleased their luxurious tastes. In the interior of their houses they sought rather the coolness and the shade.

Julia's apartment at that season was in the lower part of the house, immediately beneath the state-rooms above, and looking upon the garden, with which it was on a level. The wide door, which was glazed, alone admitted the morning rays: yet her eye, accustomed to a certain darkness, was sufficiently acute to perceive exactly what colors were the most becoming—what shade of the delicate rouge gave the brightest beam to her dark glance, and the most youthful freshness to her cheek.

On the table, before which she sat, was a small and circular
mirror of the most polished steel: round which, in precise
order, were ranged the cosmetics and the unguents—the perfumes and the paints—the jewels and the combs—the ribands
and the gold pins, which were destined to add to the natural
attractions of beauty the assistance of art and the capricious
allurements of fashion. Through the dimness of the room
glowed brightly the vivid and various colorings of the wall, in
all the dazzling frescoes of Pompeian taste. Before the dress-
ing-table, and under the feet of Julia, was spread a carpet,
woven from the looms of the East. Near at hand, on another
table, was a silver basin and ewer; an extinguished lamp, of
most exquisite workmanship, in which the artist had represented a Cupid reposing under the spreading branches of a
myrtle-tree; and a small roll of papyrus, containing the softest elegies of Tibullus. Before the door, which communicated
with the cubiculum, hung a curtain richly broidered with gold
flowers. Such was the dressing room of a beauty eighteen
centuries ago.

The fair Julia leaned indolently back on her seat, while
the ornatrix (*i. e.* hair-dresser) slowly piled, one above the
other, a mass of small curls: dexterously weaving the false
with the true, and carrying the whole fabric to a height that
seemed to place the head rather at the centre than the summit
of the human form.

Her tunic, of a deep amber, which well set off her dark
hair and somewhat embrowned complexion, swept in ample
folds to her feet, which were cased in slippers, fastened
round the slender ankle by white thongs; while a profusion
of pearls were embroidered in the slipper itself, which was of
purple, and turned slightly upward, as do the Turkish slippers
at this day. An old slave, skilled by long experience in all the
arcana of the toilet, stood beside the hair-dresser, with the
broad and studded girdle of her mistress over her arm, and
giving, from time to time (mingled with judicious flattery to
the lady herself), instructions to the mason of the ascending
pile.

"Put that pin rather more to the right—lower—stupid
one! Do you not observe how even those beautiful eyebrows
are?—One would think you were dressing Corinna, whose
face is all of one side. Now put in the flowers—what, fool!—

not that dull pink—you are not suiting colors to the dim cheek of Chloris: it must be the brightest flowers that can alone suit the cheek of the young Julia."

"Gently!" said the lady, stamping her small foot violently: "you pull my hair as if you were plucking up a weed!"

"Dull thing!" continued the directress of the ceremony. "Do you not know how delicate is your mistress?—you are not dressing the coarse horsehair of the widow Fulvia. Now, then, the riband—that's right. Fair Julia, look in the mirror; saw you ever any thing so lovely as yourself?"

When after innumerable comments, difficulties and delays, the intricate tower was at length completed, the next preparation was that of giving to the eyes the soft languish, produced by a dark powder applied to the lids and brows; a small patch cut in the form of a crescent, skilfully placed by the rosy lips, attracted attention to their dimples, and to the teeth, to which already every art had been applied in order to heighten the dazzle of their natural whiteness.

To another slave, hitherto idle, was now consigned the charge of arranging the jewels—the ear-rings of pearl (two to each ear)—the massive bracelets of gold—the chain formed of rings of the same metal, to which a talisman cut in crystals was attached—the graceful buckle on the left shoulder, in which was set an exquisite cameo of Psyche—the girdle of purple riband, richly wrought with threads of gold, and clasped by interlacing serpents—and lastly, the various rings fitted to every joint of the white and slender fingers. The toilet was now arranged, according to the last mode of Rome. The fair Julia regarded herself with a last gaze of complacent vanity, and reclining again upon her seat, she bade the youngest of her slaves, in a listless tone, read to her the enamoured couplets of Tibullus. This lecture was still proceeding, when a female slave admitted Nydia into the presence of the lady of the place.

"*Salve,* Julia!" said the flower-girl, arresting her steps within a few paces from the spot where Julia sat, and crossing her arms upon her breast. "I have obeyed your commands."

"You have done well, flower-girl," answered the lady. "Approach—you may take a seat." One of the slaves placed a stool by Julia, and Nydia seated herself.

Julia looked hard at the Thessalian for some moments

in rather an embarrassed silence. She then motioned her attendants to withdraw, and to close the door. When they were alone, she said, looking mechanically from Nydia, and forgetful that she was with one who could not observe her countenance,—"You serve the Neapolitan, Ione?" "I am with her at present," answered Nydia. "Is she as handsome as they say?" "I know not," replied Nydia. "How can *I* judge?"

"Ah! I should have remembered. But thou hast ears, if not eyes. Do thy fellow-slaves tell thee she is handsome? Slaves talking with one another forget to flatter even their mistress."

"They tell me that she is beautiful."

"Hem!—say they that she is tall?" "Yes."

"Why, so am I.—Dark-haired?" "I have heard so."

"So am I. And doth Glaucus visit her much?"

"Daily," returned Nydia, with a half-suppressed sigh.

"Daily, indeed! Does he find her handsome?"

"I should think so, since they are so soon to be wedded."

"Wedded!" cried Julia, turning pale even through the false roses on her cheek, and starting from her couch. Nydia did not, of course, perceive the emotion she had caused. Julia remained a long time silent; but her heaving breast and flashing eyes would have betrayed, to one who *could* have seen, the wound her vanity sustained.

"They tell me thou art a Thessalian," said she, at last breaking silence. "And truly!"

"Thessaly is the land of magic and of witches, of talismans and of love-philtres," said Julia. "It has ever been celebrated for its sorcerers," returned Nydia timidly. "Knowest thou, then, blind Thessalian, of any love-charms?" "I?" said the flower-girl, coloring; "*I!* how should I? No, assuredly not!"

"The worse for thee; I could have given thee gold enough to have purchased thy freedom hadst thou been more wise."

"But what," asked Nydia, "can induce the beautiful and wealthy Julia to ask that question of her servant? Has she not money, and youth, and loveliness? Are *they* not love-charms enough to dispense with magic?"

"To all but one person in the world," answered Julia, haughtily: "but methinks thy blindness is infectious; and—— But no matter." "And that one person?" said Nydia, eagerly.

"Is *not* Glaucus," replied Julia, with the customary deceit of her sex. "Glaucus—no!"

Nydia drew her breath more freely, and after a short pause Julia recommenced.

"But talking of Glaucus, and his attachment to this Neapolitan, reminded me of the influence of love-spells, which, for aught I know or care, she may have exercised upon him. Blind girl, I love, and—shall Julia live to say it?—am loved not in return! This humbles—nay, not *humbles*—but it *stings* my pride. I would see this ingrate at my feet—not in order that I might raise, but that I might spurn him. When they told me thou wert Thessalian, I imagined thy young mind might have learned the dark secrets of thy clime."

"Alas! no," murmured Nydia; "would it had!"

"Thanks, at least, for that kindly wish," said Julia, unconscious of what was passing in the breast of the flower-girl.

"But tell me,—thou hearest the gossip of slaves, always prone to these dim beliefs; always ready to apply to sorcery for their own low loves,—hast thou ever heard of any Eastern magician in this city, who possesses the art of which thou art ignorant? No vain chiromancer, no juggler of the market-place, but some more potent and mighty magician of India or of Egypt?"

"Of Egypt?—yes!" said Nydia, shuddering. "What Pompeian has not heard of Arbaces?"

"Arbaces! true," replied Julia, grasping at the recollection. "They say he is a man above all the petty and false impostures of dull pretenders,—that he is versed in the learning of the stars, and the secrets of the ancient Nox; why not in the mysteries of love?"

"If there be one magician living whose art is above that of others, it is that dread man," answered Nydia; and she felt her talisman while she spoke.

"He is too wealthy to divine for money?" continued Julia, sneeringly. "Can I not visit him?"

"It is an evil mansion for the young and the beautiful," replied Nydia. "I have heard, too, that he languishes in——"

"An evil mansion!" said Julia, catching only the first sentence. "Why so?" "The orgies of his midnight leisure are impure and polluted—at least, so says rumor."

"By Ceres, by Pan, and by Cybele! thou dost but provoke

my curiosity, instead of exciting my fears," returned the wayward and pampered Pompeian. "I will seek and question him of his lore. If to these orgies love be admitted—why the more likely that he knows its secrets!"

Nydia did not answer. "I will seek him this very day," resumed Julia; "nay, why not this very hour?"

"At daylight, and in his present state, thou hast assuredly the less to fear," answered Nydia, yielding to her own sudden and secret wish to learn if the dark Egyptian were indeed possessed of those spells to rivet and attract love, of which the Thessalian had so often heard.

"And who dare insult the rich daughter of Diomed?" said Julia, haughtily. "I will go." "May I visit thee afterwards to learn the result?" asked Nydia, anxiously.

"Kiss me for thy interest in Julia's honor," answered the lady. "Yes, assuredly. This eve we sup abroad—come hither at the same hour to-morrow, and thou shalt know all: I may have to employ thee too; but enough for the present. Stay, take this bracelet for the new thought thou hast inspired me with; remember, if thou servest Julia, she is grateful and she is generous."

"I cannot take thy present," said Nydia, putting aside the bracelet; "but young as I am, I can sympathize unbought with those who love—and love in vain."

"Sayest thou so!" returned Julia. "Thou speakest like a free woman—and thou shalt yet be free—farewell!"

CHAPTER VIII.

Julia seeks Arbaces.—The result of that interview.

ARBACES was seated in a chamber, which opened on a kind of balcony or portico, that fronted his garden. His cheek was pale and worn with the sufferings he had endured, but his iron frame had already recovered from the severest effects of that accident which had frustrated his fell designs in the moment of victory. The air that came fragrantly to his brow revived his languid senses, and the blood circulated more freely than it had done for days through his shrunken veins.

"So, then," thought he, "the storm of fate has broken and

blown over,—the evil which my lore predicted, threatening life itself, has chanced—and yet I live! It came as the stars foretold; and now the long, bright, and prosperous career which was to succeed that evil, if I survived it, smiles beyond: I have passed—I have subdued the latest danger of my destiny. Now I have but to lay out the gardens of my future fate—unterrified and secure. First, then, of all my pleasures, even before that of love, shall come revenge! This boy Greek—who has crossed my passion—thwarted my designs—baffled me even when the blade was about to drink his accursed blood—shall not a second time escape me! But for the method of my vengeance? Of that let me ponder well! Oh! Até, if thou art indeed a goddess, fill me with thy direst inspiration!" The Egyptian sank into an intent reverie, which did not seem to present to him any clear or satisfactory suggestions. He changed his position restlessly, as he revolved scheme after scheme, which no sooner occurred than it was dismissed; several times he struck his breast and groaned aloud, with the desire of vengeance, and a sense of his impotence to accomplish it. While thus absorbed, a boy slave timidly entered the chamber.

A female, evidently of rank, from her dress and that of the single slave who attended her, waited below and sought an audience with Arbaces.

"A female!" his heart beat quick. "Is she young?"

"Her face is concealed by her veil; but her form is slight, yet round as that of youth."

"Admit her," said the Egyptian; for a moment his vain heart dreamed the stranger might be Ione.

The first glance of the visitor now entering the apartment sufficed to undeceive so erring a fancy. True, she was about the same height as Ione, and perhaps the same age—true, she was finely and richly formed—but where was that undulating and ineffable grace which accompanied every motion of the peerless Neapolitan—the chaste and decorous garb, so simple even in the care of its arrangement—the dignified, yet bashful step—the majesty of womanhood and its modesty?

"Pardon me that I rise with pain," said Arbaces, gazing on the stranger: "I am still suffering from recent illness."

"Do not disturb thyself, O great Egyptian!" returned Julia, seeking to disguise the fear she already experienced beneath the ready resort of flattery; "and forgive an unfortunate female, who seeks consolation from thy wisdom."

"Draw near, fair stranger," said Arbaces; "and speak without apprehension or reserve."

Julia placed herself on a seat beside the Egyptian, and wonderingly gazed around an apartment whose elaborate and costly luxuries shamed even the ornate enrichment of her father's mansion; fearfully, too, she regarded the hieroglyphical inscriptions on the walls—the faces of the mysterious images, which at every corner gazed upon her—the tripod at a little distance—and, above all, the grave and remarkable countenance of Arbaces himself: a long white robe, like a veil, half covered his raven locks, and flowed to his feet; his face was made even more impressive by its present paleness; and his dark and penetrating eyes seemed to pierce the shelter of her veil, and explore the secrets of her vain and unfeminine soul.

"And what," said his low, deep voice, "brings thee, O maiden! to the house of the Eastern stranger?" "His fame," replied Julia. "In what?" said he, with a strange and slight smile. "Canst thou ask, O wise Arbaces? Is not thy knowledge the very gossip theme of Pompeii?"

"Some little lore have I, indeed, treasured up," replied Arbaces; "but in what can such serious and sterile secrets benefit the ear of beauty?"

"Alas!" said Julia, a little cheered by the accustomed accents of adulation; "does not sorrow fly to wisdom for relief, and they who love unrequitedly, are not they the chosen victims of grief?"

"Ha!" said Arbaces, "can unrequited love be the lot of so fair a form, whose modelled proportions are visible even beneath the folds of thy graceful robe? Deign, O maiden! to lift thy veil, that I may see at least if the face correspond in loveliness with the form."

Not unwilling, perhaps, to exhibit her charms, and thinking they were likely to interest the magician in her fate, Julia, after some slight hesitation, raised her veil, and revealed a beauty which, but for art, had been indeed attractive to the fixed gaze of the Egyptian.

"Thou comest to me for advice in unhappy love," said he;

"well, turn that face on the ungrateful one: what other love-charm can I give thee?"

"Oh, cease these courtesies!" said Julia; "it *is* a love-charm, indeed, that I would ask from thy skill?"

"Fair stranger!" replied Arbaces, somewhat scornfully, "love-spells are not among the secrets I have wasted the midnight oil to attain."

"Is it indeed so? Then pardon me, great Arbaces, and farewell."

"Stay," said Arbaces, who, despite his passion for Ione, was not unmoved by the beauty of his visitor; and had he been in the flush of a more assumed health, might have attempted to console the fair Julia by other means than those of supernatural wisdom,—

"Stay; although I confess that I have left the witchery of philtres and potions to those whose trade is in such knowledge, yet am I myself not so dull to beauty but that in earlier youth I may have employed them in my own behalf. I may give thee advice, at least, if thou wilt be candid with me. Tell me then, first, art thou unmarried, as thy dress betokens?"

"Yes," said Julia.

"And, being unblest with fortune, wouldst thou allure some wealthy suitor?" "I am richer than he who disdains me."

"Strange and more strange! And thou lovest him who loves not thee?"

"I know not if I love him," answered Julia, haughtily; "but I know that I would see myself triumph over a rival—I would see him who rejected me my suitor—I would see her whom he has preferred, in her turn despised."

"A natural ambition and a womanly," said the Egyptian, in a tone too grave for irony. "Yet more, fair maiden; wilt thou confide to me the name of thy lover? Can he be Pompeian, and despise wealth, even if blind to beauty?"

"He is of Athens," answered Julia, looking down.

"Ha!" cried the Egyptian, impetuously, as the blood rushed to his cheek; "there is but one Athenian, young and noble, in Pompeii. Can it be Glaucus of whom thou speakest!"

"Ah! betray me not—so indeed they call him."

The Egyptian sank back, gazing vacantly on the averted face of the merchant's daughter, and muttering only to himself:—this conference, with which he had hitherto only trifled,

amusing himself with the credulity and vanity of his visitor—
might it not minister to his revenge?

"I see thou canst assist me not," said Julia, offended by his
continued silence; "guard at least my secret. Once more, farewell!"

"Maiden," said the Egyptian, in an earnest and serious
tone, "thy suit hath touched me—I will minister to thy will.
Listen to me: I have not myself dabbled in these lesser mysteries, but I know one who hath. At the base of Vesuvius, less
than a league from the city, there dwells a powerful witch;
beneath the rank dews of the new moon, she has gathered the
herbs which possess the virtue to chain Love in eternal fetters.
Her art can bring thy lover to thy feet. Seek her, and mention
to her the name of Arbaces; she fears that name, and will give
thee her most potent philtres."

"Alas!" answered Julia, "I know not the road to the home
of her whom thou speakest of: the way, short though it be, is
long to traverse for a girl who leaves, unknown, the house of
her father. The country is entangled with wild vines, and
dangerous with precipitous caverns. I dare not trust to mere
strangers to guide me; the reputation of women of my rank is
easily tarnished—and though I care not who knows that I
love Glaucus, I would not have it imagined that I obtained his
love by a spell."

"Were I but three days advanced in health," said the
Egyptian, rising and walking (as if to try his strength) across
the chamber, but with irregular and feeble steps, "I myself
would accompany thee.—Well, thou must wait."

"But Glaucus is soon to wed that hated Neapolitan."

"Wed!"

"Yes; in the early part of next month."

"So soon! Art thou well advised of this?"

"From the lips of her own slave."

"It shall not be!" said the Egyptian, impetuously. "Fear
nothing, Glaucus shall be thine. Yet how, when thou obtainest
it, canst thou administer to him this potion?"

"My father has invited him, and, I believe, the Neapolitan
also, to a banquet, on the day following to-morrow: I shall
then have the opportunity to administer it."

"So be it!" said the Egyptian, with eyes flashing such

fierce joy, that Julia's gaze sank trembling beneath them. "To-morrow eve, then, order thy litter:—thou hast one at thy command?"

"Surely—yes," returned the purse-proud Julia.

"Order thy litter—at two miles' distance from the city is a house of entertainment, frequented by the wealthier Pompeians, from the excellence of its baths, and the beauty of its gardens. There canst thou pretend only to shape thy course—there, ill or dying, I will meet thee by the statue of Silenus, in the copse that skirts the garden; and I myself will guide thee to the witch. Let us wait till, with the evening star, the goats of the herdsmen are gone to rest; when the dark twilight conceals us, and none shall cross our steps. Go home, and fear not. By Hades, swears Arbaces, the sorcerer of Egypt, that Ione shall never wed with Glaucus!"

"And that Glaucus shall be mine?" added Julia, filling up the incompleted sentence.

"Thou hast said it!" replied Arbaces; and Julia, half frightened at this unhallowed appointment, but urged on by jealousy and the pique of rivalship, even more than love, resolved to fulfil it.

Left alone, Arbaces burst forth,—

"Bright stars that never lie, yet already begin the execution of your promises—success in love, and victory over foes, for the rest of my smooth existence. In the very hour when my mind could devise no clue to the goal of vengeance, have ye sent this fair fool for my guide?" He paused in deep thought. "Yes," said he again, but in a calmer voice; "I could not myself have given to her the poison, that shall be indeed a philtre! —his death might be thus tracked to my door. But the witch —ay, *there* is the fit, the natural agent of my designs!"

He summoned one of his slaves, bade him hasten to track the steps of Julia, and acquaint himself with her name and condition. This done, he stepped forth into the portico. The skies were serene and clear; but he, deeply read in the signs of their various changes, beheld in one mass of cloud, far on the horizon, which the wind began slowly to agitate, that a storm was brooding above.

"It is like my vengeance," said he, as he gazed; "the sky is clear, but the cloud moves on."

CHAPTER IX.

A storm in the south.—The witch's cavern.

IT was when the heats of noon died gradually away from the earth, that Glaucus and Ione went forth to enjoy the cooled and grateful air. At that time, various carriages were in use among the Romans; the one most used by the richer citizens, when they required no companion in their excursions, was the *biga,* already described in the early portion of this work; that appropriated to the matrons, was termed *carpentum,* which had commonly two wheels; the ancients used also a sort of litter, a vast sedan-chair, more commodiously arranged than the modern, inasmuch as the occupant thereof could lie down at ease, instead of being perpendicularly and stiffly jostled up and down. There was another carriage, used both for travelling and for excursions in the country; it was commodious, containing three or four persons with ease, having a covering which could be raised at pleasure; and, in short, answering very much the purpose of (though very different in shape from) the modern britska. It was a vehicle of this description that the lovers, accompanied by one female slave of Ione, now used in their excursion. About ten miles from the city, there was at that day an old ruin, the remains of a temple, evidently Grecian; and as for Glaucus and Ione everything Grecian possessed an interest, they had agreed to visit these ruins: it was thither they were now bound.

Their road lay among vines and olive-groves; till, winding more and more towards the higher ground of Vesuvius, the path grew rugged; the mules moved slowly, and with labor; and at every opening in the wood they beheld those grey and horrent caverns indenting the parched rock, which Strabo has described; but which the various revolutions of time and the volcano have removed from the present aspect of the mountain. The sun, sloping towards his descent, cast long and deep shadows over the mountain; here and there they still heard the rustic reed of the shepherd amongst copses of the beechwood

198

and wild-oak. Sometimes they marked the form of the silk-haired and graceful capella, with its wreathing horn and bright grey eye—which, still beneath Ausonian skies, recalls the eclogues of Maro—browsing half-way up the hills; and the grapes, already purple with the smiles of the deepening summer, glowed out from the arched festoons, which hung pendent from tree to tree. Above them, light clouds floated in the serene heavens, sweeping so slowly athwart the firmament that they scarcely seemed to stir; while, on their right they caught, ever and anon, glimpses of the waveless sea, with some light bark skimming its surface; and the sunlight breaking over the deep in those countless and softest hues so peculiar to that delicious sea.

"How beautiful!" said Glaucus, in a half-whispered tone, "is that expression by which we call Earth our Mother! With what a kindly equal love she pours her blessings upon her children! and even to those sterile spots to which Nature has denied beauty, she yet contrives to dispense her smiles; witness the arbutus and the vine, which she wreathes over the arid and burning soil of yon extinct volcano. Ah! in such an hour and scene as this, well might we imagine that the laughing face of the Faun should peep forth from those green festoons; or, that we might trace the steps of the Mountain Nymph through the thickest mazes of the glade. But the Nymphs ceased, beautiful Ione, when *thou* wert created!"

There is no tongue that flatters like a lover's; and yet, in the exaggeration of his feelings, flattery seems to him commonplace. Strange and prodigal exuberance, which soon exhausts itself by overflowing!

They arrived at the ruins: they examined them with that fondness with which we trace the hallowed and household vestiges of our own ancestry—they lingered there till Hesperus appeared in the rosy heavens; and then returning homeward in the twilight, they were more silent than they had been; for, in the shadow and beneath the stars, they felt more oppressively their mutual love.

It was at this time that the storm which the Egyptian had predicted began to creep visibly over them. At first, a low and distant thunder gave warning of the approaching conflict of the elements; and then rapidly rushed above the dark ranks of the serried clouds. The suddenness of storms in that climate is something almost preternatural, and might well suggest to early superstition the notion of a divine agency—a few large drops broke heavily among the boughs that half overhung their path, and then, swift and intolerably bright, the forked lightning darted across their very eyes, and was swallowed up by the increasing darkness. "Swifter, good Carrucarius!" cried Glaucus to the driver; "the tempest comes on apace."

The slave urged on the mules—they went swift over the uneven and stony road—the clouds thickened, near and more near broke the thunder, and fast rushed the dashing rain.

"Dost thou fear?" whispered Glaucus, as he sought excuse in the storm to come nearer to Ione.

"Not with thee," said she, softly.

At that instant, the carriage, fragile and ill-contrived (as, despite their graceful shapes, were, for practical uses, most of such inventions at that time), struck violently into a deep rut, over which lay a log of fallen wood; the driver, with a curse, stimulated his mules yet faster for the obstacle, the wheel was torn from the socket, and the carriage suddenly overset.

Glaucus quickly extricating himself from the vehicle, hastened to assist Ione, who was fortunately unhurt; with some difficulty they raised the carruca (or carriage), and found that it ceased any longer even to afford them shelter; the springs that fastened the covering were snapped asunder, and the rain poured fast and fiercely into the interior.

In this dilemma, what was to be done? They were yet some distance from the city—no house, no aid, seemed near.

"There is," said the slave, "a smith about a mile off; I could seek him, and he might fasten at least the wheel to the carruca—but, Jupiter! how the rain beats! my mistress will be wet before I come back."

"Run thither at least," said Glaucus; "we must find the best shelter we can till you return."

The lane was overshadowed with trees, beneath the amplest of which Glaucus drew Ione. He endeavored, by stripping his own cloak, to shield her yet more from the rapid rain; but it descended with a fury that broke through all puny obstacles: and suddenly, while Glaucus was yet whispering courage to his beautiful charge, the lightning struck one of the trees immediately before them, and split with a mighty crash its huge trunk in twain. This awful incident apprised them of the danger they braved in their present shelter, and Glaucus looked anxiously round for some less perilous place of refuge. "We are now," said he, "half-way up the ascent of Vesuvius; there ought to be some cavern, or hollow in the vine-clad rocks, could we but find it, in which the deserting Nymphs have left a shelter." While thus saying he moved from the trees, and looking wistfully towards the mountain, discovered through the advancing gloom a red and tremulous light at no considerable distance. "That must come," said he, "from the hearth of some shepherd or vine-dresser—it will guide us to some hospitable retreat. Wilt thou stay here, while I—yet no—that would be to leave thee to danger."

"I will go with you cheerfully," said Ione. "Open as the space seems. it is better than the treacherous shelter of these boughs."

Half leading, half carrying Ione, Glaucus, accompanied by the trembling female slave, advanced towards the light, which yet burnt red and steadfastly. At length the space was no longer open; wild vines entangled their steps, and hid from them, save by imperfect intervals, the guiding beam. But faster and fiercer came the rain, and the lightning assumed its most deadly and blasting form; they were still, therefore, impelled onward, hoping at last, if the light eluded them, to arrive at some cottage, or some friendly cavern. The vines grew more and more intricate—the light was entirely snatched from them; but a narrow path, which they trod with labor and pain, guided only by the constant and long-lingering flashes of the storm, continued to lead them towards its direction. The rain ceased suddenly; precipitous and rough crags of scorched lava frowned before them, rendered more fearful by the lightning that illumined the dark and dangerous soil. Sometimes the blaze lingered over the iron-grey heaps of scoria, covered in part with ancient mosses or stunted trees, as if seeking in vain for some gentler product of earth, more worthy of its ire; and sometimes leaving the whole of that part of the scene in darkness, the lightning, broad and sheeted, hung redly over the ocean, tossing far below until its waves seemed glowing into fire; and so intense was the blaze, that it brought vividly into view even the sharp outline of the more distant windings of the bay, from the eternal Misenum, with its lofty brow, to the beautiful Sorrentum and the giant hills behind.

Our lovers stopped in perplexity and doubt, when suddenly, as the darkness that gloomed between the fierce flashes
of lightning once more wrapped them round, they saw near,
but high, before them, the mysterious light. Another blaze,
in which heaven and earth were reddened, made visible to
them the whole expanse; no house was near, but just where
they had beheld the light, they thought they saw in the recess
of a cavern the outline of a human form. The darkness once
more returned; the light, no longer paled beneath the fires of
heaven, burned forth again: they resolved to ascend towards
it; they had to wind their way among vast fragments of stone,
here and there overhung with wild bushes; but they gained
nearer and nearer to the light, and at length they stood opposite the mouth of a kind of cavern, apparently formed by huge
splinters of rock that had fallen transversely athwart each
other: and, looking into the gloom, each drew back involuntarily with a superstitious fear and chill.

A fire burned in the far recess of the cave; and over it was
a small caldron; on a tall and thin column of iron stood a rude
lamp; over that part of the wall, at the base of which burned
the fire, hung in many rows, as if to dry, a profusion of herbs
and weeds. A fox, couched before the fire, gazed upon the
strangers with its bright and red eye—its hair bristling—and
a low growl stealing from between its teeth; in the centre of
the cave was an earthen statue, which had three heads of a
singular and fantastic cast: they were formed by the real
skulls of a dog, a horse, and a boar; a low tripod stood before
this wild representation of the popular Hecate.

But it was not these appendages and appliances of the cave
that thrilled the blood of those who gazed fearfully therein—
it was the face of its inmate. Before the fire, with the light
shining full upon her features, sat a woman of considerable
age. Perhaps in no country are there seen so many hags as in
Italy—in no country does beauty so awfully change, in age,
to hideousness the most appalling and revolting. But the old
woman now before them was not one of these specimens of the
extreme of human ugliness; on the contrary, her countenance
betrayed the remains of a regular but high and aquiline order
of feature: with stony eyes turned upon them—with a look
that met and fascinated theirs—they beheld in that fearful
countenance the very image of a corpse!—the same, the glazed

and lustreless regard, the blue and shrunken lip, the drawn and hollow jaw—the dead, lank hair, of a pale grey—the livid, green, ghastly skin, which seemed all surely tinged and tainted by the grave! "It is a dead thing!" said Glaucus. "Nay—it stirs—it is a ghost or *larva*," faltered Ione, as she clung to the Athenian's breast. "Oh, away—away!" groaned the slave, "it is the Witch of Vesuvius!" "Who are ye?" said a hollow and ghostly voice. "And what do ye here?"

The sound, terrible and death-like as it was—suiting well the countenance of the speaker, and seeming rather the voice of some bodiless wanderer of the Styx than living mortal, would have made Ione shrink back into the pitiless fury of the storm, but Glaucus, though not without some misgiving, drew her into the cavern.

"We are storm-beaten wanderers from the neighboring city," said he, "and decoyed hither by yon light; we crave shelter and the comfort of your hearth."

As he spoke, the fox rose from the ground and advanced towards the strangers, showing from end to end its white teeth, and deepening in its menacing growl.

"Down, slave!" said the witch; and at the sound of her voice the beast dropped at once, covering its face with its brush, and keeping only its quick, vigilant eye, fixed upon the invaders of its repose. "Come to the fire if ye will!" said she, turning to Glaucus and his companions. "I never welcome living thing—save the owl, the fox, the toad and the viper—so I cannot welcome ye; but come to the fire without welcome —why stand upon form?"

The language in which the hag addressed them was a strange and barbarous Latin, interlarded with many words of some more rude and ancient dialect. She did not stir from her seat, but gazed stonily upon them as Glaucus now released Ione of her outer wrapping garments, and making her place herself on a log of wood, which was the only other seat he perceived at hand—fanned with his breath the embers into a more glowing flame. The slave, encouraged by the boldness of her superiors, divested herself also of her long *palla*, and crept timorously to the opposite corner of the hearth.

"We disturb you, I fear," said the silver voice of Ione, in conciliation.

The witch did not reply—she seemed like one who has

awakened for a moment from the dead, and has then relapsed once more into the eternal slumber.

"Tell me," said she, suddenly, and after a long pause, "are ye brother and sister?" "No," said Ione, blushing.

"Are ye married?" "Not so," replied Glaucus.

"Ho, lovers!—ha!—ha!—ha!" and the witch laughed so loud and so long that the caverns rang again.

The heart of Ione stood still at that strange mirth. Glaucus muttered a rapid counter-spell to the omen—and the slave turned as pale as the cheek of the witch herself.

"Why dost thou laugh, old crone?" said Glaucus, somewhat sternly, as he concluded his invocation.

"Did I laugh?" said the hag, absently.

"She is in her dotage," whispered Glaucus: as he said this, he caught the eye of the hag fixed upon him with a malignant and vivid glare. "Thou liest" said she, abruptly.

"Thou art an uncourteous welcomer," returned Glaucus.

"Hush! provoke her not, dear Glaucus!" whispered Ione.

"I will tell thee why I laughed when I discovered ye were lovers," said the old woman. "It was because it is a pleasure to the old and withered to look upon young hearts like yours— and to know the time will come when you will loathe each other—loathe—loathe—ha!—ha!—ha!" It was now Ione's turn to pray against the unpleasing prophecy.

"The gods forbid!" said she. "Yet, poor woman, thou knowest little of love, or thou wouldst know that it never changes."

"Was I young once, think ye?" returned the hag, quickly; "and am I old, and hideous, and deathly now? Such as is the form, so is the heart." With these words she sank again into a stillness profound and fearful, as if the cessation of life itself.

"Hast thou dwelt here long?" said Glaucus, after a pause, feeling uncomfortably oppressed beneath a silence so appalling. "Ah, long!—yes." "It is but a drear abode."

"Ha! thou mayst well say that—Hell is beneath us!" replied the hag, pointing her bony finger to the earth. "And I will tell thee a secret—the dim things below are preparing wrath for ye above—you, the young, and the thoughtless, and the beautiful."

"Thou utterest but evil words, ill-becoming the hospitable," said Glaucus; "and in future I will brave the tempest rather than thy welcome."

"Thou wilt do well. None should ever seek me—save the wretched!" "And why the wretched?" asked the Athenian.

"I am the witch of the mountain," replied the sorceress, with a ghastly grin; "my trade is to give hope to the hopeless: for the crossed in love I have philtres; for the avaricious, promises of treasure; for the malicious, potions of revenge; for the happy and the good, I have only what life has—curses! Trouble me no more."

With this the grim tenant of the cave relapsed into a silence so obstinate and sullen, that Glaucus in vain endeavored to draw her into farther conversation. She did not evince, by any alteration of her locked and rigid features, that she even heard him. Fortunately, however, the storm, which was brief as violent, began now to relax; the rain grew less and less fierce; and at last, as the clouds parted, the moon burst forth in the purple opening of heaven, and streamed clear and full into that desolate abode. Never had she shone, perhaps, on a group more worthy of the painter's art. The young, the all-beautiful Ione, seated by that rude fire—her lover already forgetful of the presence of the hag, at her feet, gazing upward to her face, and whispering sweet words—the pale and affrighted slave at a little distance—and the ghastly hag resting her deadly eyes upon them; yet seemingly serene and fearless (for the companionship of love hath such power) were these beautiful beings, things of another sphere, in that dark and unholy cavern, with its gloomy quaintness of appurtenance. The fox regarded them from his corner with his keen and fiery eye; and as Glaucus now turned towards the witch, he perceived for the first time, just under her seat, the bright gaze and crested head of a large snake; whether it was that the vivid coloring of the Athenian's cloak, thrown over the shoulders of Ione, attracted the reptile's anger—its crest began to glow and rise, as if menacing and preparing itself to spring upon the Neapolitan;—Glaucus caught quickly at one of the half-burned logs upon the hearth—and, as if enraged at the action, the snake came forth from its shelter, and with a loud hiss raised itself on end till its height nearly approached that of the Greek. "Witch!" cried Glaucus, "command thy creature, or thou wilt see it dead."

"It has been despoiled of its venom!" said the witch, aroused at his threat; but ere the words had left her lip, the snake had sprung upon Glaucus; quick and watchful, the agile Greek leaped lightly aside, and struck so fell and dexterous a blow on the head of the snake, that it fell prostrate and writhing among the embers of the fire.

The hag sprang up, and stood confronting Glaucus with a face which would have befitted the fiercest of the Furies, so utterly dire and wrathful was its expression—yet even in horror and ghastliness preserving the outline and trace of beauty —and utterly free from that coarse grotesque at which the imaginations of the North have sought the source of terror.

"Thou hast," said she, in a slow and steady voice—which belied the expression of her face, so much was it passionless and calm—"thou hast had shelter under my roof, and warmth at my hearth; thou hast returned evil for good; thou hast smitten and haply slain the thing that loved me and was mine: nay, more, the creature, above all others, consecrated to gods and deemed venerable by man—now hear thy punishment. By the moon, who is the guardian of the sorceress—by Orcus, who is the treasurer of wrath—I curse thee! and thou art cursed! May thy love be blasted—may thy name be blackened —may the infernals mark thee—may thy heart wither and scorch—may thy last hour recall to thee the prophet voice of the Saga of Vesuvius! And thou"—she added, turning sharply towards Ione, and raising her right arm, when Glaucus burst impetuously on her speech: "Hag!" cried he, "forbear! Me thou hast cursed, and I commit myself to the gods—I defy and scorn thee! but breathe but one word against yon maiden, and I will convert the oath on thy foul lips to thy dying groan. Beware!"

"I have done," replied the hag, laughing wildly; "for in thy doom is she who loves thee accursed. And not the less, that I heard *her* lips breathe thy name, and know by what word to command thee to the demons. *Glaucus*—thou art doomed!" So saying, the witch turned from the Athenian, and kneeling down beside her wounded favorite, which she dragged from the hearth, she turned to them her face no more.

"O Glaucus!" said Ione, greatly terrified, "what have we done?—Let us hasten from this place; the storm has ceased.

Good mistress, forgive him—recall thy words—he meant but to defend himself—accept this peace-offering to unsay the said:" and Ione, stooping, placed her purse on the hag's lap.

"Away!" said she, bitterly—"away! The oath once woven the Fates only can untie. Away!"

"Come, dearest!" said Glaucus, impatiently: "Thinkest thou that the gods above us or below hear the impotent ravings of dotage? Come!"

Long and loud rang the echoes of the cavern with the dread laugh of the saga—she deigned no further reply.

The lovers breathed more freely when they gained the open air: yet the scene they had witnessed, the words and the laughter of the witch, still fearfully dwelt with Ione; and even Glaucus could not thoroughly shake off the impression they bequeathed. The storm had subsided—save, now and then, a low thunder muttered at the distance amidst the darker clouds, or a momentary flash of lightning affronted the sovereignty of the moon. With some difficulty they regained the road, where they found the vehicle already sufficiently repaired for their departure, and the carrucarius calling loudly upon Hercules to tell him where his charge had vanished.

Glaucus vainly endeavored to cheer the exhausted spirits of Ione; and scarce less vainly to recover the elastic tone of his own natural gaiety. They soon arrived before the gate of the city: as it opened to them, a litter borne by slaves impeded the way.

"It is too late for egress," cried the sentinel to the inmate of the litter.

"Not so," said a voice, which the lovers started to hear: it was a voice they well recognized. "I am bound to the villa of Marcus Polybius. I shall return shortly. I am Arbaces the Egyptian."

The scruples of him of the gate were removed, and the litter passed close beside the carriage that bore the lovers.

"Arbaces, at this hour!—scarce recovered too, methinks! —Whither and for what can he leave the city?" said Glaucus.

"Alas!" replied Ione, bursting into tears, "my soul feels still more and more the omen of evil. Preserve us, O ye Gods! or at least," she murmured inly, "preserve my Glaucus!"

CHAPTER X.

The lord of the burning belt and his minion.—Fate writes her prophecy in red
letters, but who shall read them?

ARBACES had tarried only till the cessation of the tempest
allowed him, under cover of night, to seek the Saga of
Vesuvius. Borne by those of his trustier slaves in whom in all
more secret expeditions he was accustomed to confide, he lay
extended along his litter, and resigning his sanguine heart to
the contemplation of vengeance gratified and love possessed.
The slaves in so short a journey moved very little slower than
the ordinary pace of mules; and Arbaces soon arrived at the
commencement of a narrow path, which the lovers had not
been fortunate enough to discover; but which, skirting the
thick vines, led at once to the habitation of the witch. Here he
rested the litter; and bidding his slaves conceal themselves and
the vehicle among the vines from the observation of any
chance passenger, he mounted alone, with steps still feeble but
supported by a long staff, the drear and sharp ascent.

Not a drop of rain fell from the tranquil heaven: but the
moisture dripped mournfully from the laden boughs of the
vine, and now and then collected in tiny pools in the crevices
and hollows of the rocky way.

"Strange passions these for a philosopher," thought
Arbaces, "that lead one like me just new from the bed of death,
and lapped even in health amidst the roses of luxury, across
such nocturnal paths as this; but Passion and Vengeance
treading to their goal can make an Elysium of a Tartarus."
High, clear, and melancholy shone the moon above the road of
that dark wayfarer, glassing herself in every pool that lay
before him, and sleeping in shadow along the sloping mount.
He saw before him the same light that had guided the steps of
his intended victims, but, no longer contrasted by the blackened
clouds, it shone less redly clear.

He paused, as at length he approached the mouth of the
208

cavern, to recover breath; and then, with his wonted collected and stately mien, he crossed the unhallowed threshold.

The fox sprang up at the ingress of this new-comer, and by a long howl announced another visitor to his mistress.

The witch had resumed her seat, and her aspect of grave-like and grim repose. By her feet, upon a bed of dry weeds which half covered it, lay the wounded snake; but the quick eye of the Egyptian caught its scales glittering in the reflected light of the opposite fire, as it writhed,—now contracting, now lengthening its folds, in pain and unsated anger.

"Down, slave!" said the witch, as before, to the fox; and, as before, the animal dropped to the ground—mute, but vigilant.

"Rise, servant of Nox and Erebus!" said Arbaces, commandingly; "a superior in thine art salutes thee! rise, and welcome him."

At these words the hag turned her gaze upon the Egyptian's towering form and dark features. She looked long and fixedly upon him, as he stood before her in his Oriental robe, and folded arms, and steadfast and haughty brow. "Who art thou," she said at last, "that callest thyself greater in art than the Saga of the Burning Fields, and the daughter of the perished Etrurian race?"

"I am he," answered Arbaces, "from whom all cultivators of magic, from north to south, from east to west, from the Ganges and the Nile to the vales of Thessaly and the shores of the yellow Tiber, have stooped to learn."

"There is but one such man in these places," answered the witch, "whom the men of the outer world, unknowing his loftier attributes and more secret fame, call Arbaces the Egyptian: to us of a higher nature and deeper knowledge, his rightful appellation is Hermes of the Burning Girdle."

"Look again," returned Arbaces: "I am he."

As he spoke he drew aside his robe, and revealed a cincture seemingly of fire, that burned around his waist, clasped in the centre by a plate whereon was engraven some sign apparently vague and unintelligible, but which was evidently not unknown to the saga. She rose hastily, and threw herself at the feet of Arbaces. "I have seen, then," said she, in a voice of deep humility, "the Lord of the Mighty Girdle—vouchsafe my homage."

"Rise," said the Egyptian; "I have need of thee."

So saying, he placed himself on the same log of wood on which Ione had rested before, and motioned to the witch to resume her seat.

"Thou sayest," said he, as she obeyed, "that thou art a daughter of the ancient Etrurian tribes; the mighty walls of whose rock-built cities yet frown above the robber race that hath seized upon their ancient reign. Partly came those tribes from Greece, partly were they exiles from a more burning and primeval soil. In either case art thou of Egyptian lineage, for the Grecian masters of the aboriginal helot were among the restless sons whom the Nile banished from her bosom. Equally then, O Saga! thy descent is from ancestors that swore allegiance to mine own. By birth as by knowledge, art thou the subject of Arbaces. Hear me, then, and obey!"

The witch bowed her head.

"Whatever art we possess in sorcery," continued Arbaces, "we are sometimes driven to natural means to attain our object. The ring† and the crystal,‡ and the ashes§ and the herbs,|| do not give unerring divinations; neither do the higher mysteries of the moon yield even the possessor of the girdle a dispensation from the necessity of employing ever and anon human measures for a human object. Mark me, then: thou art deeply skilled, methinks, in the secrets of the more deadly herbs; thou knowest those which arrest life, which burn and scorch the soul from out her citadel, or freeze the channels of young blood into that ice which no sun can melt. Do I overrate thy skill? Speak, and truly!"

"Mighty Hermes, such lore is, indeed, mine own. Deign to look at these ghostly and corpse-like features; they have waned from the hues of life merely by watching over the rank herbs which simmer night and day in yon cauldron."

The Egyptian moved his seat from so unblessed or so unhealthful a vicinity, as the witch spoke.

"It is well," said he; "thou hast learned that maxim of all the deeper knowledge which saith, 'Despise the body to make wise the mind.' But to thy task. There cometh to thee by tomorrow's star-light a vain maiden, seeking of thine art a love-charm to fascinate from another the eyes that should utter

---

† Δακτυλομαντεία.   § Τεφρομαντεία.
‡ Κρυστολομαντεία. || Βοτανομαντεία.

but soft tales to her own; instead of thy philtres, give the maiden one of thy most powerful poisons. Let the lover breathe his vows to the Shades."

The witch trembled from head to foot.

"Oh, pardon! pardon! dread master," said she, falteringly: "but this I dare not. The law in these cities is sharp and vigilant; they will seize, they will slay me."

"For what purpose, then, thy herbs and thy potions, vain Saga?" said Arbaces, sneeringly.

The witch hid her loathsome face with her hands.

"Oh! years ago," said she, in a voice unlike her usual tones, so plaintive was it, and so soft, "I was not the thing that I am now,—I loved, I fancied myself beloved."

"And what connection hath thy love, witch, with my commands?" said Arbaces, impetuously.

"Patience," resumed the witch; "patience, I implore. I loved! another and less fair than I—yes, by Nemesis! less fair —allured from me my chosen. I was of that dark Etrurian tribe to whom most of all were known the secrets of the gloomier magic. My mother was herself a saga: she shared the resentment of her child; from her hands I received the potion that was to restore me his love; and from her, also, the poison that was to destroy my rival. Oh, crush me, dread walls! my trembling hands mistook the phials, my lover fell indeed at my feet; but dead! dead! Since then, what has been life to me? I became suddenly old, I devoted myself to the sorceries of my race; still by an irresistible impulse I curse myself with an awful penance; still I seek the most noxious herbs; still I concoct the poisons; still I imagine that I am to give them to my hated rival; still I pour them into the phial; still I fancy that they shall blast her beauty to the dust; still I wake and see the quivering body, the foaming lips, the glazing eyes of my Aulus —murdered, and by me!"

The skeleton frame of the witch shook beneath strong convulsions.

Arbaces gazed upon her with a curious though contemptuous eye.

"And this foul thing has yet human emotions!" thought he; "she still cowers over the ashes of the same fire that consumes Arbaces!—Such are we all! Mystic is the tie of those mortal passions that unite the greatest and the least."

He did not reply till she had somewhat recovered herself, and now sat rocking to and fro in her seat, with glassy eyes fixed on the opposite frame, and large tears rolling down her livid cheeks.

"A grievous tale is thine, in truth," said Arbaces. "But these emotions are fit only for our youth—age should harden our hearts to all things but ourselves; as every year adds a scale to the shell-fish, so should each year wall and incrust the heart. Think of those frenzies no more! And now, listen to me again! By the revenge that was dear to thee, I command thee to obey me! it is for vengeance that I seek thee! This youth whom I would sweep from my path has crossed me, despite my spells:—this thing of purple and broidery, of smiles and glances, soulless and mindless, with no charm but that of beauty—accursed be it!—this insect—this Glaucus—I tell thee, by Orcus and by Nemesis, he must die."

And working himself up at every word, the Egyptian, forgetful of his debility—of his strange companion—of everything but his own vindictive rage, strode, with large and rapid steps, the gloomy cavern.

"Glaucus! saidst thou, mighty master!" said the witch, abruptly; and her dim eye glared at the name with all that fierce resentment at the memory of small affronts so common amongst the solitary and the shunned.

"Ay, so he is called; but what matters the name? Let it not be heard as that of a living man three days from this date!"

"Hear me!" said the witch, breaking from a short reverie into which she was plunged after this last sentence of the Egyptian. "Hear me! I am thy thing and thy slave! spare me! If I give to the maiden thou speakest of that which would destroy the life of Glaucus, I shall be surely detected—the dead ever find avengers. Nay, dread man! if thy visit to me be tracked, if thy hatred to Glaucus be known, thou mayest have need of thy archest magic to protect thyself!"

"Ha!" said Arbaces, stopping suddenly short; and as a proof of that blindness with which passion darkens the eyes even of the most acute, this was the first time when the risk that he himself ran by this method of vengeance had occurred to a mind ordinarily wary and circumspect.

"But," continued the witch, "if instead of that which shall arrest the heart, I give that which shall sear and blast the brain—which shall make him who quaffs it unfit for the uses and career of life—an abject, raving, benighted thing—smiting sense to drivelling, youth to dotage—will not thy vengeance be equally sated—thy object equally attained?"

"Oh, witch! no longer the servant, but the sister—the equal of Arbaces—how much brighter is woman's wit, even in vengeance, than ours! how much more exquisite than death is such a doom!"

"And," continued the hag, gloating over her fell scheme, "in this is but little danger: for by ten thousand methods, which men forbear to seek, can our victim become mad. He may have been among the vines and seen a nymph—or the vine itself may have had the same effect—ha, ha! they never inquire too scrupulously into these matters in which the gods may be agents. And let the worst arrive—let it be known that it is a love-charm—why, madness is a common effect of philtres; and even the fair she that gave it finds indulgence in the excuse. Mighty Hermes, have I ministered to thee cunningly?"

"Thou shalt have twenty years' longer date for this," returned Arbaces. "I will write anew the epoch of thy fate on the face of the pale stars—thou shalt not serve in vain the Master of the Flaming Belt. And here, Saga, carve thee out, by these golden tools, a warmer cell in this dreary cavern—one service to me shall countervail a thousand divinations by sieve and shears to the gaping rustics." So saying, he cast upon the floor a heavy purse, which clinked not unmusically to the ear of the hag, who loved the consciousness of possessing the means to purchase comforts she disdained. "Farewell," said Arbaces, "fail not—outwatch the stars in concocting thy beverage—thou shalt lord it over thy sisters at the Walnut-tree,* when thou tellest them that thy patron and thy friend is Hermes the Egyptian. To-morrow night we meet again."

He stayed not to hear the valediction or the thanks of the witch; with a quick step he passed into the moon-lit air, and hastened down the mountain.

The witch, who followed his steps to the threshold, stood long at the entrance of the cavern, gazing fixedly on his receding form; and as the sad moonlight streamed upon her

* The celebrated and immemorial rendezvous of the witches at Benevento. The winged serpent attached to it, long an object of idolatry in those parts, was probably consecrated by Egyptian superstitions.

shadowy form and death-like face, emerging from the dismal rocks, it seemed as if one gifted, indeed, by supernatural magic had escaped from the dreary Orcus; and, the foremost of its ghostly throng, stood at its black portals—vainly summoning his return, or vainly sighing to rejoin him. The hag then slowly re-entering the cave, groaningly picked up the heavy purse, took the lamp from its stand, and, passing to the remotest depth of her cell, a black and abrupt passage, which was not visible, save at a near approach, closed round as it was with jutting and sharp crags, yawned before her; she went several yards along this gloomy path, which sloped gradually downwards, as if towards the bowels of the earth, and, lifting a stone, deposited her treasure in a hole beneath, which, as the lamp pierced its secrets, seemed already to contain coins of various value, wrung from the credulity or gratitude of her visitors.

"I love to look at you," said she, apostrophising the moneys; "for when I see you, I feel that I am indeed of power. And I am to have twenty years' longer life to increase your store! O thou great Hermes!"

She replaced the stone, and continued her path onward for some paces, when she stopped before a deep irregular fissure in the earth. Here, as she bent—strange, rumbling, hoarse, and distant sounds might be heard, while ever and anon, with a loud and grating noise which, to use a homely but faithful simile, seemed to resemble the grinding of steel upon wheels, volumes of streaming and dark smoke issued forth, and rushed spirally along the cavern.

"The Shades are noisier than their wont," said the hag, shaking her grey locks; and, looking into the cavity, she beheld, far down, glimpses of a long streak of light, intensely but darkly red. "Strange!" she said, shrinking back; "it is only within the last two days that dull deep light hath been visible —what can it portend?"

The fox, who had attended the steps of his fell mistress, uttered a dismal howl, and ran cowering back to the inner cave; a cold shuddering seized the hag herself at the cry of the animal, which, causeless as it seemed, the superstitions of the time considered deeply ominous. She muttered her placatory charm, and tottered back into her cavern, where, amidst her herbs and incantations, she prepared to execute the orders of the Egyptian.

"He called me dotard," said she, as the smoke curled from the hissing cauldron: "when the jaws drop, and the grinders fall, and the heart scarce beats, it is a pitiable thing to dote; but when," she added, with a savage and exulting grin, "the young, and the beautiful, and the strong, are suddenly smitten into idiocy—ah, that is terrible! Burn flame—simmer herb— swelter toad—I cursed him, and he shall be cursed!"

On that night, and at the same hour which witnessed the dark and unholy interview between Arbaces and the saga, Apæcides was baptized.

CHAPTER XI.

Progress of events.—The plot thickens.—The web is woven, but the net changes hands.

"AND you have the courage then, Julia, to seek the Witch of Vesuvius this evening; in company, too, with that fearful man?"

"Why, Nydia?" replied Julia, timidly; "dost thou really think there is anything to dread? These old hags, with their enchanted mirrors, their trembling sieves, and their moon-gathered herbs, are, I imagine, but crafty impostors, who have learned, perhaps, nothing but the very charm for which I apply to their skill, and which is drawn but from the knowledge of the field's herbs and simples. Wherefore should I dread?"

"Dost thou not fear thy companion?"

"What, Arbaces? By Dian, I never saw lover more courteous than that same magician! And were he not so dark, he would be even handsome."

Blind as she was, Nydia had the penetration to perceive that Julia's mind was not one that the gallantries of Arbaces were likely to terrify. She therefore dissuaded her no more; but nursed in her excited heart the wild and increasing desire to know if sorcery had indeed a spell to fascinate love to love.

"Let me go with thee, noble Julia," said she at length; "my presence is no protection, but I should like to be beside thee to the last."

"Thine offer pleases me much," replied the daughter of Diomed. "Yet how canst thou contrive it? we may not return until late—they will miss thee."

"Ione is indulgent," replied Nydia. "If thou wilt permit me to sleep beneath thy roof, I will say that thou, an early patroness and friend, hast invited me to pass the day with thee, and sing thee my Thessalian songs; her courtesy will readily grant to thee so light a boon."

"Nay, ask for thyself!" said the haughty Julia. "*I* stoop to request no favor from the Neapolitan!"

"Well, be it so. I will take my leave now; make my request, which I know will be readily granted, and return shortly."

"Do so; and thy bed shall be prepared in my own chamber."

With that, Nydia left the fair Pompeian.

On her way back to Ione she was met by the chariot of Glaucus, on whose fiery and curveting steeds was riveted the gaze of the crowded street.

He kindly stopped for a moment to speak to the flower-girl.

"Blooming as thine own roses, my gentle Nydia! and how is thy fair mistress?—recovered, I trust, from the effects of the storm?" "I have not seen her this morning," answered Nydia, "but——"

"But what? draw back—the horses are too near thee."

"But, think you Ione will permit me to pass the day with Julia, the daughter of Diomed?—She wishes it, and was kind to me when I had few friends." "The gods bless thy grateful heart! I will answer for Ione's permission."

"Then I may stay over the night, and return to-morrow?" said Nydia, shrinking from the praise she so little merited.

"As thou and fair Julia please. Commend me to her; and, hark ye, Nydia, when thou hearest her speak, note the contrast of her voice with that of the silver-toned Ione.—*Vale!*"

His spirits entirely recovered from the effect of the past night, his locks waving in the wind, his joyous and elastic heart bounding with every spring of his Parthian steeds, a very prototype of his country's god, full of youth and of love— Glaucus was borne rapidly to his mistress.

Enjoy while ye may the present—who can read the future?

As the evening darkened, Julia, reclined within her litter, which was capacious enough also to admit her blind companion, took her way to the rural baths indicated by Arbaces. To her natural levity of disposition, her enterprise brought less of terror than of pleasurable excitement; above all, she glowed at the thought of her coming triumph over the hated Neapolitan.

A small but gay group was collected round the door of the villa, as her litter passed by it to the private entrance of the baths, appropriated to the women.

"Methinks, by this dim light," said one of the bystanders, "I recognize the slaves of Diomed."

"True, Clodius," said Sallust: "it is probably the litter of his daughter Julia. She is rich, my friend; why dost thou not proffer thy suit to her?"

"Why, I had once hoped that Glaucus would have married her. She does not disguise her attachment; and then, as he gambles freely and with ill success——"

"The sesterces would have passed to thee, wise Clodius. A wife is a good thing—when it belongs to another man!"

"But," continued Clodius, "as Glaucus is, I understand, to wed the Neapolitan, I think I must even try my chance with the dejected maid. After all, the lamp of Hymen will be gilt, and the vessel will reconcile one to the odor of the flame. I shall only protest, my Sallust, against Diomed's making *thee* trustee to his daughter's fortune."

"Ha! ha! let us within, my *comissator;* the wine and the garlands wait us."

Dismissing her slaves to that part of the house set apart for their entertainment, Julia entered the baths with Nydia, and declining the offers of the attendants, passed by a private door into the garden behind. "She comes by appointment, be sure," said one of the slaves.

"What is that to thee?" said a superintendent, sourly; "she pays for the baths, and does not waste the saffron. Such appointments are the best part of the trade. Hark! do you not hear the widow Fulvia clapping her hands? Run, fool—run!"

Julia and Nydia, avoiding the more public part of the garden, arrived at the place specified by the Egyptian. In a small circular plot of grass the stars gleamed upon the statue of Silenus:—the merry god reclined upon a fragment of rock—the lynx of Bacchus at his feet—and over his mouth he held, with extended arm, a bunch of grapes, which he seemingly laughed to welcome ere he devoured.

"I see not the magician," said Julia, looking round; when, as she spoke, the Egyptian slowly emerged from the neighboring foliage, and the light fell palely over his sweeping robes.

"*Salve,* sweet maiden!—But ha! whom hast thou here? we must have no companions!"

"It is but the blind flower-girl, wise magician," replied Julia: "herself a Thessalian." "Oh! Nydia!" said the Egyptian; "I know her well." Nydia drew back and shuddered.

"Thou hast been at my house, methinks!" said he, approaching his voice to Nydia's ear; "thou knowest the oath!—Silence and secrecy, now as then, or beware!"

"Yet," he added, musingly to himself, "why confide more than is necessary, even in the blind—Julia, canst thou trust thyself alone with me? Believe me, the magician is less formidable than he seems."

As he spoke, he gently drew Julia aside.

"The witch loves not many visitors at once," said he, "leave Nydia here till your return; she can be of no assistance to us: and, for protection—your own beauty suffices—your own beauty and your own rank; yes, Julia I know thy name and birth. Come, trust thyself with me, fair rival of the youngest of the Naiads!"

The vain Julia was not, as we have seen, easily affrighted; she was moved by the flattery of Arbaces, and she readily consented to suffer Nydia to await her return; nor did Nydia press her presence. At the sound of the Egyptian's voice all her terror of him returned, she felt a sentiment of pleasure at learning she was not to travel in his companionship.

She returned to the Bath-house, and in one of the private chambers waited their return. Many and bitter were the thoughts of this wild girl as she sat there in her eternal darkness. She thought of her own desolate fate, far from her native land, far from the bland cares that once assuaged the April sorrows of childhood;—deprived of the light of day, with none but strangers to guide her steps, accursed by the one soft feeling of her heart, loving and without hope, save the dim and unholy ray which shot across her mind, as her Thessalian fancies questioned of the force of spells and the gifts of magic!

Nature had sown in the heart of this poor girl the seeds of virtue never destined to ripen. The lessons of adversity are not always salutary—sometimes they soften and amend, but as often they indurate and pervert. If we consider ourselves more harshly treated by fate than those around us, and do not acknowledge in our own deeds the justice of the severity, we become too apt to deem the world our enemy, to case ourselves in defiance, to wrestle against our *softer self,* and to indulge the darker passions which are so easily fermented by the sense of injustice. Sold early into slavery, sentenced to a sordid task-master, exchanging her situation, only yet more to embitter her lot—the kindlier feelings, naturally profuse in the breast of Nydia, were nipped and blighted. Her sense of right and wrong was confused by a passion to which she had so madly surrendered herself; and the same intense and tragic emotions which we read of in the women of the classic age— a Myrrha, a Medea—and which hurried and swept away the whole soul when once delivered to love—ruled, and rioted in her breast.

Time passed: a light step entered the chamber where Nydia yet indulged her gloomy meditations.

"Oh, thanked be the immortal gods!" said Julia. "I have returned, I have left that terrible cavern! Come, Nydia! let us away forthwith!" It was not till they were seated in the litter that Julia again spoke.

"Oh!" said she, tremblingly, "such a scene! such fearful incantations! and the dead face of the hag!—But, let us talk not of it. I have obtained the potion—she pledges its effect. My rival shall be suddenly indifferent to his eye, and I, I alone, the idol of Glaucus!" "Glaucus!" exclaimed Nydia.

"Ay! I told thee, girl, at first, that it was *not* the Athenian whom I loved: but I see now that I may trust thee wholly— it *is* the beautiful Greek!"

What then were Nydia's emotions! she had connived, she had assisted, in tearing Glaucus from Ione; but only to transfer, by all the power of magic, his affections yet more hopelessly to another. Her heart swelled almost to suffocation —she gasped for breath—in the darkness of the vehicle, Julia did not perceive the agitation of her companion; she went on rapidly dilating on the promised effect of her acquisition, and on her approaching triumph over Ione, every now and then

abruptly digressing to the horror of the scene she had quitted
—the unmoved mien of Arbaces, and his authority over the
dreadful saga.

Meanwhile Nydia recovered her self-possession: a thought
flashed across her: she slept in the chamber of Julia—she
might possess herself of the potion.

They arrived at the house of Diomed, and descended to
Julia's apartment, where the night's repast awaited them.

"Drink, Nydia, thou must be cold; the air was chill to-
night; as for me, my veins are yet ice." And Julia unhesitatingly quaffed deep draughts of the spiced wine.

"Thou hast the potion," said Nydia; "let me hold it in my
hands. How small the phial is! of what color is the draught?"

"Clear as crystal," replied Julia, as she retook the philtre;
"thou couldst not tell it from this water. The witch assures
me it is tasteless. Small though the phial, it suffices for a life's
fidelity: it is to be poured into any liquid; and Glaucus will
only know what he has quaffed by the effect."

"Exactly like this water in appearance?"

"Yes, sparkling and colorless as this. How bright it seems!
it is as the very essence of moonlit dews. Bright thing! how
thou shinest on my hopes through thy crystal vase!"

"And how is it sealed?"

"But by one little stopper—I withdraw it now—the
draught gives no odor. Strange, that that which speaks to
neither sense should thus command all!"

"Is the effect instantaneous?" "Usually;—but sometimes
it remains dormant for a few hours."

"Oh, how sweet is this perfume!" said Nydia, suddenly,
as she took up a small bottle on the table, and bent over its
fragrant contents.

"Thinkest thou so? the bottle is set with gems of some
value. Thou wouldst not have the bracelet yestermorn; wilt
thou take the bottle?"

"It ought to be such perfumes as these that should remind
one who cannot see of the generous Julia. If the bottle be not
too costly——"

"Oh! I have a thousand costlier ones: take it, child!"

Nydia bowed her gratitude, and placed the bottle in her
vest.

"And the draught would be equally efficacious, whoever administers it?"

"If the most hideous hag beneath the sun bestowed it, such is its asserted virtue that Glaucus would deem her beautiful, and none but her!"

Julia, warmed by wine, and the reaction of her spirits, was now all animation and delight; she laughed loud, and talked on a hundred matters—nor was it till the night had advanced far towards morning that she summoned her slaves and undressed.

When they were dismissed, she said to Nydia,—

"I will not suffer this holy draught to quit my presence till the hour comes for its uses. Lie under my pillow, bright spirit, and give me happy dreams!"

So saying, she placed the potion under her pillow. Nydia's heart beat violently.

"Why dost thou drink that unmixed water, Nydia? Take the wine by its side."

"I am fevered," replied the blind girl, "and the water cools me. I will place this bottle by my bedside: it refreshes in these summer nights, when the dews of sleep fall not on our lips. Fair Julia, I must leave thee very early—so Ione bids—perhaps before thou art awake; accept, therefore, now my congratulations."

"Thanks: when next we meet, you may find Glaucus at my feet."

They had retired to their couches, and Julia, worn out by the excitement of the day, soon slept. But anxious and burning thoughts rolled over the mind of the wakeful Thessalian. She listened to the calm breathing of Julia; and her ear, accustomed to the finest distinctions of sound, speedily assured her of the deep slumber of her companion.

"Now befriend me, Venus!" said she softly.

She rose gently, and poured the perfume from the gift of Julia upon the marble floor—she rinsed it several times carefully with the water that was beside her, and then easily finding the bed of Julia (for night to her was as day), she pressed her trembling hand under the pillow and seized the potion. Julia stirred not, her breath regularly fanned the burning cheek of the blind girl. Nydia, then, opening the phial, poured its contents into the bottle, which easily contained them; and then refilling the former reservoir of the potion with that limpid water which Julia had assured her it so resembled, she once more placed the phial in its former place. She then stole again to her couch and waited—with what thoughts!—the dawning day.

The sun had risen—Julia slept still—Nydia noiselessly dressed herself, placed her treasure carefully in her vest, took up her staff, and hastened to quit the house.

The porter, Medon, saluted her kindly as she descended the steps that led to the street: she heard him not; her mind was confused and lost in the whirl of tumultuous thoughts, each thought a passion. She felt the pure morning air upon her cheek, but it cooled not her scorching veins.

"Glaucus," she murmured, "all the love-charms of the wildest magic could not make thee love me as I love thee. Ione!—ah, away hesitation! away remorse! Glaucus, my fate is in thy smile; and thine! O hope! O joy! O transport!—*thy* fate is in these hands!"

BOOK THE FOURTH.

CHAPTER I.

Reflections on the zeal of the early Christians.—Two men come to a perilous resolve.—Walls have ears—particularly sacred walls.

WHOEVER regards the early history of Christianity, will perceive how necessary to its triumph was that fierce spirit of zeal, which, fearing no danger, accepting no compromise, inspired its champions and sustained its martyrs. In a dominant church the genius of intolerance *betrays* its cause;—in a weak and a persecuted church, the same genius mainly *supports*. It was necessary to scorn, to loathe, to abhor the creeds of other men, in order to conquer the temptations which they presented—it was necessary rigidly to believe not only that the Gospel was the true faith, but the *sole* true faith that saved, in order to nerve the disciple to the austerity of its doctrine, and to encourage him to the sacred and perilous chivalry of converting the Polytheist and the Heathen. The sectarian sternness which confined virtue and heaven to a chosen few, which saw demons in other gods, and the penalties of hell in another religion—made the believer naturally anxious to convert all to whom he felt the ties of human affection; and the circle thus traced by benevolence to man was yet more widened by a desire for the glory of God. It was for the honor of the Christian faith that the Christian boldly forced his tenets upon the scepticism of some, the repugnance of others, the sage contempt of the philosopher, the pious shudder of the people;—his very intolerance supplied him with his fittest instruments of success; and the soft Heathen began at last to imagine there must indeed be something holy in a zeal wholly foreign to his experience, which stopped at no obstacle, dreaded no danger, and even at the torture, or on the scaffold, referred a dispute far other than the calm differences of speculative philosophy to the tribunal of an Eternal Judge. It was thus that the same fervor which made the Churchman of the middle age a bigot without mercy, made the Christian of the early days a hero without fear.

Of these more fiery, daring, and earnest natures, not the least ardent was Olinthus. No sooner had Apæcides been received by the rites of baptism into the bosom of the Church, than the Nazarene hastened to make him conscious of the impossibility to retain the office and robes of priesthood. He could not, it was evident, profess to worship God, and continue even outwardly to honor the idolatrous altars of the Fiend.

Nor was this all: the sanguine and impetuous mind of Olinthus beheld in the power of Apæcides the means of divulging to the deluded people the juggling mysteries of the oracular Isis. He thought Heaven had sent this instrument of his design in order to disabuse the eyes of the crowd, and prepare the way, perchance, for the conversion of a whole city. He did not hesitate then to appeal to all the new-kindled enthusiasm of Apæcides, to arouse his courage, and to stimulate his zeal. They met, according to previous agreement, the evening after the baptism of Apæcides, in the grove of Cybele, which we have before described.

"At the next solemn consultation of the oracle," said Olinthus, as he proceeded in the warmth of his address, "advance yourself to the railing, proclaim aloud to the people the deception they endure, invite them to enter, to be themselves the witness of the gross but artful mechanism of imposture thou hast described to me. Fear not—the Lord, who protected Daniel, shall protect thee; we, the community of Christians, will be amongst the crowd; we will urge on the shrinking; and in the first flush of the popular indignation and shame, I myself, upon those very altars, will plant the palm-branch typical of the Gospel—and to my tongue shall descend the rushing Spirit of the living God."

Heated and excited as he was, this suggestion was not unpleasing to Apæcides. He was rejoiced at so early an opportunity of distinguishing his faith in his new sect, and to his holier feelings were added those of a vindictive loathing at the imposition he had himself suffered, and a desire to avenge it. In that sanguine and elastic *overbound* of obstacles (the rashness necessary to all who undertake venturous and lofty actions), neither Olinthus nor the proselyte perceived the impediments to the success of their scheme, which might be found in the reverent superstition of the people themselves, who would probably be loath, before the sacred altars of the great Egyptian goddess, to believe even the testimony of her priest against her power.

Apæcides then assented to this proposal with a readiness which delighted Olinthus. They parted with the understanding that Olinthus should confer with the more important of his Christian brethren on his great enterprise, should receive their advice and the assurances of their support on the eventful day. It so chanced that one of the festivals of Isis was to be held on the second day after this conference. The festival proffered a ready occasion for the design. They appointed to meet once more on the next evening at the same spot; and in that meeting were finally to be settled the order and details of the disclosure for the following day.

It happened that the latter part of this conference had been held near the sacellum, or small chapel, which I have described in the early part of this work; and so soon as the forms of the Christian and the priest had disappeared from the grove, a dark and ungainly figure emerged from behind the chapel.

"I have tracked you with some effect, my brother flamen," soliloquized the eaves-dropper; "you, the priest of Isis, have not for mere idle discussion conferred with this gloomy Christian. Alas! that I could not hear all your precious plot: enough! I find, at least, that you meditate revealing the sacred mysteries, and that to-morrow you meet again at this place to plan the how and the when. May Osiris sharpen my ears then, to detect the whole of your unheard-of audacity! When I have learned more, I must confer at once with Arbaces. We will frustrate you, my friends, deep as you think yourselves. At present, my breast is a locked treasury of your secret."

Thus muttering, Calenus, for it was he, wrapped his robe round him, and strode thoughtfully homeward.

CHAPTER II.

A classic host, cook, and kitchen.—Apæcides seeks Ione.—Their conversation.

IT WAS then the day for Diomed's banquet to the most select of his friends. The graceful Glaucus, the beautiful Ione, the official Pansa, the high-born Clodius, the immortal Fulvius, the exquisite Lepidus, the epicurean Sallust, were not the only honorers of his festival. He expected, also, an invalid senator from Rome (a man of considerable repute and favor at court), and a great warrior from Herculaneum, who had fought with Titus against the Jews, and having enriched himself prodigiously in the wars, was always told by his friends that his country was eternally indebted to his disinterested exertions! The party, however, extended to a yet greater number: for although, critically speaking, it was, at one time, thought inelegant among the Romans to entertain less than three or more than nine at their banquets, yet this rule was easily disregarded by the ostentatious. And we are told, indeed, in history, that one of the most splendid of these entertainers usually feasted a select party of three hundred. Diomed, however, more modest, contented himself with doubling the number of the Muses. His party consisted of eighteen, no unfashionable number in the present day.

It was the morning of Diomed's banquet; and Diomed himself, though he greatly affected the gentleman and the scholar, retained enough of his mercantile experience to know that a master's eye makes a ready servant. Accordingly, with his tunic ungirdled on his portly stomach, his easy slippers on his feet, a small wand in his hand, wherewith he now directed the gaze, and now corrected the back, of some duller menial, he went from chamber to chamber of his costly villa.

He did not disdain even a visit to that sacred apartment in which the priests of the festival prepare their offerings. On entering the kitchen, his ears were agreeably stunned by the noise of dishes and pans, of oaths and commands. Small as this indispensable chamber seems to have been in all the houses of Pompeii, it was, nevertheless, usually fitted up with all that amazing variety of stoves and shapes, stew-pans and sauce-pans, cutters and moulds, without which a cook of spirit, no matter whether he be an ancient or a modern, declares it utterly impossible that he can give you anything to eat. And as fuel was then, as now, dear and scarce in those regions, great seems to have been the dexterity exercised in preparing as many things as possible with as little fire. An admirable contrivance of this nature may be still seen in the Neapolitan

Museum, viz., a portable kitchen, about the size of a folio volume, containing stoves for four dishes, and an apparatus for
heating water or other beverages.

Across the small kitchen flitted many forms which the
quick eye of the master did not recognize.

"Oh! oh!" grumbled he to himself, "that cursed Congrio
hath invited a whole legion of cooks to assist him. They won't
serve for nothing, and this is another item in the total of my
day's expenses. By Bacchus! thrice lucky shall I be if the
slaves do not help themselves to some of the drinking vessels:
ready, alas, are their hands, capacious are their tunics. *Me
miserum!*"

The cooks, however, worked on, seemingly heedless of the
apparition of Diomed.

"Ho, Euclio, your egg-pan! What, is this the largest?
it only holds thirty-three eggs: in the houses *I* usually serve,
the smallest egg-pan holds fifty, if need be!"

"The unconscionable rogue!" thought Diomed; "he talks
of eggs as if they were a sesterce a hundred!"

"By Mercury!" cried a pert little culinary disciple, scarce
in his noviciate; "whoever saw such antique sweetmeat shapes
as these?—it is impossible to do credit to one's art with such
rude materials. Why, Sallust's commonest sweetmeat shape
represents the whole siege of Troy; Hector and Paris and
Helen——with little Astyanax and the Wooden Horse into
the bargain!"

"Silence, fool!" said Congrio, the cook of the house, who
seemed to leave the chief part of the battle to his allies. "My
master, Diomed, is not one of those expensive good-for-
noughts, who must have the last fashion, cost what it will!"

"Thou liest, base slave!" cried Diomed, in a great passion,
—"and thou costest me already enough to have ruined Lucul-
lus himself! Come out of thy den, I want to talk to thee."

The slave, with a sly wink at his confederates, obeyed the
command.

"Man of three letters," said Diomed, with his face of
solemn anger, "how didst thou dare to invite all those rascals
into my house?—I see thief written in every line of their
faces."

"Yet, I assure you, master, that they are men of most respectable character—the best cooks of the place; it is a great favor to get them. But for *my* sake——"

"Thy sake, unhappy Congrio!" interrupted Diomed; "and by what purloined moneys of mine, by what reserved filchings from marketing, by what goodly meats converted into grease, and sold in the suburbs, by what false charges for bronzes marred, and earthenware broken—hast thou been enabled to make them serve thee for *thy* sake?"

"Nay, master, do not impeach my honesty! May the gods desert me if——"

"Swear not!" again interrupted the choleric Diomed, "for then the gods will smite thee for a perjurer, and I shall lose my cook on the eve of dinner. But, enough of this at present: keep a sharp eye on thy ill-favored assistants, and tell me no tales to-morrow of vases broken, and cups miraculously vanished, or thy whole back shall be one pain. And hark thee! thou knowest thou hast made me pay for those Phrygian *attagens* enough, by Hercules, to have feasted a sober man for a year together—see that they be not one iota over-roasted. The last time, O Congrio, that I gave a banquet to my friends, when thy vanity did so boldly undertake the becoming appearance of a Melian crane—thou knowest it came up like a stone from Ætna—as if all the fires of Phlegethon had been scorching out its juices. Be modest this time, Congrio—wary and modest. Modesty is the nurse of great actions; and in all other things, as in this, if thou wilt not spare thy master's purse, at least consult thy master's glory."

"There shall not be such a cœna seen at Pompeii since the days of Hercules."

"Softly, softly—thy cursed boasting again! But I say, Congrio, yon *homunculus*—yon pigmy assailant of my cranes —yon pert-tongued neophyte of the kitchen, was there aught but insolence on his tongue when he maligned the comeliness of my sweetmeat shapes? I would not be out of the fashion, Congrio."

"It is but the custom of us cooks," replied Congrio, gravely, "to undervalue our tools, in order to increase the effect of our art. The sweetmeat shape is a fair shape, and a lovely; but I would recommend my master, at the first occasion, to purchase some new ones of a——"

"That will suffice," exclaimed Diomed, who seemed resolved never to allow his slave to finish his sentences. "Now, resume thy charge—shine—eclipse thyself. Let men envy Diomed his cook—let the slaves of Pompeii style thee Congrio the great! Go! yet stay—thou hast not spent all the moneys I gave thee for the marketing?"

"'All!'—alas! the nightingales' tongues and the Roman *tomacula*,* and the oysters from Britain, and sundry other things, too numerous now to recite, are yet left unpaid for. But what matter? every one trusts the *Archimagris* of Diomed the wealthy!"

"Oh, unconscionable prodigal!—what waste!—what profusion!—I am ruined! But go, hasten—inspect!—taste!—perform!—surpass thyself! Let the Roman senator not despise the poor Pompeian. Away, slave—and remember, the Phrygian attagens."

The chief disappeared within his natural domain, and Diomed rolled back his portly presence to the more courtly chambers. All was to his liking—the flowers were fresh, the fountains played briskly, the mosaic pavements were as smooth as mirrors.

"Where is my daughter Julia?" he asked. "At the bath."

"Ah! that reminds me!—time wanes!—and I must bathe also."

Our story returns to Apæcides. On awaking that day from the broken and feverish sleep which had followed his adoption of a faith so strikingly and sternly at variance with that in which his youth had been nurtured, the young priest could scarcely imagine that he was not yet in a dream; he had crossed the fatal river—the past was henceforth to have no sympathy with the future; the two worlds were distinct and separate,—that which had been, from that which was to be. To what a bold and adventurous enterprise he had pledged his life!—to unveil the mysteries in which he had participated—to desecrate the altars he had served—to denounce the goddess whose ministering robe he wore! Slowly he became sensible of the hatred and the horror he should provoke amongst the pious, even if successful; if frustrated in his daring attempt, what penalties might he not incur for an offence hitherto unheard of—for which no specific law, derived from experience, was prepared; and which, for that very reason, precedents, dragged from the sharpest armory of obsolete and inapplicable legislation, would probably be distorted to meet! His friends,—the sister of his youth,—could he expect justice, though he might receive compassion, from them? This brave and heroic act would by their heathen eyes be regarded, perhaps, as a heinous apostasy—at the best, as a pitiable madness.

He dared, he renounced, everything in this world, in the hope of securing that eternity in the next, which had so suddenly been revealed to him. While these thoughts on the one hand invaded his breast, on the other hand his pride, his courage, and his virtue, mingled with reminiscences of revenge for deceit, of indignant disgust at fraud, conspired to raise and to support him.

The conflict was sharp and keen; but his new feelings triumphed over his old: and a mighty argument in favor of wrestling with the sanctities of old opinions and hereditary forms might be found in the conquest over both, achieved by that humble priest. Had the early Christians been more controlled by "the solemn plausibilities of custom"—less of democrats in the pure and lofty acceptation of that perverted word, —Christianity would have perished in its cradle!

As each priest in succession slept several nights together in the chambers of the temple, the term imposed on Apæcides was not yet completed; and when he had risen from his couch, attired himself, as usual, in his robes, and left his narrow chamber, he found himself before the altars of the temple.

In the exhaustion of his late emotions he had slept far into the morning, and the vertical sun already poured its fervid beams over the sacred place.

"*Salve,* Apæcides!" said a voice, whose natural asperity was smoothed by long artifice into an almost displeasing softness of tone. "Thou art late abroad; has the goddess revealed herself to thee in visions?"

"Could she reveal her true self to the people, Calenus, how incenseless would be these altars!"

"That," replied Calenus, "may possibly be true; but the deity is wise enough to hold commune with none but priests."

"A time may come when she will be unveiled without her own acquiescence."

"It is not likely: she has triumphed for countless ages. And that which has so long stood the test of time rarely succumbs to the lust of novelty. But hark ye, young brother!

these sayings are indiscreet." "It is not for thee to silence them," replied Apæcides, haughtily.

"So hot!—yet I will not quarrel with thee. Why, my Apæcides, has not the Egyptian convinced thee of the necessity of our dwelling together in unity? Has he not convinced thee of the wisdom of deluding the people and enjoying ourselves? If not, oh, brother! he is not that great magician he is esteemed."

"Thou, then, hast shared his lessons?" said Apæcides, with a hollow smile.

"Ay! but I stood less in need of them than thou. Nature had already gifted me with the love of pleasure, and the desire of gain and power. Long is the way that leads the voluptuary to the severities of life; but it is only one step from pleasant sin to sheltering hypocrisy. Beware the vengeance of the goddess, if the shortness of that step be disclosed!"

"Beware, thou, the hour when the tomb shall be rent, and the rottenness exposed," returned Apæcides, solemnly. *"Vale!"*

With these words he left the flamen to his meditations. When he got a few paces from the temple, he turned to look back. Calenus had already disappeared in the entry room of the priests, for it now approached the hour of that repast which, called *prandium* by the ancients, answers in point of date to the breakfast of the moderns. The white and graceful fane gleamed brightly in the sun. Upon the altars before it rose the incense and bloomed the garlands. The priest gazed long and wistfully upon the scene—it was the last time that it was ever beheld by him!

He then turned and pursued his way slowly towards the house of Ione; for before, possibly, the last tie that united them was cut in twain—before the uncertain peril of the next day was incurred, he was anxious to see his last surviving relative, his fondest, as his earliest friend.

He arrived at her house, and found her in the garden with Nydia.

"This is kind, Apæcides," said Ione, joyfully; "and how eagerly have I wished to see thee!—what thanks do I not owe thee? How churlish hast thou been to answer none of my letters—to abstain from coming hither to receive the expressions of my gratitude! Oh, thou hast assisted to preserve thy sister from dishonor! What, what can she say to thank thee, now thou art come at last?"

"My sweet Ione, thou owest me no gratitude, for thy cause was mine. Let us avoid that subject, let us recur not to that impious man—how hateful to both of us! I may have a speedy opportunity to teach the world the nature of his pretended wisdom and hypocritical severity. But let us sit down, my sister; I am wearied with the heat of the sun; let us sit in yonder shade, and, for a little while longer, be to each other what we have been.

Beneath a wide plane-tree, with the cistus and the arbutus clustering round them, the living fountain before, the greensward beneath their feet; the gay cicada, once so dear to Athens, rising merrily ever and anon amidst the grass; the butterfly, beautiful emblem of the soul, dedicated to Psyche, and which has continued to furnish illustrations to the Christian bard, rich in the glowing colors caught from Sicilian skies, hovering about the sunny flowers, itself like a winged flower—in this spot, and this scene, the brother and the sister sat together for the last time on earth. You may tread now on the same place; but the garden is no more, the columns are shattered, the fountain has ceased to play Let the traveller search amongst the ruins of Pompeii for the house of Ione. Its remains are yet visible; but I will not betray them to the gaze of common-place tourists. He who is more sensitive than the herd will discover them easily: when he has done so, let him keep the secret.

They sat down, and Nydia, glad to be alone, retired to the farther end of the garden.

"Ione, my sister," said the young convert, "place your hand upon my brow; let me feel your cool touch. Speak to me, too, for your gentle voice is like a breeze that hath freshness as well as music. Speak to me, but *forbear to bless me!* Utter not one word of those forms of speech which our childhood was taught to consider sacred!"

"Alas! and what then shall I say? Our language of affection is so woven with that of worship, that the words grow chilled and trite if I banish from them allusion to our gods."

"*Our gods!*" murmured Apæcides, with a shudder: "thou slightest my request already."

"Shall I speak then to thee only of Isis?"

"The Evil Spirit! No, rather be dumb for ever, unless at least thou canst—but away, away this talk! Not now will we dispute and cavil; not now will we judge harshly of each other. Thou, regarding me as an apostate! and I all sorrow and shame for thee as an idolator. No, my sister, let us avoid such topics and such thoughts. In thy sweet presence a calm falls over my spirit. For a little while I forget. As I thus lay my temples on thy bosom, as I thus feel thy gentle arm embrace me, I think that we are children once more, and that the heaven smiles equally upon both. For oh! if hereafter I escape, no matter what peril; and it be permitted me to address thee on one sacred and awful subject; should I find thine ear closed and thy heart hardened, what hope for myself could countervail the despair for thee? In thee, my sister, I behold a likeness made beautiful, made noble, of myself. Shall the mirror live for ever, and the form itself be broken as the potter's clay? Ah, no—no—thou wilt listen to me yet! Dost thou remember how we went into the fields by Baiæ, hand in hand together, to pluck the flowers of spring? Even so, hand in hand, shall we enter the Eternal Garden, and crown ourselves with imperishable asphodel!"

Wondering and bewildered by words she could not comprehend, but excited even to tears by the plaintiveness of their tone, Ione listened to these outpourings of a full and oppressed heart. In truth, Apæcides himself was softened much beyond his ordinary mood, which to outward seeming was usually either sullen or impetuous. For the noblest desires are of a jealous nature—they engross, they absorb the soul, and often leave the splenetic humors stagnant and unheeded at the surface. Unheeding the petty things around us, we are deemed morose: impatient at earthly interruption to the diviner dreams, we are thought irritable and churlish. For as there is no chimera vainer than the hope that one human heart shall find sympathy in another, so none ever interpret us with justice; and none, no, not our nearest and our dearest ties, forbear with us in mercy! When we are dead and repentance comes too late, both friend and foe may wonder to think how little there was in us to forgive!

"I will talk to thee then of our early years," said Ione. "Shall yon blind girl sing to thee of the days of childhood? Her voice is sweet and musical, and she hath a song on that theme which contains none of those allusions it pains thee to hear."

"Dost thou remember the words, my sister?" asked Apæcides. "Methinks yes; for the tune, which is simple, fixed them on my memory."

"Sing to me then thyself. My ear is not in unison with unfamiliar voices; and thine, Ione, full of household associations, has ever been to me more sweet than all the hireling melodies of Lycia or of Crete. Sing to me!"

Ione beckoned to a slave that stood in the portico, and sending for her lute, sang, when it arrived, to a tender and simple air, the following verses:—

A REGRET FOR CHILDHOOD

I.

"It is not that our earlier Heaven
    Escapes its April showers,
Or that to childhood's heart is given
    No snake amidst the flowers.
        Ah! twined with grief
        Each brightest leaf,
    That's wreath'd us by the Hours!
Young though we be, the Past may sting,
    The present feed its sorrow;
But hope shines bright on every thing
    That waits us with the morrow.
        Like sun-lit glades,
        The dimmest shades
    Some rosy beam can borrow.

II.

It is not that our later years
    Of cares are woven wholly,
But smiles less swiftly chase the tears,
    And wounds are heal'd more slowly.
        And Memory's vow
        To lost ones now,
    Makes joys too bright, unholy.
And ever fled the Iris bow
    That smiled when clouds were o'er us.
If storms should burst, uncheer'd we go,
    A drearier waste before us;—
        And with the toys
        Of childish joys,
    We've broke the staff that bore us!"

Wisely and delicately had Ione chosen that song, sad though its burthen seemed; for when we are deeply mournful, discordant above all others is the voice of mirth: the fittest spell is that borrowed from melancholy itself, for dark thoughts can be softened down when they cannot be brightened; and so they lose the precise and rigid outline of their truth, and their colors melt into the ideal. As the leech applies in remedy to the internal sore some outward irritation, which, by a gentler wound, draws away the venom of that which is more deadly, thus, in the rankling festers of the mind, our art is to divert to a milder sadness on the surface the pain that gnaweth at the core. And so with Apæcides: yielding to the influence of the silver voice that reminded him of the past, and told but of half the sorrow born to the present, he forgot his more immediate and fiery sources of anxious thought. He spent hours in making Ione alternately sing to, and converse with, him; and when he rose to leave her, it was with a calmed and lulled mind.

"Ione," said he, as he pressed her hand, "should you hear my name blackened and maligned, will you credit the aspersion?" "Never, my brother, never!"

"Dost thou not imagine, according to thy belief, that the evil-doer is punished hereafter, and the good rewarded?"

"Can you doubt it?"

"Dost thou think, then, that he who is truly good should sacrifice every selfish interest in his zeal for virtue?"

"He who doth so is the equal of the gods."

"And thou believest that, according to the purity and courage with which he thus acts, shall be his portion of bliss beyond the grave?" "So we are taught to hope."

"Kiss me, my sister. One question more.—Thou art to be wedded to Glaucus: perchance that marriage may separate us more hopelessly—but not of this speak I now;—thou art to be married to Glaucus,—dost thou love him? Nay, my sister, answer me by words." "Yes!" murmured Ione, blushing.

"Dost thou feel that, for his sake, thou couldst renounce pride, brave dishonor, and incur death? I have heard that when women really love, it is to that excess."

"My brother, all this could I do for Glaucus, and feel that it were not a sacrifice. There is no sacrifice to those who love, in what is borne for the one we love."

"Enough! shall woman feel thus for man, and man feel less devotion to his God?"

He spoke no more. His whole countenance seemed instinct and inspired with a divine life: his chest swelled proudly; his eyes glowed: on his forehead was writ the majesty of a man who can dare be noble! He turned to meet the eyes of Ione— earnest, wistful, fearful;—he kissed her fondly, strained her warmly to his breast, and in a moment more he had left the house.

Long did Ione remain in the same place, mute and thoughtful. The maidens again and again came to warn her of the deepening noon, and her engagement to Diomed's banquet. At length she woke from her reverie, and prepared, not with the pride of beauty, but listless and melancholy, for the festival: one thought alone reconciled her to the promised visit—she should meet Glaucus—she could confide to him her alarm and uneasiness for her brother.

CHAPTER III.

A fashionable party and a dinner à la mode in Pompeii.

MEANWHILE Sallust and Glaucus were slowly strolling towards the house of Diomed. Despite the habits of his life, Sallust was not devoid of many estimable qualities. He would have been an active friend, a useful citizen—in short an excellent man, if he had not taken it into his head to be a philosopher. Brought up in the schools in which Roman plagiarism worshipped the echo of Grecian wisdom, he had imbued himself with those doctrines by which the later Epicureans corrupted the simple maxims of their great master. He gave himself altogether up to pleasure, and imagined there was no sage like a boon companion. Still, however, he had a considerable degree of learning, wit, and good-nature; and the hearty frankness of his very vices seemed like virtue itself beside the utter corruption of Clodius and the prostrate effeminacy of Lepidus; and therefore Glaucus liked him the best of his companions; and he, in turn, appreciating the nobler qualities of the Athenian, loved him almost as much as a cold muræna, or a bowl of the best Falernian.

"This is a vulgar old fellow, this Diomed," said Sallust; "but he has some good qualities—in his cellar!"

"And some charming ones—in his daughter."

"True, Glaucus: but you are not much moved by them, methinks. I fancy Clodius is desirous to be your successor."

"He is welcome.—At the banquet of Julia's beauty, no guest, be sure, is considered a musca."

"You are severe: but she has, indeed, something of the Corinthian about her—they will be well-matched, after all! What good-natured fellows we are, to associate with that gambling good-for-nought!" "Pleasure unites strange varieties," answered Glaucus. "He amuses me——"

"And flatters;—but then he pays himself well! He powders his praise with gold-dust." "You often hint that he plays unfairly—think you so really?"

"My dear Glaucus, a Roman noble has his dignity to keep up—dignity is very expensive—Clodius must cheat like a scoundrel, in order to live like a gentleman."

"Ha ha!—well, of late I have renounced the dice. Ah! Sallust, when I am wedded to Ione, I trust I may yet redeem a youth of follies. We are both born for better things than those in which we sympathize now—born to render our worship in nobler temples than the sty of Epicurus."

"Alas!" returned Sallust, in rather a melancholy tone, "what do we know more than this,—life is short—beyond the grave all is dark? There is no wisdom like that which says 'enjoy.'"

"By Bacchus! I doubt sometimes if we *do* enjoy the utmost of which life is capable."

"I am a moderate man," returned Sallust, "and do not ask 'the utmost.' We are like malefactors, and intoxicate ourselves with wine and myrrh, as we stand on the brink of death; but, if we did not do so, the abyss would look very disagreeable. I own that I was inclined to be gloomy until I took so heartily to drinking—that is a new life, my Glaucus."

"Yes! but it brings us next morning to a new death."

"Why, the next morning is unpleasant, I own; but, then, if it were not so, one would never be inclined to read. I study betimes—because, by the gods! I am generally unfit for anything else till noon." "Fie, Scythian!"

"Pshaw! the fate of Pentheus to him who denies Bacchus."

"Well, Sallust, with all your faults, you are the best profligate I ever met; and verily, if I were in danger of life, you are the only man in all Italy who would stretch out a finger to save me."

"Perhaps *I* should not, if it were in the middle of supper. But, in truth, we Italians are fearfully selfish."

"So are all men who are not free," said Glaucus, with a sigh. "Freedom alone makes men sacrifice to each other."

"Freedom, then, must be a very fatiguing thing to an Epicurean," answered Sallust. "But here we are at our host's."

As Diomed's villa is one of the most considerable in point of size of any yet discovered at Pompeii, and is, moreover, built much according to the specific instructions for a suburban villa laid down by the Roman architect, it may not be uninteresting briefly to describe the plan of the apartments through which our visitors passed.

They entered, then, by the same small vestibule at which we have before been presented to the aged Medon, and passed at once into a colonnade, technically termed the peristyle; for the main difference between the suburban villa and the town mansion consisted in placing, in the first, the said colonnade in exactly the same place as that which in the town mansion was occupied by the atrium. In the centre of the peristyle was an open court, which contained the impluvium.

From this peristyle descended a staircase to the offices; another narrow passage on the opposite side communicated with a garden; various small apartments surrounded the colonnade, appropriated probably to country visitors. Another door to the left on entering communicated with a small triangular portico, which belonged to the baths; and behind was the wardrobe, in which were kept the vests of the holiday suits of the slaves, and perhaps, of the master. Seventeen centuries afterwards were found those relics of ancient finery calcined and crumbling; kept longer, alas! than their thrifty lord foresaw.

Return we to the peristyle, and endeavor now to present to the reader a *coup-d'œil* of the whole suite of apartments, which immediately stretched before the steps of the visitors.

Let him then first imagine the columns of the portico hung with festoons of flowers; the columns themselves in the lower part painted red, and the walls around glowing with various frescoes; then, looking beyond a curtain, three parts drawn aside, the eye caught the tablinum of saloon (which was closed at will by glazed doors, now slid back into the walls). On either side of this tablinum, were small rooms, one of which was a kind of cabinet of gems; and these apartments, as well as the tablinum, communicated with a long gallery, which opened at either end upon terraces; and between the terraces, and communicating with the central part of the gallery, was a hall, in which the banquet was that day prepared. All these apartments, though almost on a level with the street, were one story above the garden; and the terraces communicating with the gallery were continued into corridors, raised above the pillars, which, to the right and left, skirted the garden below.

Beneath, and on a level with the garden, ran the apartments we have already described as chiefly appropriated to Julia.

In the gallery, then, just mentioned, Diomed received his guests.

The merchant affected greatly the man of letters, and, therefore, he also affected a passion for everything Greek; he paid particular attention to Glaucus.

"You will see, my friend," said he, with a wave of his hand, "that I am a little classical here—a little Cecropian—eh? The hall in which we shall sup is borrowed from the Greeks. It is an Œcus Cyzicene. Noble Sallust, they have not, I am told, this sort of apartment in Rome."

"Oh!" replied Sallust, with a half-smile; "you Pompeians combine all that is most eligible in Greece and in Rome: may you, Diomed, combine the viands as well as the architecture!"

"You shall see—you shall see, my Sallust," replied the merchant. "We have a taste at Pompeii, and we have also money."

"They are two excellent things," replied Sallust. "But, behold, the lady Julia!"

The main difference, as I have before remarked in the manner of life observed among the Athenians and Romans, was, that with the first, the modest woman rarely or never took part in entertainments; with the latter, they were the common ornaments of the banquet; but when they were present at the feast, it usually terminated at an early hour.

Magnificently robed in white, interwoven with pearls and threads of gold, the handsome Julia entered the apartment.

Scarcely had she received the salutation of the two guests, ere Pansa and his wife, Lepidus, Clodius, and the Roman senator, entered almost simultaneously; then came the widow Fulvia; then the poet Fulvius, like to the widow in name if in nothing else; the warrior from Herculaneum, accompanied by his umbra, next stalked in; afterwards, the less eminent of the guests. Ione yet tarried.

It was the mode among the courteous ancients to flatter whenever it was in their power: accordingly it was a sign of ill-breeding to seat themselves immediately on entering the house of their host. After performing the salutation, which was usually accomplished by the same cordial shake of the right hand which we ourselves retain, and sometimes, by the yet more familiar embrace, they spent several minutes in surveying the apartment, and admiring the bronzes, the pictures, or the furniture, with which it was adorned—a mode very impolite according to our refined English notions, which place good-breeding in indifference. We would not for the world express much admiration of another man's house, for fear it should be thought we had never seen anything so fine before!

"A beautiful statue this of Bacchus!" said the Roman senator. "A mere trifle!" replied Diomed. "What charming paintings!" said Fulvia. "Mere trifles!" answered the owner.

"Exquisite candelabra!" cried the warrior. "Exquisite!" echoed his umbra. "Trifles! trifles!" reiterated the merchant.

Meanwhile, Glaucus found himself by one of the windows of the gallery, which communicated with the terraces, and the fair Julia by his side.

"Is it an Athenian virtue, Glaucus," said the merchant's daughter, "to shun those whom we once sought?"

"Fair Julia—no!"

"Yet, methinks, it is one of the qualities of Glaucus."

"Glaucus never shuns a *friend!*" replied the Greek with some emphasis on the last word.

"May Julia rank among the number of his friends?"

"It would be an honor to the emperor to find a friend in one so lovely."

"You evade my question," returned the enamoured Julia. "But tell me, is it true that you admire the Neapolitan Ione?"

"Does not beauty constrain our admiration?"

"Ah! subtle Greek, still do you fly the meaning of my words. But say, shall Julia be indeed your friend?"

"If she will so favor me, blessed be the gods! The day in which I am thus honored shall be ever marked in white."

"Yet, even while you speak, your eye is restless—your color comes and goes—you move away involuntarily—you are impatient to join Ione."

For at that moment Ione had entered, and Glaucus had indeed betrayed the emotion noticed by the jealous beauty.

"Can admiration to one woman make me unworthy the friendship of another? Sanction not so, O Julia, the libels of the poets on your sex!"

"Well, you are right—or I will learn to think so. Glaucus, yet one moment! You are to wed Ione; is it not so?"

"If the Fates permit, such is my blessed hope."

"Accept, then, from me, in token of our new friendship, a present for your bride. Nay, it is the custom of friends, you know, always to present to bride and bridegroom some such little marks of their esteem and favoring wishes."

"Julia! I cannot refuse any token of friendship from one like you. I will accept the gift as an omen from Fortune herself."

"Then, after the feast, when the guests retire, you will descend with me to my apartment, and receive it from my hands. Remember!" said Julia, as she joined the wife of Pansa and left Glaucus to seek Ione.

The widow Fulvia and the spouse of the ædile were engaged in high and grave discussion.

"O Fulvia! I assure you that the last account from Rome declares that the frizzling mode of dressing the hair is growing antiquated; they only now wear it built up in a tower, like Julia's, or arranged as a helmet—the *Galerian* fashion, like mine, you see: it has a fine effect, I think. I assure you, Vespius (Vespius was the name of the Herculaneum hero) admires it greatly."

"And nobody wears the hair like yon Neapolitan, in the Greek way."

"What, parted in front, with the knot behind? Oh, no; how ridiculous it is! it reminds one of the statue of Diana! Yet this Ione is handsome, eh?"

"So the men say; but then she is rich: she is to marry the Athenian—I wish her joy. He will not be long faithful, I suspect; those foreigners are very faithless."

"Oh, Julia!" said Fulvia, as the merchant's daughter joined them; "have you seen the tiger yet?" "No!"

"Why, all the ladies have been to see him. He is so handsome!"

"I hope we shall find some criminal or other for him and the lion," replied Julia. "Your husband (turning to Pansa's wife) is not so active as he should be in this matter."

"Why, really, the laws are too mild," replied the dame of the helmet. "There are so few offences to which the punishment of the arena can be awarded; and then, too, the gladiators are growing effeminate! The stoutest bestiarii declare they are willing enough to fight a boar or a bull; but as for a lion or a tiger, they think the game too much in earnest."

"They are worthy of a mitre," replied Julia, in disdain.

"Oh! have you seen the new house of Fulvius, the dear poet?" said Pansa's wife. "No: is it handsome?"

"Very!—such good taste. But they say, my dear, that he has such improper pictures! He won't show them to the women: how ill-bred!"

"Those poets are always odd," said the widow. "But he is an interesting man; what pretty verses he writes! We improve very much in poetry; it is impossible to read the old stuff now."

"I declare I am of your opinion," returned the lady of the helmet. "There is so much more force and energy in the modern school." The warrior sauntered up to the ladies.

"It reconciles me to peace," said he, "when I see such faces."

"Oh! you heroes are ever flatterers," returned Fulvia, hastening to appropriate the compliment specially to herself.

"By this chain, which I received from the emperor's own hand," replied the warrior, playing with a short chain which hung round the neck like a collar, instead of descending to the breast, according to the fashion of the peaceful—"By this chain, you wrong me! I am a blunt man—a soldier should be so."

"How do you find the ladies of Pompeii generally?" said Julia.

"By Venus, most beautiful! They favor me a little, it is true, and that inclines my eyes to double their charms."

"We love a warrior," said the wife of Pansa.

"I see it: by Hercules! it is even disagreeable to be too celebrated in these cities. At Herculaneum they climb the roof of my atrium to catch a glimpse of me though the compluvium; the admiration of one's citizens is pleasant at first, but burthensome afterwards."

"True, true, O Vespius!" cried the poet, joining the group: "I find it so myself."

"You!" said the stately warrior, scanning the small form of the poet with ineffable disdain. "In what legion have *you* served?"

"You may see my spoils, my exuviæ, in the forum itself," returned the poet, with a significant glance at the women. "I have been among the tent-companions, the *contubernales,* of the great Mantuan himself."

"I know no general from Mantua," said the warrior, gravely. "What campaign have you served?"

"That of Helicon." "I never heard of it."

"Nay, Vespius, he does but joke," said Julia, laughing.

"Joke! By Mars, am I a man to be joked!"

"Yes; Mars himself was in love with the mother of jokes," said the poet, a little alarmed. "Know, then, O Vespius, that I am the poet Fulvius. It is I who make warriors immortal!"

"The gods forbid!" whispered Sallust to Julia. "If Vespius were made immortal, what a specimen of tiresome braggadocio would be transmitted to posterity!"

The soldier looked puzzled; when, to the infinite relief of himself and his companions, the signal for the feast was given.

As we have already witnessed at the house of Glaucus the ordinary routine of a Pompeian entertainment, the reader is spared any second detail of the courses, and the manner in which they were introduced.

Diomed, who was rather ceremonious, had appointed a nomenclator, or appointer of places, to each guest.

The reader understands that the festive board was composed of three tables; one at the centre, and one at each wing. It was only at the outer side of these tables that the guests reclined; the inner space was left untenanted, for the greater convenience of the waiters or ministri. The extreme corner of one of the wings was appropriated to Julia as the lady of the feast; that next her, to Diomed. At one corner of the centre table was placed the ædile; at the opposite corner, the Roman senator—these were the posts of honor. The other guests were arranged, so that the young (gentleman or lady) should sit next each other, and the more advanced in years be similarly matched. An agreeable provision enough, but one which must often have offended those who wished to be thought still young.

The chair of Ione was next to the couch of Glaucus. The seats were veneered with tortoise-shell, and covered with quilts stuffed with feathers, and ornamented with costly embroideries. The modern ornaments of epergne or plateau were supplied by images of the gods, wrought in bronze, ivory, and silver. The sacred salt-cellar and the familiar Lares were not forgotten. Over the table and the seats, a rich canopy was suspended from the ceiling. At each corner of the table were lofty candelabras—for though it was early noon, the room was darkened—while from tripods, placed in different parts of the room, distilled the odor of myrrh and frankincense; and upon the abacus, or side-board, large vases and various ornaments of silver were ranged, much with the same ostentation (but with more than the same taste) that we find displayed at a modern feast.

The custom of grace was invariably supplied by that of libations to the gods; and Vesta, as queen of the household gods, usually received first that graceful homage.

This ceremony being performed, the slaves showered flowers upon the couches and the floor, and crowned each guest with rosy garlands, intricately woven with ribands, tied by the rind of the linden-tree, and each intermingled with the ivy and the amethyst—supposed preventives against the effect of wine; the wreaths of the women only were exempted from these leaves, for it was not the fashion for them to drink wine *in public*. It was then that the president Diomed thought it advisable to institute a *basileus,* or director of the feast—an important office, sometimes chosen by lot; sometimes, as now, by the master of the entertainment.

Diomed was not a little puzzled as to his election. The invalid senator was too grave and too infirm for the proper fulfilment of his duty; the ædile Pansa was adequate enough to the task; but then, to choose the next in official rank to the senator, was an affront to the senator himself. While deliberating between the merits of the others, he caught the mirthful glance of Sallust, and, by a sudden inspiration, named the jovial epicure to the rank of director, or *arbiter bibendi*.

Sallust received the appointment with becoming humility.

"I shall be a merciful king," said he, "to those who drink deep; to a recusant, Minos himself shall be less inexorable. Beware!"

The slaves handed round basins of perfumed water, by which lavation the feast commenced: and now the table groaned under the initiatory course.

The conversation, at first desultory and scattered, allowed Ione and Glaucus to carry on those sweet whispers, which are worth all the eloquence in the world. Julia watched them with flashing eyes.

"How soon shall her place be mine!" thought she.

But Clodius, who sat in the centre table, so as to observe well the countenance of Julia, guessed her pique, and resolved to profit by it. He addressed her across the table in set phrases of gallantry; and as he was of high birth and of a showy person, the vain Julia was not so much in love as to be insensible to his attentions.

The slaves, in the interim, were constantly kept upon the alert by the vigilant Sallust, who chased one cup by another with a celerity which seemed as if he were resolved upon exhausting those capacious cellars which the reader may yet see beneath the house of Diomed. The worthy merchant began to repent his choice, as amphora after amphora was pierced and emptied. The slaves, all under the age of manhood (the youngest being about ten years old,—it was they who filled the wine,—the eldest, some five years older, mingled it with water), seemed to share in the zeal of Sallust; and the face of Diomed began to glow as he watched the provoking complacency with which they seconded the exertions of the king of the feast.

"Pardon me, O senator!" said Sallust; "I see you flinch; your purple hem cannot save you—drink!"

"By the gods!" said the senator, coughing, "my lungs are already on fire; you proceed with so miraculous a swiftness, that Phaeton himself was nothing to you. I am infirm, O pleasant Sallust: you must exonerate me."

"Not I, by Vesta! I am an impartial monarch—drink!"

The poor senator, compelled by the laws of the table, was

forced to comply. Alas! every cup was bringing him nearer and nearer to the Stygian pool.

"Gently! gently! my king," groaned Diomed; "we already begin to——"

"Treason!" interrupted Sallust; "no stern Brutus here!— no interference with royalty!" "But our female guests——"

"Love a toper! Did not Ariadne dote upon Bacchus?"

The feast proceeded; the guests grew more talkative and noisy; the dessert or last course was already on the table; and the slaves bore round water with myrrh and hyssop for the finishing lavation. At the same time, a small circular table that had been placed in the space opposite the guests suddenly, and as by magic, seemed to open in the centre, and cast up a fragrant shower, sprinkling the table and the guests; while as it ceased the awning above them was drawn aside, and the guests perceived that a rope had been stretched across the ceiling, and that one of those nimble dancers for which Pompeii was so celebrated, and whose descendants add so charming a grace to the festivities of Astley's or Vauxhall, was now treading his airy measures right over their heads.

This apparition, removed but by a cord from one's pericranium, and indulging the most vehement leaps, apparently with the intention of alighting upon that cerebral region, would probably be regarded with some terror by a party in May Fair; but our Pompeian revellers seemed to behold the spectacle with delighted curiosity, and applauded in proportion as the dancer appeared with the most difficulty to miss falling upon the head of whatever guest he particularly selected to dance above. He paid the senator, indeed, the peculiar compliment of literally falling from the rope, and catching it again with his hand, just as the whole party imagined the skull of the Roman was as much fractured as ever that of the poet whom the eagle took for a tortoise. At length, to the great relief of at least Ione, who had not much accustomed herself to this entertainment, the dancer suddenly paused as a strain of music was heard from without. He danced again still more wildly; the air changed, the dancer paused again; no, it could not dissolve the charm which was supposed to possess him! He represented one who by a strange disorder is compelled to dance, and whom only a certain air of music can cure. At length the musician seemed to hit on the right tune; the dancer gave one leap, swung himself down from the rope, alighted on the floor, and vanished.

One art now yielded to another; and the musicians who were stationed without on the terrace struck up a soft and mellow air, to which were sung the following words, made almost indistinct by the barrier between, and the exceeding lowness of the minstrelsy:—

FESTIVE MUSIC SHOULD BE LOW

I.

"Hark! through these flowers our music sends its greeting
  To your loved halls, where Psilas† shuns the day;
When the young god his Cretan nymph was meeting
  He taught Pan's rustic pipe this gliding lay:
    Soft as the dews of wine
      Shed in this banquet hour,
  The rich libation of Sound's stream divine,
    O reverent harp, to Aphrodite pour!

II.

Wild rings the trump o'er ranks to glory marching;
  Music's sublimer bursts for war are meet;
But sweet lips murmuring under wreaths o'er-arching,
  Find the low whispers like their own most sweet.
    Steal, my lull'd music, steal
      Like woman's half-heard tone,
  So that whoe'er shall hear, shall think to feel
    In thee the voice of lips that love his own."

At the end of that song Ione's cheek blushed more deeply than before, and Glaucus had contrived, under cover of the table, to steal her hand.

"It is a pretty song," said Fulvius, patronizingly.

"Ah! if *you* would oblige us!" murmured the wife of Pansa.

"Do you wish Fulvius to sing?" asked the king of the feast, who had just called on the assembly to drink the health of the Roman senator, a cup to each letter of his name.

"Can you ask?" said the matron, with a complimentary glance at the poet.

Sallust snapped his fingers, and whispering the slave who came to learn his orders, the latter disappeared, and returned

† Bacchus.

in a few moments with a small harp in one hand, and a branch of myrtle in the other.

The slave approached the poet, and with a low reverence presented to him the harp. "Alas! I cannot play," said the poet.

"Then you must sing to the myrtle. It is a Greek fashion: Diomed loves the Greeks—I love the Greeks—you love the Greeks—we all love the Greeks—and between you and me this is not the only thing we have stolen from them. However, I introduce this custom—I, the king: sing, subject, sing!"

The poet, with a bashful smile, took the myrtle in his hands, and after a short prelude sang as follows, in a pleasant and well-tuned voice:—

THE CORONATION OF THE LOVES

I.

"The merry Loves one holiday
    Were all at gambols madly;
But loves too long can seldom play
    Without behaving sadly.
They laugh'd, they toy'd, they romp'd about,
And then for change they all fell out.
        Fie, fie! how can they quarrel so?
        My Lesbia—ah, for shame, love!
        Methinks 'tis scarce an hour ago
        When we did just the same, love.

II.

The Loves, 'tis thought, were free till then,
    They had no king or laws, dear;
But gods, like men, should subject be,
    Say all the ancient saws, dear.
And so our crew resolved, for quiet,
To choose a king to curb their riot.
        A kiss: ah! what a grievous thing
        For both, methinks, 'twould be, child,
        If I should take some prudish king,
        And cease to be so free, child!

III.

Among their toys a Casque they found,
    It was the helm of Ares;
With horrent plumes the crest was crown'd,
    It frighten'd all the Lares.
So fine a king was never known—
They placed the helmet on the throne.
        My girl, since Valor wins the world,

They chose a mighty master;
But thy sweet flag of smiles unfurl'd
Would win the world much faster!

IV.

The Casque soon found the Loves too wild
  A troop for him to school them;
For warriors know how *one* such child
  Has aye contrived to fool them.
They plagued him so, that in despair
He took a wife the plague to share.
    If kings themselves thus find the strife
      Of earth, unshared, severe, girl;
    Why just to halve the ills of life,
      Come, take your partner here, girl.

V.

Within that room the Bird of Love
  The whole affair had eyed then;
The monarch hail'd the royal dove,
  And placed her by his side then;
What mirth amidst the Loves was seen!
'Long live,' they cried, 'our King and Queen!'
    Ah! Lesbia, would that thrones were mine,
      And crowns to deck that brow, love!
    And yet I know that heart of thine
      For me is throne enow, love!

VI.

The urchins hoped to tease the mate
  As they had teased the hero:
But when the Dove in judgment sate,
  They found her worse than Nero!
Each look a frown, each word a law;
The little subjects shook with awe.
    In thee I find the same deceit;—
      Too late, alas! a learner!
    For where a mien more gently sweet?
      And where a tyrant sterner?"

This song, which greatly suited the gay and lively fancy of
the Pompeians, was received with considerable applause, and
the widow insisted on crowning her namesake with the very
branch of myrtle to which he had sung. It was easily twisted
into a garland, and the immortal Fulvius was crowned amidst
the clapping of hands and shouts of *Io triumphe!* The song
and the harp now circulated round the party, a new myrtle

branch being handed about, stopping at each person who could be prevailed upon to sing.

The sun began now to decline, though the revellers, who had worn away several hours, perceived it not in their darkened chamber; and the senator, who was tired, and the warrior, who had to return to Herculaneum, rising to depart, gave the signal for the general dispersion. "Tarry yet a moment, my friends," said Diomed; "if you will go so soon, you must at least take a share in our concluding game."

So saying, he motioned to one of the ministri, and whispering him, the slave went out, and presently returned with a small bowl containing various tablets carefully sealed, and, apparently, exactly similar. Each guest was to purchase one of those at the nominal price of the lowest piece of silver: and the sport of this lottery (which was the favorite diversion of Augustus, who introduced it) consisted in the inequality, and sometimes the incongruity, of the prizes, the nature and amount of which were specified within the tablets. For instance, the poet, with a wry face, drew one of his own poems (no physician ever less willingly swallowed his own draught); the warrior drew a case of bodkins, which gave rise to certain novel witticisms relative to Hercules and the distaff; the widow Fulvia obtained a large drinking-cup; Julia, a gentleman's buckle; and Lepidus, a lady's patch-box. The most appropriate lot was drawn by the gambler Clodius, who reddened with anger on being presented to a set of cogged dice. A certain damp was thrown upon the gaiety which these various lots created by an accident that was considered ominous; Glaucus drew the most valuable of all the prizes, a small marble statue of Fortune, of Grecian workmanship: on handing it to him, the slave suffered it to drop, and it broke in pieces.

A shiver went round the assembly, and each voice cried spontaneously on the gods to avert the omen.

Glaucus alone, though perhaps as superstitious as the rest, affected to be unmoved.

"Sweet Neapolitan," whispered he tenderly to Ione, who had turned pale as the broken marble itself, "I *accept* the omen. It signifies, that in obtaining thee, Fortune can give no more—she breaks *her* image when she blessed me with *thine*."

In order to divert the impression which this incident had occasioned in an assembly which, considering the civilization

of the guests, would seem miraculously superstitious, if at
the present day in a country party we did not often see a lady
grow hypochondriacal on leaving a room last of thirteen,
Sallust now crowning his cup with flowers, gave the health
of their host. This was followed by a similar compliment to
the emperor; and then, with a parting cup to Mercury to send
them pleasant slumbers, they concluded the entertainment by a
last libation, and broke up the party.

Carriages and litters were little used in Pompeii, partly
owing to the extreme narrowness of the streets, partly to the
convenient smallness of the city. Most of the guests replacing
their sandals, which they had put off in the banquet-room, and
induing their cloaks, left the house on foot attended by their
slaves.

Meanwhile, having seen Ione depart, Glaucus, turning to
the staircase which led down to the rooms of Julia, was conducted by a slave to an apartment in which he found the
merchant's daughter already seated.

"Glaucus!" said she, looking down, "I see that you really
love Ione—she is indeed beautiful."

"Julia is charming enough to be generous," replied the
Greek. "Yes, I love Ione; amidst all the youth who court you,
may you have one worshipper as sincere."

"I pray the gods to grant it! See, Glaucus, these pearls
are the present I destine to your bride: may Juno give her
health to wear them!"

So saying, she placed a case in his hand, containing a
row of pearls of some size and price. It was so much the
custom for persons about to be married to receive these gifts,
that Glaucus could have little scruple in accepting the neck-
lace, though the gallant and proud Athenian inly resolved to
requite the gift by one of thrice its value. Julia then stopping
short his thanks, poured forth some wine into a small bowl.

"You have drunk many toasts with my father," said she,
smiling,—"one now with me. Health and fortune to your
bride!"

She touched the cup with her lips and then presented it to
Glaucus. The customary etiquette required that Glaucus should
drain the whole contents; he accordingly did so. Julia, unknowing the deceit which Nydia had practised upon her,
watched him with sparkling eyes; although the witch had told

her that the effect *might* not be immediate, she yet sanguinely trusted to an expeditious operation in favor of her charms. She was disappointed when she found Glaucus coldly replace the cup, and converse with her in the same unmoved but gentle tone as before. And though she detained him as long as she decorously could do, no change took place in his manner.

"But to-morrow," thought she, exultingly recovering her disappointment,—"to-morrow, alas for Glaucus!"

Alas for him, indeed!

CHAPTER IV.

The story halts for a moment at an episode.

RESTLESS and anxious, Apæcides consumed the day in wandering through the most sequestered walks in the vicinity of the city. The sun was slowly setting as he paused beside a lonely part of the Sarnus, ere yet it wound amidst the evidences of luxury and power. Only through openings in the woods and vines were caught glimpses of the white and gleaming city, in which was heard in the distance no din, no sound, nor "busiest hum of men." Amidst the green banks crept the lizard and the grasshopper, and here and there in the brake some solitary bird burst into sudden song, as suddenly stilled. There was deep calm around, but not the calm of night; the air still breathed of the freshness and life of day; the grass still moved to the stir of the insect horde; and on the opposite bank the graceful and white capella passed browsing through the herbage, and paused at the wave to drink.

As Apæcides stood musingly gazing upon the waters, he heard beside him the low bark of a dog.

"Be still, poor friend," said a voice at hand; "the stranger's step harms not thy master." The convert recognized the voice, and, turning, he beheld the old mysterious man whom he had seen in the congregation of the Nazarenes.

The old man was sitting upon a fragment of stone covered with ancient mosses; beside him were his staff and scrip; at his feet lay a small shaggy dog, the companion in how many a pilgrimage perilous and strange.

The face of the old man was as balm to the excited spirit

of the neophyte: he approached, and craving his blessing, sat down beside him.

"Thou art provided as for a journey, father," said he: "wilt thou leave us yet?"

"My son," replied the old man, "the days in store for me on earth are few and scanty; I employ them as becomes me, travelling from place to place, comforting those whom God has gathered together in His name, and proclaiming the glory of His Son, as testified to His servant."

"Thou hast looked, they tell me, on the face of Christ?"

"And the face revived me from the dead. Know, young proselyte to the true faith, that I am he of whom thou readest in the scroll of the Apostle. In the far Judea, and in the city of Nain, there dwelt a widow, humble of spirit and sad of heart; for of all the ties of life one son alone was spared to her. And she loved him with a melancholy love, for he was the likeness of the lost. And the son died. The reed on which she leaned was broken, the oil was dried up in the widow's cruse. They bore the dead upon his bier; and near the gate of the city, where the crowd were gathered, there came a silence over the sounds of woe, for the Son of God was passing by. The mother, who followed the bier, wept,—not noisily, but all who looked upon her saw that her heart was crushed. And the Lord pitied her, and he touched the bier, and said, 'I SAY UNTO THEE, ARISE.' And the dead man woke and looked upon the face of the Lord. Oh, that calm and solemn brow, that unutterable smile, that care-worn and sorrowful face, lighted up with a God's benignity—it chased away the shadows of the grave! I rose, I spoke, I was living, and in my mother's arms—yes, *I* am the dead revived! The people shouted, the funeral horns rang forth merrily: there was a cry, 'God has visited his people!' I heard them not—I felt—I saw—nothing —but the face of the Redeemer!"

The old man paused, deeply moved; and the youth felt his blood creep, and his hair stir. He was in the presence of one who had known the Mystery of Death!

"Till that time," renewed the widow's son, "I had been as other men: thoughtless, not abandoned; taking no heed, but of the things of love and life; nay, I had inclined to the gloomy faith of the earthly Sadducee! But, raised from the dead, from awful and desert dreams that these lips never dare reveal—recalled upon earth, to testify the powers of Heaven— once more mortal, the witness of immortality; I drew a new being from the grave. O faded—O lost Jerusalem!—Him from whom came my life, I beheld adjudged to the agonized and parching death!—Far in the mighty crowd, I saw the light rest and glimmer over the cross; I heard the hooting mob, I cried aloud, I raved, I threatened—none heeded me— I was lost in the whirl and the roar of thousands! But even then, in my agony and His own, methought the glazing eye of the Son of Man sought me out—His lip smiled, as when it conquered death—it hushed me, and I became calm. He who had defied the grave for another,—what was the grave to him? The sun shone aslant the pale and powerful features, and then died away! Darkness fell over the earth; how long it endured, I know not. A loud cry came through the gloom—a sharp and bitter cry!—and all was silent.

"But who shall tell the terrors of the night? I walked along the city—the earth reeled to and fro, and the houses trembled to their base—the living had deserted the streets, but *not the Dead:* through the gloom I saw them glide—the dim and ghastly shapes, in the cerements of the grave,—with horror, and woe, and warning on their unmoving lips and lightless eyes!—they swept by me, as I passed—they glared upon me—I had been their brother; and they bowed their heads in recognition; they had risen to tell the living that the dead *can* rise!" Again the old man paused, and, when he resumed, it was in a calmer tone.

"From that night I resigned all earthly thought but that of serving HIM. A preacher and a pilgrim, I have traversed the remotest corners of the earth, proclaiming His Divinity, and bringing new converts to His fold. I come as the wind, and as the wind depart; sowing, as the wind sows, the seeds that enrich the world.

"Son, on earth we shall meet no more. Forget not this hour,—what are the pleasures and the pomps of life? As the lamp shines, so life glitters for an hour; but the soul's light is the star that burns for ever, in the heart of illimitable space."

It was then that their conversation fell upon the general and sublime doctrines of immortality; it soothed and elevated the young mind of the convert, which yet clung to many of the damps and shadows of that cell of faith which he had so lately left—it was the air of heaven breathing on the prisoner released at last. There was a strong and marked distinction between the Christianity of the old man and that of Olinthus; that of the first was more soft, more gentle, more divine. The hard heroism of Olinthus had something in it fierce and intolerant—it was necessary to the part he was destined to play—it had in it more of the courage of the martyr than the charity of the saint. It aroused, it excited, it nerved, rather than subdued and softened. But the whole heart of that divine old man was bathed in love; the smile of the Deity had burned away from it the leaven of earthlier and coarser passions, and left to the energy of the hero all the meekness of the child.

"And now," said he, rising at length, as the sun's last ray died in the west; "now, in the cool of twilight, I pursue my way towards the Imperial Rome. There yet dwell some holy men, who like me have beheld the face of Christ; and them would I see before I die."

"But the night is chill for thine age, my father, and the way is long, and the robber haunts it; rest thee till to-morrow."

"Kind son, what is there in this scrip to tempt the robber? And the Night and the Solitude!—*these* make the ladder round which angels cluster, and beneath which my spirit can dream of God. Oh! none can know what the pilgrim feels as he walks on his holy course; nursing no fear, and dreading no danger—for God is with him! He hears the winds murmur glad tidings; the woods sleep in the shadow of Almighty wings;—the stars are the Scriptures of Heaven, the tokens of love, and the witnesses of immortality. Night is the Pilgrim's day." With these words the old man pressed Apæcides to his breast, and taking up his staff and scrip, the dog bounded cheerily before him, and with slow steps and downcast eyes he went his way.

The convert stood watching his bended form, till the trees shut the last glimpse from his view; and then, as the stars broke forth, he woke from the musings with a start, reminded of his appointment with Olinthus.

CHAPTER V.

The philtre—Its effect.

WHEN Glaucus arrived at his own home, he found Nydia seated under the portico of his garden. In fact, she had sought his house in the mere chance that he *might* return at an early hour: anxious, fearful, anticipative, she resolved upon seizing the earliest opportunity of availing herself of the love-charm, while at the same time she half hoped the opportunity might be deferred.

It was then, in that fearful burning mood, her heart beating, her cheek flushing, that Nydia awaited the possibility of Glaucus's return before the night. He crossed the portico just as the first stars began to rise, and the heaven above had assumed its most purple robe.

"Ho, my child, wait you for me?"

"Nay, I have been tending the flowers, and did but linger a little while to rest myself."

"It has been warm," said Glaucus, placing himself also on one of the seats beneath the colonnade. "Very."

"Wilt thou summon Davus? The wine I have drunk heats me, and I long for some cooling drink."

Here at once, suddenly and unexpectedly, the very opportunity that Nydia awaited presented itself; of himself, at his own free choice, he afforded to her that occasion. She breathed quick—"I will prepare for you myself," said she, "the summer draught that Ione loves—of honey and weak wine cooled in snow." "Thanks," said the unconscious Glaucus. "If Ione love it, enough; it would be grateful were it poison."

Nydia frowned, and then smiled; she withdrew for a few moments, and returned with the cup containing the beverage. Glaucus took it from her hand. What would not Nydia have given then for one hour's prerogative of sight, to have watched her hopes ripening to effect;—to have seen the first dawn of the imagined love;—to have worshipped with more than Persian adoration the rising of that sun which her credulous

256

soul believed was to break upon her dreary night! Far different, as she stood then and there, were the thoughts, the emotions of the blind girl, from those of the vain Pompeian under a similar suspense. In the last, what poor and frivolous passions had made up the daring whole! What petty pique, what small revenge, what expectation of a paltry triumph, had swelled the attributes of that sentiment she dignified with the name of love! but in the wild heart of the Thessalian all was pure, uncontrolled, unmodified passion;—erring, unwomanly, frenzied, but debased by no elements of a more sordid feeling. Filled with love as with life itself, how could she resist the occasion of winning love in return!

She leaned for support against the wall, and her face, before so flushed, was now white as snow, and with her delicate hands clasped convulsively together, her lips apart, her eyes on the ground, she waited the next words Glaucus should utter.

Glaucus had raised the cup to his lips, he had already drained about a fourth of its contents, when his eye suddenly glancing upon the face of Nydia, he was so forcibly struck by its alteration, by its intense, and painful, and strange expression, that he paused abruptly, and still holding the cup near his lips, exclaimed—

"Why, Nydia! Nydia! I say, art thou ill or in pain? Nay, thy face speaks for thee. What ails my poor child?" As he spoke, he put down the cup and rose from his seat to approach her, when a sudden pang shot coldly to his heart, and was followed by a wild, confused, dizzy sensation at the brain. The floor seemed to glide from under him—his feet seemed to move on air—a mighty and unearthly gladness rushed upon his spirit—he felt too buoyant for the earth—he longed for wings, nay, it seemed in the buoyancy of his new existence, as if he possessed them. He burst involuntarily into a loud and thrilling laugh. He clapped his hands—he bounded aloft—he was as a Pythoness inspired; suddenly as it came this preternatural transport passed, though only partially, away. He now felt his blood rushing loudly and rapidly through his veins; it seemed to swell, to exult, to leap along, as a stream that has burst its bounds, and hurries to the ocean. It throbbed in his ear with a mighty sound, he felt it mount to his brow, he felt the veins in the temples stretch and swell as if they could no

longer contain the violent and increasing tide—then a kind
of darkness fell over his eyes—darkness, but not entire; for
through the dim shade he saw the opposite walls glow out,
and the figures painted thereon seemed, ghost-like, to creep
and glide. What was most strange, he did not feel himself
ill—he did not sink or quail beneath the dread frenzy that was
gathering over him. The novelty of the feelings seemed bright
and vivid—he felt as if a younger health had been infused
into his frame. He was gliding on to madness—and he knew
it not!

Nydia had not answered his first question—she had not
been able to reply—his wild and fearful laugh had roused her
from her passionate suspense: she could not see his fierce
gesture—she could not mark his reeling and unsteady step
as he paced unconsciously to and fro; but she heard the words,
broken, incoherent, insane, that gushed from his lips. She
became terrified and appalled—she hastened to him, feeling
with her arms until she touched his knees, and then falling
on the ground she embraced them, weeping with terror and
excitement.

"Oh, speak to me! speak! you do not hate me?—speak,
speak!"

"By the bright goddess, a beautiful land this Cyprus! Ho!
how they fill us with wine instead of blood! now they open
the veins of the Faun yonder, to show how the tide within
bubbles and sparkles. Come hither, jolly old god! thou ridest
on a goat, eh?—what long silky hair he has! He is worth all
the coursers of Parthia. But a word with thee—this wine of
thine is too strong for us mortals. Oh! beautiful! the boughs
are at rest! the green waves of the forest have caught the
Zephyr and drowned him! Not a breath stirs the leaves—and
I view the Dreams sleeping with folded wings upon the motionless elm; and I look beyond, and I see a blue stream sparkle
in the silent noon; a fountain—a fountain springing aloft!
Ah! my fount, thou wilt not put out the rays of my Grecian
sun, though thou triest ever so hard with thy nimble and silver
arms. And now, what form steals yonder through the boughs?
she glides like a moonbeam?—she has a garland of oak-leaves
on her head. In her hand is a vase upturned, from which she
pours pink and tiny shells, and sparkling water. Oh! look on
yon face! Man never before saw its like. See! we are alone;

only I and she in the wide forest. There is no smile upon her lips—she moves, grave and sweetly sad. Ha! fly, it is a nymph!—it is one of the wild Napææ! whoever sees her becomes mad—fly! see, she discovers me!"

"Oh! Glaucus! Glaucus! do you not know me? Rave not so wildly, or thou wilt kill me with a word!"

A new change seemed now to operate upon the jarring and disordered mind of the unfortunate Athenian. He put his hands upon Nydia's silken hair; he smoothed the locks—he looked wistfully upon her face, and then, as in the broken chain of thought one or two links were yet unsevered, it seemed that her countenance brought its associations of Ione; and with that remembrance his madness became yet more powerful, and it was swayed and tinged by passion, as he burst forth,—

"I swear by Venus, by Diana, and by Juno, that though I have now the world on my shoulders, as my countryman Hercules (ah, dull Rome! whoever was truly great was of Greece; why, you would be godless if it were not for us!)—I say, as my countryman Hercules had before me, I would let it fall into chaos for one smile from Ione. Ah, Beautiful,— Adored," he added, in a voice inexpressibly fond and plaintive, "thou lovest me not. Thou art unkind to me. The Egyptian hath belied me to thee—thou knowest not what hours I have spent beneath thy casement—thou knowest not how I have outwatched the stars, thinking thou, my sun, wouldst rise at last,—and thou lovest me not, thou forsakest me! Oh! do not leave me now! I feel that my life will not be long; let me gaze on thee at least unto the last. I am of the bright land of thy fathers—I have trod the heights of Phyle—I have gathered the hyacinth and rose amidst the olive-groves of Ilyssus. *Thou* shouldst not desert me, for thy fathers were brothers to my own. And they say this land is lovely, and these climes serene, but I will bear thee with me—Ho! dark form, why risest thou like a cloud between me and mine? Death sits calmly dread upon thy brow—on thy lip is the smile that slays: thy name is Orcus, but on earth men call thee Arbaces. See, I know thee! fly, dim shadow, thy spells avail not!"

"Glaucus! Glaucus!" murmured Nydia, releasing her hold

and falling, beneath the excitement of her dismay, remorse, and anguish, insensible on the floor.

"Who calls?" said he, in a loud voice. "Ione, it is she! they have borne her off—we will save her—where is my stilus? Ha, I have it! I come, Ione, to thy rescue! I come! I come!"

So saying, the Athenian with one bound passed the portico, he traversed the house, and rushed with swift but vacillating steps, and muttering audibly to himself, down the star-lit streets. The direful potion burnt like fire in his veins, for its effect was made, perhaps, still more sudden from the wine he had drunk previously. Used to the excesses of nocturnal revellers, the citizens, with smiles and winks, gave way to his reeling steps; they naturally imagined him under the influence of the Bromian god, not vainly worshipped at Pompeii; but they who looked twice upon his face started in a nameless fear, and the smile withered from their lips. He passed the more populous streets; and, pursuing mechanically the way to Ione's house, he traversed a more deserted quarter, and entered now the lonely grove of Cybele, in which Apæcides had held his interview with Olinthus.

CHAPTER VI.

A reunion of different actors.—Streams that flowed apparently apart rush into one gulf.

Impatient to learn whether the fell drug had yet been administered by Julia to his hated rival, and with what effect, Arbaces resolved, as the evening came on, to seek her house, and satisfy his suspense. It was customary, as I have before said, for men at that time to carry abroad with them the tablets and the stilus attached to their girdle; and with the girdle they were put off when at home. In fact, under the appearance of a literary instrument, the Romans carried about with them in that same stilus a very sharp and formidable weapon. It was with his stilus that Cassius stabbed Cæsar in the senate-house. Taking, then, his girdle and his cloak, Arbaces left his house, supporting his steps, which were still somewhat feeble (though hope and vengeance had conspired greatly with his own medical science, which was profound, to restore his natural strength) by his long staff: Arbaces took his way to the villa of Diomed.

And beautiful is the moonlight of the south! In those climes the night so quickly glides into the day, that twilight scarcely makes a bridge between them. One moment of darker purple in the sky—of a thousand rose-hues in the water—of shade half victorious over light; and then burst forth at once the countless stars—the moon is up—night has resumed her reign!

Brightly then, and softly bright, fell the moonbeams over the antique grove consecrated to Cybele—the stately trees, whose date went beyond tradition, cast their long shadows over the soil, while through the openings in their boughs the stars shone, still and frequent. The whiteness of the small sacellum in the centre of the grove, amidst the dark foliage, had in it something abrupt and startling; it recalled at once the purpose to which the wood was consecrated,—its holiness and solemnity.

With a swift and stealthy pace, Calenus, gliding under the shade of the trees, reached the chapel, and gently putting back the boughs that completely closed around its rear, settled himself in his concealment; a concealment so complete, what with the fane in front and the trees behind, that no unsuspicious passenger could possibly have detected him. Again, all was apparently solitary in the grove; afar off you heard faintly the voices of some noisy revellers, or the music that played cheerily to the groups that then, as now in those climates, during the nights of summer, lingered in the streets, and enjoyed, in the fresh air and the liquid moonlight, a milder day.

From the height on which the grove was placed, you saw through the intervals of the trees the broad and purple sea, rippling in the distance, the white villas of Stabiæ in the curving shore, and the dim Lectiarian hills mingling with the delicious sky. Presently the tall figure of Arbaces, on his way to the house of Diomed, entered the extreme end of the grove; and at the same instant Apæcides, also bound to his appointment with Olinthus, crossed the Egyptian's path.

"Hem! Apæcides," said Arbaces, recognizing the priest at a glance; "when last we met, you were my foe. I have wished since then to see you, for I would have you still my pupil and my friend."

Apæcides started at the voice of the Egyptian; and halting abruptly, gazed upon him with a countenance full of contending, bitter, and scornful emotions.

"Villain and impostor!" said he at length; "thou hast recovered then from the jaws of the grave! But think not again to weave around me thy guilty meshes.—*Retiarius,* I am armed against thee!"

"Hush!" said Arbaces, in a very low voice—but his pride, which in that descendant of kings was great, betrayed the wound it received from the insulting epithets of the priest in the quiver of his lip and the flush of his tawny brow. "Hush! more low! thou mayest be overheard, and if other ears than mine had drunk those sounds—why——"

"Dost thou threaten?—what if the whole city had heard me?"

"The manes of my ancestors would not have suffered me to forgive thee. But, hold, and hear me. Thou art enraged that I would have offered violence to thy sister.—Nay, peace, peace, but one instant, I pray thee. Thou art right; it was the frenzy of passion and of jealousy—I have repented bitterly of my madness. Forgive me; I, who never implored pardon of living man, beseech thee now to forgive me. Nay, I will atone the insult—I ask thy sister in marriage;—start not, consider, —what is the alliance of yon holiday Greek compared to mine? Wealth unbounded—birth that in its far antiquity leaves your Greek and Roman names the things of yesterday—science— but that thou knowest! Give me thy sister, and my whole life shall atone a moment's error."

"Egyptian, were even I to consent, my sister loathes the very air thou breathest: but I have my own wrongs to forgive —I may pardon thee that thou hast made me a tool to thy deceits, but never that thou hast seduced me to become the abettor of thy vices—a—polluted and a perjured man. Tremble!—even now I prepare the hour in which thou and thy false gods shall be unveiled. Thy lewd and Circéan life shall be dragged to day,—thy mumming oracles disclosed— the fane of the idol Isis shall be a by-word and a scorn—the name of Arbaces a mark for the hisses of execration! Tremble!"

The flush on the Egyptian's brow was succeeded by a livid paleness. He looked behind, before, around, to feel assured that none were by; and then he fixed his dark and dilating eye on the priest, with such a gaze of wrath and menace, that one, perhaps, less supported than Apæcides by the fervent daring of a divine zeal, could not have faced with unflinching look that lowering aspect. As it was, however, the young convert met it unmoved, and returned it with an eye of proud defiance.

"Apæcides," said the Egyptian, in a tremulous and inward tone, "beware! What is it thou wouldst meditate? Speakest thou—reflect, pause before thou repliest—from the hasty influences of wrath, as yet divining no settled purpose, or from some fixed design?"

"I speak from the inspiration of the True God, whose servant I now am," answered the Christian, boldly; "and in the knowledge that by His grace human courage has already fixed the date of thy hypocrisy and thy demon's worship; ere thrice the sun has dawned, thou wilt know all! Dark sorcerer, tremble, and farewell!"

All the fierce and lurid passions which he inherited from his nation and his clime, at all times but ill concealed beneath the blandness of craft and the coldness of philosophy, were released in the breast of the Egyptian. Rapidly one thought chased another; he saw before him an obstinate barrier to even a lawful alliance with Ione—the fellow-champion of Glaucus in the struggle which had baffled his designs—the reviler of his name—the threatened desecrator of the goddess he served while he disbelieved—the avowed and approaching revealer of his own impostures and vices. His love, his repute, nay, his very life, might be in danger—the day and hour seemed even to have been fixed for some design against him. He knew by the words of the convert that Apæcides had adopted the Christian faith: he knew the indomitable zeal which led on the proselytes of that creed. Such was his enemy; he grasped his stilus,—that enemy was in his power! They were now before the chapel; one hasty glance once more he cast around; he saw none near,—silence and solitude alike tempted him. "Die, then, in thy rashness!" he muttered; "away, obstacle to my rushing fates!"

And just as the young Christian had turned to depart, Arbaces raised his hand high over the left shoulder of Apæcides, and plunged his sharp weapon twice into his breast.

Apæcides fell to the ground pierced to the heart,—he fell mute, without even a groan at the very base of the sacred chapel.

Arbaces gazed upon him for a moment with the fierce animal joy of conquest over a foe. But presently the full sense of the danger to which he was exposed flashed upon him; he wiped his weapon carefully in the long grass, and with the very garments of his victim; drew his cloak round him, and was about to depart, when he saw, coming up the path, right before him, the figure of a young man, whose steps reeled and vacillated strangely as he advanced: the quiet moonlight streamed full upon his face, which seemed, by the whitening ray, colorless as marble. The Egyptian recognized the face and form of Glaucus. The unfortunate and benighted Greek was chanting a disconnected and mad song, composed from snatches of hymns and sacred odes, all jarringly woven together.

"Ha!" thought the Egyptian, instantaneously divining his state and its terrible cause; "so, then, the hell-draught works, and destiny hath sent thee hither to crush two of my foes at once!"

Quickly, even ere this thought occurred to him, he had withdrawn on one side of the chapel, and concealed himself amongst the boughs; from that lurking-place he watched, as a tiger in his lair, the advance of his second victim. He noted the wandering and restless fire in the bright and beautiful eyes of the Athenian; the convulsions that distorted his statue-like features, and writhed his hueless lip. He saw that the Greek was utterly deprived of reason. Nevertheless, as Glaucus came up to the dead body of Apæcides, from which the dark red stream flowed slowly over the grass, so strange and ghastly a spectacle could not fail to arrest him, benighted and erring as was his glimmering sense. He paused, placed his hand to his brow, as if to collect himself, and then saying,—

"What, ho! Endymion, sleepest thou so soundly? What

has the moon said to thee? Thou makest me jealous; it is time to wake,"—he stooped down with the intention of lifting up the body.

Forgetting—feeling not—his own debility, the Egyptian sprang from his hiding-place, and, as the Greek bent, struck him forcibly to the ground, over the very body of the Christian; then, raising his powerful voice to its loudest pitch, he shouted—

"Ho, citizens—oh! help me!—run hither—hither!—A murder—a murder before your very fane! Help, or the murderer escapes!" As he spoke, he placed his foot on the breast of Glaucus: an idle and superfluous precaution; for the potion operating with the fall, the Greek lay there motionless and insensible, save that now and then his lips gave vent to some vague and raving sounds.

As he there stood awaiting the coming of those his voice still continued to summon, perhaps some remorse, some compunctious visitings—for despite his crimes he was human— haunted the breast of the Egyptian; the defenceless state of Glaucus—his wandering words—his shattered reason, smote him even more than the death of Apæcides, and he said, half audibly, to himself—

"Poor clay!—poor human reason! *where is the soul now?* I could spare thee, O my rival—rival never more! But destiny must be obeyed—my safety demands thy sacrifice." With that, as if to drown compunction, he shouted yet more loudly; and drawing from the girdle of Glaucus the stilus it contained, he steeped it in the blood of the murdered man, and laid it beside the corpse.

And now, fast and breathless, several of the citizens came thronging to the place, some with torches, which the moon rendered unnecessary, but which flared red and tremulously against the darkness of the trees: they surrounded the spot.

"Lift up yon corpse," said the Egyptian, "and guard well the murderer."

They raised the body, and great was their horror and sacred indignation to discover in that lifeless clay a priest of the adored and venerable Isis; but still greater, perhaps, was their surprise, when they found the accused in the brilliant and admired Athenian. "Glaucus!" cried the by-standers, with one accord; "it is even credible?"

"I would sooner," whispered one man to his neighbor, "believe it to be the Egyptian himself."

Here a centurion thrust himself into the gathering crowd, with an air of authority.

"How! blood spilt! who the murderer?"

The by-standers pointed to Glaucus. "He!—by Mars, he has rather the air of being the victim! Who accuses him?"

"*I*," said Arbaces, drawing himself up haughtily; and the jewels which adorned his dress flashing in the eyes of the soldier, instantly convinced that worthy warrior of the witness's respectability.

"Pardon me—your name?" said he.

"Arbaces; it is well known, methinks, in Pompeii. Passing through the grove, I beheld before me the Greek and the priest in earnest conversation. I was struck by the reeling motions of the first, his violent gestures, and the loudness of his voice; he seemed to me either drunk or mad. Suddenly I saw him raise his stilus—I darted forward—too late to arrest the blow. He had twice stabbed his victim, and was bending over him, when, in my horror and indignation, I struck the murderer to the ground. He fell without a struggle, which makes me yet more suspect that he was not altogether in his senses when the crime was perpetrated; for, recently recovered from a severe illness, my blow was comparatively feeble, and the frame of Glaucus, as you see, is strong and youthful."

"His eyes are open now—his lips move," said the soldier. "Speak, prisoner, what sayest thou to the charge?"

"The charge—ha—ha! Why, it was merrily done; when the old hag set her serpent at me, and Hecate stood by laughing from ear to ear—what could I do? But I am ill—I faint—the serpent's fiery tongue hath bitten me. Bear me to bed, and send for your physician; old Æsculapius himself will attend me, if you let him know that I am Greek. Oh, mercy—mercy—I burn!—marrow and brain, I burn!"

And, with a thrilling and fierce groan, the Athenian fell back in the arms of the by-standers.

"He raves," said the officer, compassionately; "and in his

delirium he has struck the priest. Hath any one present seen him to-day?"

"I," said one of the spectators, "beheld him in the morning. He passed my shop and accosted me. He seemed well and sane as the stoutest of us."

"And I saw him half an hour ago," said another, "passing up the streets, muttering to himself with strange gestures, and just as the Egyptian has described."

"A corroboration of the witness! it must be too true. He must at all events to the prætor; a pity, so young, and so rich! But the crime is dreadful: a priest of Isis, in his very robes, too, and at the base itself of our most ancient chapel!"

At these words the crowd were reminded more forcibly, than in their excitement and curiosity they had yet been, of the heinousness of the sacrilege. They shuddered in pious horror.

"No wonder the earth has quaked," said one, "when it held such a monster!"

"Away with him to prison—away!" cried they all.

And one solitary voice was heard shrilly and joyously above the rest:—

"The beasts will not want a gladiator now,

'Ho! ho! for the merry, merry show!'"

It was the voice of the young woman whose conversation with Medon has been repeated.

"True—true—it chances in season for the games!" cried several; and at that thought all pity for the accused seemed vanished. His youth—his beauty, but fitted him better for the purpose of the arena.

"Bring hither some planks—or if at hand, a litter—to bear the dead," said Arbaces; "a priest of Isis ought scarcely to be carried to his temple by vulgar hands, like a butchered gladiator."

At this the by-standers reverently laid the corpse of Apæcides on the ground, with the face upwards; and some of them went in search of some contrivance to bear the body, untouched by the profane.

It was just at that time that the crowd gave way to right and left as a sturdy form forced itself through, and Olinthus the Christian stood immediately confronting the Egyptian. But his eyes, at first, only rested with inexpressible grief and horror on that gory side and upturned face, on which the agony of violent death yet lingered.

"Murdered!" he said. "Is it thy zeal that has brought thee to this? Have they detected thy noble purpose, and by death prevented their own shame?"

He turned his head abruptly, and his eyes fell full on the solemn features of the Egyptian.

As he looked, you might see in his face, and even the slight shiver of his frame, the repugnance and aversion which the Christian felt for one whom he knew to be so dangerous and so criminal. It was indeed the gaze of the bird upon the basilisk—so silent was it and so prolonged. But shaking off the sudden chill that had crept over him, Olinthus extended his right arm towards Arbaces, and said, in a deep and loud voice:—

"Murder hath been done upon this corpse! Where is the murderer? Stand forth, Egyptian! For, as the Lord liveth, I believe *thou* art the man!"

An anxious and perturbed change might for one moment be detected on the dusky features of Arbaces; but it gave way to the frowning expression of indignation and scorn, as, awed and arrested by the suddenness and vehemence of the charge, the spectators pressed nearer and nearer upon the two more prominent actors.

"I know," said Arbaces, proudly, "who is my accuser, and I guess wherefore he thus arraigns me. Men and citizens, know this man for the most bitter of the Nazarenes, if that or Christians be their proper name! What marvel that in his malignity he dares accuse even an Egyptian of the murder of a priest of Egypt!"

"I know him! I know the dog!" shouted several voices. "It is Olinthus the Christian—or rather the Atheist;—he denies the gods!"

"Peace, brethren," said Olinthus, with dignity, "and hear me! This murdered priest of Isis before his death embraced the Christian faith—he revealed to me the dark sins, the sorceries of yon Egyptian—the mummeries and delusions of the fane of Isis. He was about to declare them publicly. *He,* a stranger, unoffending, without enemies! who should shed his blood but one of those who feared his witness? Who might fear that testimony the most?—Arbaces, the Egyptian!"

"You hear him!" said Arbaces; "you hear him! he blasphemes! Ask him if he believes in Isis?"

"Do I believe in an evil demon?" returned Olinthus boldly.

A groan and shudder passed through the assembly. Nothing daunted, for prepared at every time for peril, and in the present excitement losing all prudence, the Christian continued—

"Back, idolaters! this clay is not for your vain and polluting rites—it is to us—to the followers of Christ, that the last offices due to a Christian belong. I claim this dust in the name of the great Creator who has recalled the spirit!"

With so solemn and commanding a voice and aspect the Christian spoke these words, that even the crowd forbore to utter aloud the execration of fear and hatred which in their hearts they conceived. And never, perhaps, since Lucifer and the Archangel contended for the body of the mighty Lawgiver, was there a more striking subject for the painter's genius than that scene exhibited. The dark trees—the stately fane—the moon full on the corpse of the deceased—the torches tossing wildly to and fro in the rear—the various faces of the motley audience—the insensible form of the Athenian, supported, in the distance; and in the foreground, and above all, the forms of Arbaces and the Christian; the first drawn to its full height, far taller than the herd around; his arms folded, his brow knit, his eyes fixed, his lip slightly curled in defiance and disdain. The last bearing, on a brow worn and furrowed, the majesty of an equal command—the features stern, yet frank—the aspect bold, yet open—the quiet dignity of the whole form impressed with an ineffable earnestness, hushed, as it were, in a solemn sympathy with the awe he himself had created. His left hand pointing to the corpse—his right hand raised to heaven. The centurion pressed forward again.

"In the first place, hast thou, Olinthus, or whatever be thy name, any proof of the charge thou hast made against Arbaces, beyond thy vague suspicions?" Olinthus remained silent—the Egyptian laughed contemptuously.

"Dost thou claim the body of a priest of Isis as one of the Nazarene or Christian sect?" "I do."

"Swear then by yon fane, yon statue of Cybele, by yon most ancient sacellum in Pompeii, that the dead man embraced your faith!" "Vain man! I disown your idols! I abhor your temples! How can I swear by Cybele then?"

"Away, away with the atheist! away! the earth will swallow us, if we suffer these blasphemers in a sacred grove— away with him to death!"

"To the beasts!" added a female voice in the centre of the crowd: *"we shall have one a-piece now for the lion and tiger!"*

"If, O Nazarene, thou disbelievest in Cybele, which of our gods dost thou own?" resumed the soldier, unmoved by the cries around. "None!"

"Hark to him! hark!" cried the crowd.

"O vain and blind!" continued the Christian, raising his voice; "can you believe in images of wood and stone? Do you imagine that they have eyes to see, or ears to hear, or hands to help ye? Is yon mute thing carved by man's art a goddess!—hath it made mankind?—alas! by mankind was it made. Lo! convince yourselves of its nothingness—of your folly."

And as he spoke, he strode across to the fane, and ere any of the by-standers were aware of his purpose, he, in his compassion or his zeal, struck the statue of wood from its pedestal.

"See!" cried he, "your goddess cannot avenge herself. Is this a thing to worship?"

Further words were denied to him: so gross and daring a sacrilege—of one, too, of the most sacred of their places of worship—filled even the most lukewarm with rage and horror. With one accord the crowd rushed upon him, seized, and but for the interference of the centurion, they would have torn him to pieces.

"Peace!" said the soldier, authoritatively,—"refer we this insolent blasphemer to the proper tribunal—time has been already wasted. Bear we both the culprits to the magistrates; place the body of the priest on the litter—carry it to his own home."

At this moment a priest of Isis stepped forward. "I claim

these remains, according to the custom of the priesthood."

"The flamen be obeyed," said the centurion. "How is the murderer?" "Insensible or asleep."

"Were his crimes less, I could pity him. On!"

Arbaces, as he turned, met the eye of that priest of Isis—it was Calenus; and something there was in that glance, so significant and sinister, that the Egyptian muttered to himself—"Could he have witnessed the deed?"

A girl darted from the crowd, and gazed hard on the face of Olinthus. *"By Jupiter, a stout knave! I say, we shall have a man for the tiger now; one for each beast!"*

"Ho!" shouted the mob; "a man for the lion, and another for the tiger! What luck? Io Pæan!"

CHAPTER VII.

In which the reader learns the condition of Glaucus.—Friendship tested.—Enmity softened.—Love the same;—because the one loving is blind.

THE night was somewhat advanced, and the gay lounging-places of the Pompeians were still crowded. You might observe in the countenances of the various idlers a more earnest expression than usual. They talked in large knots and groups, as if they sought by numbers to divide the half-painful, half-pleasurable anxiety which belonged to the subject on which they conversed:—it was a subject of life and death.

A young man passed briskly by the graceful portico of the Temple of Fortune—so briskly, indeed, that he came with no slight force full against the rotund and comely form of that respectable citizen Diomed, who was retiring homeward to his suburban villa.

"Holloa!" groaned the merchant, recovering with some difficulty his equilibrium; "have you no eyes? or do you think I have no feeling? By Jupiter! you have well-nigh driven out the divine particle; such another shock, and my soul will be in Hades!"

"Ah, Diomed! is it you? forgive my inadvertence. I was absorbed in thinking of the reverses of life. Our poor friend, Glaucus, eh! who could have guessed it?" "Well, but tell me, Clodius, is he really to be tried by the senate?"

"Yes: they say the crime is of so extraordinary a nature, that the senate itself must adjudge it; and so the lictors are to induct him formally."

"He has been accused publicly, then?"

"To be sure; where have you been, not to hear that?"

"Why, I have only just returned from Neapolis, whither I went on business the very morning after his crime;—so shocking, and at my house the same night that it happened!"

"There is no doubt of his guilt," said Clodius, shrugging his shoulders; "and as these crimes take precedence of all little undignified peccadilloes, they will hasten to finish the sentence previous to the games."

"The games! Good gods!" replied Diomed, with a slight shudder; "can they adjudge him to the beasts?—so young, so rich!"

"True; but, then, he is a Greek. Had he been a Roman, it would have been a thousand pities. These foreigners can be borne with in their prosperity; but in adversity we must not forget that they are in reality slaves. However, we of the upper classes are always tender-hearted; and he would certainly get off tolerably well, if he were left to us: for, between ourselves, what is a paltry priest of Isis!—what Isis herself? But the common people are superstitious; they clamor for the blood of the sacrilegious one. It is dangerous not to give way to public opinion."

"And the blasphemer—the Christian, or Nazarene, or whatever else he be called?"

"Oh, poor dog! if he will sacrifice to Cybele, or Isis, he will be pardoned—if not, the tiger has him. At least, so I suppose; but the trial will decide. We talk while the urn's still empty. And the Greek may yet escape the deadly Θ* of his own alphabet. But enough of this gloomy subject. How is the fair Julia?"

"Well, I fancy."

"Commend me to her. But hark! the door yonder creaks on its hinges; it is the house of the prætor. Who comes forth?

---

* Θ, the initial of θάνατος (death), the condemning letter of the Greeks, as C was of the Romans.

By Pollux! it is the Egyptian! What can he want with our official friend!"

"Some conference touching the murder, doubtless," replied Diomed; "but what was supposed to be the inducement to the crime? Glaucus was to have married the priest's sister."

"Yes: some say Apæcides refused the alliance. It might have been a sudden quarrel. Glaucus was evidently drunk;—nay, so much so as to have been quite insensible when taken up, and I hear is still delirious—whether with wine, terror, remorse, the Furies, or the Bacchanals, I cannot say."

"Poor fellow!—he has good counsel?"

"The best—Caius Pollio, an eloquent fellow enough. Pollio has been hiring all the poor gentlemen and well-born spend-thrifts of Pompeii to dress shabbily and sneak about, swearing their friendship to Glaucus (who would not have spoken to them to be made emperor!—I will do him justice, he was a gentleman in his choice of acquaintance), and trying to melt the stony citizens into pity. But it will not do; Isis is mightily popular just at this moment."

"And, by the by, I have some merchandise at Alexandria. Yes, Isis ought to be protected."

"True; so farewell, old gentleman: we shall meet soon; if not, we must have a friendly bet at the Amphitheatre. All my calculations are confounded by this cursed misfortune of Glaucus! He had bet on Lydon the gladiator; I must make up my tablets elsewhere. *Vale!*"

Leaving the less active Diomed to regain his villa, Clodius strode on, humming a Greek air, and perfuming the night with the odors that steamed from his snowy garments and flowing locks.

"If," thought he, "Glaucus feed the lion, Julia will no longer have a person to love better than me; she will certainly dote on me;—and so, I suppose, I must marry. By the gods! the twelve lines begin to fail—men look suspiciously at my hand when it rattles the dice. That infernal Sallust insinuates cheating; and if it be discovered that the ivory is cogged, why farewell to the merry supper and the perfumed billet;—Clodius is undone! Better marry, then, while I may, renounce gaming, and push my fortune (or rather the gentle Julia's) at the imperial court."

Thus muttering the schemes of his ambition, if by that

high name the projects of Clodius may be called, the gamester found himself suddenly accosted; he turned and beheld the dark brow of Arbaces.

"Hail, noble Clodius! pardon my interruption; and inform me, I pray you, which is the house of Sallust?"

"It is but a few yards hence, wise Arbaces. But does Sallust entertain to-night?"

"I know not," answered the Egyptian; "nor am I, perhaps, one of those whom he would seek as a boon companion. But thou knowest that his house holds the person of Glaucus, the murderer."

"Ay! he, good-hearted epicure, believes in the Greek's innocence! You remind me that he has become his surety; and, therefore, till the trial, is responsible for his appearance. Well, Sallust's house is better than a prison, especially that wretched hole in the forum. But for what can *you* seek Glaucus?"

"Why, noble Clodius, if we could save him from execution, it would be well. The condemnation of the rich is a blow upon society itself. I should like to confer with him—for I hear he has recovered his senses—and ascertain the motives of his crime; they may be so extenuating as to plead in his defence."

"You are benevolent, Arbaces."

"Benevolence is the duty of one who aspires to wisdom," replied the Egyptian, modestly. "Which way lies Sallust's mansion?"

"I will show you," said Clodius, "if you will suffer me to accompany you a few steps. But, pray what has become of the poor girl who was to have wed the Athenian—the sister of the murdered priest?"

"Alas! well-nigh insane. Sometimes she utters imprecations on the murderer—then suddenly stops short—then cries, 'But *why* curse? Oh, my brother! Glaucus was *not* thy murderer—never will I believe it!' Then she begins again, and again stops short, and mutters awfully to herself, 'Yet if it were indeed he?'" "Unfortunate Ione!"

"But it is well for her that those solemn cares to the dead which religion enjoins have hitherto greatly absorbed her attention from Glaucus and herself: and, in the dimness of her senses, she scarcely seems aware that Glaucus is apprehended and on the eve of trial. When the funeral rites due to Apæcides are performed, her apprehension will return; and then I fear me much that her friends will be revolted by seeing her run to succor and aid the murderer of her brother!"

"Such scandal should be prevented."

"I trust I *have* taken precautions to that effect. I am her lawful guardian, and have just succeeded in obtaining permission to escort her, after the funeral of Apæcides, to my own house; there, please the gods! she will be secure."

"You have done well, sage Arbaces. And now, yonder is the house of Sallust. The gods keep you! Yet, hark you, Arbaces—why so gloomy and unsocial? Men say you *can* be gay—why not let me initiate you into the pleasures of Pompeii?—I flatter myself no one knows them better."

"I thank you, noble Clodius; under your auspices I might venture, I think, to wear the philyra: but, at my age, I should be an awkward pupil."

"Oh, never fear; I have made converts of fellows of seventy. The rich, too, are never old."

"You flatter me. At some future time, I will remind you of your promise." "You may command Marcus Clodius at all times:—and so, *vale!*"

"Now," said the Egyptian, soliloquizing, "I am not wantonly a man of blood; I would willingly save this Greek, if by confessing the crime, he will lose himself for ever to Ione, and for ever free me from the chance of discovery; and I *can* save him by persuading Julia to own the philtre, which will be held his excuse. But if he do not confess the crime, why Julia must be shamed from the confession, and he must die! —die, lest he prove my rival with the living—die, that he may be my proxy with the dead! Will he confess?—can he not be persuaded that in his delirium he struck the blow? To me it would give far greater safety than even his death. Hem! we must hazard the experiment."

Sweeping along the narrow street, Arbaces now approached the house of Sallust, when he beheld a dark form wrapped in a cloak, and stretched at length across the threshold of the door.

So still lay the figure, and so dim was its outline, that any other than Arbaces might have felt a superstitious fear, lest he beheld one of those grim *lemures,* who, above all other spots, haunted the threshold of the homes they formerly possessed. But not for Arbaces were such dreams.

"Rise!" said he, touching the figure with his foot; "thou obstructest the way!"

"Ha! who art thou?" cried the form, in a sharp tone; and as she raised herself from the ground, the star-light fell full on the pale face and fixed but sightless eyes of Nydia the Thessalian. "Who art thou? I know the burden of thy voice."

"Blind girl! what dost thou here at this late hour? Fie!— is this seeming thy sex or years? Home, girl."

"I know thee," said Nydia, in a low voice, "thou art Arbaces the Egyptian:" then, as if inspired by some sudden impulse, she flung herself at his feet, and clasping his knees, exclaimed, in a wild and passionate tone, "Oh, dread and potent man! save him—save him! He is not guilty—it is I! He lies within, ill—dying, and I—I am the hateful cause! And they will not admit me to him—they spurn the blind girl from the hall. Oh, heal him! thou knowest some herb—some spell—some counter-charm, for it is a potion that hath wrought this frenzy!"

"Hush, child! I know all!—thou forgettest that ı accompanied Julia to the saga's home. Doubtless her hand administered the draught; but her reputation demands thy silence. Reproach not thyself—what must be, must: meanwhile, I seek the criminal—he may yet be saved. Away!"

Thus saying, Arbaces extricated himself from the clasp of the despairing Thessalian, and knocked loudly at the door.

In a few moments the heavy bars were heard suddenly to yield, and the porter, half opening the door, demanded who was there. "Arbaces—the important business to Sallust relative to Glaucus. I come from the prætor."

The porter, half yawning, half groaning, admitted the tall form of the Egyptian. Nydia sprang forward. "How is he?" she cried; "tell me—tell me!"

"Ho, mad girl! is it thou still?—for shame! Why, they say he is sensible." "The gods be praised!—and you will not admit me? Ah, I beseech thee——"

"Admit thee!—no. A pretty salute I should prepare for these shoulders, were I to admit such things as thou! Go home!"

The door closed, and Nydia, with a deep sigh, laid herself

down once more on the cold stones; and, wrapping her cloak round her face, resumed her weary vigil.

Meanwhile, Arbaces had already gained the triclinium, where Sallust, with his favorite freedman, sat late at supper.

"What! Arbaces! and at this hour!—Accept this cup."

"Nay, gentle Sallust; it is on business, not pleasure, that I venture to disturb thee. How doth thy charge?—they say in the town that he has recovered sense."

"Alas! and truly," replied the good-natured but thoughtless Sallust, wiping the tear from his eyes; "but so shattered are his nerves and frame, that I scarcely recognize the brilliant and gay carouser I was wont to know. Yet, strange to say, he cannot account for the cause of the sudden frenzy that seized him—he retains but a dim consciousness of what hath passed; and, despite thy witness, wise Egyptian, solemnly upholds his innocence of the death of Apæcides."

"Sallust," said Arbaces, gravely, "there is much in thy friend's case that merits a peculiar indulgence; and could we learn from his lips the confession and the cause of his crime, much might be yet hoped from the mercy of the senate; for the senate, thou knowest, hath the power either to mitigate or to sharpen the law. Therefore it is that I have conferred with the highest authority of the city, and obtained his permission to hold a private conference this night with the Athenian. To-morrow thou knowest, the trial comes on."

"Well," said Sallust, "thou wilt be worthy of thy Eastern name and fame if thou canst learn aught from him; but thou mayst try. Poor Glaucus!—and he had such an excellent appetite! He eats nothing now!"

The benevolent epicure was moved sensibly at this thought. He sighed, and ordered his slaves to refill his cup.

"Night wanes," said the Egyptian; "suffer me to see thy ward now."

Sallust nodded assent, and led the way to a small chamber, guarded without by two dozing slaves. The door opened; at the request of Arbaces, Sallust withdrew—the Egyptian was alone with Glaucus.

One of those tall and graceful candelabra common to that day, supporting a single lamp, burned beside the narrow bed. Its rays fell palely over the face of the Athenian, and Arbaces was moved to see how sensibly that countenance had changed. The rich color was gone, the cheek was sunk, the lips were convulsed and pallid; fierce had been the struggle between reason and madness, life and death. The youth, the strength of Glaucus had conquered; but the freshness of blood and soul—the life of life, its glory and its zest, were gone for ever.

The Egyptian seated himself quietly beside the bed; Glaucus still lay mute and unconscious of his presence. At length, after a considerable pause, Arbaces thus spoke:—

"Glaucus, we have been enemies. I come to thee alone, and in the dead of night—thy friend, perhaps thy savior."

As the steed starts from the path of the tiger, Glaucus sprang up breathless—alarmed, panting at the abrupt voice, the sudden apparition of his foe. Their eyes met, and neither, for some moments, had power to withdraw his gaze. The flush went and came over the face of the Athenian, and the bronzed cheek of the Egyptian grew a shade more pale. At length, with an inward groan, Glaucus turned away, drew his hand across his brow, sunk back, and muttered—

"Am I still dreaming?"

"No, Glaucus, thou art awake. By this right hand and my father's head, thou seest one who may save thy life. Hark! I know what thou hast done, but I know also its excuse, of which thou thyself art ignorant. Thou hast committed murder, it is true—a sacrilegious murder: frown not—start not —these eyes saw it. But I can save thee—I can prove how thou wert bereaved of sense, and made not a free-thinking and free-acting man. But in order to save thee, thou must confess thy crime. Sign but this paper, acknowledging thy hand in the death of Apæcides, and thou shalt avoid the fatal urn."

"What words are these?—Murder and Apæcides!—Did I not see him stretched on the ground bleeding and a corpse? and wouldst thou persuade me that I did the deed? Man, thou liest! Away!"

"Be not rash—Glaucus, be not hasty; the deed is proved. Come, come, thou mayst well be excused for not recalling the act of thy delirium, and which thy sober senses would have shunned even to contemplate. But let me try to refresh thy exhausted and weary memory. Thou knowest thou wert walking with the priest, disputing about his sister; thou knowest he was intolerant, and half a Nazarene, and he sought to convert thee, and ye had hot words; and he calumniated thy mode of life, and swore he would not marry Ione to thee—and then, in thy wrath and thy frenzy, thou didst strike the sudden blow. Come, come; you can recollect this!—read this papyrus, it runs to that effect—sign it, and thou art saved."

"Barbarian, give me the written lie, that I may tear it! *I* the murderer of Ione's brother! *I* confess to have injured one hair of the head of him she loved! Let me rather perish a thousand times!"

"Beware!" said Arbaces, in a low and hissing tone; "there is but one choice—thy confession and thy signature, or the amphitheatre and the lion's maw!"

As the Egyptian fixed his eyes upon the sufferer, he hailed with joy the signs of evident emotion that seized the latter at these words. A slight shudder passed over the Athenian's frame—his lip fell—an expression of sudden fear and wonder betrayed itself in his brow and eye.

"Great gods," he said, in a low voice, "what reverse is this? It seems but a little day since life laughed out from amidst roses—Ione mine—youth, health, love, lavishing on me their treasures; and now—pain, madness, shame, death! And for what? what have I done? Oh, I am mad still?"

"Sign, and be saved!" said the soft, sweet voice of the Egyptian.

"Tempter, never!" cried Glaucus, in the reaction of rage. "Thou knowest me not: thou knowest not the haughty soul of an Athenian! The sudden face of death might appal me for a moment, but the fear is over. Dishonor appals for ever! Who will debase his name to save his life? who exchange clear thoughts for sullen days? who will belie himself to shame, and stand blackened in the eyes of glory and of love? If to earn a few years of polluted life there be so base a coward, dream not, dull barbarian of Egypt! to find him in one who has trod the same sod as Harmodius, and breathed the same air as Socrates. Go! leave me to live without self-reproach—or to perish without fear!"

"Bethink thee well! the lion's fangs: the hoots of the brutal mob: the vulgar gaze on thy dying agony and mutilated limbs; thy name degraded; thy corpse unburied; the shame thou wouldst avoid clinging to thee for aye and ever!"

"Thou ravest! *thou* art the madman! shame is not in the loss of other men's esteem,—it is in the loss of our own. Wilt thou go?—my eyes loathe the sight of thee! hating ever, I despise thee now!"

"I go," said Arbaces, stung and exasperated, but not without some pitying admiration of his victim,—"I go; we meet twice again—once at the Trial, once at the Death! Farewell!"

The Egyptian rose slowly, gathered his robes about him, and left the chamber. He sought Sallust for a moment, whose eyes began to reel with the vigils of the cup: "He is still unconscious, or still obstinate; there is no hope for him."

"Say not so," replied Sallust, who felt but little resentment against the Athenian's accuser, for he possessed no great austerity of virtue, and was rather moved by his friend's reverses than persuaded of his innocence,—"say not so, my Egyptian! so good a drinker shall be saved if possible. Bacchus against Isis!"

"We shall see," said the Egyptian.

Suddenly the bolts were again withdrawn—the door unclosed; Arbaces was in the open street; and poor Nydia once more started from her long watch.

"Wilt thou save him?" she cried, clasping her hands.

"Child, follow me home; I would speak to thee—it is for his sake I ask it."

"And thou wilt save him?"

No answer came forth to the thirsting ear of the blind girl; Arbaces had already proceeded far up the street; she hesitated a moment, and then followed his steps in silence.

"I must secure this girl," said he, musingly, "lest she give evidence of the philtre; as to the vain Julia, she will not betray herself."

CHAPTER VIII.

A classic funeral.

WHILE Arbaces had been thus employed, Sorrow and Death were in the house of Ione. It was the night preceding the morn in which the solemn funeral rites were to be decreed to the remains of the murdered Apæcides. The corpse had been removed from the temple of Isis to the house of the nearest surviving relative, and Ione had heard, in the same breath, the death of her brother and the accusation against her betrothed. That first violent anguish which blunts the sense to all but herself, and the forbearing silence of her slaves, had prevented her learning minutely the circumstances attendant on the fate of her lover. His illness, his frenzy, and his approaching trial, were unknown to her. She learned only the accusation against him, and at once indignantly rejected it; nay, on hearing that Arbaces was the accuser, she required no more to induce her firmly and solemnly to believe that the Egyptian himself was the criminal. But the vast and absorbing importance attached by the ancients to the performance of every ceremonial connected with the death of a relation, had, as yet, confined her woe and her convictions to the chamber of the deceased. Alas! it was not for her to perform that tender and touching office, which obliged the nearest relative to endeavor to catch the last breath—the parting soul—of the beloved one: but it was hers to close the straining eyes, the distorted lips: to watch by the consecrated clay, as, fresh bathed and anointed, it lay in festive robes upon the ivory bed; to strew the couch with leaves and flowers, and to renew the solemn cypress-branch at the threshold of the door. And in these sad offices, in lamentation and in prayer, Ione forgot herself. It was among the loveliest customs of the ancients to bury the young at the morning twilight; for, as they strove to give the softest interpretation to death, so they poetically imagined that Aurora, who loved the young, had stolen them to her embrace; and though in the instance of the murdered priest this fable could not appropriately cheat the fancy, the general custom was still preserved.*

The stars were fading one by one from the grey heavens, and night slowly receding before the approach of morn, when a dark group stood motionless before Ione's door. High and slender torches, made paler by the unmellowed dawn, cast their light over various countenances, hushed for the moment in one

---

* This was rather a Greek than a Roman custom; but the reader will observe that in the cities of Magna Græcia the Greek customs and susperstitions were much mingled with the Roman.

solemn and intent expression. And now there arose a slow
and dismal music, which accorded sadly with the rite, and
floated far along the desolate and breathless streets; while a
chorus of female voices (the Præficæ so often cited by the
Roman poets), accompanying the Tibicen and the Mysian
flute, woke the following strain:—

THE FUNERAL DIRGE.

"O'er the sad threshold, where the cypress bough
    Supplants the rose that should adorn thy home,
On the last pilgrimage on earth that now
    Awaits thee, wanderer to Cocytus, come!
Darkly we woo, and weeping we invite—
    Death is thy host—his banquet asks thy soul;
Thy garlands hang within the House of Night,
    And the black stream alone shall fill thy bowl.

No more for thee the laughter and the song,
    The jocund night—the glory of the day!
The Argive daughters at their labors long:
    The hell-bird swooping on its Titan prey—
The false Æolides upheaving slow,
    O'er the eternal hill, the eternal stone;
The crowned Lydian, in his parching woe,
    And green Callirrhoe's monster-headed son—

These shalt thou see, dim shadow'd through the dark,
    Which makes the sky of Pluto's dreary shore;
Lo! where thou stand'st, pale-gazing on the bark,
    That waits our rite to bear thee trembling o'er!
Come, then! no more delay!—the phantom pines
    Amidst the Unburied for its latest home;
O'er the grey sky the torch impatient shines—
    Come, mourner, forth!—the lost one bids thee come!"

As the hymn died away, the group parted in twain; and
placed upon a couch, spread with a purple pall, the corpse of
Apæcides was carried forth, with the feet foremost. The
designator, or marshal of the sombre ceremonial, accompanied
by his torch-bearers, clad in black, gave the signal, and the
procession moved dreadly on.

First went the musicians, playing a slow march—the solemnity of the lower instruments broken by many a louder and
wilder burst of the funeral trumpet: next followed the hired
mourners, chanting their dirges to the dead; and the female
voices were mingled with those of boys, whose tender years

made still more striking the contrast of life and death—the fresh leaf and the withered one. But the players, the buffoons, the archimimus (whose duty it was to personate the dead)— these, the customary attendants at ordinary funerals, were banished from a funeral attended with so many terrible associations.

The priests of Isis came next in their snowy garments, barefooted, and supporting sheaves of corn; while before the corpse were carried the images of the deceased and his many Athenian forefathers. And behind the bier followed, amidst her women, the sole surviving relative of the dead—her head bare, her locks dishevelled, her face paler than marble, but composed and still, save ever and anon, as some tender thought, awakened by the music, flashed upon the dark lethargy of woe, she covered that countenance with her hands, and sobbed unseen: for hers were not the noisy sorrow, the shrill lament, the ungoverned gesture, which characterized those who honored less faithfully. In that age, as in all, the channel of deep grief flowed hushed and still.

And so the procession swept on, till it had traversed the streets, passed the city gate, and gained the Place of Tombs without the wall, which the traveller yet beholds.

Raised in the form of an altar—of unpolished pine, amidst whose interstices were placed preparations of combustible matter—stood the funeral pyre; and around it drooped the dark and gloomy cypresses so consecrated by song to the tomb.

As soon as the bier was placed upon the pile, the attendants parting on either side, Ione passed up to the couch, and stood before the unconscious clay for some moments motionless and silent. The features of the dead had been composed from the first agonized expression of violent death. Hushed for ever the terror and the doubt, the contest of passion, the awe of religion, the struggle of the past and present, the hope and the horror of the future!—of all that racked and desolated the breast of that young aspirant to the Holy of Life, what trace was visible in the awful serenity of that impenetrable brow and unbreathing lip? The sister gazed, and not a sound was heard amidst the crowd; there was something terrible, yet softening, also, in the silence; and when it broke, it broke

sudden and abrupt—it broke with a loud and passionate cry
—the vent of long-smothered despair.

"My brother! my brother!" cried the poor orphan, falling
upon the couch; "thou whom the worm on thy path feared not
—what enemy couldst thou provoke? Oh, is it in truth come
to this? Awake! awake! We grew together! Are we thus
torn asunder? Thou art not dead—thou sleepest. Awake!
awake!"

The sound of her piercing voice aroused the sympathy of
the mourners, and they broke into loud and rude lament. This
startled, this recalled Ione; she looked up hastily and confusedly, as if for the first time sensible of the presence of
those around.

"*Ah!*" she murmured with a shiver, "*we are not then
alone!*"

With that, after a brief pause, she rose: and her pale and
beautiful countenance was again composed and rigid. With
fond and trembling hands, she unclosed the lids of the
deceased; but when the dull glazed eye, no longer beaming
with love and life, met hers, she shrieked aloud, as if she had
seen a spectre. Once more recovering herself, she kissed again
and again the lids, the lips, the brow; and with mechanic and
unconscious hand, received from the high-priest of her
brother's temple the funeral torch.

The sudden burst of music, the sudden song of the
mourners, announced the birth of the sanctifying flame.

HYMN TO THE WIND

I.

"On thy couch of cloud reclined,
Wake, O soft and sacred Wind!
Soft and sacred will we name thee,
Whosoe'er the sire that claim thee,—
Whether old Auster's dusky child,
Or the loud son of Eurus wild;
Or his* who o'er the darkling deeps,
From the bleak North, in tempest sweeps
Still shalt thou seem as dear to us
As flowery-crowned Zephyrus,
When, through twilight's starry dew,
Trembling, he hastes his nymph† to woo.

* Boreas.
† Flora.

II.

Lo! our silver censers swinging,
Perfumes o'er thy path are flinging,—
Ne'er o'er Tempe's breathless valleys,
Ne'er o'er Cypria's cedarn alleys,
Or the Rose-isle's moon-lit sea,
Floated sweets more worthy thee.
Lo! around our vases sending
Myrrh and nard with cassia blending;
Paving air with odors meet,
For thy silver-sandall'd feet!

III.

August and everlasting air!
    The source of all that breathe and be,
From the mute clay before thee bear
    The seeds it took from thee!
Aspire, bright Flame! aspire!
    Wild wind!—awake, awake!
Thine own, O solemn Fire!
    O Air, thine own retake!

IV.

It comes! it comes! Lo! it sweeps,
    The Wind we invoke the while!
And crackles, and darts, and leaps
    The light on the holy pile!
It rises! its wings interweave
With the flames—how they howl and heave!
        Toss'd, whirl'd to and fro,
        How the flame-serpents glow!
        Rushing higher and higher,
        On—on, fearful Fire!
        Thy giant limbs twined
        With the arms of the Wind!
Lo! the elements meet on the throne
Of death—to reclaim their own!

V.

Swing, swing the censer round—
Tune the strings to a softer sound!
From the chains of thy earthly toil,
From the clasp of thy mortal coil,
From the prison where clay confined thee,
The hands of the flame unbind thee!
        O soul! thou art free—all free!

* Rhodes.

As the winds in their ceaseless chase,
  When they rush o'er their airy sea,
Thou mayst speed through the realms of space,
  No fetter is forged for thee!
Rejoice! o'er the sluggard tide
Of the Styx thy bark can glide,
And thy steps evermore shall rove
Through the glades of the happy grove;
Where, far from the loath'd Cocytus,
The loved and the lost invite us.
Thou art slave to the earth no more!
  O soul, thou art freed!—and we?—
Ah! when shall our toil be o'er?
Ah! when shall we rest with thee?"

And now high and far into the dawning skies broke the
fragrant fire; it flashed luminously across the gloomy cypresses—it shot above the massive walls of the neighboring
city; and the early fishermen started to behold the blaze
reddening on the waves of the creeping sea.

But Ione sat down apart and alone, and, leaning her face
upon her hands, saw not the flame, nor heard the lamentation
of the music: she felt only one sense of loneliness—she had
not yet arrived to that hallowing sense of comfort, when we
know that we are *not* alone—that the dead are with us!

The breeze rapidly aided the effect of the combustibles
placed within the pile. By degrees the flame wavered, lowered,
dimmed, and slowly, by fits and unequal starts, died away—
emblem of life itself; where, just before, all was restlessness
and flame, now lay the dull and smouldering ashes.

The last sparks were extinguished by the attendants—the
embers were collected. Steeped in the rarest wine and the
costliest odors, the remains were placed in a silver urn, which
was solemnly stored in one of the neighboring sepulchres
beside the road; and they placed within it the vial full of tears,
and the small coin which poetry still consecrated to the grim
boatmen. And the sepulchre was covered with flowers and
chaplets, and incense kindled on the altar, and the tomb hung
round with many lamps.

But the next day, when the priest returned with fresh
offerings to the tomb, he found that to the relics of heathen
superstition some unknown hands had added a green palm-

branch. He suffered it to remain, unknowing that it was the sepulchral emblem of Christianity.

When the above ceremonies were over, one of the Præficæ three times sprinkled the mourners from the purifying branch of laurel, uttering the last word, *"Ilicet!"*—Depart!—and the rite was done.

But first they paused to utter—weepingly and many times —the affecting farewell, *"Salve Eternum!"* And as Ione yet lingered, they woke the parting strain.

SALVE ETERNUM.

I.

"Farewell! O soul departed!
　　Farewell! O sacred urn!
Bereaved and broken-hearted,
　　To earth the mourners turn!
To the dim and dreary shore,
Thou art gone our steps before!
But thither the swift Hours lead us,
And thou dost but a while precede us!
　　　　　Salve—salve!
Loved urn, and thou solemn cell,
Mute ashes!—farewell, farewell!
　　　　　Salve—salve!

II.

Ilicet—ire licet—
Ah, vainly would we part!
Thy tomb is the faithful heart.
About evermore we bear thee;
For who from the heart can tear thee?
Vainly we sprinkle o'er us
　　The drops of the cleansing stream;
And vainly bright before us
　　The lustral fire shall beam.
For where is the charm expelling
Thy thought from its sacred dwelling?
Our griefs are thy funeral feast.
And Memory thy mourning priest,
　　　　　Salve—salve!

III.

Ilicet—ire licet!
The spark from the hearth is gone
　　Wherever the air shall bear it;

The elements take their own—
    The shadows receive thy spirit.
It will soothe thee to feel our grief.
    As thou glid'st by the Gloomy River!
If love may in life be brief,
    In death it is fixed for ever.
                Salve—salve!
In the hall which our feasts illume
The rose for an hour may bloom;
But the cypress that decks the tomb—
The cypress is green for ever!
                Salve—salve!"

CHAPTER IX.

In which an adventure happens to Ione.

WHILE some stayed behind to share with the priests the funeral banquet, Ione and her handmaids took homeward their melancholy way. And now (the last duties to her brother performed) her mind awoke from its absorption, and she thought of her affianced, and the dread charge against him. Not—as we have before said—attaching even a momentary belief to the unnatural accusation, but nursing the darkest suspicion against Arbaces, she felt that justice to her lover and to her murdered relative demanded her to seek the prætor, and communicate her impression, unsupported as it might be. Questioning her maidens, who had hitherto—kindly anxious, as I have said, to save her the additional agony—refrained from informing her of the state of Glaucus, she learned that he had been dangerously ill; that he was in custody, under the roof of Sallust; that the day of his trial was appointed.

"Averting gods!" she exclaimed; "and have I been so long forgetful of him? Have I seemed to shun him? Oh! let me hasten to do him justice—to show that I, the nearest relative of the dead, believe him innocent of the charge. Quick! quick! let us fly. Let me soothe—tend—cheer him! and if they will not believe me; if they will not yield to my conviction; if they sentence him to exile or to death, let me share the sentence with him!"

Instinctively she hastened her pace, confused and bewildered, scarce knowing whither she went; now designing first to seek the prætor, and now to rush to the chamber of Glaucus. She hurried on—she passed the gate of the city—she was in the long street leading up the town. The houses were opened, but none were yet astir in the streets; the life of the city was scarce awake—when lo! she came suddenly upon a small knot of men standing beside a covered litter. A tall figure stepped from the midst of them, and Ione shrieked aloud to behold Arbaces.

"Fair Ione!" said he, gently, and appearing not to heed her alarm; "my ward, my pupil! forgive me if I disturb thy pious sorrows; but the prætor, solicitous of thy honor, and anxious that thou mayst not rashly be implicated in the coming trial; knowing the strange embarrassment of thy state (seeking justice for thy brother, but dreading punishment to thy betrothed)—sympathizing, too, with thy unprotected and friendless condition, and deeming it harsh that thou shouldst be suffered to act unguided and mourn alone—hath wisely and paternally confided thee to the care of thy lawful guardian. Behold the writing which intrusts thee to my charge!"

"Dark Egyptian!" cried Ione, drawing herself proudly aside; "begone! It is thou that hast slain my brother! Is it to thy care, thy hands yet reeking with his blood, that they will give the sister? Ha! thou turnest pale! thy conscience smites thee! thou tremblest at the thunderbolt of the avenging god! Pass on, and leave me to my woe!"

"Thy sorrows unstring thy reason, Ione," said Arbaces, attempting in vain his usual calmness of tone. "I forgive thee. Thou wilt find me now, as ever, thy surest friend. But the public streets are not the fitting place for us to confer— for me to console thee. Approach, slaves! Come, my sweet charge, the litter awaits thee."

The amazed and terrified attendants gathered round Ione, and clung to her knees.

"Arbaces," said the eldest of the maidens, "this is surely not the law! For nine days after the funeral, is it not written that the relatives of the deceased shall not be molested in their homes, or interrupted in their solitary grief?"

"Woman!" returned Arbaces, imperiously waving his hand, "to place a ward under the roof of her guardian is not against the funeral laws. I tell thee I have the fiat of the prætor. This delay is indecorous. Place her in the litter."

So saying, he threw his arm firmly round the shrinking form of Ione. She drew back, gazed earnestly in his face, and then burst into hysterical laughter:—

"Ha, ha! this is well—well! Excellent guardian—paternal law! Ha, ha!" And, startled herself at the dread echo of that shrill and maddened laughter, she sank, as it died away, lifeless upon the ground. . . . A minute more, and Arbaces had lifted her into the litter. The bearers moved swiftly on, and the unfortunate Ione was soon borne from the sight of her weeping handmaids.

CHAPTER X.

What becomes of Nydia in the house of Arbaces.—The Egyptian feels compassion for Glaucus.—Compassion is often a very useless visitor to the guilty.

IT will be remembered that, at the command of Arbaces, Nydia followed the Egyptian to his home, and conversing there with her, he learned from the confession of her despair and remorse, that her hand, and not Julia's, had administered to Glaucus the fatal potion. At another time the Egyptian might have conceived a philosophical interest in sounding the depths and origin of the strange and absorbing passion which, in blindness and in slavery, this singular girl had dared to cherish; but at present he spared no thought from himself. As, after her confession, the poor Nydia threw herself on her knees before him, and besought him to restore the health and save the life of Glaucus—for in her youth and ignorance she imagined the dark magician all-powerful to effect both—Arbaces, with unheeding ears, was noting only the new expediency of detaining Nydia a prisoner until the trial and fate of Glaucus were decided. For if, when he judged her merely the accomplice of Julia in obtaining the philtre, he had felt it was dangerous to the full success of his vengeance to allow her to be at large—to appear, perhaps, as a witness—to avow the manner in which the sense of Glaucus had been darkened, and thus win indulgence to the crime of which he was accused— how much more was she likely to volunteer her testimony when she herself had administered the draught, and, inspired by love, would be only anxious, at any expense of shame, to retrieve her error and preserve her beloved! Besides, how unworthy of the rank and repute of Arbaces to be implicated in the disgrace of pandering to the passion of Julia, and assisting in the unholy rites of the Saga of Vesuvius! Nothing less, indeed, than his desire to induce Glaucus to own the murder of Apæcides, as a policy evidently the best both for his own permanent safety and his successful suit with Ione, could ever have led him to contemplate the confession of Julia.

As for Nydia, who was necessarily cut off by her blindness from much of the knowledge of active life, and who, a slave and a stranger, was naturally ignorant of the perils of the Roman law, she thought rather of the illness and delirium of her Athenian, than the crime of which she had vaguely heard him accused, or the chances of the impending trial. Poor wretch that she was, whom none addressed, none cared for, what did she know of the senate and the sentence—the hazard of the law—the ferocity of the people—the arena and the lion's den? She was accustomed only to associate with the thought of Glaucus everything that was prosperous and lofty—she could not imagine that any peril, save from the madness of her love, could menace that sacred head. He seemed to her set apart for the blessings of life. *She* only had disturbed the current of his felicity; she knew not, she dreamed not, that the stream, once so bright, was dashing on to darkness and to death. It was therefore to restore the brain that *she* had marred, to save the life that *she* had endangered, that she implored the assistance of the great Egyptian.

"Daughter," said Arbaces, waking from his reverie, "thou must rest here; it is not meet for thee to wander along the streets, and be spurned from the threshold by the rude feet of slaves. I have compassion on thy soft crime—I will do all to remedy it. Wait here patiently for some days, and Glaucus shall be restored." So saying, and without waiting for her reply, he hastened from the room, drew the bolt across the door and consigned the care and wants of his prisoner to the slave who had the charge of that part of the mansion.

Alone, then, and musingly, he waited the morning light, and with it repaired, as we have seen, to possess himself of the person of Ione.

His primary object, with respect to the unfortunate Neapolitan, was that which he had really stated to Clodius, viz., to prevent her interesting herself actively in the trial of Glaucus, and also to guard against her accusing him (which she would, doubtless, have done) of his former act of perfidy and violence towards her, his ward—denouncing his causes for vengeance against Glaucus—unveiling the hypocrisy of his character— and casting any doubt upon his veracity in the charge which he had made against the Athenian. Not till he had encountered her that morning—not till he had heard her loud denunciations—was he aware that he had also another danger to apprehend in her suspicion of his crime. He hugged himself now in the thought that these ends were effected; that one, at once the object of his passion and his fear, was in his power. He believed more than ever the flattering promises of the stars; and when he sought Ione in that chamber in the inmost recesses of his mysterious mansion to which he had consigned her—when he found her overpowered by blow upon blow, and passing from fit to fit, from violence to torpor, in all the alternations of hysterical disease—he thought more of the loveliness which no frenzy could distort, than of the woe which he had brought upon her. In that sanguine vanity common to men who through life have been invariably successful, whether in fortune or love, he flattered himself that when Glaucus had perished—when his name was solemnly blackened by the award of a legal judgment, his title to her love for ever forfeited by condemnation to death for the murder of her own brother—her affection would be changed to horror; and that his tenderness and his passion, assisted by all the arts with which he well knew how to dazzle woman's imagination, might elect him to that throne in her heart from which his rival would be so awfully expelled. This was his hope: but should it fail, his unholy and fervid passion whispered, "At the worst, *now* she is in my power."

Yet, withal, he felt that uneasiness and apprehension which attend upon the chance of detection, even when the criminal is insensible to the voice of conscience—that vague terror of the consequences of crime, which is often mistaken for remorse at the crime itself. The buoyant air of Campania weighed heavily upon his breast; he longed to hurry from a scene where danger might not sleep eternally with the dead;

and, having Ione now in his possession, he secretly resolved, as soon as he had witnessed the last agony of his rival, to transport his wealth—and her, the costliest treasure of all, to some distant shore.

"Yes," said he, striding to and fro his solitary chamber —"yes, the law that gave me the person of my ward gives me the possession of my bride. Far across the broad main will we sweep on our search after novel luxuries and inexperienced pleasures. Cheered by my stars, supported by the omens of my soul, we will penetrate to those vast and glorious worlds which my wisdom tells me lie yet untracked in the recesses of the circling sea. There may this heart, possessed of love, grow once more alive to ambition—there, amongst nations uncrushed by the Roman yoke, and to whose ear the name of Rome has not yet been wafted, I may found an empire, and transplant my ancestral creed; renewing the ashes of the dead Theban rule: continuing on yet grander shores the dynasty of my crowned fathers, and waking in the noble heart of Ione the grateful consciousness that she shares the lot of one who, far from the aged rottenness of this slavish civilization, restores the primal elements of greatness, and units in one mighty soul, the attributes of the prophet and the king."

From this exultant soliloquy, Arbaces was awakened to attend the trial of the Athenian.

The worn and pallid cheek of his victim touched him less than the firmness of his nerves and the dauntlessness of his brow; for Arbaces was one who had little pity for what was unfortunate, but a strong sympathy for what was bold. The congenialities that bind us to others ever assimilate to the qualities of our own nature. The hero weeps less at the reverses of his enemy than at the fortitude with which he bears them. All of us are human, and Arbaces, criminal as he was, had his share of our common feelings and our mother-clay. Had he but obtained from Glaucus the written confession of his crime, which would, better than even the judgment of others, have lost him with Ione, and removed from Arbaces the chance of future detection, the Egyptian would have strained every nerve to save his rival. Even now his hatred was over—his desire of revenge was slaked; he crushed his prey, not in enmity, but as an obstacle in his path. Yet was he not the less resolved, the less crafty and persevering, in the course he pursued, for the destruction of one whose doom was become necessary to the attainment of his objects; and while, with apparent reluctance and compassion, he gave against Glaucus the evidence which condemned him, he secretly, and through the medium of the priesthood, fomented that popular indignation which made an effectual obstacle to the pity of the senate. He had sought Julia; he had detailed to her the confession of Nydia; he had easily, therefore, lulled any scruple of conscience which might have led her to extenuate the offence of Glaucus by avowing her share in his frenzy: and the more readily, for her vain heart had loved the fame and the prosperity of Glaucus—not Glaucus himself; she felt no affection for a disgraced man—nay, she almost rejoiced in a disgrace that humbled the hated Ione. If Glaucus could not be her slave, neither could he be the adorer of her rival. This was sufficient consolation for any regret at his fate. Volatile and fickle, she began again to be moved by the sudden and earnest suit of Clodius, and was not willing to hazard the loss of an alliance with that base but high-born noble by any public exposure of her past weakness and immodest passion for another. All things then smiled upon Arbaces—all things frowned upon the Athenian.

CHAPTER XI.

Nydia affects the sorceress.

WHEN the Thessalian found that Arbaces returned to her no more—when she was left, hour after hour, to all the torture of that miserable suspense which was rendered by blindness doubly intolerable, she began, with outstretched arms, to feel around her prison for some channel of escape; and finding the only entrance secure, she called aloud, and with the vehemence of a temper naturally violent, and now sharpened by impatient agony.

"Ho, girl!" said the slave in attendance, opening the door; "art thou bit by a scorpion? or thinkest thou that we are dying of silence here, and only to be preserved, like the infant Jupiter, by a hullabaloo?"

"Where is thy master? and wherefore am I caged here? I want air and liberty: let me go forth!"

"Alas! little one, hast thou not seen enough of Arbaces to know that his will is imperial? He hath ordered thee to be caged; and caged thou art, and I am thy keeper. Thou canst not have air and liberty; but thou mayst have what are much better things—food and wine."

"Proh Jupiter!" cried the girl, wringing her hands; "and why am I thus imprisoned? What can the great Arbaces want with so poor a thing as I am?"

"That I know not, unless it be to attend on thy new mistress, who has been brought hither this day."

"What! Ione here?"

"Yes, poor lady; she liked it little, I fear. Yet, by the Temple of Castor! Arbaces is a gallant man to the women. Thy lady is his ward, thou knowest." "Wilt thou take me to her?"

"She is ill—frantic with rage and spite. Besides, I have no orders to do so; and I never think for myself. When Arbaces made me slave of these chambers, he said, 'I have but one lesson to give thee;—while thou servest me, thou must have neither ears, eyes, nor thought; thou must be but one quality —obedience.'" "But what harm is there in seeing Ione?"

"That I know not; but if thou wantest a companion, I am willing to talk to thee, little one, for I am solitary enough in my dull cubiculum. And, by the way, thou art Thessalian— knowest thou not some cunning amusement of knife and shears, some pretty trick of telling fortunes, as most of thy race do, in order to pass the time?"

"Tush, slave, hold thy peace! or, if thou wilt speak, what hast thou heard of the state of Glaucus?"

"Why, my master has gone to the Athenian's trial; Glaucus will smart for it!" "For what?"

"The murder of the priest Apæcides."

"Ha!" said Nydia, pressing her hands to her forehead; "something of this I have indeed heard, but understand not. Yet, who will dare to touch a hair of his head?"

"That will the lion, I fear."

"Averting gods! what wickedness dost thou utter?"

"Why, only that, if he be found guilty, the lion, or may be the tiger, will be his executioner."

Nydia leaped up as if an arrow had entered her heart; she uttered a piercing scream; then, falling before the feet of the slave, she cried, in a tone that melted even his rude heart—

"Ah! tell me thou jestest—thou utterest not the truth—speak, speak!"

"Why, by my faith, blind girl, I know nothing of the law; it may not be so bad as I say. But Arbaces is his accuser, and the people desire a victim for the arena. Cheer thee! But what hath the fate of the Athenian to do with thine?"

"No matter, no matter—he has been kind to me. Thou knowest not, then, what they will do? Arbaces his accuser! O fate! The people—the people! Ah! *they* can look upon his face—who will be cruel to the Athenian!—Yet was not Love itself cruel to him?"

So saying, her head drooped upon her bosom: she sank into silence; scalding tears flowed down her cheeks; and all the kindly efforts of the slave were unable either to console her or distract the absorption of her reverie.

When his household cares obliged the ministrant to leave her room, Nydia began to re-collect her thoughts. Arbaces was the accuser of Glaucus; Arbaces had imprisoned her here; was not that a proof that her liberty might be serviceable to Glaucus? Yes, she was evidently inveigled into some snare; she was contributing to the destruction of her beloved! Oh, how she panted for release! Fortunately, for her sufferings, all sense of pain became merged in the desire of escape; and as she began to revolve the possibility of deliverance, she grew calm and thoughtful. She possessed much of the craft of her sex, and it had been increased in her breast by her early servitude. What slave was ever destitute of cunning? She resolved to practise upon her keeper; and, calling suddenly to mind his superstitious query as to her Thessalian art, she hoped by that handle to work out some method of release. These doubts occupied her mind during the rest of the day and the long hours of night; and, accordingly, when Sosia visited her the following morning, she hastened to divert his garrulity into that channel in which it had before evinced a natural disposition to flow.

She was aware, however, that her only chance of escape was at night; and accordingly she was obliged, with a bitter pang at the delay, to defer till then her purposed attempt.

"The night," said she, "is the sole time in which we can well decipher the decrees of Fate—then it is thou must seek me. But what desirest thou to learn?"

"By Pollux! I should like to know as much as my master; but that is not to be expected. Let me know, at least, whether I shall save enough to purchase my freedom, or whether this Egyptian will give it me for nothing. He does such generous things sometimes. Next, supposing that be true, shall I possess myself of that snug taberna among the Myropolia* which I have long had in my eye? 'Tis a genteel trade that of a perfumer, and suits a retired slave who has something of a gentleman about him!"

"Ay! so you would have precise answers to those questions?—there are various ways of satisfying you. There is the Lithomanteia, or Speaking-stone, which answers your prayer with an infant's voice; but, then, we have not that precious stone with us—costly is it and rare. Then there is the Gastromanteia, whereby the demon casts pale and deadly images upon water, prophetic of the future. But this art requires also glasses of a peculiar fashion, to contain the consecrated liquid, which we have not. I think, therefore, that the simplest method of satisfying your desire would be by the Magic of Air."

"I trust," said Sosia, tremulously, "that there is nothing very frightful in the operation? I have no love for apparitions."

"Fear not; thou wilt see nothing; thou wilt only hear by the bubbling of water whether or not thy suit prospers. First, then, be sure, from the rising of the evening star, that thou leavest the garden-gate somewhat open, so that the demon may feel himself invited to enter therein; and place fruits and water near the gate as a sign of hospitality; then, three hours after twilight, come here with a bowl of the coldest and purest water, and thou shalt learn all, according to the Thessalian lore my mother taught me. But forget not the garden-gate—all rests upon that: it must be open when you come, and for three hours previously."

"Trust me," replied the unsuspecting Sosia; "I know what a gentleman's feelings are when a door is shut in his face, as the cook-shop's hath been in mine many a day; and I know also, that a person of respectability, as a demon of course is, cannot but be pleased, on the other hand, with any little mark of courteous hospitality. Meanwhile, pretty one, here is thy morning's meal." "And what of the trial?"

"Oh, the lawyers are still at it—talk, talk—it will last over till to-morrow." "To-morrow?—you are sure of that?"

"So I hear." "And Ione?"

"By Bacchus! she must be tolerably well, for she was strong enough to make my master stamp and bite his lip this morning. I saw him quit her apartment with a brow like a thunder-storm."

"Lodges she near this?"

"No—in the upper apartments. But I must not stay prating here longer.—*Vale!*"

CHAPTER XII.

A wasp ventures into the spider's web.

THE second night of the trial had set in; and it was nearly the time in which Sosia was to brave the dread Unknown, when there entered, at that very garden-gate which the slave had left ajar—not, indeed, one of the mysterious spirits of earth or air, but the heavy and most human form of Calenus, the priest of Isis. He scarcely noted the humble offerings of indifferent fruit and still more indifferent wine, which the pious Sosia had deemed good enough for the invisible stranger they were intended to allure. "Some tribute," thought he, "to the garden god. By my father's head! if his deityship were never better served, he would do well to give up the godly profession. Ah! were it not for us priests, the gods would have a sad time of it. And now for Arbaces—I am treading a quicksand, but it ought to cover a mine. I have the Egyptian's life in my power—what will he value it at?"

As he thus soliloquized, he crossed through the open court into the peristyle, where a few lamps here and there broke upon the empire of the star-lit night; and, issuing from one of the chambers that bordered the colonnade, suddenly encountered Arbaces.

"Ho! Calenus—seekest thou me?" said the Egyptian; and there was a little embarrassment in his voice.

"Yes, wise Arbaces—I trust my visit is not unreasonable?"

"Nay—it was but this instant that my freedman Callias sneezed thrice at my right hand; I knew, therefore, some good fortune was in store for me—and, lo! the gods have sent me Calenus."

"Shall we within to your chamber, Arbaces?"

"As you will; but the night is clear and balmy—I have some remains of languor yet lingering on me from my recent illness—the air refreshes me—let us walk in the garden—we are equally alone there."

"With all my heart," answered the priest; and the two *friends* passed slowly to one of the many terraces which, bordered by marble vases and sleeping flowers, intersected the garden.

"It is a lovely night," said Arbaces—"blue and beautiful as that on which, twenty years ago, the shores of Italy first broke upon my view. My Calenus, age creeps upon us—let us, at least, feel that we have lived."

"Thou, at least, mayst arrogate that boast," said Calenus, beating about, as it were, for an opportunity to communicate the secret which weighed upon him, and feeling his usual awe of Arbaces still more impressively that night, from the quiet and friendly tone of dignified condescension which the Egyptian assumed—"Thou, at least, mayst arrogate that boast. Thou hast had countless wealth—a frame on whose close-woven fibres disease can find no space to enter—prosperous love—inexhaustible pleasure—and. even at this hour, triumphant revenge."

"Thou alludest to the Athenian. Ay, to-morrow's sun the fiat of his death will go forth. The senate does not relent. But thou mistakest: his death gives me no other gratification than that it releases me from a rival in the affections of Ione. I entertain no other sentiment of animosity against that unfortunate homicide."

"Homicide!" repeated Calenus, slowly and meaningly; and, halting as he spoke, he fixed his eyes upon Arbaces. The stars shone pale and steadily on the proud face of their prophet, but they betrayed there no change: the eyes of Cale-

nus fell disappointed and abashed. He continued rapidly—
"Homicide! it is well to charge him with that crime; but thou,
of all men, knowest that he is innocent."

"Explain thyself," said Arbaces, coldly; for he had prepared himself for the hint his secret fears had foretold.

"Arbaces," answered Calenus, sinking his voice into a
whisper, "I was in the sacred grove, sheltered by the chapel
and the surrounding foliage. I overheard—I marked the
whole. I saw thy weapon pierce the heart of Apæcides. I
blame not the deed—it destroyed a foe and an apostate."

"Thou sawest the whole!" said Arbaces, drily; "so I
imagined—thou wert alone?" "Alone!" returned Calenus,
surprised at the Egyptian's calmness. "And wherefore wert
thou hid behind the chapel at that hour?"

"Because I had learned the conversion of Apæcides to the
Christian faith—because I knew that on that spot he was to
meet the fierce Olinthus—because they were to meet there to
discuss plans for unveiling the sacred mysteries of our goddess
to the people—and I was there to detect, in order to defeat
them." "Hast thou told living ear what thou didst witness?"

"No, my master; the secret is locked in thy servant's
breast."

"What! even thy kinsman Burbo guesses it not! Come, the
truth!" "By the gods——"

"Hush! we know each other—what are the gods to us!"

"By the fear of thy vengeance, then—no!"

"And why hast thou hitherto concealed from me this secret? Why hast thou waited till the eve of the Athenian's condemnation before thou hast ventured to tell me that Arbaces
is a murderer? And, having tarried so long, why revealest
thou now that knowledge?" "Because—because——" stam-
mered Calenus, coloring and in confusion.

"Because," interrupted Arbaces, with a gentle smile, and
tapping the priest on the shoulder with a kindly and familiar
gesture—"because, my Calenus (see now, I will read thy heart,
and explain its motives)—because thou didst wish thoroughly
to commit and entangle me in the trial, so that I might have
no loop-hole of escape; that I might stand firmly pledged to
perjury and to malice, as well as to homicide; that having
myself whetted the appetite of the populace to blood, no wealth,

no power, could prevent my becoming their victim; and thou
tellest me thy secret now, ere the trial be over, and the innocent
condemned, to show what a desperate web of villainy thy word
to-morrow could destroy; to enhance in this, the ninth hour,
the price of thy forbearance; to show that my own arts, in
arousing the popular wrath, would, at thy witness, recoil upon
myself; and that, if not for Glaucus, for *me* would gape the
jaws of the lion! Is it not so?"

"Arbaces," replied Calenus, losing all the vulgar audacity
of his natural character, "verily thou *art* a Magian; thou readest the heart as it were a scroll."

"It is my vocation," answered the Egyptian, laughing
gently. "Well, then, forbear; and when all is over, I will
make thee rich."

"Pardon me," said the priest, as the quick suggestion of
that avarice, which was his master-passion, bade him trust no
future chance of generosity; "pardon me; thou saidst right—
we know each other. If thou wouldst have me silent, thou must
pay something in advance, as an offer to Harpocrates. If the
rose, sweet emblem of discretion, is to take root firmly, water
her this night with a stream of gold."

"Witty and poetical!" answered Arbaces, still in that bland
voice which lulled and encouraged, when it ought to have
alarmed and checked, his griping comrade. "Wilt thou not
wait the morrow?"

"Why this delay? Perhaps, when I can no longer give
my testimony without shame for not having given it ere the
innocent man suffered, thou wilt forget my claim; and, indeed,
thy present hesitation is a bad omen of thy future gratitude."

"Well, then, Calenus, what wouldst thou have me pay
thee?"

"Thy life is very precious, and thy wealth is very great,"
returned the priest, grinning.

"Wittier and more witty. But speak out—what shall be the
sum?"

"Arbaces, I have heard that in thy secret treasury below,
beneath those rude Oscan arches which prop thy stately halls,
thou hast piles of gold, of vases, and of jewels, which might
rival the receptacles of the wealth of the deified Nero. Thou
mayst easily spare out of those piles enough to make Calenus

among the richest priests of Pompeii, and yet not miss the loss."

"Come, Calenus," said Arbaces, winningly, and with a frank and generous air, "thou art an old friend, and hast been a faithful servant. Thou canst have no wish to take away my life, nor I a desire to stint thy reward: thou shalt descend with me to that treasury thou referrest to, thou shalt feast thine eyes with the blaze of uncounted gold and the sparkle of priceless gems; and thou shalt, for thy own reward, bear away with thee this night as much as thou canst conceal beneath thy robes. Nay, when thou hast once seen what thy friend possesses, thou wilt learn how foolish it would be to injure one who has so much to bestow. When Glaucus is no more, thou shalt pay the treasury another visit. Speak I frankly and as a friend?"

"Oh, greatest, best of men!" cried Calenus, almost weeping with joy, "canst thou thus forgive my injurious doubts of thy justice, thy generosity?

"Hush! one other turn, and we will descend to the Oscan arches."

CHAPTER XIII.

The slave consults the oracle.—They who blind themselves the blind may fool.— Two new prisoners made in one night.

IMPATIENTLY Nydia awaited the arrival of the no less anxious Sosia. Fortifying his courage by plentiful potations of a better liquor than that provided for the demon, the credulous ministrant stole into the blind girl's chamber.

"Well, Sosia, and art thou prepared? Hast thou the bowl of pure water?"

"Verily, yes: but I tremble a little. You are sure I shall not see the demon? I have heard that those gentlemen are by no means of a handsome person or a civil demeanor."

"Be assured! And hast thou left the garden-gate gently open?"

"Yes; and placed some beautiful nuts and apples on a little table close by."

"That's well. And the gate is open now, so that the demon may pass through it?"

"Surely it is."

"Well, then, open this door; there—leave it just ajar. And now, Sosia, give me the lamp."

"What! you will not extinguish it?"

"No; but I must breathe my spell over its ray. There is a spirit in fire. Seat thyself."

The slave obeyed; and Nydia, after bending for some moments silently over the lamp, rose, and in a low voice chanted the following rude

INVOCATION TO THE SPECTRE OF THE AIR

"Loved alike by Air and Water,
Aye must be Thessalia's daughter;
To us, Olympian hearts, are given
Spells that draw the moon from heaven.
All that Egypt's learning wrought—
All that Persia's Magian taught—
Won from song, or wrung from flowers,
Or whisper'd low by fiend—are ours.

Spectre of the viewless air,
Hear the blind Thessalian's prayer;
By Erictho's art, that shed
Dews of life when life was fled:—
By lone Ithaca's wise king,
Who could wake the crystal spring
To the voice of prophecy?
By the lost Eurydice,
Summon'd from the shadowy throng,
At the muse-son's magic song—
By the Colchian's awful charms,
When fair-hair'd Jason left her arms;—
Spectre of the airy halls,
One who owns thee duly calls!
Breathe along the brimming bowl,
And instruct the fearful soul
In the shadowy things that lie
Dark in dim futurity.
Come, wild demon of the air,
Answer to thy votary's prayer;
    Come! oh, come!

And no god on heaven or earth—
Not the Paphian Queen of Mirth,
Nor the vivid Lord of Light,

Nor the triple Maid of Night,
Nor the Thunderer's self, shall be
Blest and honor'd more than thee!
Come! oh, come!"

"The spectre *is* certainly coming," said Sosia. "I feel him running along my hair!"

"Place thy bowl of water on the ground. Now, then, give me thy napkin, and let me fold up thy face and eyes."

"Ay! that's always the custom with these charms. Not so tight, though: gently—gently!" "There—thou canst not see?" "See, by Jupiter! No! nothing but darkness."

"Address, then, to the spectre whatever question thou wouldst ask him, in a low-whispered voice, three times. If thy question is answered in the affirmative, thou wilt hear the water ferment and bubble before the demon breathes upon it; if in the negative, the water will be quite silent."

"But you will not play any trick with the water, eh?"

"Let me place the bowl under thy feet—so. Now thou wilt perceive that I cannot touch it without thy knowledge."

"Very fair. Now, then, O Bacchus! befriend me. Thou knowest that I have always loved thee better than all the other gods, and I will dedicate to thee that silver cup I stole last year from the burly carptor (butler), if thou wilt but befriend me with this water-loving demon. And thou, O Spirit! listen and hear me. Shall I be enabled to purchase my freedom next year? Thou knowest: for, as thou livest in the air, the birds have doubtless acquainted thee with every secret of this house,— thou knowest that I have filched and pilfered all that I honestly —that is, safely—could lay finger upon for the last three years, and I yet want two thousand sesterces of the full sum. Shall I be able, O good Spirit! to make up the deficiency in the course of this year? Speak—Ha! does the water bubble? No; all is still as a tomb.—Well, then, if not this year, in two years? —Ah! I hear something; the demon is scratching at the door; he'll be here presently.—In two years, my good fellow? come now, two; that's a very reasonable time. What! dumb still! Two years and a half—three—four? Ill fortune to you, friend demon! You are not a lady, that's clear, or you would not keep silence so long. Five—six—sixty years? and may Plato seize you! I'll ask no more." And Sosia, in a rage, kicked down the water over his legs. He then, after much fumbling, and more cursing, managed to extricate his head from the napkin in which it was completely folded—stared round—and discovered that he was in the dark.

"What, ho! Nydia; the lamp is gone. Ah, traitress; and thou art gone too; but I'll catch thee—thou shalt smart for this!"

The slave groped his way to the door; it was bolted from without: he was a prisoner instead of Nydia. What could he do? He did not dare to knock loud—to call out—lest Arbaces should overhear him, and discover how he had been duped; and Nydia, meanwhile, had probably already gained the garden-gate, and was fast on her escape.

"But," thought he, "she will go home, or, at least, be somewhere in the city. To-morrow, at dawn, when the slaves are at work in the peristyle, I can make myself heard; then I can go forth and seek her. I shall be sure to find and bring her back, before Arbaces knows a word of the matter. Ah! that's the best plan. Little traitress my fingers itch at thee: and to leave only a bowl of water, too! Had it been wine, it would have been some comfort."

While Sosia, thus entrapped, was lamenting his fate, and revolving his schemes to repossess himself of Nydia, the blind girl, with that singular precision and dexterous rapidity of motion, which, we have before observed, was peculiar to her, had passed lightly along the peristyle, threaded the opposite passage that led into the garden, and, with a beating heart, was about to proceed towards the gate, when she suddenly heard the sound of approaching steps, and distinguished the dreaded voice of Arbaces himself. She paused for a moment in doubt and terror; then suddenly it flashed across her recollection that there was another passage which was little used except for the admission of the fair partakers of the Egyptian's secret revels, and which wound along the basement of that massive fabric towards a door which also communicated with the garden. By good fortune it might be open. At that thought, she hastily retraced her steps, descended the narrow stairs at the right, and was soon at the entrance of the passage. Alas! the door at the entrance was closed and secured. While she was yet assuring herself that it was indeed locked, she heard behind her the voice of Calenus, and, a moment after, that of Arbaces in low reply. She could not stay there; they were probably passing to that very door. She sprang onward, and felt herself in unknown ground. The air grew damp and chill; this reassured her. She thought she might be among the cellars of the luxurious mansion, or, at least, in some rude spot not likely to be visited by its haughty lord, when, again, her quick ear caught steps and the sound of voices. On, on, she hurried, extending her arms, which now frequently encountered pillars of thick and massive form. With a tact, doubled in acuteness by her fear, she escaped these perils, and continued her way, the air growing more and more damp as she proceeded; yet, still, as she ever and anon paused for breath, she heard the advancing steps and the indistinct murmur of voices. At length she was abruptly stopped by a wall that seemed the limit of her path. Was there no spot in which she could hide? No aperture? no cavity? There was none! She stopped and wrung her hands in despair; then again, nerved as the voices neared upon her, she hurried on by the side of the wall; and coming suddenly against one of the sharp buttresses that here and there jutted boldly forth, she fell to the ground. Though much bruised, her senses did not leave her; she uttered no cry; nay, she hailed the accident that had led her to something like a screen; and creeping close up to the angle formed by the buttress, so that on one side at least she was sheltered from view, she gathered her slight and small form into its smallest compass, and breathlessly awaited her fate.

Meanwhile Arbaces and the priest were taking their way to that secret chamber whose stores were so vaunted by the Egyptian. They were in a vast subterranean atrium, or hall; the low roof was supported by short, thick pillars of an architecture far remote from the Grecian graces of that luxuriant period. The single and pale lamp, which Arbaces bore, shed but an imperfect ray over the bare and rugged walls, in which the huge stones, without cement, were fitted curiously and uncouthly into each other. The disturbed reptiles glared dully on the intruders, and then crept into the shadow of the walls.

Calenus shivered as he looked around and breathed the damp, unwholesome air.

"Yet," said Arbaces, with a smile, perceiving his shudder, "it is these rude abodes that furnish the luxuries of the halls above. They are like the laborers of the world—we despise their ruggedness, yet they feed the very pride that disdains them."

"And whither goes yon dim gallery to the left?" asked Calenus; "in this depth of gloom it seems without limit, as if winding into Hades."

"On the contrary, it does but conduct to the upper day," answered Arbaces, carelessly: "it is to the right that we steer to our bourn."

The hall, like many in the more habitable regions of Pompeii, branched off at the extremity into two wings or passages; the length of which, not really great, was to the eye considerably exaggerated by the sullen gloom against which the lamp so faintly struggled. To the right of these *alæ* the two comrades now directed their steps.

"The gay Glaucus will be lodged to-morrow in apartments not much drier, and far less spacious than this," said Calenus, as they passed by the very spot where, completely wrapped in the shadow of the broad, projecting buttress, cowered the Thessalian.

"Ay, but then he will have dry room, and ample enough, in the arena on the following day. And to think," continued Arbaces, slowly, and very deliberately—"to think that a word of thine could save him, and consign Arbaces to his doom!"

"That word shall never be spoken," said Calenus.

"Right, my Calenus! it never shall," returned Arbaces, familiarly leaning his arm on the priest's shoulder: "and now, halt—we are at the door."

The light trembled against a small door deep set in the wall, and guarded strongly by many plates and bindings of iron, that intersected the rough and dark wood. From his girdle Arbaces now drew a small ring, holding three or four short but strong keys. Oh, how beat the griping heart of Calenus, as he heard the rusty wards growl, as if resenting the admission to the treasures they guarded!

"Enter, my friend," said Arbaces, "while I hold the lamp on high, that thou mayst glut thine eyes on the yellow heaps."

The impatient Calenus did not wait to be twice invited; he hastened towards the aperture.

Scarce had he crossed the threshold, when the strong hand of Arbaces plunged him forwards.

"The word shall never be spoken!" said the Egyptian, with a loud, exultant laugh, and closed the door upon the priest.

Calenus had been precipitated down several steps, but not feeling at the moment the pain of his fall, he sprang up again to the door, and beating at it fiercely with his clenched fist, he cried aloud in what seemed more a beast's howl than a human voice, so keen was his agony and despair: "Oh, release me, release me, and I will ask no gold!"

The words but imperfectly penetrated the massive door, and Arbaces again laughed. Then, stamping his foot violently, rejoined, perhaps to give vent to his long-stifled passions—

"All the gold of Dalmatia," cried he, "will not buy thee a crust of bread. Starve, wretch! thy dying groans will never wake even the echo of these vast halls: nor will the air ever reveal, as thou gnawest, in thy desperate famine, thy flesh from thy bones, that so perishes the man who threatened, and could have undone, Arbaces! Farewell!"

"Oh, pity—mercy! Inhuman villain; was it for this——"

The rest of the sentence was lost to the ear of Arbaces as he passed backward along the dim hall. A toad, plump and bloated, lay unmoving before his path; the rays of the lamp fell upon its unshaped hideousness and red upward eye. Arbaces turned aside that he might not harm it.

"Thou art loathsome and obscene," he muttered, "but thou canst not injure me; therefore thou art safe in my path."

The cries of Calenus, dulled and choked by the barrier that confined him, yet faintly reached the ear of the Egyptian. He paused and listened intently.

"This is unfortunate," thought he; "for I cannot sail till that voice is dumb for ever. My stores and treasures lie, not in yon dungeon, it is true, but in the opposite wing. My slaves, as they move them, must not hear his voice. But what fear of that? In three days, if he still survive, his accents, by my father's beard, must be weak enough, then!—no, they could not pierce even through his tomb. By Isis, it is cold!—I long for a deep draught of the spiced Falernian."

With that the remorseless Egyptian drew his gown closer round him, and resought the upper air.

CHAPTER XIV.

Nydia accosts Calenus.

WHAT words of terror, yet of hope, had Nydia overheard! The next day Glaucus was to be condemned; yet there lived one who could save him, and adjudge Arbaces to his doom, and that one breathed within a few steps of her hiding-place! She caught his cries and shrieks—his imprecations—his prayers, though they fell choked and muffled on her ear. He was imprisoned, but she knew the secret of his cell: could she but escape—could she but seek the prætor, he might yet in time be given to light, and preserve the Athenian. Her emotions almost stifled her; her brain reeled—she felt her sense give way —but by a violent effort she mastered herself, and, after listening intently for several minutes, till she was convinced that Arbaces had left the space to solitude and herself, she crept on as her ear guided her to the very door that had closed upon Calenus. Here she more distinctly caught his accents of terror and despair. Thrice she attempted to speak, and thrice her voice failed to penetrate the folds of the heavy door. At length finding the lock, she applied her lips to its small aperture, and the prisoner distinctly heard a soft tone breathe his name.

His blood curdled—his hair stood on end. That awful solitude, what mysterious and preternatural being could penetrate! "Who's there?" he cried, in new alarm; "what spectre—what dread *larva,* calls upon the lost Calenus?"

"Priest," replied the Thessalian, "unknown to Arbaces, I have been, by the permission of the gods, a witness to his perfidy. If I myself can escape from these walls, I may save thee. But let thy voice reach my ear through this narrow passage, and answer what I ask."

"Ah, blessed spirit," said the priest, exultingly, and obeying the suggestion of Nydia, "save me, and I will sell the very cups on the altar to pay thy kindness."

"I want not thy gold—I want thy secret. Did I hear aright?

—Canst thou save the Athenian Glaucus from the charge against his life?"

"I can—I can!—therefore (may the Furies blast the foul Egyptian!) hath Arbaces snared me thus, and left me to starve and rot!" "They accuse the Athenian of murder; canst thou disprove the accusation?"

"Only free me, and the proudest head of Pompeii is not more safe than his. I saw the deed done—I saw Arbaces strike the blow; I can convict the true murderer and acquit the innocent man. But if I perish, he dies also. Dost thou interest thyself for him? Oh, blessed stranger, in my heart is the urn which condemns or frees him!"

"And thou wilt give full evidence of what thou knowest?"

"Will!—Oh! were hell at my feet—yes! Revenge on the false Egyptian!—revenge! revenge! revenge!"

As through his ground teeth Calenus shrieked forth those last words, Nydia felt that in his worst passions was her certainty of his justice to the Athenian. Her heart beat: was it—was it to be her proud destiny to preserve her idolized—her adored? "Enough," said she; "the powers that conducted me hither will carry me through all. Yes, I feel that I shall deliver thee. Wait in patience and hope."

"But be cautious, be prudent, sweet stranger. Attempt not to appeal to Arbaces—he is marble. Seek the prætor—say what thou knowest—obtain his writ of search; bring soldiers, and smiths of cunning—these locks are wondrous strong! Time flies—I may starve—starve! if you are not quick! Go—go! Yet stay—it is horrible to be alone!—the air is like a charnel—and the scorpions—ha! and the pale larvæ! Oh! stay, stay!"

"Nay," said Nydia, terrified by the terror of the priest, and anxious to confer with herself,—"nay, for thy sake, I must depart. Take Hope for thy companion—farewell!"

So saying, she glided away, and felt with extended arms along the pillared space until she had gained the farther end of the hall and the mouth of the passage that led to the upper air. But there she paused; she felt that it would be more safe to wait awhile, until the night was so far blended with the morning that the whole house would be buried in sleep, and so that she might quit it unobserved. She, therefore, once more laid herself down, and counted the weary moments. In her sanguine heart, joy was the predominant emotion. Glaucus was in deadly peril—but *she* should save him!

CHAPTER XV.

Arbaces and Ione.—Nydia gains the garden.—Will she escape and save the Athenian?

When Arbaces had warmed his veins by large draughts of that spiced and perfumed wine so valued by the luxurious, he felt more than usually elated and exultant of heart. There is a pride in triumphant ingenuity, not less felt, perhaps, though its object be guilty. Our vain human nature hugs itself in the consciousness of superior craft and self-obtained success—afterwards comes the horrible reaction of remorse.

But remorse was not a feeling which Arbaces was likely ever to experience for the fate of the base Calenus. He swept from his remembrance the thought of the priest's agonies and lingering death: he felt only that a great danger was passed, and a possible foe silenced; all left to him now would be to account to the priesthood for the disappearance of Calenus; and this he imagined it would not be difficult to do. Calenus had often been employed by him in various religious missions to the neighboring cities. On some such errand he could now assert that he had been sent, with offerings to the shrines of Isis at Herculaneum and Neapolis, placatory of the goddess for the recent murder of her priest Apæcides. When Calenus had expired, his body might be thrown, previous to the Egyptian's departure from Pompeii, into the deep stream of the Sarnus; and when discovered, suspicion would probably fall upon the Nazarene atheists, as an act of revenge for the death of Olinthus at the arena. After rapidly running over these plans for screening himself, Arbaces dismissed at once from his mind all recollection of the wretched priest; and, animated by the success which had lately crowned all his schemes, he surrendered his thoughts to Ione. The last time he had seen her, she had driven him from her presence by a reproachful and bitter scorn, which his arrogant nature was unable to endure. He now felt emboldened once more to renew that interview; for his passion for her was like similar feelings in other men—it made him restless for her presence, even though in that presence he was exasperated and humbled. From delicacy to her grief he laid not aside his dark and unfestive robes, but, renewing the perfumes on his raven locks, and arranging his tunic in its most becoming folds, he sought the chamber of the Neapolitan. Accosting the slave in attendance without, he inquired if Ione had yet retired to rest; and learning that she was still up, and unusually quiet and composed, he ventured into her presence. He found his beautiful ward sitting before a small table, and leaning her face upon both her hands in the attitude of thought. Yet the expression of the face itself possessed not its wonted bright and Psyche-like expression of sweet intelligence; the lips were apart—the eye vacant and unheeding—and the long dark hair, falling neglected and dishevelled upon her neck, gave by the contrast additional paleness to a cheek which had already lost the roundness of its contour.

Arbaces gazed upon her a moment ere he advanced. She, too, lifted up her eyes; and when she saw who was the intruder, shut them with an expression of pain, but did not stir.

"Ah!" said Arbaces, in a low and earnest tone, as he respectfully, nay, humbly, advanced and seated himself at a little distance from the table—"Ah! that my death could remove thy hatred, then would I gladly die! Thou wrongest me, Ione; but I will bear the wrong without a murmur, only let me see thee sometimes. Chide, reproach, scorn me, if thou wilt—I will teach myself to bear it. And is not even thy bitterest tone sweeter to me than the music of the most artful lute? In thy silence the world seems to stand still—a stagnation curdles up the veins of the earth—there is no earth, no life, without the light of thy countenance and the melody of thy voice."

"Give me back my brother and my betrothed," said Ione, in a calm and imploring tone, and a few large tears rolled unheeded down her cheeks.

"Would that I could restore the one and save the other!" returned Arbaces, with apparent emotion. "Yes; to make thee happy I would renounce my ill-fated love, and gladly join thy hand to the Athenian's. Perhaps he will yet come unscathed from his trial [Arbaces had prevented her learning that the trial had already commenced]; if so, thou art free to judge or condemn him thyself. And think not, O Ione, that I would follow thee longer with a prayer of love. I know it is in vain. Suffer me only to weep—to mourn with thee. Forgive a violence deeply repented, and that shall offend no more. Let me be to thee only what I once was—a friend, a father, a protector. Ah, Ione! spare me and forgive."

"I forgive thee. Save but Glaucus, and I will renounce him. O mighty Arbaces! thou are powerful in evil or in good: save the Athenian, and the poor Ione will never see him more." As she spoke, she rose with weak and trembling limbs, and falling at his feet, she clasped his knees: "Oh! if thou really lovest me—if thou art human—remember my father's ashes, remember my childhood, think of all the hours we passed happily together, and save my Glaucus!"

Strange convulsions shook the frame of the Egyptian; his features worked fearfully—he turned his face aside, and said, in a hollow voice, "If I could save him, even now, I would; but the Roman law is stern and sharp. Yet if I *could* succeed —if I *could* rescue and set him free—wouldst thou be mine— my bride?"

"Thine?" repeated Ione, rising: "thine!—thy bride? My brother's blood is unavenged: *who* slew him? O Nemesis, can I even sell, for the life of Glaucus, thy solemn trust? Arbaces —*thine?* Never." "Ione, Ione!" cried Arbaces, passionately; "why these mysterious words?—why dost thou couple my name with the thought of thy brother's death?"

"My dreams couple it—and dreams are from the gods."

"Vain fantasies all! Is it for a dream that thou wouldst wrong the innocent, and hazard thy sole chance of saving thy lover's life?"

"Hear me!" said Ione, speaking firmly, and with a deliberate and solemn voice: "if Glaucus be saved by thee, I will never be borne to his home a bride. But I cannot master the horror of other rites: I cannot wed with thee. Interrupt me not; but mark me, Arbaces!—if Glaucus die, on that same day I baffle thine arts, and leave to thy love only my dust! Yes —thou mayst put the knife and the poison from my reach— thou mayst imprison—thou mayst chain me, but the brave soul resolved to escape is never without means. These hands, naked and unarmed though they be, shall tear away the bonds of life. Fetter them, and these lips shall firmly refuse the air. Thou art learned—thou hast read how women have died rather than meet dishonor. If Glaucus perish, I will not unworthily linger behind him. By all the gods of the heaven, and the ocean, and the earth, I devote myself to death! I have said!"

High, proud, dilating in her stature, like one inspired, the air and voice of Ione struck an awe into the breast of her listener.

"Brave heart!" said he, after a short pause; "thou art indeed worthy to be mine. Oh! that I should have dreamed of such a partner in my lofty destinies, and never found it but in thee! Ione," he continued rapidly, "dost thou not see that we are born for each other? Canst thou not recognize something kindred to thine own energy—thine own courage —in this high and self-dependent soul? We were formed to unite our sympathies—formed to breathe a new spirit into this hackneyed and gross world—formed for the mighty ends which my soul, sweeping down the gloom of time, foresees with a prophet's vision. With a resolution equal to thine own, I defy thy threats of an inglorious suicide. I hail thee as my own! Queen of climes undarkened by the eagle's wing, unravaged by his beak, I bow before thee in homage and in awe— but I claim thee in worship and in love! Together will we cross the ocean—together will we found our realm; and far-distant ages shall acknowledge the long race of kings born from the marriage-bed of Arbaces and Ione!"

"Thou ravest! These mystic declamations are suited rather to some palsied crone selling charms in the market-place than to the wise Arbaces. Thou hast heard my resolution —it is fixed as the Fates themselves. Orcus has heard my vow, and it is written in the book of the unforgetful Hades. Atone, then, O Arbaces!—atone the past: convert hatred into regard —vengeance into gratitude; preserve one who shall never be thy rival. These are acts suited to thy original nature, which gives forth sparks of something high and noble. They weigh in the scales of the Kings of Death: they turn the balance on that day when the disembodied soul stands shivering and dismayed between Tartarus and Elysium: they gladden the heart in life, better and longer than the reward of a momentary passion. Oh, Arbaces! hear me, and be swayed!"

"Enough, Ione. All that I can do for Glaucus shall be done; but blame me not if I fail. Inquire of my foes, even, if I have not sought, if I do not seek, to turn aside the sentence from his head; and judge me accordingly. Sleep, then, Ione. Night wanes; I leave thee to its rest—and mayst thou have kinder dreams of one who has no existence but in thine."

Without waiting a reply, Arbaces hastily withdrew; afraid, perhaps, to trust himself further to the passionate prayer of Ione, which racked him with jealousy, even while it touched him to compassion. But compassion itself came too late. Had Ione even pledged him her hand as his reward, he could not now—his evidence given—the populace excited—have saved the Athenian. Still, made sanguine by his very energy of mind, he threw himself on the chances of the future, and believed he should yet triumph over the woman that had so entangled his passions.

As his attendants assisted to unrobe him for the night, the thought of Nydia flashed across him. He felt it was necessary that Ione should never learn of her lover's frenzy, lest it might excuse his imputed crime; and it was possible that her attendants might inform her that Nydia was under his roof, and she might desire to see her. As this idea crossed him, he turned to one of his freedmen—

"Go, Callias," said he, "forthwith to Sosia, and tell him that on no pretence is he to suffer the blind slave Nydia out of her chamber. But, stay—first seek those in attendance upon my ward, and caution them not to inform her that the blind girl is under my roof. Go—quick!"

The freedman hastened to obey. After having discharged his commission with respect to Ione's attendants, he sought the worthy Sosia. He found him not in the little cell which was apportioned for his cubiculum; he called his name aloud, and from Nydia's chamber, close at hand, he heard the voice of Sosia reply—

"Oh, Callias, is it you that I hear?—the gods be praised! Open the door, I pray you!"

Callias withdrew the bolt, and the rueful face of Sosia hastily obtruded itself.

"What!—in the chamber with that young girl, Sosia! *Proh pudor!* Are there not fruits ripe enough on the wall, but that thou must tamper with such green——"

"Name not the little witch!" interrupted Sosia, impatiently; "she will be my ruin!" And he forthwith imparted to Callias the history of the Air Demon, and the escape of the Thessalian.

"Hang thyself, then, unhappy Sosia! I am just charged from Arbaces with a message to thee;—on no account art thou to suffer her, even for a moment, from that chamber!"

"*Me miserum!*" exclaimed the slave. "What can I do!—by this time she may have visited half Pompeii. But to-morrow I will undertake to catch her in her old haunts. Keep but my counsel, my dear Callias."

"I will do all that friendship can, consistent with my own safety. But are you sure she has left the house?—she may be hiding here yet."

"How is that possible? She could easily have gained the garden; and the door, as I told thee, was open."

"Nay, not so; for, at that very hour thou specifiest, Arbaces was in the garden with the priest Calenus. I went there in search of some herbs for my master's bath to-morrow. I saw the table set out; but the gate I am sure was shut: depend upon it, that Calenus entered by the garden, and naturally closed the door after him." "But it was not locked."

"Yes; for I myself, angry at a negligence which might expose the bronzes in the peristyle to the mercy of any robber, turned the key, took it away, and—as I did not see the proper slave to whom to give it, or I should have rated him finely —here it actually is, still in my girdle."

"Oh, merciful Bacchus! I did not pray to thee in vain, after all. Let us not lose a moment! Let us to the garden instantly—she may yet be there!"

The good-natured Callias consented to assist the slave; and after vainly searching the chambers at hand, and the recesses of the peristyle, they entered the garden.

It was about this time that Nydia had resolved to quit her hiding-place, and venture forth on her way. Lightly, tremulously, holding her breath, which ever and anon broke forth in quick convulsive gasps,—now gliding by the flower-wreathed columns that bordered the peristyle—now darkening the still moonshine that fell over its tessellated centre—now ascending the terrace of the garden—now gliding amidst the gloomy and breathless trees, she gained the fatal door—to find it locked! We have all seen that expression of pain, of uncertainty, of fear, which a sudden disappointment of touch, if I may use the expression, casts over the face of the blind. But what words can paint the intolerable woe, the sinking of the whole heart, which was now visible on the features of the Thessalian? Again and again her small, quivering hands wandered to and fro the inexorable door. Poor thing that thou wert! in vain had been all thy noble courage, thy innocent craft, thy doublings to escape the hound and huntsman? Within but a few yards from thee, laughing at thy endeavors—thy despair—knowing thou wert now their own, and watching with cruel patience their own moment to seize their prey—thou art saved from seeing thy pursuers!

"Hush, Callias!—let her go on. Let us see what she will do when she has convinced herself that the door is honest."

"Look! she raises her face to the heavens—she mutters—she sinks down despondent! No! by Pollux, she has some new scheme! She will not resign herself! By Jupiter, a tough spirit! See, she springs up—she retraces her steps—she thinks of some other chance! I advise thee, Sosia, to delay no longer: seize her ere she quit the garden,—now!"

"Ah! runaway! I have thee—eh?" said Sosia, seizing upon the unhappy Nydia.

As a hare's last *human* cry in the fangs of the dogs—as the sharp voice of terror uttered by a sleep-walker suddenly awakened—broke the shriek of the blind girl, when she felt the abrupt gripe of her gaoler. It was a shriek of such utter agony, such entire despair, that it might have rung hauntingly in your ears for ever. She felt as if the last plank of the sinking Glaucus were torn from his clasp. It had been a suspense of life and death; and death had now won the game.

"Gods! that cry will alarm the house! Arbaces sleeps full lightly. Gag her!" cried Callias.

"Ah! here is the very napkin with which the young witch conjured away my reason! Come! that's right; now thou art dumb as well as blind."

And, catching the light weight in his arms, Sosia soon gained the house, and reached the chamber from which Nydia had escaped. There, removing the gag, he left her to a solitude so racked and terrible, that out of Hades its anguish could scarcely be exceeded.

CHAPTER XVI.

The sorrow of boon companions for our afflictions.—The dungeon and its victims.

It was now late on the third and last day of the trial of Glaucus and Olinthus. A few hours after the court had broken up and judgment been given, a small party of the fashionable youth at Pompeii were assembled round the fastidious board of Lepidus.

"So Glaucus denies his crime to the last?" said Clodius.

"Yes; but the testimony of Arbaces was convincing; he saw the blow given," answered Lepidus.

"What could have been the cause?"

"Why, the priest was a gloomy and sullen fellow. He probably rated Glaucus soundly about his gay life and gaming habits, and ultimately swore he would not consent to his marriage with Ione. High words arose; Glaucus seems to have been full of the passionate god, and struck in sudden exasperation. The excitement of wine, the desperation of abrupt remorse, brought on the delirium under which he suffered for some days; and I can readily imagine, poor fellow! that, yet confused by that delirium, he is even now unconscious of the crime he committed! Such, at least, is the shrewd conjecture of Arbaces, who seems to have been most kind and forbearing in his testimony."

"Yes; he has made himself generally popular by it. But, in consideration of these extenuating circumstances, the senate should have relaxed the sentence."

"And they *would* have done so, but for the people; but *they* were outrageous. The priest had spared no pains to excite them; and they imagined—the ferocious brutes!—because Glaucus was a rich man and a gentleman, that he was likely to escape; and therefore they were inveterate against him, and doubly resolved upon his sentence. It seems, by some accident or other, that he was never formally enrolled as a Roman citizen; and thus the senate is deprived of the power to resist the people, though, after all, there was but a majority of three against him. Ho! the Chian!"

"He looks sadly altered; but how composed and fearless!"

"Ay, we shall see if his firmness will last over to-morrow. But what merit in courage, when that atheistical hound, Olinthus, manifested the same?"

"The blasphemer! Yes," said Lepidus, with pious wrath, "no wonder that one of the decurions was, but two days ago, struck dead by lightning in a serene sky. The gods feel vengeance against Pompeii while the vile desecrator is alive within its walls."

"Yet so lenient was the senate, that had he but expressed his penitence, and scattered a few grains of incense on the altar of Cybele, he would have been let off. I doubt whether these Nazarenes, had they the state religion, would be as tolerant to us, supposing we had kicked down the image of their Deity, blasphemed their rites, and denied their faith."

"They give Glaucus one chance, in consideration of the circumstances; they allow him, against the lion, the use of the same stilus wherewith he smote the priest."

"Hast thou seen the lion? hast thou looked at his teeth and fangs, and wilt thou call *that* a chance? Why, sword and buckler would be mere reed and papyrus against the rush of the mighty beast! No, I think the true mercy has been, not to leave him long in suspense; and it was therefore fortunate for him that our benign laws are slow to pronounce, but swift to execute; and that the games of the amphitheatre had been, by a sort of providence, so long since fixed for to-morrow. He who awaits death, dies twice."

"As for the Atheist," said Clodius, "he is to cope the grim tiger naked-handed. Well, these combats are past betting on. Who will take the odds?"

A peal of laughter announced the ridicule of the question.

"Poor Clodius!" said the host; "to lose a friend is something; but to find no one to bet on the chance of his escape is a worse misfortune to thee."

"Why, it is provoking; it would have been some consolation to him and to me to think he was useful to the last."

"The people," said the grave Pansa, "are all delighted with the result. They were so much afraid the sports at the amphitheatre would go off without a criminal for the beasts; and now, to get two *such* criminals is indeed a joy for the poor fellows! They work hard; they ought to have some amusement."

"There speaks the popular Pansa, who never moves without a string of clients as long as an Indian triumph. He is always prating about the people. Gods! he will end by being a Gracchus!" "Certainly I am no insolent patrician," said Pansa, with a generous air.

"Well," observed Lepidus, "it would have been assuredly dangerous to have been merciful at the eve of a beast-fight. If ever *I*, though a Roman bred and born, come to be tried, pray Jupiter there may be either no beasts in the *vivaria,* or plenty of criminals in the gaol."

"And pray," said one of the party, "what has become of the poor girl whom Glaucus was to have married? A widow without being a bride—that is hard!"

"Oh," returned Clodius, "she is safe under the protection of her guardian, Arbaces. It was natural she should go to him when she had lost both lover and brother."

"By sweet Venus, Glaucus was fortunate among the women! They say the rich Julia was in love with him."

"A mere fable, my friend," said Clodius, coxcombically; "I was with her to-day. If any feeling of the sort she ever conceived, I flatter myself that *I* have consoled her."

"Hush, gentlemen!" said Pansa; "do you not know that Clodius is employed at the house of Diomed in blowing hard at the torch? It begins to burn, and will soon shine bright on the shrine of Hymen."

"Is it so?" said Lepidus. "What! Clodius become a married man?—Fie!"

"Never fear," answered Clodius; "old Diomed is delighted at the notion of marrying his daughter to a nobleman, and will come down largely with the sesterces. You will see that I shall not lock them up in the atrium. It will be a white day for his jolly friends, when Clodius marries an heiress."

"Say you so?" cried Lepidus; "come, then, a full cup to the health of the fair Julia!"

While such was the conversation—one not discordant to

the tone of mind common among the dissipated of that day, and which might perhaps, a century ago, have found an echo in the looser circles of Paris—while such, I say, was the conversation in the gaudy triclinium of Lepidus, far different the scene which scowled before the young Athenian.

After his condemnation, Glaucus was admitted no more to the gentle guardianship of Sallust, the only friend of his distress. He was led along the forum till the guards stopped at a small door by the side of the temple of Jupiter. You may see the place still. The door opened in the centre in a somewhat singular fashion, revolving round on its hinges, as it were, like a modern turnstile, so as only to leave half the threshold open at the same time. Through this narrow aperture they thrust the prisoner, placed before him a loaf and a pitcher of water, and left him to darkness, and, as he thought, to solitude. So sudden had been that revolution of fortune which had prostrated him from the palmy height of youthful pleasure and successful love to the lowest abyss of ignominy, and the horror of a most bloody death, that he could scarcely convince himself that he was not held in the meshes of some fearful dream. His elastic and glorious frame had triumphed over a potion, the greater part of which he had fortunately not drained. He had recovered sense and consciousness, but still a dim and misty depression clung to his nerves and darkened his mind. His natural courage, and the Greek nobility of pride, enabled him to vanquish all unbecoming apprehension, and, in the judgment-court, to face his awful lot with a steady mien and unquailing eye. But the consciousness of innocence scarcely sufficed to support him when the gaze of men no longer excited his haughty valor, and he was left to loneliness and silence. He felt the damps of the dungeon sink chillingly into his enfeebled frame. *He*—the fastidious, the luxurious, the refined—he who had hitherto braved no hardship and known no sorrow. Beautiful bird that he was! why had he left his far and sunny clime—the olive-groves of his native hills—the music of immemorial streams? Why had he wantoned on his glittering plumage amidst these harsh and ungenial strangers, dazzling the eyes with his gorgeous hues, charming the ear with his blithesome song—thus suddenly to be arrested—caged in darkness—a victim and a prey—his gay

flights for ever over—his hymns of gladness for ever stilled!
The poor Athenian! his very faults the exuberance of a gentle
and joyous nature, how little had his past career fitted him
for the trials he was destined to undergo! The hoots of the
mob, amidst whose plaudits he had so often guided his graceful car and bounding steeds, still rang gratingly in his ear.
The cold and stony faces of his former friends (the co-mates
of his merry revels) still rose before his eye. None now were
by to soothe, to sustain, the admired, the adulated stranger.
These walls opened but on the dread arena of a violent and
shameful death. And Ione! of her, too, he had heard naught;
no encouraging word, no pitying message; she, too, had forsaken him; she believed him guilty—and of what crime?—
the murder of a brother! He ground his teeth—he groaned
aloud—and ever and anon a sharp fear shot across him. In
that fell and fierce delirium which had so unaccountably seized
his soul, which had so ravaged the disordered brain, *might he
not,* indeed, unknowing to himself, have committed the crime
of which he was accused? Yet, as the thought flashed upon
him, it was as suddenly checked; for, amidst all the darkness
of the past, he thought distinctly to recall the dim grove of
Cybele, the upward face of the pale dead, the pause that he
had made beside the corpse, and the sudden shock that felled
him to the earth. He felt convinced of his innocence; and yet
who, to the latest time, long after his mangled remains were
mingled with the elements, would believe him guiltless, or
uphold his fame? As he recalled his interview with Arbaces,
and the causes of revenge which had been excited in the heart
of that dark and fearful man, he could not but believe that he
was the victim of some deep-laid and mysterious snare—the
clue and train of which he was lost in attempting to discover:
and Ione—Arbaces loved her—might his rival's success be
founded upon his ruin? That thought cut him more deeply
than all; and his noble heart was more stung by jealousy than
appalled by fear. Again he groaned aloud.

A voice from the recess of the darkness answered that
burst of anguish. "Who [it said] is my companion in this
awful hour? Athenian Glaucus, is it thou?"

"So, indeed, they called me in mine hour of fortune: they

may have other names for me now. And *thy* name, stranger?"

"Is Olinthus, thy co-mate in the prison as the trial."

"What, he whom they call the Atheist? Is it the injustice of men that hath taught thee to deny the providence of the gods?"

"Alas!" answered Olinthus: "thou, not I, art the true Atheist, for thou deniest the sole true God—the Unknown One—to whom thy Athenian fathers erected an altar. It is in this hour that I know my God. He is with me in the dungeon; His smile penetrates the darkness; on the eve of death my heart whispers immortality, and earth recedes from me but to bring the weary soul nearer unto heaven."

"Tell me," said Glaucus, abruptly, "did I not hear thy name coupled with that of Apæcides in my trial? Dost thou believe me guilty?"

"God alone reads the heart! but my suspicion rested not upon thee." "On whom, then?" "They accuser, Arbaces."

"Ha! thou cheerest me: and wherefore?"

"Because I know the man's evil breast, and he had cause to fear him who is now dead."

With that, Olinthus proceeded to inform Glaucus of those details which the reader already knows, the conversion of Apæcides, the plan they had proposed for the detection of the impostures of the Egyptian priestcraft, and of the seductions practised by Arbaces upon the youthful weakness of the proselyte. "Therefore," concluded Olinthus, "had the deceased encountered Arbaces, reviled his treasons, and threatened detection, the place, the hour, might have favored the wrath of the Egyptian, and passion and craft alike dictated the fatal blow." "It must have been so!" cried Glaucus, joyfully. "I am happy."

"Yet what, O unfortunate! avails to thee now the discovery? Thou art condemned and fated; and in thine innocence thou wilt perish."

"But I shall *know myself* guiltless; and in my mysterious madness I had fearful, though momentary, doubts. Yet tell me, man of a strange creed, thinkest thou that, for small errors, or for ancestral faults, we are for ever abandoned and accursed by the powers above, whatever name thou allottest to them?"

"God is just, and abandons not His creatures for their mere human frailty. God is merciful, and curses none but the wicked who repent not."

"Yet it seemeth to me as if, in the divine anger, I had been smitten by a sudden madness, a supernatural and solemn frenzy, wrought not by human means."

"There are demons on earth," answered the Nazarene, fearfully, "as well as there are God and His Son in heaven; and since thou acknowledgest not the last, the first may have had power over thee."

Glaucus did not reply, and there was a silence for some minutes. At length the Athenian said, in a changed, and soft, and half-hesitating voice, "Christian, believest thou, among the doctrines of thy creed, that the dead live again—that they who have loved here are united hereafter—that beyond the grave our good name shines pure from the mortal mists that unjustly dim it in the gross-eyed world—and that the streams which are divided by the desert and the rock meet in the solemn Hades, and flow once more into one?"

"Believe I that, O Athenian? No, I do not believe—I *know!* and it is that beautiful and blessed assurance which supports me now. O Cyllene!" continued Olinthus, passionately, "bride of my heart! torn from me in the first month of our nuptials, shall I not see thee yet, and ere many days be past? Welcome, welcome death, that will bring me to heaven and thee!"

There was something in this sudden burst of human affection which struck a kindred chord in the soul of the Greek. He felt, for the first time, a sympathy greater than mere affliction between him and his companion. He crept nearer towards Olinthus; for the Italians, fierce in some points, were not unnecessarily cruel in others: they spared the separate cell and the superfluous chain, and allowed the victims of the arena the sad comfort of such freedom and such companionship as the prison would afford.

"Yes," continued the Christian with holy fervor, "the immortality of the soul—the resurrection—the reunion of the dead—is the great principle of our creed—the great truth a God suffered death itself to attest and proclaim. No fabled

Elysium—no poetic Orcus—but a pure and radiant heritage of heaven itself, is the portion of the good."

"Tell me, then, thy doctrines, and expound to me thy hopes," said Glaucus, earnestly.

Olinthus was not slow to obey that prayer; and there—as oftentimes in the early ages of the Christian creed—it was in the darkness of the dungeon, and over the approach of death, that the dawning Gospel shed its soft and consecrating rays.

CHAPTER XVII.

A change for Glaucus.

THE hours passed in lingering torture over the head of Nydia from the time in which she had been replaced in her cell.

Sosia, as if afraid he should be again outwitted, had refrained from visiting her until late in the morning of the following day, and then he but thrust in the periodical basket of food and wine, and hastily reclosed the door. That day rolled on, and Nydia felt herself pent—barred—inexorably confined, when that day was the judgment day of Glaucus, and when her release would have saved him! Yet knowing, almost impossible as seemed her escape, that the sole chance for the life of Glaucus rested on her, this young girl, frail, passionate, and acutely susceptible as she was—resolved not to give way to a despair that would disable her from seizing whatever opportunity *might* occur. She kept her senses whenever, beneath the whirl of intolerable thought, they reeled and tottered; nay, she took food and wine that she might sustain her strength—that she might be prepared!

She revolved scheme after scheme of escape, and was forced to dismiss all. Yet Sosia was her only hope, the only instrument with which she could tamper. He had been superstitious in the desire of ascertaining whether he could eventually purchase his freedom. Blessed gods! might he not be won by the bribe of freedom itself? was she not nearly rich enough to purchase it? Her slender arms were covered with bracelets, the presents of Ione; and on her neck she yet wore that very chain which, it may be remembered, had occasioned

her jealous quarrel with Glaucus, and which she had afterwards promised vainly to wear for ever. She waited burningly
till Sosia should again appear; but as hour after hour passed,
and he came not, she grew impatient. Every nerve beat with
fever; she could endure the solitude no longer—she groaned,
she shrieked aloud—she beat herself against the door. Her
cries echoed along the hall, and Sosia, in peevish anger, hastened to see what was the matter, and silence his prisoner if
possible.

"Ho! ho! what is this?" said he, surlily. "Young slave, if
thou screamest out thus, we must gag thee again. My shoulders will smart for it, if thou art heard by my master."

"Kind Sosia, chide me not—I cannot endure to be so long
alone," answered Nydia; "the solitude appals me. Sit with
me, I pray, a little while. Nay, fear not that I should attempt
to escape; place thy seat before the door. Keep thine eye on
me—I will not stir from this spot."

Sosia, who was a considerable gossip himself, was moved
by this address. He pitied one who had nobody to talk with
—it was his case too; he pitied—and resolved to relieve *himself*. He took the hint of Nydia, placed a stool before the door,
leaned his back against it, and replied,—

"I am sure I do not wish to be churlish; and so far as a
little innocent chat goes, I have no objection to indulge you.
But mind, no tricks—no more conjuring!"

"No, no; tell me, dear Sosia, what is the hour?"

"It is already evening—the goats are going home."

"O gods! how went the trial?"

"Both condemned!"

Nydia repressed the shriek. "Well—well, I thought it
would be so. When do they suffer?"

"To-morrow, in the amphitheatre. If it were not for thee,
little wretch! I should be allowed to go with the rest and
see it."

Nydia leant back for some moments. Nature could endure
no more—she had fainted away. But Sosia did not perceive
it, for it was the dusk of eve, and he was full of his own priva-
tions. He went on lamenting the loss of so delightful a show,
and accusing the injustice of Arbaces for singling him out
from all his fellows to be converted into a gaoler; and ere he

had half finished, Nydia, with a deep sigh, recovered the sense of life.

"Thou sighest, blind one, at my loss! Well, that is some comfort. So long as you acknowledge how much you cost me, I will endeavor not to grumble. It is hard to be ill-treated, and yet not pitied."

"Sosia, how much dost thou require to make up the purchase of thy freedom?"

"How much? Why, about two thousand sesterces."

"The gods be praised! not more? Seest thou these bracelets and this chain? They are well worth double that sum. I will give them thee if——"

"Tempt me not: I cannot release thee. Arbaces is a severe and awful master. Who knows but I might feed the fishes of the Sarnus? Alas! all the sesterces in the world would not buy me back into life. Better a live dog than a dead lion."

"Sosia, thy freedom! Think well! If thou wilt let me out, only for one little hour!—let me out at midnight—I will return ere to-morrow's dawn; nay, thou canst go with me."

"No," said Sosia, sturdily, "a slave once disobeyed Arbaces, and he was never more heard of."

"But the law gives a master no power over the life of a slave."

"The law is very obliging, but more polite than efficient. I know that Arbaces always gets the law on his side. Besides, if I am once dead, what law can bring me to life again!"

Nydia wrung her hands. "Is there no hope, then?" said she, convulsively.

"None of escape, till Arbaces gives the word."

"Well, then," said Nydia, quickly, "thou wilt not, at least, refuse to take a letter for me: thy master cannot kill thee for that." "To whom?" "The prætor."

"To a magistrate? No—not I. I should be made a witness in court, for what I know; and the way they cross-examine the slave is by the torture."

"Pardon: I meant not the prætor—it was a word that escaped me unawares; I meant quite another person—the gay Sallust."

"Oh! and what want you with him?"

"Glaucus was my master; he purchased me from a cruel

lord. He alone has been kind to me. He is to die. I shall never live happily if I cannot, in his hour of trial and doom, let him know that one heart is grateful to him. Sallust is his friend; he will convey my message."

"I am sure he will do no such thing. Glaucus will have enough to think of between this and to-morrow without troubling his head about a blind girl."

"Man," said Nydia, rising, "wilt thou become free? Thou hast the offer in thy power; to-morrow it will be too late. Never was freedom more cheaply purchased. Thou canst easily and unmissed leave home: less than half an hour will suffice for thine absence. And for such a trifle wilt thou refuse liberty?"

Sosia was greatly moved. It was true that the request was remarkably silly; but what was that to him? So much the better. He could lock the door on Nydia, and, if Arbaces should learn his absence, the offence was venial, and would merit but a reprimand. Yet, should Nydia's letter contain something more than what she had said—should it speak of her imprisonment, as he shrewdly conjectured it would do— what then! It need never be known to Arbaces that *he* had carried the letter. At the worst the bribe was enormous— the risk light—the temptation irresistible. He hesitated no longer—he assented to the proposal.

"Give me the trinkets, and I will take the letter. Yet stay —thou art a slave—thou hast no right to these ornaments— they are thy master's."

"They were the gifts of Glaucus; he is my master. What chance hath he to claim them? Who else will know they are in my possession?"

"Enough—I will bring thee the papyrus."

"No, not papyrus—a tablet of wax and a stilus."

Nydia, as the reader will have seen, was born of gentle parents. They had done all to lighten her calamity, and her quick intellect seconded their exertions. Despite her blindness, she had therefore acquired in childhood, though imperfectly, the art to write with the sharp stilus upon waxen tablets, in which her exquisite sense of touch came to her aid. When the tablets were brought to her, she thus painfully traced some words in Greek, the language of her childhood, and which almost every Italian of the higher ranks was then supposed

to know. She carefully wound round the epistle the protecting
thread, and covered its knot with wax; and ere she placed it
in the hands of Sosia, she thus addressed him:—

"Sosia, I am blind and in prison. Thou mayst think to
deceive me—thou mayst pretend only to take the letter to
Sallust—thou mayst not fulfil thy charge: but here I solemnly
dedicate thy head to vengeance, thy soul to the infernal powers,
if thou wrongest thy trust; and I call upon thee to place thy
right hand of faith in mine, and repeat after me these words:
—'By the ground on which we stand—by the elements which
contain life and can curse life—by Orcus, the all-avenging—
by the Olympian Jupiter, the all-seeing—I swear that I will
honestly discharge my trust, and faithfully deliver into the
hands of Sallust this letter! And if I perjure myself in this
oath, may the full curses of heaven and hell be wreaked upon
me!' Enough!—I trust thee—take thy reward. It is already
dark—depart at once."

"Thou art a strange girl, and thou hast frightened me
terribly; but it is all very natural: and if Sallust is to be
found, I give him this letter as I have sworn. By my faith,
I may have my little peccadilloes! but perjury—no! I leave
that to my betters."

With this Sosia withdrew, carefully passing the heavy bolt
athwart Nydia's door—carefully locking its wards: and,
hanging the key to his girdle, he retired to his own den, envel-
oped himself from head to foot in a huge disguising cloak,
and slipped out by the back way undisturbed and unseen.

The streets were thin and empty. He soon gained the house
of Sallust. The porter bade him leave his letter, and be gone;
for Sallust was so grieved at the condemnation of Glaucus,
that he could not on any account be disturbed.

"Nevertheless, I have sworn to give this letter into his
own hands—do so I must!" And Sosia, well knowing by
experience that Cerberus loves a sop, thrust some half a dozen
sesterces into the hand of the porter.

"Well, well," said the latter, relenting, "you may enter if
you will; but, to tell you the truth, Sallust is drinking himself
out of his grief. It is his way when anything disturbs him.
He orders a capital supper, the best wine, and does not give
over till everything is out of his head—but the liquor."

"An excellent plan—excellent! Ah, what it is to be rich! If I were Sallust, I would have some grief or another every day. But just say a kind word for me with the atriensis—I see him coming."

Sallust was too sad to receive company; he was too sad, also, to drink alone; so, as was his wont, he admitted his favorite freedman to his entertainment, and a stranger banquet never was held. For ever and anon, the kind-hearted epicure sighed, whimpered, wept outright, and then turned with double zest to some new dish or his refilled goblet.

"My good fellow," said he to his companion, "it was a most awful judgment—heighho!—it is not bad that kid, eh? Poor, dear Glaucus!—what a jaw the lion has too! Ah, ah, ah!"

And Sallust sobbed loudly—the fit was stopped by a counteraction of hiccups.

"Take a cup of wine," said the freedman.

"A thought too cold; but then how cold Glaucus must be! Shut up the house to-morrow—not a slave shall stir forth— none of my people shall honor that cursed arena—No, no!"

"Taste the Falernian—your grief distracts you. By the gods it does—a piece of that cheesecake."

It was at this auspicious moment that Sosia was admitted to the presence of the disconsolate carouser.

"Ho!—what art thou?"

"Merely a messenger to Sallust. I give him this billet from a young female. There is no answer that I know of. May I withdraw?"

Thus said the discreet Sosia, keeping his face muffled in his cloak, and speaking with a feigned voice, so that he might not hereafter be recognized.

"By the gods—a pimp! Unfeeling wretch!—do you not see my sorrows? Go!—and the curses of Pandarus with you!"

Sosia lost not a moment in retiring.

"Will you read the letter, Sallust?" said the freedman.

"Letter!—which letter?" said the epicure, reeling, for he began to see double. "A curse on these wenches, say I! Am I a man to think of—(hiccup)—pleasure, when—when—my friend is going to be eat up?"

"Eat another tartlet."

"No, no! My grief chokes me!"

"Take him to bed," said the freedman; and Sallust's head
now declining fairly on his breast, they bore him off to his
cubiculum, still muttering lamentations for Glaucus, and imprecations on the unfeeling overtures of ladies of pleasure.

Meanwhile Sosia strode indignantly homeward. "Pimp,
indeed!" quoth he to himself. "Pimp! a scurvy-tongued fellow
that Sallust! Had I been called knave, or thief. I could have
forgiven it; but pimp! Faugh! there is something in the word
which the toughest stomach in the world would rise against.
A knave is a knave for his own pleasure, and a thief a thief
for his own profit; and there is something honorable and
philosophical in being a rascal for one's own sake: that is
doing things upon principle—upon a grand scale. But a pimp
is a thing that defiles itself for another—a pipkin that is put
on the fire for another man's pottage! a napkin, that every
guest wipes his hands upon! and the scullion says, 'by your
leave,' too. A pimp! I would rather he had called me parricide! But the man was drunk, and did not know what he said;
and, besides, I disguised myself. Had he seen it had been
Sosia who addressed him, it would have been 'honest Sosia!'
and, 'worthy man!' I warrant. Nevertheless, the trinkets have
been won easily—that's some comfort! and, O goddess Fe-
ronia! I shall be a freedman soon! and then I should like to see
who'll call me pimp!—unless, indeed, he pay me pretty handsomely for it!"

While Sosia was soliloquizing in this high-minded and
generous vein, his path lay along a narrow lane that led
towards the amphitheatre and its adjacent palaces. Suddenly,
as he turned a sharp corner he found himself in the midst
of a considerable crowd. Men, women, and children, all were
hurrying on, laughing, talking, gesticulating; and, ere he was
aware of it, the worthy Sosia was borne away with the noisy
stream.

"What now?" he asked of his nearest neighbor, a young
artificer; "what now? Where are all these good folks thronging? Does any rich patron give away alms or viands
to-night?"

"Not so, man—better still," replied the artificer; "the noble
Pansa—the people's friend—has granted the public leave to

see the beasts in their *vivaria*. By Hercules! they will not be
seen so safely by some persons to-morrow!"

" 'Tis a pretty sight," said the slave, yielding to the throng
that impelled him onward; "and since I may not go to the
sports to-morrow, I may as well take a peep at the beasts to-
night."

"You will do well," returned his new acquaintance; "a lion
and a tiger are not to be seen at Pompeii every day."

The crowd had now entered a broken and wide space of
ground, on which, as it was only lighted scantily and from a
distance, the press became dangerous to those whose limbs and
shoulders were not fitted for a mob. Nevertheless, the women
especially—many of them with children in their arms, or even
at the breast—were the most resolute in forcing their way; and
their shrill exclamations of complaint or objurgation were
heard loud above the more jovial and masculine voices. Yet,
amidst them was a young and girlish voice, that appeared to
come from one too happy in her excitement to be alive to the
inconvenience of the crowd.

"Aha!" cried the young woman, to some of her companions, "I always told you so; I always said we should have a
man for the lion; and now we have one for the tiger too! I
wish to-morrow were come!

> "Ho! ho! for the merry, merry show,
> With a forest of faces in every row!
> Lo! the swordsmen, bold as the son of Alcmæna,
> Sweep, side by side, o'er the hushed arena.
> Talk while you may, you will hold your breath
> When they meet in the grasp of the glowing death!
> Tramp! tramp! how gaily they go!
> Ho! ho! for the merry, merry show!"

"A jolly girl!" said Sosia.

"Yes," replied the young artificer, a curly-headed, handsome youth. "Yes," replied he, enviously; "the women love a
gladiator. If I had been a slave, I would have soon found my
schoolmaster in the lanista!"

"Would you, indeed?" said Sosia, with a sneer. "People's
notions differ!"

The crowd had now arrived at the place of destination;
but as the cell in which the wild beasts were confined was ex-

tremely small and narrow, tenfold more vehement than it
hitherto had been was the rush of the aspirants to obtain ad-
mittance. Two of the officers of the amphitheatre, placed at
the entrance, very wisely mitigated the evil by dispensing to
the foremost only a limited number of tickets at a time, and
admitting no new visitors till their predecessors had sated
their curiosity. Sosia, who was a tolerably stout fellow, and
not troubled with any remarkable scruples of diffidence or
good-breeding, contrived to be among the first of the in-
itiated.

Separated from his companion the artificer, Sosia found
himself in a narrow cell of oppressive heat and atmosphere,
and lighted by several rank and flaring torches.

The animals, usually kept in different vivaria, or dens,
were now, for the greater entertainment of the visitors, placed
in one, but equally indeed divided from each other by strong
cages protected by iron bars.

There they were, the fell and grim wanderers of the desert,
who have now become almost the principal agents of this
story. The lion, who, as being more gentle by nature than his
fellow-beast, had been more incited to ferocity by hunger,
stalked restlessly and fiercely to and fro his narrow confines:
his eyes were lurid with rage and famine; and as, every now
and then, he paused and glared around, the spectators fearfully pressed backward, and drew their breath more quickly.
But the tiger lay quiet and extended at full length in his cage,
and only by an occasional play of his tail, or a long impatient
yawn, testified any emotion at his confinement, or at the crowd
which honored him with their presence.

"I have seen no fiercer beast than yon lion even in the
amphitheatre of Rome," said a gigantic and sinewy fellow
who stood at the right hand of Sosia.

"I feel humbled when I look at his limbs," replied, at the
left of Sosia, a slighter and younger figure, with his arms
folded on his breast.

The slave looked first at one, and then at the other. *"Virtus
in medio!*—virtue is ever in the middle!" muttered he to himself; "a goodly neighborhood for thee, Sosia—a gladiator on
each side!" "That is well said, Lydon," returned the huger
gladiator; "I feel the same."

"And to think," observed Lydon, in a tone of deep feeling, "to think that the noble Greek, he whom we saw but a day or two since before us, so full of youth, and health, and joyousness, is to feast yon monster!"

"Why not?" growled Niger savagely; "many an honest gladiator has been compelled to a like combat by the emperor —why not a wealthy murderer by the law?"

Lydon sighed, shrugged his shoulders, and remained silent. Meanwhile the common gazers listened with staring eyes and lips apart: the gladiators were objects of interest as well as the beasts—they were animals of the same species; so the crowd glanced from one to the other—the men and the brutes:—whispering their comments and anticipating the morrow.

"Well!" said Lydon, turning away, "I thank the gods that it is not the lion or the tiger *I* am to contend with; even you, Niger, are a gentler combatant than they."

"But equally dangerous," said the gladiator, with a fierce laugh; and the by-standers, admiring his vast limbs and ferocious countenance, laughed too.

"That as it may be," answered Lydon, carelessly, as he pressed through the throng and quitted the den.

"I may as well take advantage of his shoulders," thought the prudent Sosia, hastening to follow him: "the crowd always give way to a gladiator, so I will keep close behind, and come in for a share of his consequence."

The son of Medon strode quickly through the mob, many of whom recognized his features and profession. "That is young Lydon, a brave fellow; he fights to-morrow," said one. "Ah! I have a bet on him," said another; "see how firmly he walks!" "Good luck to thee, Lydon!" said a third.

"Lydon, you have my wishes," half whispered a fourth, smiling (a comely woman of the middle class)—"and if you win, why, you may hear more of me."

"A handsome man, by Venus!" cried a fifth, who was a girl scarcely in her teens. "Thank you," returned Sosia, gravely taking the compliment to himself.

However strong the purer motives of Lydon, and certain

though it be that he would never have entered so bloody a calling but from the hope of obtaining his father's freedom, he was not altogether unmoved by the notice he excited. He forgot that the voices now raised in commendation might, on the morrow, shout over his death-pangs. By nature fierce and reckless, as well as generous and warm-hearted, he was already imbued with the pride of a profession that he fancied he disdained, and affected by the influence of a companionship that in reality he loathed. He saw himself now a man of importance; his step grew yet lighter, and his mien more elate.

"Niger," said he, turning suddenly, as he had now threaded the crowd; "we have often quarrelled; we are not matched against each other, but one of us, at least, may reasonably expect to fall—give us thy hand."

"Most readily," said Sosia, extending his palm.

"Ha! what fool is this? Why, I thought Niger was at my heels!"

"I forgive the mistake," replied Sosia, condescendingly: "don't mention it; the error was easy—I and Niger are somewhat of the same build."

"Ha! ha! that is excellent! Niger would have slit thy throat, had he heard thee!"

"You gentlemen of the arena have a most disagreeable mode of talking," said Sosia: "let us change the conversation."

"Vah! Vah!" said Lydon, impatiently; "I am in no humor to converse with thee!"

"Why, truly," returned the slave, "you must have serious thoughts enough to occupy your mind: to-morrow is, I think, your first essay in the arena? Well, I am sure you will die bravely!"

"May thy words fall on thine own head!" said Lydon, superstitiously, for he by no means liked the blessing of Sosia. "Die! No—I trust my hour is not yet come."

"He who plays at dice with death must expect the dog's throw," replied Sosia, maliciously. "But you are a strong fellow, and I wish you all imaginable luck; and so vale!"

With that the slave turned on his heel, and took his way homeward.

"I trust the rogue's words are not ominous," said Lydon,

musingly. "In my zeal for my father's liberty, and my confidence in my own thews and sinews, I have not contemplated the possibility of death. My poor father! I am thy only son! —if I were to fall——"

As the thought crossed him, the gladiator strode on with a more rapid and restless pace, when suddenly, in an opposite street, he beheld the very object of his thoughts. Leaning on his stick, his form bent by care and age, his eyes downcast, and his steps trembling, the grey-haired Medon slowly approached towards the gladiator. Lydon paused a moment: he divined at once the cause that brought forth the old man at that late hour.

"Be sure, it is I whom he seeks," thought he; "he is horror-struck at the condemnation of Olinthus—he more than ever esteems the arena criminal and hateful—he comes again to dissuade me from the contest. I must shun him—I cannot brook his prayers—his tears."

These thoughts, so long to recite, flashed across the young man like lightning. He turned abruptly and fled swiftly in an opposite direction. He paused not till, almost spent and breathless, he found himself on the summit of a small acclivity which overlooked the most gay and splendid part of that miniature city; and as there he paused, and gazed along the tranquil streets glittering in the rays of the moon (which had just arisen, and brought partially and picturesquely into light the crowd around the amphitheatre at a distance, murmuring, and swaying to and fro), the influence of the scene affected him, rude and unimaginative though his nature. He sat himself down to rest upon the steps of a deserted portico, and felt the calm of the hour quiet and restore him. Opposite and near at hand, the lights gleamed from a palace in which the master now held his revels. The doors were open for coolness, and the gladiator beheld the numerous and festive group gathered round the tables in the atrium; while behind them, closing the long vista of the illumined rooms beyond, the spray of the distant fountain sparkled in the moonbeams. There, the garlands wreathed around the columns of the hall—there, gleamed still and frequent the marble statue—there, amidst peals of jocund laughter, rose the music and the lay.

EPICUREAN SONG.

"Away with your stories of Hades,
    Which the Flamen has forged to affright us—
We laugh at your three Maiden Ladies,
    Your Fates—and your sullen Cocytus.

Poor Jove has a troublesome life, sir,
    Could we credit your tales of his portals—
In shutting his ears on his wife, sir,
    And opening his eyes upon mortals.

Oh, blest be the bright Epicurus!
    Who taught us to laugh at such fables;
On Hades they wanted to moor us,
    And his hand cut the terrible cables.

If, then, there's a Jove or a Juno,
    They vex not their heads about us, man:
Besides, if they did, I and you know
    'Tis the life of a god to live *thus,* man!

What! think you the gods place their bliss—eh?—
    In playing the spy on a sinner?
In counting the girls that we kiss, eh?
    Or the cups that we empty at dinner?

Content with the soft lips that love us,
    This music, this wine, and this mirth, boys
We care not for gods up above us—
    We know there's no god for this earth, boys!"

While Lydon's piety (which, accommodating as it might be, was in no slight degree disturbed by these verses, which embodied the fashionable philosophy of the day) slowly recovered itself from the shock it had received, a small party of men, in plain garments and of the middle class, passed by his resting-place. They were in earnest conversation, and did not seem to notice or heed the gladiator as they moved on.

"O horror on horrors!" said one; "Olinthus is snatched from us! our right arm is lopped away! When will Christ descend to protect his own?"

"Can human atrocity go farther?" said another; "to sentence an innocent man to the same arena as a murderer! But let us not despair; the thunder of Sinai may yet be heard, and the Lord preserve his saint. 'The fool has said in his heart, There is no God.'"

At that moment out broke again, from the illumined palace, the burden of the revellers' song:—

"We care not for gods up above us—
We know there's no god for this earth, boys!" .

Ere the words died away, the Nazarenes, moved by sudden indignation, caught up the echo, and, in the words of one of their favorite hymns, shouted aloud—

THE WARNING HYMN OF THE NAZARENES.

"Around—about—for ever near thee,
God—OUR GOD—shall mark and hear thee!
On His car of storm He sweeps!
Bow, ye heavens, and shrink, ye deeps!
Woe to the proud ones who defy Him!—
Woe to the dreamers who deny Him!
          Woe to the wicked, woe!
The proud stars shall fail—
The sun shall grow pale—
The heavens shrivel up like a scroll—
Hell's ocean shall bare
Its depths of despair,
Each wave an eternal soul!
For the only thing, then,
That shall *not* live again,
          Is the corpse of the giant TIME!
Hark, the trumpet of thunder!
Lo, earth rent asunder!
And, forth, on his Angel-throne,
He comes through the gloom,
The Judge of the Tomb,
To summon and save His own!
          Oh, joy to Care, and woe to Crime
He comes to save His own!
Woe to the proud ones who defy Him!
Woe to the dreamers who deny Him!
          Woe to the wicked, woe!"

A sudden silence from the startled hall of revel succeeded these ominous words: the Christians swept on, and were soon hidden from the sight of the gladiator. Awed, he scarce knew why, by the mystic denunciations of the Christians, Lydon, after a short pause, now rose to pursue his way homeward.

Before him, how serenely slept the star-light on that lovely

city! how breathlessly its pillared streets reposed in their security!—how softly rippled the dark-green waves beyond!—
how cloudless spread, aloft and blue, the dreaming Campanian
skies! Yet this was the last night for the gay Pompeii! the
colony of the hoar Chaldean! the fabled city of Hercules! the
delight of the voluptuous Roman! Age after age had rolled,
indestructive, unheeded, over its head; and now the last ray
quivered on the dial-plate of its doom! The gladiator heard
some light steps behind—a group of females were wending
homeward from their visit to the amphitheatre. As he turned,
his eye was arrested by a strange and sudden apparition. From
the summit of Vesuvius, darkly visible at the distance, there
shot a pale, meteoric, livid light—it trembled an instant and
was gone. And at the same moment that his eye caught it, the
voice of one of the youngest of the women broke out hilari-
ously and shrill:—

> "TRAMP! TRAMP! HOW GAILY THEY GO!
> HO, HO! FOR THE MORROW'S MERRY SHOW!"

BOOK THE FIFTH.
CHAPTER I.

The dream of Arbaces.—A visitor and a warning to the Egyptian.

THE awful night preceding the fierce joy of the amphitheatre rolled drearily away, and greyly broke forth the dawn of THE LAST DAY OF POMPEII! The air was uncommonly calm and sultry—a thin and dull mist gathered over the valleys and hollows of the broad Campanian fields. But yet it was remarked in surprise by the early fishermen, that, despite the exceeding stillness of the atmosphere, the waves of the sea were agitated, and seemed, as it were, to run disturbedly back from the shore; while along the blue and stately Sarnus, whose ancient breadth of channel the traveller now vainly seeks to discover, there crept a hoarse and sullen murmur, as it glided by the laughing plains and the gaudy villas of the wealthy citizens. Clear above the low mist rose the time-worn towers of the immemorial town, the red-tiled roofs of the bright streets, the solemn columns of many temples, and the statue-crowned portals of the Forum and the Arch of Triumph. Far in the distance, the outline of the circling hills soared above the vapors, and mingled with the changeful hues of the morning sky. The cloud that had so long rested over the crest of Vesuvius had suddenly vanished, and its rugged and haughty brow looked without a frown over the beautiful scenes below.

Despite the earliness of the hour, the gates of the city were already opened. Horseman upon horseman, vehicle after vehicle, poured rapidly in; and the voices of numerous pedestrian groups, clad in holiday attire, rose high in joyous and excited merriment; the streets were crowded with citizens and strangers from the populous neighborhood of Pompeii; and noisily—fast—confusedly swept the many streams of life towards the fatal show.

Despite the vast size of the amphitheatre, seemingly so dis-

340

proportioned to the extent of the city, and formed to include nearly the whole population of Pompeii itself, so great, on extraordinary occasions, was the concourse of strangers from all parts of Campania, that the space before it was usually crowded for several hours previous to the commencement of the sports, by such persons as were not entitled by their rank to appointed and especial seats. And the intense curiosity which the trial and sentence of two criminals so remarkable had occasioned, increased the crowd on this day to an extent wholly unprecedented.

While the common people, with the lively vehemence of their Campanian blood, were thus pushing, scrambling, hurrying on,—yet, amidst all their eagerness, preserving, as is now the wont with Italians in such meetings, a wonderful order and unquarrelsome good-humor,—a strange visitor to Arbaces was threading her way to his sequestered mansion. At the sight of her quaint and primæval garb—of her wild gait and gestures—the passengers she encountered touched each other and smiled; but as they caught a glimpse of her countenance, the mirth was hushed at once, for the face was as the face of the dead; and, what with the ghastly features and obsolete robes of the stranger, it seemed as if one long entombed had risen once more amongst the living. In silence and awe each group gave way as she passed along, and she soon gained the broad porch of the Egyptian's palace.

The black porter, like the rest of the world, astir at an unusual hour, started as he opened the door to her summons.

The sleep of the Egyptian had been unusually profound during the night; but, as the dawn approached, it was disturbed by strange and unquiet dreams, which impressed him the more as they were colored by the peculiar philosophy he embraced.

He thought that he was transported to the bowels of the earth, and that he stood alone in a mighty cavern, supported by enormous columns of rough and primæval rock, lost, as they ascended, in the vastness of a shadow athwart whose eternal darkness no beam of day had ever glanced. And in the space between these columns were huge wheels, that whirled round and round unceasingly, and with a rushing and roaring noise. Only to the right and left extremities of the cavern, the space between the pillars was left bare, and the apertures stretched away into galleries—not wholly dark, but dimly lighted by wandering and erratic fires, that meteor-like, now crept (as the snake creeps) along the rugged and dank soil; and now leaped fiercely to and fro, darting across the vast gloom in wild gambols—suddenly disappearing, and as suddenly bursting into tenfold brilliancy and power. And while he gazed wonderingly upon the gallery to the left, thin, mist-like, ærial shapes passed slowly up; and when they had gained the hall they seemed to rise aloft, and to vanish, as the smoke vanishes, in the measureless ascent.

He turned in fear towards the opposite extremity—and behold! there came swiftly, from the gloom above, similar shadows, which swept hurriedly along the gallery to the right, as if borne involuntarily adown the tides of some invisible stream; and the faces of these spectres were more distinct than those that emerged from the opposite passage; and on some was joy, and on others sorrow—some were vivid with expectation and hope, some unutterably dejected by awe and horror. And so they passed swift and constantly on, till the eyes of the gazer grew dizzy and blinded with the whirl of an ever-varying succession of things impelled by a power apparently not their own.

Arbaces turned away; and, in the recess of the hall, he saw the mighty form of a giantess seated upon a pile of skulls, and her hands were busy upon a pale and shadowy woof; and he saw that the woof communicated with the numberless wheels, as if it guided the machinery of their movements. He thought his feet, by some secret agency, were impelled towards the female, and that he was borne onwards till he stood before her, face to face. The countenance of the giantess was solemn and hushed, and beautifully serene. It was as the face of some colossal sculpture of his own ancestral sphinx. No passion —no human emotion, disturbed its brooding and unwrinkled brow; there was neither sadness, nor joy, nor memory, nor hope; it was free from all with which the wild human heart can sympathize. The mystery of mysteries rested on its beauty,—it awed, but terrified not; it was the Incarnation of the Sublime. And Arbaces felt the voice leave his lips, without an impulse of his own; and the voice asked—

"Who art thou, and what is thy task?"

"I am That which thou hast acknowledged," answered, without desisting from its work, the mighty phantom. "My name is NATURE! These are the wheels of the world, and my hand guides them for the life of all things."

"And what," said the voice of Arbaces, "are these galleries, that, strangely and fitfully illumined, stretch on either hand into the abyss of gloom?"

"That," answered the giant-mother, "which thou beholdest to the left, is the gallery of the Unborn. The shadows that flit onward and upward into the world, are the souls that pass from the long eternity of being to their destined pilgrimage on earth. That which thou beholdest to thy right, wherein the shadows descending from above sweep on, equally unknown and dim, is the gallery of the Dead!"

"And, wherefore," said the voice of Arbaces, "yon wandering lights, that so wildly break the darkness; but only *break,* not *reveal?*"

"Dark fool of the human sciences! dreamer of the stars, and would-be decipherer of the heart and origin of things! those lights are but the glimmerings of such knowledge as is vouchsafed to Nature to work her way, to trace enough of the past and future to give providence to her designs. Judge, then, puppet as thou art, what lights are reserved for thee!"

Arbaces felt himself tremble as he asked again, "Wherefore am I here?"

"It is the forecast of thy soul—the prescience of thy rushing doom—the shadow of thy fate lengthening into eternity as it declines from earth."

Ere he could answer, Arbaces felt a rushing WIND sweep down the cavern, as the winds of a giant god. Borne aloft from the ground, and whirled on high as a leaf in the storms of autumn, he beheld himself in the midst of the Spectres of the Dead, and hurrying with them along the length of gloom. As in vain and impotent despair he struggled against the impelling power, he thought the WIND grew into something like a shape—a spectral outline of the wings and talons of an eagle, with limbs floating far and indistinctly along the air, and eyes that, alone clearly and vividly seen, glared stonily and remorselessly on his own.

"What art thou?" again said the voice of the Egyptian.

"I am That which thou hast acknowledged;" and the spectre laughed aloud—"and my name is NECESSITY."

"To what dost thou bear me?" "To the Unknown."

"To happiness or to woe?"

"As thou hast sown, so shalt thou reap."

"Dread thing, not so! If thou art the Ruler of life, *thine* are my misdeeds, not mine."

"I am but the breath of God!" answered the mighty WIND.

"Then is my wisdom vain!" groaned the dreamer.

"The husbandman accuses not fate, when, having sown thistles, he reaps not corn. Thou hast sown crime, accuse not fate if thou reapest not the harvest of virtue."

The scene suddenly changed. Arbaces was in a place of human bones; and lo! in the midst of them was a skull, and the skull, still retaining its fleshless hollows, assumed slowly, and in the mysterious confusion of a dream, the face of Apæcides; and forth from the grinning jaws there crept a small worm, and it crawled to the feet of Arbaces. He attempted to stamp on it and crush it; but it became longer and larger with that attempt. It swelled and bloated till it grew into a vast serpent: it coiled itself round the limbs of Arbaces; it crunched his bones; it raised its glaring eyes and poisonous jaws to his face. He writhed in vain; he withered—he gasped—beneath the influence of the blighting breath—he felt himself blasted into death. And then a voice came from the reptile, which still bore the face of Apæcides, and rang in his reeling ear,—

"THY VICTIM IS THY JUDGE! THE WORM THOU WOULDST CRUSH BECOMES THE SERPENT THAT DEVOURS THEE!"

With a shriek of wrath, and woe, and despairing resistance, Arbaces awoke—his hair on end—his brow bathed in dew—his eyes glazed and staring—his mighty frame quivering as an infant's, beneath the agony of that dream. He awoke—he collected himself—he blessed the gods whom he disbelieved, that he *was* in a dream;—he turned his eyes from side to side—he saw the dawning light break through his small but lofty window—he was in the Precincts of Day—he rejoiced—he smiled;—his eyes fell, and opposite to him he beheld the ghastly features, the lifeless eye, the livid lip—of the Hag of Vesuvius!

"Ha!" he cried, placing his hands before his eyes, as to shut out the grisly vision, "do I dream still?—Am I with the dead?"

"Mighty Hermes—no! Thou art with one death-like, but not dead. Recognize thy friend and slave."

There was a long silence. Slowly the shudders that passed over the limbs of the Egyptian chased each other away, faintlier and faintlier dying till he was himself again.

"It was a dream, then," said he. "Well—let me dream no more, or the day cannot compensate for the pangs of night. Woman, how camest thou here, and wherefore?"

"I came to warn thee," answered the sepulchral voice of the saga.

"Warn me! The dream lied not, then? Of what peril?"

"Listen to me. Some evil hangs over this fated city. Fly while it be time. Thou knowest that I hold my home on that mountain beneath which old tradition saith there yet burn the fires of the river of Phlegethon; and in my cavern is a vast abyss, and in that abyss I have of late marked a red and dull stream creep slowly, slowly on; and heard many and mighty sounds hissing and roaring through the gloom. But last night, as I looked thereon, behold the stream was no longer dull, but intensely and fiercely luminous; and while I gazed, the beast that liveth with me, and was cowering by my side, uttered a shrill howl, and fell down and died,* and the slaver and froth were round his lips. I crept back to my lair; but I distinctly heard, all the night, the rock shake and tremble; and, though the air was heavy and still, there were the hissing of pent winds, and the grinding as of wheels, beneath the ground. So, when I rose this morning at the very birth of dawn, I looked again down the abyss, and I saw vast fragments of stone borne black and floatingly over the lurid stream; and the stream itself was broader, fiercer, redder than the night before. Then I went forth, and ascended to the summit of the rock; and in that summit there appeared a sudden and vast hollow, which I had never perceived before, from which curled a dim, faint smoke; and the vapor was deathly, and I gasped, and sickened, and nearly died. I returned home, I took my gold

---

* We may suppose that the exhalations were similar in effect to those of the *Grotto del Cane.*

and my drugs, and left the habitation of many years; for I remembered the dark Etruscan prophecy which saith, 'When the mountain opens, the city shall fall—when the smoke crowns the Hill of the Parched Fields, there shall be woe and weeping in the hearths of the Children of the Sea.' Dread master, ere I leave these walls for some more distant dwelling, I come to thee. As thou livest, know I in my heart that the earthquake that sixteen years ago shook this city to its solid base, was but the forerunner of more deadly doom. The walls of Pompeii are built above the fields of the Dead, and the rivers of the sleepless Hell. Be warned and fly!"

"Witch, I thank thee for thy care of one not ungrateful. On yon table stands a cup of gold; take it, it is thine. I dreamt not that there lived one, out of the priesthood of Isis, who would have saved Arbaces from destruction. The signs thou hast seen in the bed of the extinct volcano," continued the Egyptian, musingly, "surely tell of some coming danger to the city; perhaps another earthquake fiercer than the last. Be that as it may, there is a new reason for my hastening from these walls. After this day I will prepare my departure. Daughter of Etruria, whither wendest thou?"

"I shall cross over to Herculaneum this day, and wandering thence along the coast, shall seek out a new home. I am friendless; my two companions, the fox and the snake, are dead. Great Hermes, thou hast promised me twenty additional years of life!"

"Ay," said the Egyptian, "I have promised thee. But, woman," he added, lifting himself upon his arm, and gazing curiously on her face, "tell me, I pray thee, wherefore thou wishest to live? What sweets dost thou discover in existence?"

"It is not life that is sweet, but death that is awful," replied the hag, in a sharp, impressive tone, that struck forcibly upon the heart of the vain star-seer. He winced at the truth of the reply; and, no longer anxious to retain so uninviting a companion, he said, "Time wanes; I must prepare for the solemn spectacle of this day. Sister, farewell! enjoy thyself as thou canst over the ashes of life."

The hag, who had placed the costly gift of Arbaces in the loose folds of her vest, now rose to depart. When she had gained the door she paused, turned back, and said, "This may

be the last time we meet on earth; but whither flieth the flame
when it leaves the ashes?—Wandering to and fro, up and
down, as an exhalation on the morass, the flame may be seen in
the marshes of the lake below; and the witch and the Magian,
the pupil and the master, the great one and the accursed one,
may meet again, Farewell!"

"Out, croaker!" muttered Arbaces, as the door closed on
the hag's tattered robes; and, impatient of his own thoughts,
not yet recovered from the past dream, he hastily summoned
his slaves.

It was the custom to attend the ceremonials of the amphitheatre in festive robes, and Arbaces arrayed himself that day
with more than usual care. His tunic was of the most dazzling
white; his many fibulae were formed from the most precious
stones; over his tunic flowed a loose eastern robe, half-gown,
half-mantle, glowing in the richest hues of the Tyrian dye;
and the sandals, that reached half-way up the knee, were
studded with gems, and inlaid with gold. In the quackeries
that belonged to his priestly genius, Arbaces never neglected,
on great occasions, the arts which dazzle and impose upon
the vulgar; and on this day, that was for ever to release him,
by the sacrifice of Glaucus, from the fear of a rival and the
chance of detection, he felt that he was arraying himself as
for a triumph or a nuptial feast.

It was customary for men of rank to be accompanied to
the shows of the amphitheatre by a procession of their slaves
and freedmen; and the long "family" of Arbaces were already
arranged in order, to attend the litter of their lord.

Only, to their great chagrin, the slaves in attendance on
Ione, and the worthy Sosia, as gaoler to Nydia, were condemned to remain at home.

"Callias," said Arbaces, apart to his freedman, who was
buckling on his girdle, "I am weary of Pompeii; I propose to
quit it in three days, should the wind favor. Thou knowest
the vessel that lies in the harbor which belonged to Narses, of
Alexandria; I have purchased it of him. The day after to-
morrow, we shall begin to remove my stores."

"So soon! 'Tis well. Arbaces shall be obeyed;—and his
ward, Ione?"

"Accompanies me. Enough!—Is the morning fair?"

"Dim and oppressive; it will probably be intensely hot in the forenoon."

"The poor gladiators, and more wretched criminals! Descend, and see that the slaves are marshalled."

Left alone, Arbaces stepped into his chamber of study, and thence upon the portico without. He saw the dense masses of men pouring fast into the amphitheatre, and heard the cry of the assistants, and the cracking of the cordage, as they were straining aloft the huge awning under which the citizens, molested by no discomforting ray, were to behold, at luxurious ease, the agonies of their fellow-creatures. Suddenly a wild, strange sound went forth, and as suddenly died away—it was the roar of the lion. There was a silence in the distant crowd; but the silence was followed by joyous laughter—they were making merry at the hungry impatience of the royal beast.

"Brutes!" muttered the disdainful Arbaces, "are ye less homicides than I am? *I* slay but in self-defence—*ye* make murder pastime."

He turned, with a restless and curious eye, towards Vesuvius. Beautifully glowed the green vineyards round its breast, and tranquil as eternity lay in the breathless skies the form of the mighty hill.

"We have time yet, if the earthquake be nursing," thought Arbaces; and he turned from the spot. He passed by the table which bore his mystic scrolls and Chaldean calculations.

"August art!" he thought, "I have not consulted thy decrees since I passed the danger and the crisis they foretold. What matter?—I know that *henceforth* all in my path is bright and smooth. Have not events already proved it? Away, doubt—away, pity! Reflect, O my heart—reflect, for the future, but two images—Empire and Ione!"

CHAPTER II.

The amphitheatre.

NYDIA, assured by the account of Sosia, on his return home, and satisfied that her letter was in the hands of Sallust, gave herself up once more to hope. Sallust would surely lose no time in seeking the prætor—in coming to the house of the

Egyptian—in releasing her—in breaking the prison of
Calenus. That very night Glaucus would be free. Alas! the
night passed—the dawn broke; she heard nothing but the
hurried footsteps of the slaves along the hall and peristyle,
and their voices in preparation for the show. By-and-by, the
commanding voice of Arbaces broke on her ear—a flourish of
music rang out cheerily; the long processions were sweeping
to the amphitheatre to glut their eyes on the death-pangs of
the Athenian!

The procession of Arbaces moved along slowly, and with
much solemnity, till now, arriving at the place where it was
necessary for such as came in litters or chariots to alight,
Arbaces descended from his vehicle, and proceeded to the entrance by which the more distinguished spectators were admitted. His slaves, mingling with the humbler crowd, were
stationed by officers who received their tickets (not much unlike our modern Opera ones), in places in the *popularia* (the
seats apportioned to the vulgar). And now, from the spot
where Arbaces sat, his eyes scanned the mighty and impatient
crowd that filled the stupendous theatre.

On the upper tier (but apart from the male spectators) sat
the women, their gay dresses resembling some gaudy flower-
bed; it is needless to add that they were the most talkative part
of the assembly; and many were the looks directed up to them,
especially from the benches appropriated to the young and the
unmarried men. On the lower seats round the arena sat the
more high-born and wealthy visitors—the magistrates and
those of senatorial or equestrian* dignity: the passages which,
by corridors at the right and left, gave access to these seats,
at either end of the oval arena, were also the entrances for the
combatants. Strong palings at these passages prevented any
unwelcome eccentricity in the movements of the beasts, and
confined them to their appointed prey. Around the parapet
which was raised above the arena, and from which the seats
gradually rose, were gladiatorial inscriptions, and paintings
wrought in fresco, typical of the entertainments for which the
place was designed. Throughout the whole building wound invisible pipes, from which, as the day advanced, cooling and
fragrant showers were to be sprinkled over the spectators.

* The equites sat immediately behind the senators.

The officers of the amphitheatre were still employed in the task of fixing the vast awning (or *velaria*) which covered the whole, and which luxurious invention the Campanians arrogated to themselves: it was woven of the whitest Apulian wool, and variegated with broad stripes of crimson. Owing either to some inexperience on the part of the workmen, or to some defect in the machinery, the awning, however, was not arranged that day so happily as usual; indeed from the immense space of the circumference, the task was always one of great difficulty and art—so much so, that it could seldom be adventured in rough or windy weather. But the present day was so remarkably still, that there seemed to the spectators no excuse for the awkwardness of the artificers; and when a large gap in the back of the awning was still visible, from the obstinate refusal of one part of the velaria to ally itself with the rest, the murmurs of discontent were loud and general.

The ædile Pansa, at whose expense the exhibition was given, looked particularly annoyed at the defect, and vowed bitter vengeance on the head of the chief officer of the show, who fretting, puffing, perspiring, busied himself in idle orders and unavailing threats.

The hubbub ceased suddenly—the operators desisted—the crowd were stilled—the gap was forgotten—for now, with a loud and warlike flourish of trumpets, the gladiators, marshalled in ceremonious procession, entered the arena. They swept round the oval space very slowly and deliberately, in order to give the spectators full leisure to admire their stern serenity of feature—their brawny limbs and various arms, as well as to form such wagers as the excitement of the moment might suggest.

"Oh!" cried the widow Fulvia to the wife of Pansa, as they leaned down from their lofty bench, "do you see that gigantic gladiator? how drolly he is dressed!"

"Yes," said the ædile's wife with complacent importance, for she knew all the names and qualities of each combatant; "he is a retiarius or netter; he is armed only, you see, with a three-pronged spear like a trident, and a net; he wears no armor, only the fillet and the tunic. He is a mighty man, and is to fight with Sporus, yon thick-set gladiator, with the round shield and drawn sword, but without body armor; he has not his helmet on now, in order that you may see his face—how fearless it is!—by-and-by he will fight with his vizor down."

"But surely a net and a spear are poor arms against a shield and sword?"

"That shows how innocent you are, my dear Fulvia; the retiarius has generally the best of it."

"But who is yon handsome gladiator, nearly naked—is it not quite improper? By Venus! but his limbs are beautifully shaped!"

"It is Lydon, a young untried man! he has the rashness to fight yon other gladiator similarly dressed, or rather undressed—Tetraides. They fight first in the Greek fashion, with the cestus; afterwards they put on armor, and try sword and shield."

"He is a proper man, this Lydon; and the women, I am sure, are on his side."

"So are not the experienced betters; Clodius offers three to one against him."

"Oh, Jove! how beautiful!" exclaimed the widow, as two gladiators, armed *cap-à-pié,* rode round the arena on light and prancing steeds. Resembling much the combatants in the tilts of the middle age, they bore lances and round shields beautifully inlaid: their armor was woven intricately with bands of iron, but it covered only the thighs and the right arms; short cloaks, extending to the seat, gave a picturesque and graceful air to their costume; their legs were naked with the exception of sandals, which were fastened a little above the ankle. "Oh, beautiful! Who are these?" asked the widow.

"The one is named Berbix—he has conquered twelve times; the other assumes the arrogant name of Nobilior. They are both Gauls."

While thus conversing, the first formalities of the show were over. To these succeeded a feigned combat with wooden swords between the various gladiators matched against each other. Amongst these, the skill of two Roman gladiators, hired for the occasion, was the most admired; and next to them the most graceful combatant was Lydon. This sham contest did not last above an hour, nor did it attract any very lively interest, except among those connoisseurs of the arena to whom art was preferable to more coarse excitement; the body of the spectators were rejoiced when it was over; and when the sympathy rose to terror. The combatants were now arranged in pairs, as agreed beforehand; their weapons examined; and the grave sports of the day commenced amidst the deepest silence —broken only by an exciting and preliminary blast of warlike music.

It was often customary to begin the sports by the most cruel of all, and some bestiarius, or gladiator appointed to the beasts, was slain first, as an initiatory sacrifice. But in the present instance, the experienced Pansa thought it better that the sanguinary drama should advance, not decrease, in interest; and, accordingly, the execution of Olinthus and Glaucus was reserved for the last. It was arranged that the two horsemen should first occupy the arena; that the foot gladiators, paired off, should then be loosed indiscriminately on the stage; that Glaucus and the lion should next perform their part in the bloody spectacle; and the tiger and the Nazarene be the grand finale. And, in the spectacles of Pompeii, the reader of Roman history must limit his imagination, nor expect to find those vast and wholesale exhibitions of magnificent slaughter with which a Nero or a Caligula regaled the inhabitants of the Imperial City. The Roman shows, which absorbed the more celebrated gladiators, and the chief proportion of foreign beasts, were indeed the very reason why, in the lesser towns of the empire, the sports of the amphitheatre were comparatively humane and rare; and in this, as in other respects, Pompeii was but the miniature, the microcosm of Rome. Still, it was an awful and imposing spectacle, with which modern times have, happily, nothing to compare;—a vast theatre, rising row upon row, and swarming with human beings, from fifteen to eighteen thousand in number, intent upon no fictitious representation—no tragedy of the stage—but the actual victory or defeat, the exultant life or the bloody death, of each and all who entered the arena!

The two horsemen were now at either extremity of the lists (if so they might be called); and at a given signal from Pansa, the combatants started simultaneously as in full collision, each advancing his round buckler, each poising on high his light yet sturdy javelin; but just when within three paces of his opponent, the steed of Berbix suddenly halted, wheeled round, and, as Nobilior was borne rapidly by, his antagonist spurred upon him. The buckler of Nobilior, quickly and skilfully extended, received a blow which otherwise would have been fatal.

"Well done, Nobilior!" cried the prætor, giving the first vent to the popular excitement.

"Bravely struck, my Berbix!" answered Clodius from his seat.

And the wild murmur, swelled by many a shout, echoed from side to side.

The vizors of both the horsemen were completely closed (like those of the knights in after times), but the head was, nevertheless, the great point of assault; and Nobilior, now wheeling his charger with no less adroitness than his opponent, directed his spear full on the helmet of his foe. Berbix raised his buckler to shield himself, and his quick-eyed antagonist, suddenly lowering his weapon, pierced him through the breast. Berbix reeled and fell.

"Nobilior! Nobilior!" shouted the populace.

"I have lost ten sestertia," said Clodius, between his teeth.

"*Habet!*—he has it," said Pansa, deliberately.

The populace, not yet hardened into cruelty, made the signal of mercy; but as the attendants of the arena approached, they found the kindness came too late;—the heart of the Gaul had been pierced, and his eyes were set in death. It was his life's blood that flowed so darkly over the sand and sawdust of the arena.

"It is a pity it was so soon over—there was little enough for one's trouble," said the widow Fulvia.

"Yes—I have no compassion for Berbix. Any one might have seen that Nobilior did but feint. Mark, they fix the fatal hook to the body—they drag him away to the spoliarium— they scatter new sand over the stage! Pansa regrets nothing more than that he is not rich enough to strew the arena with borax and cinnabar, as Nero used to do."

"Well, if it has been a brief battle, it is quickly succeeded. See my handsome Lydon on the arena—ay, and the net-bearer too, and the swordsmen! Oh, charming!"

There were now on the arena six combatants: Niger and his net, matched against Sporus with his shield and his short broadsword; Lydon and Tetraides, naked save by a cincture round the waist, each armed only with a heavy Greek cestus—and two gladiators from Rome, clad in complete steel, and evenly matched with immense bucklers and pointed swords.

The initiatory contest between Lydon and Tetraides being less deadly than that between the other combatants, no sooner had they advanced to the middle of the arena than, as by common consent, the rest held back, to see how that contest should be decided, and wait till fiercer weapons might replace the cestus, ere they themselves commenced hostilities. They stood leaning on their arms and apart from each other, gazing on the show, which, if not bloody enough thoroughly to please the populace, they were still inclined to admire, because its origin was of their ancestral Greece.

No person could, at first glance, have seemed less evenly matched than the two antagonists. Tetraides, though not taller than Lydon, weighed considerably more; the natural size of his muscles was increased, to the eyes of the vulgar, by masses of solid flesh; for, as it was a notion that the contest of the cestus fared easiest with him who was plumpest, Tetraides had encouraged to the utmost his hereditary predisposition to the portly. His shoulders were vast, and his lower limbs thickset, double-jointed, and slightly curved outward, in that formation which takes so much from beauty to give so largely to strength. But Lydon, except that he was slender even almost to meagreness, was beautifully and delicately proportioned; and the skilful might have perceived that, with much less compass of muscle than his foe, that which he had was more seasoned—iron and compact. In proportion, too, as he wanted flesh, he was likely to possess activity; and a haughty smile on his resolute face, which strongly contrasted the solid heaviness of his enemy's, gave assurance to those who beheld it, and united their hope to their pity: so that, despite the disparity of their seeming strength, the cry of the multitude was nearly as loud for Lydon as for Tetraides.

Whoever is acquainted with the modern prize-ring—whoever has witnessed the heavy and disabling strokes which the human fist, skilfully directed, hath the power to bestow—may easily understand how much that happy facility would be increased by a band carried by thongs of leather round the arm as high as the elbow, and terribly strengthened about the knuckles by a plate of iron, and sometimes a plumpet of lead. Yet this, which was meant to increase, perhaps rather diminished, the interest of the fray: for it necessarily shortened its duration. A very few blows, successfully and scientifically *planted,* might suffice to bring the contest to a close; and the battle did not, therefore, often allow full scope for the energy, fortitude, and dogged perseverance, that we technically style *pluck,* which not unusually wins the day against superior science, and which heightens to so painful a delight the interest in the battle and the sympathy for the brave.

"Guard thyself!" growled Tetraides, moving nearer and nearer to his foe, who rather shifted round him than receded.

Lydon did not answer, save by a scornful glance of his quick, vigilant eye. Tetraides struck—it was as the blow of a smith on a vise; Lydon sank suddenly on one knee—the blow passed over his head. Not so harmless was Lydon's retaliation: he quickly sprang to his feet, and aimed his cestus full on the broad breast of his antagonist. Tetraides reeled—the populace shouted.

"You are unlucky to-day," said Lepidus to Clodius: "you have lost one bet—you will lose another."

"By the gods! my bronzes go to the auctioneer if that is the case. I have no less than a hundred sestertia upon Tetraides. Ha, ha! see how he rallies! That was a home stroke: he has cut open Lydon's shoulder.—A Tetraides!—a Tetraides!"

"But Lydon is not disheartened. By Pollux! how well he keeps his temper! See how dexterously he avoids those hammer-like hands!—dodging now here, now there—circling round and round. Ah, poor Lydon! he has it again."

"Three to one still on Tetraides! What say you, Lepidus?"

"Well—nine sestertia to three—be it so! What! again, Lydon? He stops—he gasps for breath. By the gods, he is down! No—he is again on his legs. Brave Lydon! Tetraides is encouraged—he laughs loud—he rushes on him."

"Fool—success blinds him—he should be cautious. Lydon's eye is like a lynx's!" said Clodius, between his teeth.

"Ha, Clodius! saw you that? Your man totters! Another blow—he falls—he falls!"

"Earth revives him, then. He is once more up; but the blood rolls down his face."

"By the thunderer! Lydon wins it. See how he presses on him! That blow on the temple would have crushed an ox! it *has* crushed Tetraides. He falls again—he cannot move— *habet!—habet!"*

"*Habet!"* repeated Pansa. "Take them out and give them the armor and swords."

"Noble editor," said the officers, "we fear that Tetraides will not recover in time; howbeit, we will try."

"Do so."

In a few minutes the officers, who had dragged off the stunned and insensible gladiator, returned with rueful countenances. They feared for his life; he was utterly incapacitated from re-entering the arena.

"In that case," said Pansa, "hold Lydon a *subditius;* and the first gladiator that is vanquished, let Lydon supply his place with the victor."

The people shouted their applause at this sentence; then they again sunk into deep silence. The trumpet sounded loudly. The four combatants stood each against each in prepared and stern array.

"Dost thou recognize the Romans, my Clodius; are they among the celebrated, or are they merely *ordinarii?"*

"Eumolpus is a good second-rate swordsman, my Lepidus. Nepimus, the lesser man, I have never seen before; but he is the son of one of the imperial fiscales, and brought up in a proper school; doubtless they will show sport, but I have no heart for the game; I cannot win back my money—I am undone. Curses on that Lydon! who could have supposed he was so dexterous or so lucky?"

"Well, Clodius, shall I take compassion on you, and accept your own terms with these Romans?"

"An even ten sestertia on Eumolpus, then?"

"What! when Nepimus is untried? Nay, nay; that is too bad." "Well—ten to eight?" "Agreed."

While the contest in the amphitheatre had thus commenced, there was one in the loftier benches for whom it had assumed, indeed, a poignant—a stifling interest. The aged father of Lydon, despite his Christian horror of the spectacle, in his agonized anxiety for his son, had not been able to resist being the spectator of his fate. One amidst a fierce crowd of strangers—the lowest rabble of the populace—the old man saw, felt nothing, but the form—the presence of his brave son! Not a sound had escaped his lips when twice he had seen him fall to the earth;—only he had turned paler, and his limbs trembled. But he had uttered one low cry when he saw him victorious; unconscious, alas! of the more fearful battle to which that victory was but a prelude.

"My gallant boy!" said he, and wiped his eyes.

"Is he thy son?" said a brawny fellow to the right of the Nazarene; "he has fought well: let us see how he does by-and-by. Hark! he is to fight the first victor. Now, old boy, pray the gods that that victor be neither of the Romans! nor, next to them, the giant Niger."

The old man sat down again and covered his face. The fray for the moment was indifferent to him—Lydon was not one of the combatants. Yet—yet—the thought flashed across him—the fray was indeed of deadly interest—the first who fell was to make way for Lydon! He started, and bent down, with straining eyes and clasped hands, to view the encounter.

The first interest was attracted towards the combat of Niger with Sporus; for this species of contest, from the fatal result which usually attended it, and from the great science it required in either antagonist, was always peculiarly inviting to the spectators.

They stood at a considerable distance from each other. The singular helmet which Sporus wore (the vizor of which was down) concealed his face; but the features of Niger attracted a fearful and universal interest from their compressed and vigilant ferocity. Thus they stood for some moments, each eyeing each, until Sporus began slowly, and with great caution, to advance, holding his sword pointed, like a modern fencer's, at the breast of his foe. Niger retreated as his antagonist advanced, gathering up his net with his right hand, and never taking his small glittering eye from the movements of the swordsman. Suddenly, when Sporus had approached nearly at arm's length, the retiarius threw himself forward, and cast his net. A quick inflection of body saved the gladiator from the deadly snare! he uttered a sharp cry of joy and rage, and rushed upon Niger: but Niger had already drawn in his net, thrown it across his shoulders, and now fled round the lists with a swiftness which the *secutor* in vain endeavored to equal. The people laughed and shouted aloud, to see the ineffectual efforts of the broad-shouldered gladiator to overtake the flying giant: when, at that moment, their attention was turned from these to the two Roman combatants.

They had placed themselves at the onset face to face, at the distance of modern fencers from each other: but the extreme caution which both evinced at first had prevented any warmth of engagement, and allowed the spectators full leisure to interest themselves in the battle between Sporus and his foe. But the Romans were now heated into full and fierce encounter: they pushed—returned—advanced on—retreated from—each other with all that careful yet scarcely perceptible caution which characterizes men well experienced and equally matched. But at this moment, Eumolpus, the elder gladiator, by that dexterous back-stroke which was considered in the arena so difficult to avoid, had wounded Nepimus in the side. The people shouted; Lepidus turned pale.

"Ho!" said Clodius, "the game is nearly over. If Eumolpus fights now the quiet fight, the other will gradually bleed himself away."

"But, thank the gods! he does *not* fight the backward fight. See!—he presses hard upon Nepimus. By Mars! but Nepimus had him there! the helmet rang again!—Clodius, I shall win!"

"Why do I ever bet but at the dice?" groaned Clodius to himself;—"or why cannot one cog a gladiator?"

"A Sporus!—a Sporus!" shouted the populace, as Niger, having now suddenly paused, had again cast his net, and again unsuccessfully. He had not retreated this time with sufficient agility—the sword of Sporus had inflicted a severe wound upon his right leg; and, incapacitated to fly, he was pressed hard by the fierce swordsman. His great height and length of arm still continued, however, to give him no despicable advantages; and steadily keeping his trident at the front of his foe, he repelled him successfully for several minutes. Sporus now tried, by great rapidity of evolution, to get round his antagonist, who necessarily moved with pain and slowness. In so doing, he lost his caution—he advanced too near to the giant—raised his arm to strike, and received the three points of the fatal spear full in his breast! He sank on his knee. In a moment more, the deadly net was cast over him,—he struggled against its meshes in vain; again—again—again he writhed mutely beneath the fresh strokes of the trident—his blood flowed fast through the net and redly over the sand. He lowered his arms in acknowledgment of defeat.

The conquering retiarius withdrew his net, and leaning on his spear, looked to the audience for their judgment. Slowly, too, at the same moment, the vanquished gladiator rolled his dim and despairing eyes around the theatre. From row to row, from bench to bench, there glared upon him but merciless and unpitying eyes.

Hushed was the roar—the murmur! The silence was dread, for in it was no sympathy; not a hand—no, not even a woman's hand—gave the signal of charity and life! Sporus had never been popular in the arena; and, lately, the interest of the combat had been excited on behalf of the wounded Niger. The people were warmed into blood—the *mimic* fight had ceased to charm; the interest had mounted up to the desire of sacrifice and the thirst of death!

The gladiator felt that his doom was sealed: he uttered no prayer—no groan. The people gave the signal of death! In dogged but agonized submission, he bent his neck to receive the fatal stroke. And now, as the spear of the retiarius was not a weapon to inflict instant and certain death, there stalked into the arena a grim and fatal form, brandishing a short, sharp sword, and with features utterly concealed beneath its vizor. With slow and measured steps, this dismal headsman approached the gladiator, still kneeling—laid the left hand on his humbled crest—drew the edge of the blade across his neck —turned round to the assembly, lest, in the last moment, remorse should come upon them; the dread signal continued the same: the blade glittered brightly in the air—fell—and the gladiator rolled upon the sand; his limbs quivered—were still, —he was a corpse.*

His body was dragged at once from the arena through the gate of death, and thrown into the gloomy den termed techni-

---

* See the engraving from the friezes of Pompeii, in the work on that city published in the "Library of Entertaining Knowledge," vol. ii. p. 311.

cally the spoliarium. And ere it had well reached that destination, the strife between the remaining combatants was decided. The sword of Eumolpus had inflicted the death-wound upon the less experienced combatant. A new victim was added to the receptacle of the slain.

Throughout that mighty assembly there now ran a universal movement; the people breathed more freely, and resettled themselves in their seats. A grateful shower was cast over every row from the concealed conduits. In cool and luxurious pleasure they talked over the late spectacle of blood. Eumolpus removed his helmet, and wiped his brows; his close-curled hair and short beard, his noble Roman features and bright dark eye, attracted the general admiration. He was fresh, unwounded, unfatigued.

The editor paused, and proclaimed aloud that, as Niger's wound disabled him from again entering the arena, Lydon was to be the successor to the slaughtered Nepimus, and the new combatant of Eumolpus.

"Yet Lydon," added he, "if thou wouldst decline the combat with one so brave and tried, thou mayst have full liberty to do so. Eumolpus is not the antagonist that was originally decreed for thee. Thou knowest best how far thou canst cope with him. If thou failest, thy doom is honorable death; if thou conquerest, out of my own purse I will double the stipulated prize."

The people shouted applause. Lydon stood in the lists, he gazed around; high above he beheld the pale face, the straining eyes, of his father. He turned away irresolute for a moment. No! the conquest of the cestus was not sufficient—he had not yet won the prize of victory—his father was still a slave!

"Noble ædile!" he replied, in a firm and deep tone, "I shrink not from this combat. For the honor of Pompeii, I demand that one trained by its long-celebrated lanista shall do battle with this Roman."

The people shouted louder than before.

"Four to one against Lydon!" said Clodius to Lepidus.

"I would not take twenty to one! Why, Eumolpus is a very Achilles, and this poor fellow is but a *tyro!*"

Eumolpus gazed hard on the face of Lydon; he smiled:

yet the smile was followed by a slight and scarce audible sigh —a touch of compassionate emotion, which custom conquered the moment the heart acknowledged it.

And now both, clad in complete armor, the sword drawn, the vizor closed, the two last combatants of the arena (ere man, at least, was matched with beast), stood opposed to each other.

It was just at this time that a letter was delivered to the prætor by one of the attendants of the arena; he removed the cincture—glanced over it for a moment—his countenance betrayed surprise and embarrassment. He re-read the letter, and then muttering,—"Tush! it is impossible!—the man must be drunk, even in the morning, to dream of such follies!"—threw it carelessly aside, and gravely settled himself once more in the attitude of attention to the sports.

The interest of the public was wound up very high. Eumolpus had at first won their favor; but the gallantry of Lydon, and his well-timed allusion to the honor of the Pompeian lanista, had afterwards given the latter the preference in their eyes.

"Holla, old fellow!" said Medon's neighbor to him. "Your son is hardly matched; but never fear, the editor will not permit him to be slain—no, nor the people neither; he has behaved too bravely for that. Ha! that was a home thrust!—well averted, by Pollux! At him again, Lydon!—they stop to breathe! What art thou muttering, old boy?"

"Prayers!" answered Medon, with a more calm and hopeful mien than he had yet maintained.

"Prayers!—trifles! The time for gods to carry a man away in a cloud is gone now. Ha, Jupiter!—what a blow! Thy side —thy side!—take care of thy side, Lydon!"

There was a convulsive tremor throughout the assembly. A fierce blow from Eumolpus, full on the crest, had brought Lydon to his knee.

"*Habet!*—he has it!" cried a shrill female voice; "he has it!"

It was the voice of the girl who had so anxiously anticipated the sacrifice of some criminal to the beasts.

"Be silent, child!" said the wife of Pansa, haughtily. "*Non habet!*—he is *not* wounded!"

"I wish he were, if only to spite old surly Medon," muttered the girl.

Meanwhile Lydon, who had hitherto defended himself with great skill and valor, began to give way before the vigorous assaults of the practised Roman; his arm grew tired, his eye dizzy, he breathed hard and painfully. The combatants paused again for breath.

"Young man," said Eumolpus, in a low voice, "desist; I will wound thee slightly—then lower thy arms; thou hast propitiated the editor and the mob—thou wilt be honorably saved!" "And my father still enslaved!" groaned Lydon to himself. "No! death or his freedom."

At that thought, and seeing that, his strength not being equal to the endurance of the Roman, everything depended on a sudden and desperate effort, he threw himself fiercely on Eumolpus; the Roman warily retreated—Lydon thrust again —Eumolpus drew himself aside—the sword grazed his cuirass —Lydon's breast was exposed—the Roman plunged his sword through the joints of the armor, not meaning, however, to inflict a deep wound; Lydon, weak and exhausted, fell forward, fell right on the point: it passed through and through, even to the back. Eumolpus drew forth his blade; Lydon still made an effort to regain his balance—his sword left his grasp—he struck mechanically at the gladiator with his naked hand, and fell prostrate on the arena. With one accord, editor and assembly made the signal of mercy—the officers of the arena approached—they took off the helmet of the vanquished. He still breathed; his eyes rolled fiercely on his foe; the savageness he had acquired in his calling glared from his gaze, and lowered upon the brow darkened already with the shades of death; then, with a convulsive groan, with a half-start, he lifted his eyes above. They rested not on the face of the editor nor on the pitying brows of his relenting judges. He saw them not; they were as if the vast space was desolate and bare; one pale agonizing face alone was all he recognized—one cry of a broken heart was all that, amidst the murmurs and the shouts of the populace, reached his ear. The ferocity vanished from his brow: a soft, a tender expression of sanctifying but despairing filial love played over his features—played—waned—

darkened! His face suddenly became locked and rigid, resuming its former fierceness. He fell upon the earth.

"Look to him," said the ædile; "he has done his duty!"

The officers dragged him off to the spoliarium.

"A true type of glory, and of its fate!" murmured Arbaces to himself; and his eye, glancing round the amphitheatre, betrayed so much of disdain and scorn, that whoever encountered it felt his breath suddenly arrested, and his emotions frozen into one sensation of abasement and of awe.

Again rich perfumes were wafted around the theatre; the attendants sprinkled fresh sand over the arena.

"Bring forth the lion and Glaucus the Athenian," said the editor.

And a deep and breathless hush of overwrought interest, and intense (yet, strange to say, not unpleasing) terror lay, like a mighty and awful dream, over the assembly.

CHAPTER III.

Sallust and Nydia's letter.

THRICE had Sallust wakened from his morning sleep, and thrice, recollecting that his friend was that day to perish, had he turned himself with a deep sigh once more to court oblivion. His sole object in life was to avoid pain; and where he could not avoid, at least to forget it.

At length, unable any longer to steep his consciousness in slumber, he raised himself from his incumbent posture, and discovered his favorite freedman sitting by his bedside as usual; for Sallust, who, as I have said, had a gentleman-like taste for the polite letters, was accustomed to be read to for an hour or so previous to his rising in the morning.

"No books to-day! no more Tibullus! no more Pindar for me! Pindar! alas, alas! the very name recalls those games to which our arena is the savage successor. Has it begun—the amphitheatre? are its rites commenced?"

"Long since, O Sallust! Did you not hear the trumpets and the trampling feet?"

"Ay, ay; but the gods be thanked, I was drowsy, and had only to turn round to fall asleep again."

"The gladiators must have been long in the ring?"

"The wretches! None of my people have gone to the spectacle?" "Assuredly not; your orders were too strict!"

"That is well—would the day were over! What is that letter yonder on the table?"

"That! Oh, the letter brought to you last night, when you were too—too——"

"Drunk to read it, I suppose. No matter, it cannot be of much importance." "Shall I open it for you, Sallust?"

"Do: anything to divert my thoughts. Poor Glaucus!"

The freedman opened the letter. "What! Greek?" said he; "some learned lady, I suppose." He glanced over the letter, and for some moments the irregular lines traced by the blind girl's hand puzzled him. Suddenly, however, his countenance exhibited emotion and surprise. "Good gods! noble Sallust! what have we done not to attend to this before? Hear me read!

" 'Nydia, the slave, to Sallust, the friend of Glaucus! I am a prisoner in the house of Arbaces. Hasten to the prætor! procure my release, and we shall yet save Glaucus from the lion. There is another prisoner within these walls, whose witness can exonerate the Athenian from the charge against him;— one who saw the crime—who can prove the criminal in a villain hitherto unsuspected. Fly! hasten! quick! quick! Bring with you armed men, lest resistance be made,—and a cunning and dexterous smith; for the dungeon of my fellow-prisoner is thick and strong. Oh! by thy right hand, and thy father's ashes, lose not a moment!' "

"Great Jove!" exclaimed Sallust, starting, "and this day —nay, within this hour, perhaps he dies. What is to be done? I will instantly to the prætor."

"Nay; not so. The prætor (as well as Pansa, the editor himself,) is the creature of the mob; and the mob will not hear of delay; they will not be balked in the very moment of expectation. Besides, the publicity of the appeal would forewarn the cunning Egyptian. It is evident that he has some interest in these concealments. No; fortunately thy slaves are in thy house."

"I seize thy meaning," interrupted Sallust; "arm the slaves instantly. The streets are empty. We will ourselves hasten to the house of Arbaces, and release the prisoners. Quick! quick! What ho! Davus there! My gown and sandals, the papyrus and a reed. I will write to the prætor, to beseech him to delay the sentence of Glaucus, for that, within an hour, we may yet prove him innocent. So, so; that is well. Hasten with this, Davus, to the prætor, at the amphitheatre. See it given to his own hand. Now then, O ye gods! whose providence Epicurus denied, befriend me, and I will call Epicurus a liar!"

CHAPTER IV.

The amphitheatre once more.

GLAUCUS and Olinthus had been placed together in that gloomy and narrow cell in which the criminals of the arena awaited their last and fearful struggle. Their eyes, of late accustomed to the darkness, scanned the faces of each other in this awful hour, and by that dim light, the paleness, which chased away the natural hues from either cheek, assumed a yet more ashy and ghastly whiteness. Yet their brows were erect and dauntless—their limbs did not tremble—their lips were compressed and rigid. The religion of the one, the pride of the other, the conscious innocence of both, and it may be the support derived from their mutual companionship, elevated the victim into the hero.

"Hark! hearest thou that shout? They are growling over their human blood," said Olinthus.

"I hear; my heart grows sick; but the gods support me."

"The gods! O rash young man! in this hour recognize only the One God. Have I not taught thee in the dungeon, wept for thee, prayed for thee?—in my zeal and in my agony, have I not thought more of thy salvation than my own?"

"Brave friend!" answered Glaucus, solemnly, "I have listened to thee with awe, with wonder, and with a secret tendency towards conviction. Had our lives been spared, I might gradually have weaned myself from the tenets of my own faith, and inclined to thine; but, in this last hour, it were a craven thing, and a base, to yield to hasty terror what should only be the result of lengthened meditation. Were I to embrace thy creed, and cast down my father's gods, should I not be bribed by thy promise of heaven, or awed by thy threats of hell? Olinthus, no! Think we of each other with equal charity —I honoring thy sincerity—thou pitying my blindness or my obdurate courage. As have been my deeds, such will be my reward; and the Power of Powers above will not judge harshly of human error, when it is linked with honesty of purpose and truth of heart. Speak we no more of this. Hush! Dost thou hear them drag yon heavy body through the passage? Such as that clay will be ours soon."

"O Heaven! O Christ! already I behold ye!" cried the fervent Olinthus, lifting up his hands; "I tremble not—I rejoice that the prison-house shall be soon broken."

Glaucus bowed his head in silence. He felt the distinction between his fortitude and that of his fellow-sufferer. The heathen did not tremble; but the Christian exulted.

The door swung gratingly back—the gleam of spears shot along the walls.

"Glaucus the Athenian, thy time has come," said a loud and clear voice, "the lion awaits thee."

"I am ready," said the Athenian. "Brother and co-mate, one last embrace! Bless me—and, farewell!"

The Christian opened his arms—he clasped the young heathen to his breast—he kissed his forehead and cheek—he sobbed aloud—his tears flowed fast and hot over the features of his new friend.

"Oh! could I have converted thee, I had not wept. Oh! that I might say to thee, "We two shall sup this night in Paradise!' "

"It may be so yet," answered the Greek with a tremulous voice. "They whom death parts now, may yet meet beyond the grave: on the earth—on the beautiful, the beloved earth, farewell for ever!—Worthy officer, I attend you."

Glaucus tore himself away; and when he came forth into the air, its breath, which, though sunless, was hot and arid, smote witheringly upon him. His frame, not yet restored from the effects of the deadly draught, shrank and trembled. The officers supported him.

"Courage!" said one; "thou art young, active, well knit.

They give thee a weapon! despair not, and thou mayst yet conquer."

Glaucus did not reply; but, ashamed of his infirmity, he made a desperate and convulsive effort, and regained the firmness of his nerves. They anointed his body, completely naked save by a cincture round the loins, placed the stilus (vain weapon!) in his hand, and led him into the arena.

And now when the Greek saw the eyes of thousands and tens of thousands upon him, he no longer felt that he was mortal. All evidence of fear—all fear itself—was gone. A red and haughty flush spread over the paleness of his features— he towered aloft to the full of his glorious stature. In the elastic beauty of his limbs and form, in his intent but unfrowning brow, in the high disdain, and in the indomitable soul, which breathed visibly, which spoke audibly, from his attitude, his lip, his eye,—he seemed the very incarnation, vivid and corporeal, of the valor of his land—of the divinity of its worship —at once a hero and a god!

The murmur of hatred and horror at his crime, which had greeted his entrance, died into the silence of involuntary admiration and half-compassionate respect; and, with a quick and convulsive sigh, that seemed to move the whole mass of life as if it were one body, the gaze of the spectators turned from the Athenian to a dark uncouth object in the centre of the arena. It was the grated den of the lion!

"By Venus, how warm it is!" said Fulvia; "yet there is no sun. Would that those stupid sailors could have fastened up that gap in the awning!"

"Oh! it is warm, indeed. I turn sick—I faint!" said the wife of Pansa; even her experienced stoicism giving way at the struggle about to take place.

The lion had been kept without food for twenty-four hours, and the animal had, during the whole morning, testified a singular and restless uneasiness, which the keeper had attributed to the pangs of hunger. Yet its bearing seemed rather that of fear than of rage; its roar was painful and distressed; it hung its head—snuffed the air through the bars—then lay down—started again—and again uttered its wild and far-resounding cries. And now, in its den, it lay utterly dumb and mute, with distended nostrils forced hard against the grating, and disturbing, with a heaving breath the sand below on the arena.

The editor's lip quivered, and his cheek grew pale; he looked anxiously around—hesitated—delayed; the crowd became impatient. Slowly he gave the sign; the keeper, who was behind the den, cautiously removed the grating, and the lion leaped forth with a mighty and glad roar of release. The keeper hastily retreated through the grated passage leading from the arena, and left the lord of the forest—and his prey.

Glaucus had bent his limbs so as to give himself the firmest posture at the expected rush of the lion, with his small and shining weapon raised on high, in the faint hope that *one* well-directed thrust (for he knew that he should have time but for *one*,) might penetrate through the eye to the brain of his grim foe.

But, to the unutterable astonishment of all, the beast seemed not even aware of the presence of the criminal.

At the first moment of its release it halted abruptly in the arena, raised itself half on end, snuffing the upward air with impatient sighs; then suddenly it sprang forward, but not on the Athenian. At half-speed it circled round and round the space, turning its vast head from side to side with an anxious and perturbed gaze, as if seeking only some avenue of escape; once or twice it endeavored to leap up the parapet that divided it from the audience, and, on failing, uttered rather a baffled howl than its deep-toned and kingly roar. It evinced no sign, either of wrath or hunger; its tail drooped along the sand, instead of lashing its gaunt sides; and its eye, though it wandered at times to Glaucus, rolled again listlessly from him. At length, as if tired of attempting to escape, it crept with a moan into its cage, and once more laid itself down to rest.

The first surprise of the assembly at the apathy of the lion soon grew converted into resentment at its cowardice; and the populace already merged their pity for the fate of Glaucus into angry compassion for their own disappointment.

The editor called to the keeper.

"How is this? Take the goad, prick him forth, and then close the door of the den."

As the keeper, with some fear, but more astonishment, was

preparing to obey, a loud cry was heard at one of the entrances of the arena; there was a confusion, a bustle—voices of remonstrance suddenly breaking forth, and suddenly silenced at the reply. All eyes turned in wonder at the interruption, towards the quarter of the disturbance; the crowd gave way, and suddenly Sallust appeared on the senatorial benches, his hair dishevelled—breathless—heated—half-exhausted. He cast his eyes hastily round the ring. "Remove the Athenian!" he cried; "haste—he is innocent! Arrest Arbaces the Egyptian—HE is the murderer of Apæcides!"

"Art thou mad, O Sallust!" said the prætor, rising from his seat. "What means this raving?"

"Remove the Athenian!—Quick! or his blood be on your head. Prætor, delay, and you answer with your own life to the emperor! I bring with me the eye-witness to the death of the priest Apæcides. Room there!—stand back!—give way! People of Pompeii, fix every eye upon Arbaces—there he sits! Room there for the priest Calenus!"

Pale, haggard, fresh from the jaws of famine and of death, his face fallen, his eyes dull as a vulture's, his broad frame gaunt as a skeleton,—Calenus was supported into the very row in which Arbaces sat. His releasers had given him sparingly of food; but the chief sustenance that nerved his feeble limbs was revenge!

"The priest Calenus!—Calenus!" cried the mob. "*Is* it he? No—it is a dead man!" "It *is* the priest Calenus," said the prætor, gravely. "What hast thou to say?"

"Arbaces of Egypt is the murderer of Apæcides, the priest of Isis; these eyes saw him deal the blow. It is from the dungeon into which he plunged me—it is from the darkness and horror of death by famine—that the gods have raised me to proclaim his crime! Release the Athenian—*he* is innocent!"

"It is for this then, that the lion spared him.—A miracle! a miracle!" cried Pansa.

"A miracle! a miracle!" shouted the people; "remove the Athenian—*Arbaces to the lion!*"

And that shout echoed from hill to vale—from coast to sea—*"Arbaces to the lion!"*

"Officers, remove the accused Glaucus—remove, but guard

him yet," said the prætor. "The gods lavish their wonders upon this day."

As the prætor gave the word of release, there was a cry of joy—a female voice—a child's voice—and it was of joy! It rang through the heart of the assembly with electric force —it was touching, it was holy, that child's voice! And the populace echoed it back with sympathizing congratulation!

"Silence!" said the grave prætor—"who is there?"

"The blind girl—Nydia," answered Sallust; "it is her hand that has raised Calenus from the grave, and delivered Glaucus from the lion."

"Of this hereafter," said the prætor. "Calenus, priest of Isis, thou accusest Arbaces of the murder of Apæcides?"

"I do?" "Thou didst behold the deed?"

"Prætor—with these eyes——"

"Enough at present—the details must be reserved for more suiting time and place. Arbaces of Egypt, thou hearest the charge against thee—thou hast not yet spoken—what hast thou to say?"

The gaze of the crowd had been long riveted on Arbaces: but not until the confusion which he had betrayed at the first charge of Sallust and the entrance of Calenus had subsided. At the shout, "Arbaces to the lion!" he had indeed trembled, and the dark bronze of his cheek had taken a paler hue. But he had soon recovered his haughtiness and self-control. Proudly he returned the angry glare of the countless eyes around him; and replying now to the question of the prætor, he said, in that accent so peculiarly tranquil and commanding, which characterized his tones,—

"Prætor, this charge is so mad that it scarcely deserves reply. My first accuser is the noble Sallust—the most intimate friend of Glaucus! my second is a priest; I revere his garb and calling—but, people of Pompeii! ye know somewhat of the character of Calenus—he is griping and gold-thirsty to a proverb; the witness of such men is to be bought! Prætor, I am innocent!"

"Sallust," said the magistrate, "where found you Calenus!"

"In the dungeons of Arbaces."

"Egyptian," said the prætor, frowning, "thou didst, then, dare to imprison a priest of the gods—and wherefore?"

"Hear me," answered Arbaces, rising calmly, but with agitation visible in his face. "This man came to threaten that he would make against me the charge he has now made, unless I would purchase his silence with half my fortune: I remonstrated—in vain. Peace there—let not the priest interrupt me! Noble prætor—and ye, O people! I was a stranger in the land—I knew myself innocent of crime—but the witness of a priest against me might yet destroy me. In my perplexity I decoyed him to the cell whence he has been released, on pretence that it was the coffer-house of my gold. I resolved to detain him there until the fate of the true criminal was sealed, and his threats could avail no longer; but I meant no worse. I may have erred—but who amongst ye will not acknowledge the equity of self-preservation? Were I guilty, why was the witness of this priest silent at the trial?—*then* I had not detained or concealed him. Why did he not proclaim my guilt when I proclaimed that of Glaucus? Prætor, this needs an answer. For the rest, I throw myself on your laws. I demand their protection. Remove hence the accused and the accuser. I will willingly meet, and cheerfully abide by, the decision of the legitimate tribunal. This is no place for further parley."

"He says right," said the prætor. "Ho! guards—remove Arbaces—guard Calenus! Sallust, we hold you responsible for your accusation. Let the sports be resumed."

"What!" cried Calenus, turning round to the people, "shall Isis be thus contemned? Shall the blood of Apæcides yet cry for vengeance? Shall justice be delayed now, that it may be frustrated hereafter? Shall the lion be cheated of his lawful prey? A god! a god!—I feel the god rush to my lips! *To the lion—to the lion with Arbaces!*"

His exhausted frame could support no longer the ferocious malice of the priest; he sank on the ground in strong convulsions—the foam gathered to his mouth—he was as a man, indeed, whom a supernatural power had entered! The people saw, and shuddered.

"It is a god that inspires the holy man!—*To the lion with the Egyptian!*"

With that cry up sprang—on moved—thousands upon thousands! They rushed from the heights—they poured down in the direction of the Egyptian. In vain did the ædile command—in vain did the prætor lift his voice and proclaim the law. The people had been already rendered savage by the exhibition of blood—they thirsted for more—their superstition was aided by their ferocity. Aroused—inflamed by the spectacle of their victims, they forgot the authority of their rulers. It was one of those dread popular convulsions common to crowds wholly ignorant, half free and half servile; and which the peculiar constitution of the Roman provinces so frequently exhibited. The power of the prætor was as a reed beneath the whirlwind; still, at his word the guards had drawn themselves along the lower benches, on which the upper classes sat separate from the vulgar. They made but a feeble barrier—the waves of the human sea halted for a moment, to enable Arbaces to count the exact moment of his doom! In despair, and in a terror which beat down even pride, he glanced his eyes over the rolling and rushing crowd—when, right above them, through the wide chasm which had been left in the velaria, he beheld a strange and awful apparition—he beheld—and his craft restored his courage!

He stretched his hand on high; over his lofty brow and royal features there came an expression of unutterable solemnity and command.

"Behold!" he shouted with a voice of thunder, which stilled the roar of the crowd; "behold how the gods protect the guiltless! The fires of the avenging Orcus burst forth against the false witness of my accusers!"

The eyes of the crowd followed the gesture of the Egyptian, and beheld, with ineffable dismay, a vast vapor shooting from the summit of Vesuvius, in the form of a gigantic pine-tree; the trunk, blackness,—the branches fire!—a fire that shifted and wavered in its hues with every moment, now fiercely luminous, now of a dull and dying red, that again blazed terrifically forth with intolerable glare!

There was a dead, heart-sunken silence—through which there suddenly broke the roar of the lion, which was echoed back from within the building by the sharper and fiercer yells of its fellow-beast. Dread seers were they of the Burden of the Atmosphere, and wild prophets of the wrath to come!

Then there arose on high the universal shrieks of women; the men stared at each other, but were dumb. At that moment they felt the earth shake beneath their feet; the walls of the theatre trembled; and, beyond in the distance, they heard the crash of falling roofs; an instant more, and the mountain-cloud seemed to roll towards them, dark and rapid, like a torrent; at the same time, it cast forth from its bosom a shower of ashes mixed with vast fragments of burning stone! Over the crushing vines,—over the desolate streets,—over the amphitheatre itself,—far and wide,—with many a mighty splash in the agitated sea,—fell that awful shower!

No longer thought the crowd of justice or of Arbaces; safety for themselves was their sole thought. Each turned to fly—each dashing, pressing, crushing, against the other. Trampling recklessly over the fallen—amidst groans, and oaths, and prayers and sudden shrieks, the enormous crowd vomited itself forth through the numerous passages. Whither should they fly? Some, anticipating a second earthquake, hastened to their homes to load themselves with their most costly goods, and escape while it was yet time; others, dreading the showers of ashes that now fell fast, torrent upon torrent, over the streets, rushed under the roofs of the nearest houses, or temples, or sheds—shelter of any kind—for protection from the terrors of the open air. But darker, and larger, and mightier, spread the cloud above them. It was a sudden and more ghastly Night rushing upon the realm of Noon!

CHAPTER V.

The cell of the prisoner and the den of the dead.—Grief unconscious of horror.

STUNNED by his reprieve, doubting that he was awake, Glaucus had been led by the officers of the arena into a small cell within the walls of the theatre. They threw a loose robe over his form, and crowded round in congratulation and wonder. There was an impatient and fretful cry without the cell; the throng gave way, and the blind girl, led by some gentler hand, flung herself at the feet of Glaucus.

"It is *I* who have saved thee," she sobbed; "now let me die!"

"Nydia, my child!—my preserver!"

"Oh, let me feel thy touch—thy breath! Yes, yes, thou livest! We are not too late! That dread door, methought it would never yield! and Calenus—oh! his voice was as the dying wind among tombs:—we had to wait,—gods! it seemed hours ere food and wine restored to him something of strength. But thou livest! thou livest yet! And I—*I* have saved thee!"

This affecting scene was soon interrupted by the event just described.

"The mountain! the earthquake!" resounded from side to side. The officers fled with the rest; they left Glaucus and Nydia to save themselves as they might.

As the sense of the dangers around them flashed on the Athenian, his generous heart recurred to Olinthus. He, too, was reprieved from the tiger by the hand of the gods; should he be left to a no less fatal death in the neighboring cell? Taking Nydia by the hand, Glaucus hurried across the passages; he gained the den of the Christian. He found Olinthus kneeling, and in prayer.

"Arise! arise! my friend," he cried. "Save thyself, and fly! See! Nature is thy dread deliverer!" He led forth the bewildered Christian, and pointed to a cloud which advanced darker and darker, disgorging forth showers of ashes and pumice stones;—and bade him hearken to the cries and trampling rush of the scattered crowd.

"This is the hand of God—God be praised!" said Olinthus, devoutly. "Fly! seek thy brethren! Concert with them thy escape. Farewell!"

Olinthus did not answer, neither did he mark the retreating form of his friend. High thoughts and solemn absorbed his soul; and in the enthusiasm of his kindling heart, he exulted in the mercy of God rather than trembled at the evidence of His power.

At length he roused himself, and hurried on, he scarce knew whither.

The open doors of a dark, desolate cell suddenly appeared on his path; through the gloom within there flared and flickered a single lamp; and by its light he saw three grim and naked forms stretched on the earth in death. His feet were suddenly arrested; for, amidst the terrors of that drear recess

—the spoliarium of the arena—he heard a low voice calling on the name of Christ.

He could not resist lingering at that appeal; he entered the den, and his feet were dabbled in the slow streams of blood that gushed from the corpses over the sand.

"Who," said the Nazarene, "calls upon the Son of God?"

No answer came forth; and turning round, Olinthus beheld, by the light of the lamp, an old grey-headed man sitting on the floor, and supporting in his lap the head of one of the dead. The features of the dead man were firmly and rigidly locked in the last sleep; but over the lip there played a fierce smile—not the Christian's smile of hope, but the dark sneer of hatred and defiance. Yet on the face still lingered the beautiful roundness of early youth. The hair curled thick and glossy over the unwrinkled brow; and the down of manhood but slightly shaded the marble of the hueless cheek. And over this face bent one of such unutterable sadness—of such yearning tenderness—of such fond, and such deep despair! The tears of the old man fell fast and hot, but he did not feel them; and when his lips moved, and he mechanically uttered the prayer of his benign and hopeful faith, neither his heart nor his sense responded to the words: it was but the involuntary emotion that broke from the lethargy of his mind. His boy was dead, and had died for him!—and the old man's heart was broken!

"Medon!" said Olinthus, pityingly, "arise, and fly! God is forth upon the wings of the elements! The New Gomorrah is doomed!—Fly, ere the fires consume thee!"

"He was ever so full of life!—he *cannot* be dead! Come hither!—place your hand on his heart!—sure it beats yet?"

"Brother, the soul has fled!—we will remember it in our prayers! Thou canst not reanimate the dumb clay! Come, come,—hark! while I speak, yon crashing walls!—hark! yon agonizing cries! Not a moment is to be lost!—Come!"

"I hear nothing!" said Medon, shaking his grey hair. "The poor boy, his love murdered him!"

"Come! come! forgive this friendly force."

"What! Who would sever the father from the son?" And Medon clasped the body tightly in his embrace, and covered it with passionate kisses. "Go!" said he, lifting up his face for one moment. "Go!—we must be alone!" "Alas!" said the compassionate Nazarene, "Death hath severed ye already!"

The old man smiled very calmly. "No, no, no!" he muttered, his voice growing lower with each word,—"Death has been more kind!"

With that his head drooped on his son's breast—his arms relaxed their grasp. Olinthus caught him by the hand—the pulse had ceased to beat! The last words of the father were the words of truth,—*Death had been more kind!*

Meanwhile Glaucus and Nydia were pacing swiftly up the perilous and fearful streets. The Athenian had learned from his preserver that Ione was yet in the house of Arbaces. Thither he fled, to release—to save her! The few slaves whom the Egyptian had left at his mansion when he had repaired in long procession to the amphitheatre, had been able to offer no resistance to the armed band of Sallust; and when afterwards the volcano broke forth they had huddled together, stunned and frightened, in the inmost recesses of the house. Even the tall Ethiopian had forsaken his post at the door; and Glaucus (who left Nydia without—the poor Nydia, jealous once more, even in such an hour!) passed on through the vast hall without meeting one from whom to learn the chamber of Ione. Even as he passed, however, the darkness that covered the heavens increased so rapidly, that it was with difficulty he could guide his steps. The flower-wreathed columns seemed to reel and tremble; and with every instant he heard the ashes fall cranchingly into the roofless peristyle. He ascended to the upper rooms—breathless he paced along, shouting out aloud the name of Ione; and at length he heard, at the end of a gallery, a voice—*her* voice, in wondering reply! To rush forward—to shatter the door—to seize Ione in his arms—to hurry from the mansion—seemed to him the work of an instant! Scarce had he gained the spot where Nydia was, than he heard steps advancing towards the house, and recognized the voice of Arbaces, who had returned to seek his wealth and Ione ere he fled from the doomed Pompeii. But so dense was already the reeking atmosphere, that the foes saw not each other, though so near,—save that, dimly in the gloom, Glaucus caught the moving outline of the snowy robes of the Egyptian.

They hastened onward—those three! Alas!—whither? They now saw not a step before them—the blackness became utter. They were encompassed with doubt and horror!—and the death he had escaped seemed to Glaucus only to have changed its form and augmented its victims.

CHAPTER VI.

Calenus and Burbo.—Diomed and Clodius.—The girl of the amphitheatre and Julia.

THE sudden catastrophe which had, as it were, riven the very bonds of society, and left prisoner and gaoler alike free, had soon rid Calenus of the guards to whose care the prætor had consigned him. And when the darkness and the crowd separated the priest from his attendants, he hastened with trembling steps towards the temple of his goddess. As he crept along, and ere the darkness was complete, he felt himself suddenly caught by the robe, and a voice muttered in his ear,—

"Hist!—Calenus!—an awful hour!"

"Ay, by my father's head! Who art thou?—thy face is dim, and thy voice is strange!"

"Not know thy Burbo?—fie!"

"Gods!—how the darkness gathers! Ho, ho;—by yon terrific mountain, what sudden blazes of lightning!*—How they dart and quiver! Hades is loosed on earth!"

"Tush!—thou believest not these things, Calenus! Now is the time to make our fortune!" "Ha!"

"Listen! Thy temple is full of gold and precious mummeries!—let us load ourselves with them, and then hasten to the sea and embark! None will ever ask an account of the doings of this day."

"Burbo, thou art right! Hush! and follow me into the temple. Who cares now—who sees now—whether thou art a priest or not? Follow, and we will share."

In the precincts of the temple were many priests gathered around the altars, praying, weeping, grovelling in the dust.

* Volcanic lightnings. These phenomena were especially the characteristic of the long-subsequent eruption of 1779, and their evidence is visible in the tokens of that more awful one, now so imperfectly described.

Imposters in safety, they were not the less superstitious in danger! Calenus passed them, and entered the chamber yet to be seen in the south side of the court. Burbo followed him— the priest struck a light. Wine and viands strewed the table; the remains of a sacrificial feast.

"A man who has hungered forty-eight hours," muttered Calenus, "has an appetite even in such a time." He seized on the food, and devoured it greedily. Nothing could, perhaps, be more unnaturally horrid than the selfish baseness of these villains; for there is nothing more loathsome than the valor of avarice. Plunder and sacrilege while the pillars of the world tottered to and fro! What an increase to the terrors of nature can be made by the vices of man!

"Wilt thou never have done?" said Burbo, impatiently, "thy face purples and thine eyes start already."

"It is not every day one has such a right to be hungry. Oh, Jupiter! what sound is that?—the hissing of fiery water! What! does the cloud give rain as well as flame! Ha!—what! shrieks? And, Burbo, how silent all is now! Look forth!"

Amidst the other horrors, the mighty mountain now cast up columns of boiling water. Blent and kneaded with the half-burning ashes, the streams fell like seething mud over the streets in frequent intervals. And full, where the priests of Isis had now cowered around the altars, on which they had vainly sought to kindle fires and pour incense, one of the fiercest of those deadly torrents, mingled with immense fragments of scoria, had poured its rage. Over the bended forms of the priests it dashed, that cry had been of death—that silence had been of eternity! The ashes—the pitchy stream— sprinkled the altars, covered the pavement, and half concealed the quivering corpses of the priests!

"They are dead," said Burbo, terrified for the first time, and hurrying back into the cell. "I thought not the danger was so near and fatal."

The two wretches stood staring at each other—you might have heard their hearts beat! Calenus, the less bold by nature, but the most griping, recovered first.

"We must to our task, and away!" he said, in a low whisper, frightened at his own voice. He stepped to the threshold, paused, crossed over the heated floor and his dead brethren to the sacred chapel, and called to Burbo to follow. But the gladiator quaked, and drew back.

"So much the better," thought Calenus; "the more will be *my* booty." Hastily he loaded himself with the more portable treasures of the temple; and thinking no more of his comrade, hurried from the sacred place. A sudden flash of lightning from the mount showed to Burbo, who stood motionless at the threshold, the flying and laden form of the priest. He took heart; he stepped forth to join him, when a tremendous shower of ashes fell right before his feet. The gladiator shrank back once more. Darkness closed him in. But the shower continued fast—fast; its heaps rose high and suffocatingly—deathly vapors steamed from them. The wretch gasped for breath—he sought in despair again to fly—the ashes had blocked up the threshold—he shrieked as his feet shrank from the boiling fluid. How could he escape? —he could not climb to the open space; nay, were he able, he could not brave its horrors. It were best to remain in the cell, protected, at least, from the fatal air. He sat down and clenched his teeth. By degrees, the atmosphere from without—stifling and venomous—crept into the chamber. He could endure it no longer. His eyes, glaring round, rested on a sacrificial axe, which some priest had left in the chamber: he seized it. With the desperate strength of his gigantic arm, he attempted to hew his way through the walls.

Meanwhile, the streets were already thinned; the crowd had hastened to disperse itself under shelter; the ashes began to fill up the lower parts of the town; but, here and there, you heard the steps of fugitives cranching them warily, or saw their pale and haggard faces by the blue glare of the lightning, or the more unsteady glare of torches, by which they endeavored to steer their steps. But ever and anon, the boiling water, or the straggling ashes, mysterious and gusty winds, rising and dying in a breath, extinguished these wandering lights, and with them the last living hope of those who bore them.

In the street that leads to the gate of Herculaneum, Clodius now bent his perplexed and doubtful way. "If I can gain the open country," thought he, "doubtless there will be various vehicles beyond the gate, and Herculaneum is not far distant.

Thank Mercury! I have little to lose, and that little is about me!"

"Holla!—help there—help!" cried a querulous and frightened voice. "I have fallen down—my torch has gone out—my slaves have deserted me. I am Diomed—the rich Diomed;—ten thousand sesterces to him who helps me!"

At the same moment, Clodius felt himself caught by the feet. "Ill fortune to thee,—let me go, fool!" said the gambler.

"Oh, help me up!—give me thy hand!"

"There—rise!"

"Is this Clodius? I know the voice! Whither fliest thou?"

"Towards Herculaneum."

"Blessed be the gods! our way is the same, then, as far as the gate. Why not take refuge in my villa? Thou knowest the long range of subterranean cellars beneath the basement, —that shelter, what shower can penetrate?"

"You speak well," said Clodius, musingly. "And by storing the cellar with food, we can remain there even some days, should these wondrous storms endure so long."

"Oh, blessed be he who invented gates to a city!" cried Diomed. "See!—they have placed a light within yon arch: by that let us guide our steps."

The air was now still for a few minutes: the lamp from the gate streamed out far and clear: the fugitives hurried on—they gained the gate—they passed by the Roman sentry; the lightning flashed over his livid face and polished helmet, but his stern features were composed even in their awe! He remained erect and motionless at his post. That hour itself had not animated the machine of the ruthless majesty of Rome into the reasoning and self-acting man. There he stood, amidst the crashing elements: he had not received the permission to desert his station and escape.*

Diomed and his companion hurried on, when suddenly a female form rushed athwart their way. It was the girl whose ominous voice had been raised so often and so gladly in anticipation of "the merry show!"

"Oh, Diomed!" she cried, "shelter! shelter! See,"—pointing to an infant clasped to her breast—"see this little one!—it is mine!—the child of shame! I have never owned it till

---

* The skeletons of more than one sentry were found at their posts.

this hour. But *now* I remember I am a mother! I have plucked it from the cradle of its nurse: *she* had fled! Who could think of the babe in such an hour but she who bore it? Save it! save it!"

"Curses on thy shrill voice! Away, harlot!" muttered Clodius between his ground teeth.

"Nay, girl," said the more humane Diomed; "follow if thou wilt. This way—this way—to the vaults!"

They hurried on—they arrived at the house of Diomed— they laughed aloud as they crossed the threshold, for they deemed the danger over.

Diomed ordered his slaves to carry down into the subterranean gallery before described, a profusion of food and oil for lights; and there Julia, Clodius, the mother and her babe, the greater part of the slaves, and some frightened visitors and clients of the neighborhood, sought their shelter.

CHAPTER VII.

The progress of the destruction.

THE cloud, which had scattered so deep a murkiness over the day, had now settled into a solid and impenetrable mass. It resembled less even the thickest gloom of a night in the open air than the close and blind darkness of some narrow room. But in proportion as the blackness gathered, did the lightnings around Vesuvius increase in their vivid and scorching glare. Nor was their horrible beauty confined to the usual hues of fire; no rainbow ever rivalled their varying and prodigal dyes. Now brightly blue as the most azure depth of a southern sky— now of a livid and snake-like green, darting restlessly to and fro as the folds of an enormous serpent—now of a lurid and intolerable crimson, gushing forth through the columns of smoke, far and wide, and lighting up the whole city from arch to arch—then suddenly dying into a sickly paleness, like the ghost of their own life!

In the pauses of the showers, you heard the rumbling of the earth beneath, and the groaning waves of the tortured sea; or, lower still, and audible but to the watch of intensest fear, the grinding and hissing murmur of the escaping gases through the chasms of the distant mountain. Sometimes the cloud appeared to break from its solid mass, and, by the lightning, to assume quaint and vast mimicries of human or of monster shapes, striding across the gloom, hurtling one upon the other, and vanishing swiftly into the turbulent abyss of shade; so that, to the eyes and fancies of the affrighted wanderers, the unsubstantial vapors were as the bodily forms of gigantic foes—the agents of terror and of death.

The ashes in many places were already knee-deep; and the boiling showers which came from the steaming breath of the volcano forced their way into the houses, bearing with them a strong and suffocating vapor. In some places, immense fragments of rock, hurled upon the house roofs, bore down along the streets masses of confused ruin, which yet more and more, with every hour, obstructed the way; and, as the day advanced, the motion of the earth was more sensibly felt—the footing seemed to slide and creep—nor could chariot or litter be kept steady, even on the most level ground.

Sometimes the huger stones striking against each other as they fell, broke into countless fragments, emitting sparks of fire, which caught whatever was combustible within their reach; and along the plains beyond the city the darkness was now terribly relieved; for several houses, and even vineyards, had been set on flames; and at various intervals, the fires rose sullenly and fiercely against the solid gloom. To add to this partial relief of the darkness, the citizens had, here and there, in the more public places, such as the porticos of temples and the entrances to the forum, endeavored to place rows of torches; but these rarely continued long; the showers and the winds extinguished them, and the sudden darkness into which their fitful light was converted had something in it doubly terrible and doubly impressive on the impotence of human hopes, the lesson of despair.

Frequently, by the momentary light of these torches, parties of fugitives encountered each other, some hurrying towards the sea, others flying from the sea back to the land; for the ocean had retreated rapidly from the shore—an utter darkness lay over it, and, upon its groaning and tossing waves, the storm of cinders and rocks fell without the protection

which the streets and roofs afforded to the land. Wild—
haggard—ghastly with supernatural fears, these groups encountered each other, but without the leisure to speak, to
consult, to advise; for the showers fell now frequently, though
not continuously, extinguishing the lights, which showed to
each band the death-like faces of the other, and hurrying all to
seek refuge beneath the nearest shelter. The whole elements of
civilization were broken up. Ever and anon, by the flickering
lights, you saw the thief hastening by the most solemn authorities of the law, laden with, and fearfully chuckling over, the
produce of his sudden gains. If in the darkness, wife was
separated from husband, or parent from child, vain was the
hope of reunion. Each hurried blindly and confusedly on.
Nothing in all the various and complicated machinery of social
life was left save the primal law of self-preservation!

Through this awful scene did the Athenian wade his way,
accompanied by Ione and the blind girl. Suddenly, a rush of
hundreds, in their path to the sea, swept by them. Nydia was
torn from the side of Glaucus, who, with Ione, was borne
rapidly onward; and when the crowd (whose forms they saw
not, so thick was the gloom) were gone, Nydia was still
separated from their side. Glaucus shouted her name. No answer came. They retraced their steps—in vain: they could not
discover her—it was evident she had been swept along in some
opposite direction by the human current. Their friend, their
preserver, was lost! And hitherto Nydia had been their guide.
Her blindness rendered the scene familiar to her alone. Accustomed, through a perpetual night, to thread the windings
of the city, she had led them unerringly towards the sea-shore,
by which they had resolved to hazard an escape. Now, which
way could they wend? all was rayless to them—a maze without
a clue. Wearied, despondent, bewildered, they, however, passed
along, the ashes falling upon their heads, the fragmentary
stones, dashing up in sparkles before their feet.

"Alas! alas!" murmured Ione, "I can go no farther; my
steps sink among the scorching cinders. Fly, dearest!—beloved, fly! and leave me to my fate!"

"Hush, my betrothed! my bride! Death with thee is
sweeter than life without thee! Yet, whither—oh! whither,
can we direct ourselves through the gloom? Already, it seems

that we have made but a circle, and are in the very spot which we quitted an hour ago."

"O gods! yon rock—see, it hath riven the roof before us! It is death to move through the streets!"

"Blessed lightning! See, Ione—see! the portico of the Temple of Fortune is before us. Let us creep beneath it; it will protect us from the showers."

He caught his beloved in his arms, and with difficulty and labor gained the temple. He bore her to the remoter and more sheltered part of the portico, and leaned over her, that he might shield her, with his own form, from the lightning and the showers! The beauty and the unselfishness of love could hallow even that dismal time!

"Who is there?" said the trembling and hollow voice of one who had preceded them in their place of refuge. "Yet, what matters?—the crush of the ruined world forbids to us friends or foes."

Ione turned at the sound of the voice, and, with a faint shriek, cowered again beneath the arms of Glaucus: and he, looking in the direction of the voice, beheld the cause of her alarm. Through the darkness glared forth two burning eyes —the lightning flashed and lingered athwart the temple—and Glaucus, with a shudder, perceived the lion to which he had been doomed couched beneath the pillars;—and, close beside it, unwitting of the vicinity, lay the giant form of him who had accosted them—the wounded gladiator, Niger.

That lightning had revealed to each other the form of beast and man; yet the instinct of both was quelled. Nay, the lion crept near and nearer to the gladiator, as for companionship; and the gladiator did not recede or tremble. The revolution of Nature had dissolved her lighter terrors as well as her wonted ties.

While they were thus terribly protected, a group of men and women, bearing torches, passed by the temple. They were of the congregation of the Nazarenes; and a sublime and unearthly emotion had not, indeed, quelled their awe, but it had robbed awe of fear. They had long believed, according to the error of the early Christians, that the Last Day was at hand; they imagined now that the Day had come.

"Woe! woe!" cried, in a shrill and piercing voice, the elder at their head. "Behold! the Lord descendeth to judgment! He maketh fire come down from heaven in the sight of men! Woe! woe! ye strong and mighty! Woe to ye of the fasces and the purple! Woe to the idolater and the worshipper of the beast! Woe to ye who pour forth the blood of saints, and gloat over the death-pangs of the sons of God! Woe to the harlot of the sea!—woe! woe!"

And with a loud and deep chorus, the troop chanted forth along the wild horrors of the air,—"Woe to the harlot of the sea!—woe! woe!"

The Nazarenes paced slowly on, their torches still flickering in the storm, their voices still raised in menace and solemn warning, till, lost amid the windings in the streets, the darkness of the atmosphere and the silence of death again fell over the scene.

There was one of the frequent pauses in the showers, and Glaucus encouraged Ione once more to proceed. Just as they stood, hesitating, on the last step of the portico, an old man, with a bag in his right hand and leaning upon a youth, tottered by. The youth bore a torch. Glaucus recognized the two as father and son—miser and prodigal.

"Father," said the youth, "if you cannot move more swiftly, I must leave you, or we *both* perish!"

"Fly, boy, then, and leave thy sire!"

"But I cannot fly to starve; give me thy bag of gold!" And the youth snatched at it.

"Wretch! wouldst thou rob thy father?"

"Ay! who can tell the tale in this hour? Miser, perish!"

The boy struck the old man to the ground, plucked the bag from his relaxing hand, and fled onward with a shrill yell.

"Ye gods!" cried Glaucus: "are ye blind, then, even in the dark? Such crimes may well confound the guiltless with the guilty in one common ruin. Ione, on!—on!"

CHAPTER VIII.

Arbaces encounters Glaucus and Ione.

ADVANCING, as men grope for escape in a dungeon, Ione and her lover continued their uncertain way. At the moments

when the volcanic lightnings lingered over the streets, they were
enabled, by that awful light, to steer and guide their progress:
yet, little did the view it presented to them cheer or encourage
their path. In parts, where the ashes lay dry and uncommixed
with the boiling torrents, cast upward from the mountain at
capricious intervals, the surface of the earth presented a lep-
rous and ghastly white. In other places, cinder and rock lay
matted in heaps, from beneath which emerged the half-hid
limbs of some crushed and mangled fugitive. The groans of
the dying were broken by wild shrieks of women's terror—
now near, now distant—which, when heard in the utter darkness, were rendered doubly appalling by the crushing sense of
helplessness and the uncertainty of the perils around; and clear
and distinct through all were the mighty and various noises
from the Fatal Mountain; its rushing winds; its whirling
torrents; and, from time to time, the burst and roar of some
more fiery and fierce explosion. And ever as the winds swept
howling along the street, they bore sharp streams of burning
dust, and such sickening and poisonous vapors, as took away,
for the instant, breath and consciousness, followed by a rapid
revulsion of the arrested blood, and a tingling sensation of
agony trembling through every nerve and fibre of the frame.

"Oh, Glaucus! my beloved! my own!—take me to thy
arms! One embrace! let me feel thy arms around me—and in
that embrace let me die—I can no more!"

"For my sake, for my life—courage, yet, sweet Ione—my
life is linked with thine; and see—torches—this way! Lo!
how they brave the wind! Ha! they live through the storm—
doubtless, fugitives to the sea!—we will join them."

As if to aid and reanimate the lovers, the winds and
showers came to a sudden pause; the atmosphere was pro-
foundly still—the mountain seemed at rest, gathering, perhaps, fresh fury for its next burst: the torch-bearers moved
quickly on. "We are nearing the sea," said, in a calm voice,
the person at their head. "Liberty and wealth to each slave
who survives this day; Courage!—I tell you that the gods
themselves have assured me of deliverance—On!"

Redly and steadily the torches flashed full on the eyes of
Glaucus and Ione, who lay trembling and exhausted on his
bosom. Several slaves were bearing, by the light, panniers

and coffers, heavily laden; in front of them,—a drawn sword in his hand,—towered the lofty form of Arbaces.

"By my fathers!" cried the Egyptian, "Fate smiles upon me even through these horrors, and, amidst the dreadest aspects of woe and death, bodes me happiness and love. Away, Greek! I claim my ward, Ione!"

"Traitor and murderer!" cried Glaucus, glaring upon his foe, "Nemesis hath guided thee to my revenge!—a just sacrifice to the shades of Hades, that now seem loosed on earth. Approach—touch but the hand of Ione, and thy weapon shall be as a reed—I will tear thee limb from limb!"

Suddenly, as he spoke, the place became lighted with an intense and lurid glow. Bright and gigantic through the darkness, which closed around it like the walls of hell, the mountain shone—a pile of fire! Its summit seemed riven in two; or rather, above its surface there seemed to rise two monster shapes, each confronting each, as Demons contending for a World. These were of one deep blood-red hue of fire, which lighted up the whole atmosphere far and wide; but *below,* the nether part of the mountain was still dark and shrouded, save in three places, adown which flowed, serpentine and irregular, rivers of the molten lava. Darkly red through the profound gloom of their banks, they flowed slowly on, as towards the devoted city. Over the broadest there seemed to spring a cragged and stupendous arch, from which, as from the jaws of hell, gushed the sources of the sudden Phlegethon. And through the stilled air was heard the rattling of the fragments of rock, hurtling one upon another as they were borne down the fiery cataracts—darkening, for one instant, the spot where they fell, and suffused the next, in the burnished hues of the flood along which they floated!

The slaves shrieked aloud, and, cowering, hid their faces. The Egyptian himself stood transfixed to the spot, the glow lighting up his commanding features and jewelled robes. High behind him rose a tall column that supported the bronze statue of Augustus; and the imperial image seemed changed to a shape of fire!

With his left hand circled round the form of Ione—with his right arm raised in menace, and grasping the stilus which was to have been his weapon in the arena, and which he still fortunately bore about him, with his brow knit, his lips apart, the wrath and menace of human passions arrested as by a charm, upon his features, Glaucus fronted the Egyptian!

Arbaces turned his eyes from the mountain—they rested on the form of Glaucus! He paused a moment: "Why," he muttered, "should I hesitate? Did not the stars foretell the only crisis of imminent peril to which I was subjected?—Is not that peril past?

"The soul," cried he aloud, "can brave the wreck of worlds and the wrath of imaginary gods! By that soul will I conquer to the last! Advance, slaves!—Athenian, resist me, and thy blood be on thine own head! Thus, then, I regain Ione!"

He advanced one step—it was his last on earth! The ground shook beneath him with a convulsion that cast all around upon its surface. A simultaneous crash resounded through the city, as down toppled many a roof and pillar!— the lightning, as if caught by the metal, lingered an instant on the Imperial Statue—then shivered bronze and column! Down fell the ruin, echoing along the street, and riving the solid pavement where it crashed!—The prophecy of the stars was fulfilled!

The sound—the shock, stunned the Athenian for several moments. When he recovered, the light still illumined the scene—the earth still slid and trembled beneath! Ione lay senseless on the ground; but he saw her not yet—his eyes were fixed upon a ghastly face that seemed to emerge, without limbs or trunk, from the huge fragments of the shattered column—a face of unutterable pain, agony, and despair! The eyes shut and opened rapidly, as if sense were not yet fled; the lips quivered and grinned—then sudden stillness and darkness fell over the features, yet retaining that aspect of horror never to be forgotten!

So perished the wise Magician—the great Arbaces—the Hermes of the Burning Belt—the last of the royalty of Egypt!

CHAPTER IX.

The despair of the lovers.—The condition of the multitude.

GLAUCUS turned in gratitude but in awe, caught Ione once more in his arms, and fled along the street, that was yet intensely luminous. But suddenly a duller shade fell over the air. Instinctively he turned to the mountain, and behold! one of the two gigantic crests, into which the summit had been divided, rocked and wavered to and fro; and then, with a sound, the mightiness of which no language can describe, it fell from its burning base, and rushed, an avalanche of fire, down the sides of the mountain! At the same instant gushed forth a volume of blackest smoke—rolling on, over air, sea, and earth.

Another—and another—and another shower of ashes, far more profuse than before, scattered fresh desolation along the streets. Darkness once more wrapped them as a veil; and Glaucus, his bold heart at last quelled and despairing, sank beneath the cover of an arch, and, clasping Ione to his heart —a bride on that couch of ruin—resigned himself to die.

Meanwhile Nydia, when separated by the throng from Glaucus and Ione, had in vain endeavored to regain them. In vain she raised that plaintive cry so peculiar to the blind; it was lost amidst a thousand shrieks of more selfish terror. Again and again she returned to the spot where they had been divided—to find her companions gone, to seize every fugitive —to inquire of Glaucus—to be dashed aside in the impatience of distraction. Who in that hour spared one thought to his neighbor? Perhaps in scenes of universal horror, nothing is more horrid than the unnatural selfishness they engender. At length it occurred to Nydia, that as it had been resolved to seek the sea-shore for escape, her most probable chance of rejoining her companions would be to persevere in that direction. Guiding her steps, then, by the staff which she always carried, she continued, with incredible dexterity, to avoid the

masses of ruin that encumbered the path—to thread the streets
—and unerringly (so blessed now was that accustomed darkness, so afflicting in ordinary life!) to take the nearest direction to the sea-side.

Poor girl! her courage was beautiful to behold!—and Fate
seemed to favor one so helpless! The boiling torrents touched
her not, save by the general rain which accompanied them;
the huge fragments of scoria shivered the pavement before
and beside her, but spared that frail form: and when the lesser
ashes fell over her, she shook them away with a slight
tremor, and dauntlessly resumed her course.

Weak, exposed, yet fearless, supported but by one wish,
she was a very emblem of Psyche in her wanderings; of Hope,
walking through the Valley of the Shadow; of the Soul itself
—lone but undaunted, amidst the dangers and the snares of
life!

Her path was, however, constantly impeded by the crowds
that now groped amidst the gloom, now fled in the temporary
glare of the lightnings across the scene; and, at length, a
group of torch-bearers rushing full against her, she was
thrown down with some violence.

"What!" said the voice of one of the party, "is this the
brave blind girl! By Bacchus, she must not be left here to
die! Up! my Thessalian! So—so. Are you hurt? That's
well! Come along with us! we are for the shore!"

"O Sallust! it is thy voice! The gods be thanked! Glaucus!
Glaucus! have ye seen him?"

"Not I. He is doubtless out of the city by this time. The
gods who saved him from the lion will save him from the
burning mountain."

As the kindly epicure thus encouraged Nydia, he drew her
along with him towards the sea, heeding not her passionate
entreaties that he would linger yet awhile to search for
Glaucus; and still, in the accent of despair, she continued to
shriek out that beloved name, which, amidst all the roar of
the convulsed elements, kept alive a music at her heart.

The sudden illumination, the bursts of the floods of lava,
and the earthquake, which we have already described, chanced
when Sallust and his party had just gained the direct path
leading from the city to the port; and here they were arrested

by an immense crowd, more than half the population of the city. They spread along the field without the walls, thousands upon thousands, uncertain whither to fly. The sea had retired far from the shore; and they who had fled to it had been so terrified by the agitation and preternatural shrinking of the element, the gasping forms of the uncouth sea things which the waves had left upon the sand, and by the sound of the huge stones cast from the mountain into the deep, that they had returned again to the land, as presenting the less frightful aspect of the two. Thus the two streams of human beings, the one seaward, the other *from* the sea, had met together, feeling a sad comfort in numbers; arrested in despair and doubt.

"The world is to be destroyed by fire," said an old man in long loose robes, a philosopher of the Stoic school: "Stoic and Epicurean wisdom have alike agreed in this prediction; and the hour is come!"

"Yea; the hour is come!" cried a loud voice, solemn but not fearful.

Those around turned in dismay. The voice came from above them. It was the voice of Olinthus, who, surrounded by his Christian friends, stood upon an abrupt eminence on which the old Greek colonists had raised a temple to Apollo, now time-worn and half in ruin.

As he spoke, there came that sudden illumination which had heralded the death of Arbaces, and glowing over that mighty multitude, awed, crouching, breathless—never on earth had the faces of men seemed so haggard!—never had meeting of mortal beings been so stamped with the horror and sublimity of dread!—never till the last trumpet sounds, shall such meeting be seen again! And above those the form of Olinthus, with outstretched arm and prophet brow, girt with the living fires. And the crowd knew the face of him they had doomed to the fangs of the beast—*then* their victim—*now* their warner; and through the stillness again came his ominous voice—

"The hour is come!"

The Christians repeated the cry. It was caught up—it was echoed from side to side—woman and man, childhood and old age repeated, not aloud, but in a smothered and dreary murmur—

"THE HOUR IS COME!"

At that moment, a wild yell burst through the air;—and, thinking only of escape, whither it knew not, the terrible tiger of the desert leaped amongst the throng, and hurried through its parted streams. And so came the earthquake,—and so darkness once more fell over the earth!

And now new fugitives arrived. Grasping the treasures no longer destined for their lord, the slaves of Arbaces joined the throng. One only of all their torches yet flickered on. It was borne by Sosia; and its light falling on the face of Nydia, he recognized the Thessalian.

"What avails thy liberty now, blind girl?" said the slave.

"Who art thou? canst thou tell me of Glaucus?"

"Ay; I saw him but a few minutes since."

"Blessed be thy head! where?"

"Couched beneath the arch of the forum—dead or dying! —gone to rejoin Arbaces, who is no more!"

Nydia uttered not a word, she slid from the side of Sallust; silently she glided through those behind her, and retraced her steps to the city. She gained the forum—the arch; she stooped down—she felt around—she called on the name of Glaucus.

A weak voice answered—"Who calls on me? Is it the voice of the Shades? Lo! I am prepared!"

"Arise! follow me! Take my hand! Glaucus, thou shalt be saved!"

In wonder and sudden hope, Glaucus arose—"Nydia still? Ah thou, then, art safe!"

The tender joy of his voice pierced the heart of the poor Thessalian, and she blessed him for his thought of her.

Half leading, half carrying Ione, Glaucus followed his guide. With admirable discretion, she avoided the path which led to the crowd she had just quitted, and, by another route, sought the shore.

After many pauses and incredible perseverance, they gained the sea, and joined a group, who, bolder than the rest, resolved to hazard any peril rather than continue in such a scene. In darkness they put forth to sea; but, as they cleared

the land and caught new aspects of the mountain, its channels
of molten fire threw a partial redness over the waves.

Utterly exhausted and worn out, Ione slept on the breast
of Glaucus, and Nydia lay at his feet. Meanwhile the showers
of dust and ashes, still borne aloft, fell into the wave, and
scattered their snows over the deck. Far and wide, borne
by the winds, those showers descended upon the remotest
climes, startling even the swarthy African; and whirled along
the antique soil of Syria and of Egypt.

CHAPTER X.

The next morning.—The fate of Nydia.

'And meekly, softly, beautifully, dawned at last the light
over the trembling deep!—the winds were sinking into rest—
the foam died from the glowing azure of that delicious sea.
Around the east, thin mists caught gradually the rosy hues
that heralded the morning; Light was about to resume her
reign. Yet, still, dark and massive in the distance, lay the
broken fragments of the destroying cloud, from which red
streaks, burning dimlier and more dim, betrayed the yet rolling
fires of the mountain of the "Scorched Fields." The white
walls and gleaming columns that had adorned the lovely coasts
were no more. Sullen and dull were the shores so lately crested
by the cities of Herculaneum and Pompeii. The darlings of
the Deep were snatched from her embrace! Century after
century shall the mighty Mother stretch forth her azure arms,
and know them not—moaning round the sepulchres of the
Lost!

There was no *shout* from the mariners at the dawning
light—it had come too gradually, and they were too wearied
for such sudden bursts of joy—but there was a low, deep
murmur of thankfulness amidst those watchers of the long
night. They looked at each other and smiled—they took heart
—they felt once more that there was a world around, and a
God above them! And in the feeling that the worst was passed,
the over-wearied ones turned round, and fell placidly to sleep.
In the growing light of the skies there came the silence which

night had wanted: and the bark drifted calmly onward to its port. A few other vessels, bearing similar fugitives, might be seen in the expanse, apparently motionless, yet gliding also on. There was a sense of security, or companionship, and of hope, in the sight of their slender masts and white sails. What beloved friends, lost and missed in the gloom, might they not bear to safety and to shelter!

In the silence of the general sleep, Nydia rose gently. She bent over the face of Glaucus—she inhaled the deep breath of his heavy slumber,—timidly and sadly she kissed his brow— his lips; she felt for his hand—it was locked in that of Ione; she sighed deeply, and her face darkened. Again she kissed his brow, and with her hair wiped from it the damps of night. "May the gods bless you, Athenian!" she murmured: "may you be happy with your beloved one!—may you sometimes remember Nydia! Alas! she is of no further use on earth!"

With these words, she turned away. Slowly she crept along by the *fori,* or platforms, to the farther side of the vessel and, pausing, bent low over the deep; the cool spray dashed upward on her feverish brow. "It is the kiss of death," she said—"it is welcome." The balmy air played through her waving tresses—she put them from her face, and raised those eyes—so tender, though so lightless—to the sky, whose soft face she had never seen!

"No, no!" she said, half aloud, and in a musing and thoughtful tone, "I cannot endure it; this jealous, exacting love—it shatters my whole soul in madness! I might harm him again—wretch that I was! I have saved him—twice saved him—happy, happy thought:—why not *die* happy?—it is the last glad thought I can ever know. Oh! sacred Sea! I hear thy voice invitingly—it hath a freshening and joyous call. They say that in thy embrace is dishonor—that thy victims cross not the fatal Styx—be it so!—I would not meet him in the Shades, for I should meet him still with *her!* Rest—rest —rest!—there is no other Elysium for a heart like mine!"

A sailor, half dozing on the deck, heard a slight splash on the waters. Drowsily he looked up, and behind, as the vessel merrily bounded on, he fancied he saw something white above the waves; but it vanished in an instant. He turned round again, and dreamed of his home and children.

When the lovers awoke, their first thought was of each other—their next of Nydia! She was not to be found—none had seen her since the night. Every crevice of the vessel was searched—there was no trace of her. Mysterious from first to last, the blind Thessalian had vanished for ever from the living world! They guessed her fate in silence: and Glaucus and Ione, while they drew nearer to each other (feeling each other the world itself) forgot their deliverance, and wept as for a departed sister.

CHAPTER THE LAST.

Wherein all things cease.

Letter from Glaucus to Sallust, ten years after the destruction of Pompeii.
"Athens.

"GLAUCUS to his beloved Sallust—greeting and health! —You request me to visit you at Rome—no, Sallust, come rather to me at Athens! I have forsworn the Imperial City, its mighty tumult and hollow joys. In my own land henceforth I dwell for ever. The ghost of our departed greatness is dearer to me than the gaudy life of your loud prosperity. There is a charm to me which no other spot can supply, in the porticos hallowed still by holy and venerable shades. In the olive-groves of Ilyssus I still hear the voice of poetry—on the heights of Phyle, the clouds of twilight seem yet the shrouds of departed freedom—the heralds—the heralds—of the morrow that shall come! You smile at my enthusiasm, Sallust!— better be hopeful in chains than resigned to their glitter. You tell me you are sure that I cannot enjoy life in these melancholy haunts of a fallen majesty. You dwell with rapture on the Roman splendors, and the luxuries of the imperial court. My Sallust—*'non sum qualis eram'*—I am not what I was! The events of my life have sobered the bounding blood of my youth. My health has never quite recovered its wonted elasticity ere it felt the pangs of disease, and languished in the damps of a criminal's dungeon. My mind has never shaken off the dark shadow of the Last Day of Pompeii—the horror and the desolation of that awful ruin!—Our beloved, our

SIR EDWARD BULWER LYTTON

remembered Nydia! I have reared a tomb to her shade, and I see it every day from the window of my study. It keeps alive in me a tender recollection—a not unpleasing sadness— which are but a fitting homage to her fidelity, and the mysteriousness of her early death. Ione gathers the flowers, but my own hand wreathes them daily around the tomb. She was worthy of a tomb in Athens!

"You speak of the growing sect of the Christians in Rome. Sallust, to you I may confide my secret; I have pondered much over that faith—I have adopted it. After the destruction of Pompeii, I met once more with Olinthus—saved, alas! only for a day, and falling afterwards a martyr to the indomitable energy of his zeal. In my preservation from the lion and the earthquake he taught me to behold the hand of the unknown God! I listened—believed—adored! My own, my more than ever beloved Ione, has also embraced the creed!—a creed, Sallust, which, shedding light over this world, gathers its concentrated glory, like a sunset, over the next! We know that we are united in the soul, as in the flesh, for ever and for ever! Ages may roll on, our very dust be dissolved, the earth shrivelled like a scroll; but round and round the circle of eternity rolls the wheel of life—imperishable—unceasing! And as the earth from the sun, so immortality drinks happiness from virtue, which is the smile upon the face of God! Visit me, then, Sallust; bring with you the learned scrolls of Epicurus, Pythagoras, Diogenes; arm yourself for defeat; and let us, amidst the groves of Academus, dispute, under a surer guide than any granted to our fathers, on the mighty problem of the true ends of life and the nature of the soul.

"Ione—at that name my heart yet beats!—Ione is by my side as I write: I lift my eyes, and meet her smile. The sunlight quivers over Hymettus: and along my garden I hear the hum of the summer bees. Am I happy, ask you? Oh, what can Rome give me equal to what I possess at Athens? Here, everything awakens the soul and inspires the affections—the trees, the waters, the hills, the skies, are those of Athens!— fair, though mourning—mother of the Poetry and the Wisdom of the World. In my hall I see the marble faces of my ancestors. In the Ceramicus, I survey their tombs! In the streets, I behold the hand of Phidias and the soul of Pericles.

Harmodius, Aristogiton—*they* are everywhere—but in our hearts!—in *mine,* at least, they shall not perish! If anything can make me forget that I am an Athenian and not free, it is partly the soothing—the love—watchful, vivid, sleepless—of Ione:—a love that has taken a new sentiment in our new creed—a love which none of our poets, beautiful though they be, had shadowed forth in description; for mingled with religion, it partakes of religion; it is blended with pure and unworldly thoughts; it is that which we may hope to carry through eternity, and keep, therefore, white and unsullied, that we may not blush to confess it to our God! This is the true type of the dark fable of our Grecian Eros and Psyche —it is, in truth, the soul asleep in the arms of love. And if this, our love, support me partly against the fever of the desire for freedom, my religion supports me more; for whenever I would grasp the sword and sound the shell, and rush to a new Marathon (but Marathon without victory), I feel my despair at the chilling thought of my country's impotence—the crashing weight of the Roman yoke, comforted, at least, by the thought that earth is but the beginning of life—that the glory of a few years matters little in the vast space of eternity—that there is no perfect freedom till the chains of clay fall from the soul, and all space, all time, become its heritage and domain. Yet, Sallust, some mixture of the soft Greek blood still mingles with my faith. I can share not the zeal of those who see crime and eternal wrath in men who cannot believe as they. I shudder not at the creed of others. I dare not *curse* them—I pray the Great Father to *convert.* This lukewarmness exposes me to some suspicion amongst the Christians: but I forgive it; and, not offending openly the prejudices of the crowd, I am thus enabled to protect my brethren from the danger of the law, and the consequences of their own zeal. If moderation seem to me the natural creature of benevolence, it gives, also, the greatest scope to beneficence.

"Such, then, O Sallust! is my life—such my opinions. In this manner I greet existence and await death. And thou, glad-hearted and kindly pupil of Epicurus, thou—— But come hither, and see what enjoyments, what hopes are ours—and not the splendor of imperial banquets, nor the shouts of the crowded circus, nor the noisy forum, nor the glittering theatre,

nor the luxuriant gardens, nor the voluptuous baths of Rome
—shall seem to thee to constitute a life of more vivid and
uninterrupted happiness than that which thou so unseasonably
pitiest as the career of Glaucus the Athenian!—Farewell!"

*   *   *   *   *   *

Nearly Seventeen Centuries had rolled away when the City
of Pompeii was disinterred from its silent tomb,* all vivid
with undimmed hues; its walls fresh as if painted yesterday—
not a hue faded on the rich mosaic of its floors—in its forum
the half-finished columns as left by the workman's hand—in
its gardens the sacrificial tripod—in its halls the chest of
treasure—in its baths the strigil—in its theatres the counter
of admission—in its saloons the furniture and the lamp—in its
triclinia the fragments of the last feast—in its cubicula the
perfumes and the rouge of faded beauty—and everywhere the
bones and skeletons of those who once moved the springs of
that minute yet gorgeous machine of luxury and of life!

In the house of Diomed, in the subterranean vaults, twenty
skeletons (one of a babe) were discovered in one spot by the
door, covered by a fine ashen dust, that had evidently been
wafted slowly through the apertures, until it had filled the
whole space. There were jewels and coins, candelabra for
unavailing light, and wine hardened in the amphoræ for a
prolongation of agonized life. The sand, consolidated by
damps, had taken the forms of the skeletons as in a cast; and
the traveller may yet see the impression of a female neck and
bosom of young and round proportions—the trace of the fated
Julia! It seems to the inquirer as if the air had been gradually
changed into a sulphurous vapor; the inmates of the vaults had
rushed to the door, to find it closed and blocked up by the
scoria without, and in their attempts to force it, had been
suffocated with the atmosphere.

In the garden was found a skeleton with a key by its bony
hand, and near it a bag of coins. This is believed to have been
the master of the house—the unfortunate Diomed, who had
probably sought to escape by the garden, and been destroyed
either by the vapors or some fragment of stone. Beside some
silver vases lay another skeleton, probably of a slave.

The houses of Sallust and of Pansa, the Temple of Isis,

---

* Destroyed A. D. 79; first discovered A. D. 1750.

with the juggling concealments behind the statues—the lurking-place of its holy oracles,—are now bared to the gaze of the
curious. In one of the chambers of that temple was found a
huge skeleton with an axe beside it: two walls had been pierced
by the axe—the victim could penetrate no farther. In the
midst of the city was found another skeleton, by the side of
which was a heap of coins, and many of the mystic ornaments
of the fane of Isis. Death had fallen upon him in his avarice,
and Calenus perished simultaneously with Burbo! As the
excavators cleared on through the mass of ruin, they found
the skeleton of a man literally severed in two by a prostrate
column; the skull was of so striking a conformation, so boldly
marked in its intellectual, as well as its worse physical develop-
ments, that it has excited the constant speculation of every
itinerant believer in the theories of Spurzheim who has gazed
upon that ruined palace of the mind. Still, after the lapse of
ages, the traveller may survey that airy hall within whose cunning galleries and elaborate chambers once thought, reasoned,
dreamed, and sinned, the soul of Arbaces the Egyptian.

Viewing the various witnesses of a social system which has
passed from the world for ever—a stranger, from that remote
and barbarian Isle which the imperial Roman shivered when
he named, paused amidst the delights of the soft Campania
and composed this history!